The Erol's Guide to Cyberspace

By
Ronald L. Wagner

Published by:
Citapei Communications, Inc.
Herndon, Virginia
Distributed by:
Erol's Computers & Internet
Springfield, Virginia

Published by Citapei Communications, Inc.

Distributed by Erol's Computers and Internet.

The Erol's Guide to Cyberspace
by Ronald L. Wagner

ISBN 0-9654604-0-1

Editors: Lisa M. Kauffman
Bob Kleinfeld

Cover Art: Rob Turner

Technical Consultant: Steve Zlatos

Publishing Consultants: Orhan Onaran
Corinne Rogers
Steve Taft

Contents

Phase 2: The Launch 55

Phase 3: Cyberspace 137

Introduction

> "Once a photograph of the Earth, taken from the outside, is available... a new idea as powerful as any in history will let loose."
>
> **Sir Fred Hoyle, 1948**

Twenty years after Sir Fred Hoyle made this prediction, an "earthrise" was seen for the first time when Apollo 8 orbited the moon on Christmas Eve, 1968. Many of the people who saw that earthrise were building a global computer networking system that today brings you the Internet.

Certainly the Internet qualifies as Sir Hoyle's new idea. It is as powerful as any idea in history and it's no coincidence that the Internet was created by the first generation to see an earthrise. That historic celestial event illustrated the concept that we all are joined in global unity—and the Internet has turned this into reality.

And now, through your Erol's Internet service, you are hooked up to participate in this sweeping, global communications revolution—*the waiting is over!*

Not your everyday Internet service

Your Erol's Internet service brings you much more than what most Internet service subscribers get today. In addition to basic services such as Web browsing, electronic mail and Internet news, we bring you:

- **The Erol's Home page:** Erol's links you to an exciting array of on-line services. By merely double-clicking the Netscape Navigator icon on your computer, you'll be able to jump to local news and weather, sports, entertainment and traffic cameras.

- **Great content and incredible speed**: The biggest problem most people have on the Internet today is it's too slow. That's because most home users access the Internet through an Internet service provider with a slow Internet connection. But with Erol's high-speed Internet lines, you won't nod off waiting for things to happen on your computer screen.

- **The Erol's Guide to Cyberspace**: Most Internet services simply give you access and leave you on your own. But you're not on your own with us because—in addition to our unprecedented, 7 day-a-week, 24-hour-a-day telephone technical support services—we give you *The Erol's Guide to Cyberspace*. We understand that you need more than simple Internet access. You need it to be useful, valuable and enjoyable. This book will help with all of that as it walks you through cyberspace and shows you a few thousand good reasons to use Erol's.

What's in the book?

We thought you might ask, so here's an overview of what we've included:

- **Phase 1 - Preflight**: This is the ground school for your cyber-journey, which includes an introduction to our exclusive Erol's Home Page service, a quick tour of the Internet and some help with Internet etiquette and cyberspace security issues.

- **Phase 2 - The Launch**: Here's where you actually lift-off and go into cyberspace as we present Step-By-Step lessons on how to use the software applications that will carry you as you explore cyberspace on your own.

- **Phase 3 - Cyberspace**: This is a tour guide to what's out there in cyberspace. As you explore these valuable Web sites and services, you'll be thrilled that you became a cyber-naut.

- **Phase 4 - Web Publishing**: Here's where we help you handle the "what's next?" question by showing you how to create your own little place in cyberspace—a Web site of your own.

Finally, we wrap up this book with a glossary of Internet, Web and computer terms, plus a mini-lesson on Windows—in case you're new to computers and need a quick lesson to keep up with the exercises we give you in Phase 2.

Orbiting in Cyberspace

Check out our end-of-chapter modules called "Orbiting in Cyberspace"—listings of Internet resources that will keep you up-to-the-second-informed on the chapter's topic. These sections will keep you abreast of the topics that affect your personal interests, your hobbies, your profession, and your business organization.

A closing note: Internet access speed

We know that one of the reasons you subscribed to Erol's was for our super, high-speed connection to the Internet. And you've made the right choice because we can deliver the Internet to you faster than normal service providers. But getting the Internet into your computer isn't the total solution to fast Internet access. There are many other performance factors that can mask the high-speed Internet capability you have on tap.

If you're not happy with the speed of your system, ask our technical support staff to evaluate your video card, monitor, processor power, RAM memory and hard drive. You might need to upgrade some components to enjoy the full power that Erol's can deliver. And, we not only can recommend a computer system that will do the job, but we can deliver it and set it up because we're your one-stop Internet solution.

But that's enough build-up: Turn now to Phase 1 and let's start ground school!

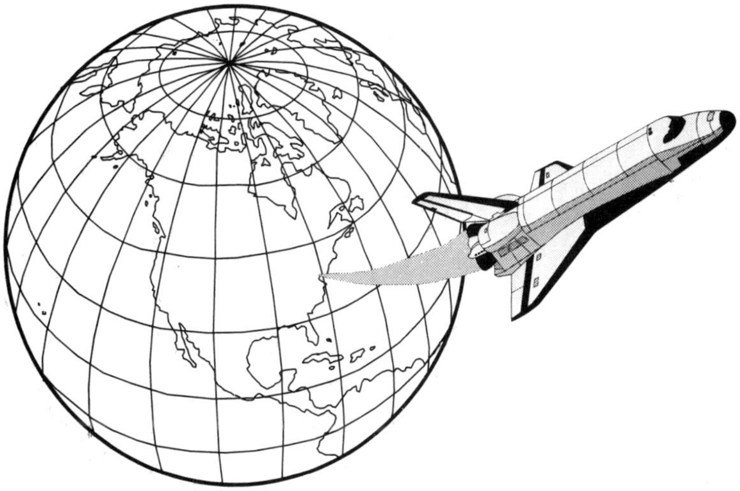

Phase 1

Phase 1: Preflight

Winston Churchill said, "I love learning. But I hate being taught." Believing that you might agree with Churchill, we have strived in this book to create opportunities for you to enjoy something you love—the pleasures of learning something new. This book is not constrained to the technical nuts-and-bolts. After all, volumes of technical computer tomes already crowd computer store bookshelves.

Of course we'll give you some technical material, but we'll do so in a way that will help you integrate your technical needs with your human needs. This book is different from any you can buy in the stores because it's targeted toward Erol's subscribers. You'll get the information you need to get the most out of your Erol's Internet access service.

Reading the first four chapters here in Phase 1 before going on-line, will prepare you for the dramatic transformation that the Internet will bring to your life. The changes will be unprecedented. After you've prepared yourself by learning the basics about the Internet, you'll move into Phase 2 for our "Step-by-Step" exercises that will walk you through the most important functions of most of the Internet software you'll use.

After you've finished these chapters, you'll be all set to explore the Web and learn how it can serve as a powerful enhancement to your daily work and to your personal and family life at home.

- **Chapter 1** presents the exclusive **Erol's Home Page** Internet service.

- **Chapter 2** gives you an **Internet quick tour** and a map of your new on-line environment so you'll know the lay of this new cyber-land before you jump in. Rather than being an in-depth technical report, it's an easy-reading overview that will introduce you to the basic technical aspects of the Internet.

- **Chapter 3** gives you the highlights of **netiquette** (Internet etiquette) that will help you steer clear of a serious electronic faux pas. The Internet is a revolutionary communication tool and you need to know the rules of the road to keep from being blasted out of cyberspace by irate fellow travelers.

- **Chapter 4** will put you at peace with **Internet security**. You may have heard horror stories about Internet security problems. But we'll show you that most of the news is good and that the Internet is as safe a place for your financial transactions as anywhere else.

1

A Cyber•Space Shuttle: Erol's Internet

Welcome to Erol's Internet! And thank you for signing up for our remarkable service: a localized on-line system that helps you make sense of the Internet from the very first day you try it.

You've been hearing a lot about on-line technology and the Internet recently. But if you've tried to get on-line without help, you know how frustrating it can be to find information on the Internet that's of real value. Well, the waiting is over! The Erol's system leads you in the right direction from your first day on-line by giving you an enticing menu of valuable on-line resources.

Countless early Internet users have spent millions of hours wandering through cyber-space trying to find something of value to see, or something of interest to do. *You* won't have that problem because with Erol's you can make extensive connections to your local community, download encyclopedic volumes of valuable information and communicate with anyone else on the Internet, anywhere in the world. And it all starts just by jumping to the Erol's home page.

Now you can go on-line whenever you want, as often as you want, and stay on for as long as you want—for one low price. Of course there's much more to the Internet than our home page and we've given you full, unrestricted, regular Internet access. But you always have our exclusive Erol's information system at your fingertips when-ever you'd like to see a familiar face. Thanks for selecting Erol's and we hope you're as excited about using Erol's Internet service as we are about providing it!

Internet jargon

In this book, we've used as few technical terms as we could, but the Internet involves a lot of technical jargon. Learning it can bewilder an Internet beginner. In fact, there's even a jargon term for an Internet beginner. The term is "Newbie." And, as you'll see later, there's a whole Internet site dedicated to helping newbies.

Jargon is an integral part of the Internet and it's useful because once you understand the terms, the shorthand will save time when communicating about the Internet. Besides, you're going to see it everywhere so you might as well learn it anyway.

To help you out, this book includes an Internet glossary in the Appendix section that starts on page 259. The glossary defines a lot of terms about the Internet, computers and telecommunications and covers most of the jargon you need. With this handy guide next to your computer you'll always be able to look up new terms. In addition to this glossary, we've created an on-line version for the Erol's Web site—you can use it by visiting *www.erols.com* and looking for the links to our glossary.

Throughout the book, we've tried to anticipate your need to use our glossaries. In those places, when we use jargon to explain some new Internet concept, you'll see a feature we call a *Jargon Cutter* that defines the term on-the-spot. Here's an example:

Jargon Cutter

Jargon Cutter - Throughout the book, we'll use these little inserts to buzzsaw through some of the techno-confusion when we need to spring a new term on you. And, there's always the glossary in the back of this book, or the on-line glossary on the Erol's home page.

We've also sprinkled the book liberally with valuable "Inside Info" tips that will help smooth the information superhighway for you. Here's an example of one:

Inside Info

If you're a new Windows user, you can read the Windows Primer in the Appendix of this book. It's got several short lessons that can help you get acquainted with some basic Windows terms and functions. So, if you need some help using Windows, read our Windows Primer, then return to where you left off and try again.

Erol's history

Erol Onaran left Turkey as a young man with little money in his pocket and dreams in his head. On his way to America, he spent half of his money in Italy, so when he landed here he had only $16 with which to build a new life. Within just a few years, he was in business for himself, having begun his own classic American dream.

The business we know today as Erol's began modestly enough in November of 1963 as a TV and radio repair shop, started on a borrowed $500 investment. After developing a loyal customer base and a reputation for unmatched service, Erol expanded into sales of new TVs in 1967. In 1976, Erol's began to sell the machine that would change the world of entertainment forever—the VCR.

Erol's Video Club was born in 1980 amid little fanfare. Soon the chain would be the home of unparalleled and remarkable growth. By the late eighties there seemed to be an Erol's in every neighborhood in the Washington area. At the time, Erol's was in ten markets, and for more than five years, was the largest video club in the country. Erol's Video Club set an unmatched standard for customer service, with its helpful employees and family atmosphere. The chain grew to 220 stores before being sold to Blockbuster in 1991.

By August of 1992, Erol grew lonesome for the customers he had become so fond of serving. Along with his son Orhan, he bought back the TV/VCR Service Department from Blockbuster and was once again reunited with his former employees and customers. The company began selling TVs and VCRs by the end of the year, and the familiar Washington institution of Erol's customer service was back.

But the Onarans didn't rest on the laurels of the Erol's comeback. In April 1994, Erol's began building and selling computers. Praised by the press for their innovative style of custom-building computers to fit the individual customer's needs, Erol's once again set the standard by which customer service should be judged.

Erol's is now in the midst of its most exciting endeavor yet. In August of 1995 the company entered the growing Internet business with the goal of bringing Erol's kind of customer service to the Internet. From the outset, Erol's aimed to become *the* Internet provider by guaranteeing low prices, high volume, and unbeatable customer service. This particular venture proved to be wildly popular. And with recruitment of the most talented Internet staff available, our service is now well on its way to perfection. At Erol's there is no excuse for customer dissatisfaction, and we make every effort to provide peerless service.

Erol Onaran abides by a simple philosophy: *the customer comes first, his employees come second, his suppliers come third, and he comes last.*

Erol's services

We offer far more than a simple connection to the Internet as you can see in the graphic rundown of our services and products (see Figure 1). Erol's can handle nearly all of your computing needs, both on-line and off-line. We can sell you a tailored, custom computer for less than a generic computer purchased from the large, brand-name dealers—and we back it up with our outstanding Erol's parts and labor warranty. We'll even configure your new computer to work with your Erol's Internet account.

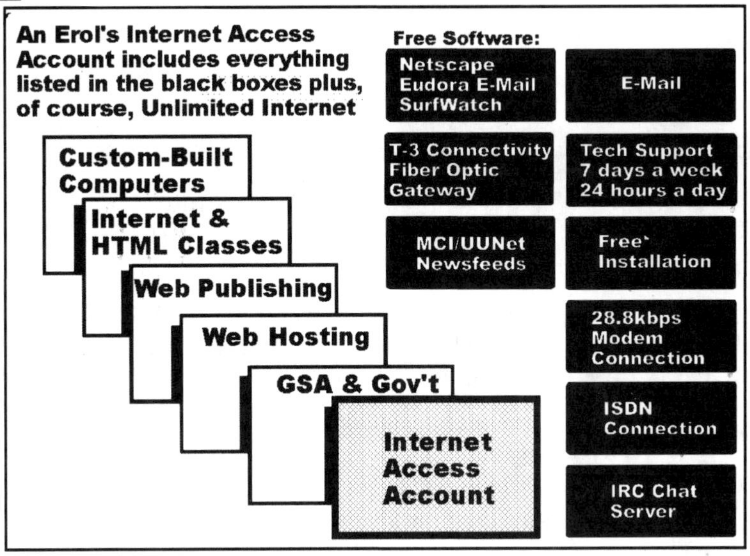

Figure 1 Erol's Internet services

As your on-line needs grow, we can fill them. We can host your personal Web site or even host your large, interactive corporate Web site. And we can handle commercial, educational and government accounts.

Our technicians and programmers can deliver a turn-key Web site, or help with a site you've already got underway. We can enhance your present Web site with form mail or other interactive programming tools. We've attracted some of the best local computer talent available. They'll know *exactly* how to work with your Erol's account!

Internet access account

With an Erol's Internet account, you enjoy **unlimited** access to the Internet, the World Wide Web and e-mail 24 hours per day, 7 days a week. At Erol's, there's never a charge for overtime; in fact, there are no hidden costs or charges, ever! In addition, we offer a wide range of free services that often cost extra at other Internet service providers—and may not even be available at all:

- Free technical support 24 hours a day, 7 days a week.
- Free installation package with a fully-licensed, non-expiring copy of Netscape Navigator and Eudora e-mail, with clear, easy-to-follow installation instructions.
- Free installation of your Internet software at Erol's (by appointment)
- Free T-3 connectivity that provides up to 28 times the capacity of what most Internet service providers offer with T-1 connectivity. Moreover, Erol's has its own fiber optic gateway to the Internet, assuring you of the clearest data transfer possible.
- No extra charge for 28.8kbps modem connection or even for high-speed 128kbps ISDN access.
- Free MCI/UUNet Newsfeed that gives you free access to the most up-to-the-minute news.
- Free access to Erol's own IRC Chat Server.
- Free SurfWatch software upon request as a part of our family Internet package.
- Free extra months of Internet service can be earned through our customer referral program.

Web hosting services

With Erol's International Web Hosting Program, your personal home page or corporate Web site can be on the Net at a fraction of the price charged by most providers. And we offer virtual domain hosting, which means that your Erol's Web site can use your own domain name. Thus, instead of an address of *www.erols.com/yourdomain*, your site can be located at *www.yourdomain.com*. That's a **huge** plus for businesses and a very cool feature even for families.

Web publishing

To help our customers gain an edge in the expanding Internet market, Erol's offers complete Web page design and development, including graphics, CGI scripting and Java. When you're ready to establish an attractive, professional and successful Web site, contact Erol's Web Publishing Department at (703) 321-8000 x2447.

Custom-built computers

Erol's offers the best computing systems, service, price and performance in the region. From the initial contact with our technical staff to determine the system that's just right for you, to testing and post-delivery support for two years, Erol's does everything possible to make your computing experience a pleasure.

Internet and HTML classes

Erol's is pleased to offer Internet, e-mail and HTML courses. These are hands-on classes! You will be on a computer and on the Web as you learn!

GSA, Government Division

For government purchases, please call (703) 321-8000 and ask for GSA ordering information.

Potholes on the "superhighway"

Speaking of superhighways, the term *information superhighway* is way ahead of its time—even though we use the term ourselves. The Internet is really much more like a winding country road with a lot of potholes. In truth, information traveling over the Internet experiences a pretty bumpy ride. It's a miracle than anything ever gets through intact.

You're going to experience traffic jams on the Internet, just as you do on real highways. Sometimes the slowdowns will be due to just normal rush hour problems and sometimes they'll be caused by accidents and weather problems. So, there are times when the best thing is to wait and try again later, or try another Web site.

Internet rush hour

Rush hour on the Internet starts a little before noon on the East Coast as workers begin using their lunch hour to surf the Net. Traffic steadily increases as the lunch hour sweeps across the U.S. By about 5 PM on the East Coast, people are heading home from work and lunch is over on the West Coast, so traffic begins to thin out. Then there's another traffic surge in the evening as people surf the Net after dinner.

Inside Info

Sometimes Erol's does have temporary system problems that will prevent you from logging on or downloading data. It doesn't happen often, but brief outages are a normal part of Internet life today. So, if you try a couple of quick troubleshooting techniques and still can't download anything, call us and listen to our recording. We'll tell you if we're experiencing a temporary system problem. These temporary problems sometimes are Internet-wide outages that prevent anyone in your entire area from using the Internet for awhile. In either case, it's a good idea to check with our recording before you try to reconfigure your system because it's not working.

Gremlins

Occasionally, you'll experience problems that an army of experts couldn't figure out. Call it gremlins, call it Murphy's Law, but sometimes things just go awry. We've found that a good troubleshooting technique is simply to disconnect from the Internet and reconnect. You might be surprised at how many times this does the trick and everything works perfectly, even though no system changes were made. So, if you can't quickly trace the source of your troubles, log off, reconnect, log back on and try again. With our fast, new servers this is a pretty quick procedure.

Try a different number

If you've done everything we've said so far, and you still cannot get anything to download, disconnect and call us again on one of the alternate phone numbers we've given you. Rarely do we experience problems on all of our lines at the same time. And, sometimes, it's not really any trouble, just too many people calling one number. Calling another number may be the equivalent of taking an alternate route. Don't worry about the alternate number being slower, though, because all of our numbers deliver data at the same rate.

The telephone company

Sometimes trouble with the telephone system may cause you difficulty in connecting to your Erol's account. Telephone line problems can become acute during inclement weather. During heavy rain, winds, snow or ice, don't be surprised at telephone line problems. Call our recording for a status check because we work closely with your local phone company and we'll tell you if we're aware of a widespread telephone system problem. The recording may direct you to use an alternate number or let you know how long you can expect to wait for the trouble to clear.

Use some common sense on this. If you're snowed in and you decide to surf the Net because there's nothing else to do and nothing good on television, you can bet that lots of other people have the same idea. Then you've got a jammed telephone system that's also experiencing weather-related problems. Be patient during bad weather!

Troubleshooting

If you have an external modem or use the Windows 95 operating system, you'll have indicators that let you see what's going on with your Internet connection. These indicators can help you diagnose connection problems. Don't worry, we're not going to ask you to memorize all the lights on your modem. But if you understand just three of them, you'll spare yourself some confusion. Many times your system will appear to be stuck, when, in fact, everything is working fine and it's merely busy receiving data.

The three important lights on your modem are the ones that tell you if you're *connected*, if data is being *sent* and if data is being *received*.

Off-hook

One light on an external modem indicates if the modem is "off-hook." This light might be labeled **OH**. Being off-hook doesn't mean that the modem is connected to another computer. It's just telling you that the modem has opened the phone line as if you had taken a telephone off-hook, but it's still an important light. If you're not receiving data from Erol's, check your off-hook light. If the off-hook light is out, then there is *absolutely no chance* that you are connected to Erol's.

Send data

One light on an external modem indicates that the modem is sending data. This light might be labeled **SD** (for send data) or **TX** (for transmit). For this light to be useful to you, you need to know when your modem *should* be sending data. Naturally, the send light will flash when you send an e-mail message. But it also needs to send a short burst of data every time you request anything from the Internet. For example, if you visit a Web site, your modem must send to the Web site a request for information. Periodically, during long downloads, this light will blink occasionally as your modem acknowledges receipt of downloaded information.

Receive data

One light on an external modem indicates that the modem is receiving data. This light might be labeled **RD** (for receive data) or **RX** (for receive). The use of this light will be obvious when you're downloading data. It will flash very rapidly and may even appear to be on steadily.

But even while you're receiving a steady data stream, you'll see your send light flash occasionally. And that will be the normal mode during steady downloads: the receive light flashing rapidly with occasional blips of the send light.

If it seems that your system has frozen when you're expecting data to be downloading, look at these three lights. First, check that your modem has not unexpectedly hung up on you. If it's still off-hook, then watch the receive light—if it's not flashing, then check the send light. If the send light is showing occasional blips, that means that your system is sending out requests to receive information but no data is coming in. In this situation, your system is working fine but an Internet traffic jam is preventing the information from arriving. Just be patient and wait, or try another Web site.

Most Frequently Asked Questions (FAQs)

Erol's technical support is unsurpassed in the industry. We answer our calls quickly and we have talented technical staff that's familiar with almost every software package in use on the Internet. If you give us enough detail, we can usually solve your connection problems. But, as good as we are, it's even faster to fix problems yourself. To help save you calls to technical support, we've included our technical support list of the most frequently-asked questions that we get on our phone lines.

Number 1
What are my Internet configuration settings?

Primary DNS:	205.252.116.61
Secondary DNS:	205.252.116.62
POP3 User Name:	Your Erol's user ID
POP Server:	pop.erols.com
SMTP Server:	smtp.erols.com
NNTP Server:	news.erols.com

Number 2
I have a 14.4kbps modem and still have trouble getting on. What can I do?

Windows 3.x
Click on **Erol's Internet v4.4d Dialer**.
Click on **Properties**, **General**, then select **Manual** login.
Click on **Bring up TTY Window** and **Enable Dial on demand**.

Windows 95
Right-click **My Computer**, then double-click **Dial-Up Networking**.
Right-click the **Erol's** icon, then click **Properties.**.
Click **Configure, Options**.
Click **Bring up Terminal Window After Dialing**.
Click **OK, OK**, then close the Control Panel.

Number 3
I've been on before, surfed the Web and used e-mail, but now I get an error message. What do I do?

The best thing to is to disconnect and try connecting later to Erol's if you get any of these messages:

- Unable to establish a compatible set of network preferences as specified by the server type setting in the Control Panel.
- Unable to establish a dial-Up network connection.
- Unable to establish a dial-in connection.
- Computer you are calling is not answering/responding (or is hanging up modem)
- The line/telephone number you are trying is busy.
- Any POP or SMTP error (for example, "Error connecting to POP server).
- Authentication error (password seems not to work).

Inside Info
Any time you encounter an error message, be sure to either keep it on the screen until you've read it to an Erol's tech support specialist, or write it down *exactly* as it reads on the screen so you can tell us later what it said. We often can't help you if you call and simply say you had some sort of error message.

Number 4
I'm connected but I can't get to any Web pages. What can I do?

Search your hard drive to make sure you've got a file called *winsock.dll*. With Windows 3.x, use the File Manager. With Windows 95, use the Explorer. Be sure that you search for hidden files.

Number 5
How do I get to the IRC chat lines?

First you must download, install and configure an IRC client, such as Netscape Chat. Then connect to a server. Our Web page has step-by-step instructions on installing and configuring IRC. Erol's has its own chat server located at *irc.erols.com*.

Inside Info
You can download an IRC client from us at *www.erols.com/erols/support/irc.htm*. Or you can search the Web for other sources by visiting Yahoo! (*www.yahoo.com*) or Lycos (*www.lycos.com*) and searching for "IRC client software."

Number 6
Why can't I see my mail in Netscape?

You need to maximize the mail window, or switch to it using **ALT+TAB**.

Number 7
How do I connect to Erol's, and surf and look up objects on the Net?

Dial-up Erol's Internet by double-clicking on the Erol's icon and, after connecting, start Netscape. In the location bar, you may enter the address of any Web site and press **ENTER**. To look up locations of Web sites on any subject, choose the **Net Search** button in Netscape. For more detailed information, refer to the chapter on Netscape, beginning on page 57.

Number 8
My settings are correct, Erol's is working fine and I have my paper from Erol's with my password, but this is the first time I am getting on and Erol's is saying "password error." What could be wrong?

Erol's passwords are case-sensitive. For example, if your password were "Sample," entering "sample" would fail. Make sure you've typed correctly and that the **Caps Lock** key is *not* on.

Number 9
What information will I need when I call Erol's Tech Support?

You should have the User ID you've chosen, your password, the Erol's telephone number you are trying to use and your installation disks. You also may need your DOS, Windows 3.x, Windows 95, or Windows NT disks. You will need to know the brand name of your modem (for example, U.S. Robotics Courier) and speed (28.8kbps). If you do not know what your brand name is, ask the dealer from whom you purchased the modem or the system.

Digital telephone service

Most of our subscribers connect to us via normal, analog telephone modems. These modems generally have a maximum connection speed of 28.8kbps. That means that the modem can download 28,800 bits of information per second. That's an adequate speed for many Internet services and lots of people are happy with it.

But you can use digital telephone service and a digital modem to experience speeds far higher than you get with an analog modem. Technically there's no such thing as a digital modem because when it's digital it's called a terminal adapter (TA). But as far as the function is concerned, an ISDN terminal adapter is essentially a digital modem. The digital phone service is called ISDN (Integrated Services Digital Network). With an Erol's ISDN connection, you'll log on at speeds up to 128kbps.

Erol's does not charge extra for ISDN service, although the telephone company does charge extra for the ISDN phone line into your home. And, you'll need to buy a terminal adapter. Once the ISDN phone line and the terminal adapter are installed, you can connect to Erol's through the normal phone numbers. Our equipment will automatically detect that you're using ISDN and will connect you at the higher speed. As a bonus to using ISDN, you'll be pleased to discover that connection time is reduced to about 4 seconds—no more waiting for your analog modem to connect.

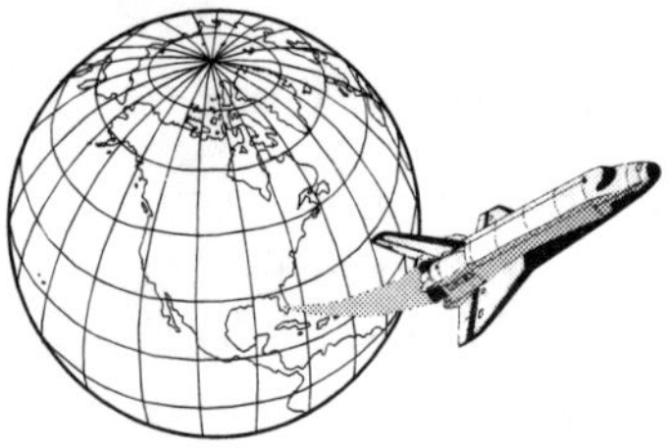

Orbiting in Cyberspace

Motorola
http://www.mot.com

Motorola makes the most popular ISDN terminal adapters, the BitSURFR and the BitSURFR Pro. The BitSURFRs are highly recommended by Bell Atlantic Info-Speed. And their technical support staff are experts at configuring Bell Atlantic Info-Speed ISDN service with Motorola products. Motorola's home page will keep you up to date with their ISDN products. They also include several links to other sites that deal with telecommunications issues. And, you'll find a helpful FAQs file that might answer some of your ISDN questions. While you're visiting them, you can complete their on-line survey to tell them what you think about ISDN Internet service.

Microsoft
http://www.microsoft.com/windows/software/isdn.htm

Microsoft has downloadable utility packages that can help you get connected to the Internet via ISDN. If you use an external ISDN terminal adapter (TA), Windows 95 will configure your system with no problem because it treats an external TA as a regular modem. But if you use an internal TA, you'll need to update your Windows 95 with Microsoft's latest ISDN utility.

Why Choose Erol's as Your ISP?

You'll get an unlimited combination of benefits and value, with unsurpassed service and an ironclad guarantee of satisfaction. ***That's why!***

- **The best software** - Free Internet Netscape Navigator™ and E-mail software
- **Free SurfWatch™** software so you can control what your children can access (upon request)
- **Macintosh and PC access** available
- **Free, easy-to-use custom setup disks** and CD-ROM
- **No hidden costs,** charges, or cancellation fees, ever
- **Fastest access,** with 28.8 to 33.6kbps, v.34, digital modems on our gateway
- **64kbps ISDN** for the same price as a standard account
- **Custom computers** for less than major brands

Here's a summary of Erol's Internet Services:

Internet Access Account (http://www.erols.com/erols/services.htm)

- Unlimited, 24-hour-a-day access to the Internet, the World Wide Web, and E-mail, with never a charge for overtime. In fact, there are no hidden costs or charges, ever!
- Free technical support 24 hours a day, 7 days a week.
- A fully-licensed, non-expiring copy of Netscape Navigator with E-mail software, and clear, easy-to-follow installation instructions.
- Free installation of your Internet software at any Erol's retail location (by appointment only).
- T-3 connectivity, giving you up to 28 times the capacity of what most providers offer with their T-1s. Erol's has its own fiber optic gateway to the Internet, assuring you of the clearest data transfer possible.
- 28.8 to 33.6kbps modem connection; 64kbps ISDN available at same price as regular dial-up account.
- More than 28,000 newsgroups, giving you free access to the most up-to-the-minute news.
- Free access to our IRC Chat Server (currently in beta testing).
- Free SurfWatch software ($29.95 value) upon request as a part of our family Internet package.
- Free months of service available through our Referral Program.

Web Hosting Programs (http://www.erols.com/erols/hosting.htm) (webhost@erols.com)
With Erol's World Wide Web Hosting Program, your personal home page or corporate Web site can be on the Net at a fraction of the price charged by most providers.

Web Publishing (http://www.erols.com/erols/webpub.htm) (webpub@erols.com)
To help our customers gain an edge in the expanding Internet market, Erol's offers complete Web page design and development, including graphics, CGI scripting, and Java. When you're ready for an attractive, professional, successful Web site, contact Erol's Web Publishing at (703) 321-8000 X2447.

Custom Built Computers (http://www.erols.com/erols/products/computers.htm)
Erol's offers the best computing systems, service, price, and performance in the region. From initial contact with our technical staff to determine the system that's right for you, to testing and post-delivery support for two years, Erol's does everything possible to make your computing experience a pleasure.

Internet and HTML Classes (http://www.erols.com/erols/classes.htm) (sales@erols.com)
Erol's offers hands-on Internet, E-mail, and HTML courses starting at $49. You'll be on a computer and on the Web as you learn.

Further questions? Call 1-800-EROLS PC (1-800-376-5722) or E-mail to webhost@erols.com for Web Hosting questions

See Erol's on the Web! www.erols.com

2

Ground School: Internet Quick Tour

In case you want to be included in Internet discussions at parties or around the office, we've included this chapter to help you get a quick overview of that famous *information superhighway*. If you want to know how it came to be, then this chapter will give you just enough of the Internet's origin, history and current status so that you can chat about it, but you'll not be burdened with a lot of geeky details. After all, many drivers on our regular highways have no idea how the U.S. Interstate highway system was built. Similarly, you don't *need to read* this chapter—but it's short and really pretty simple.

If you enjoy details and want even more, you can find out more about the Internet from the Internet itself. The end of this chapter lists a wide selection of Internet sites that can help you peek under the hood of the Internet. There's no reason to include a lot of information in this book that's available on the Internet.

But let's not worry about details now, we're just out for a scenic tour. So, we'll begin by defining one term important now, the term "internet" itself.

internet versus The Internet

There are internets and then there is The Internet. A small "i" internet could be any two computer *networks* that are interconnected so that users on both networks can share resources on either network. A network is at least two computers connected locally to each other—but some networks have thousands of computers. An internet is at least two connected networks—regardless of the size of either one. Here, we've depicted two connected networks as icons and have labeled them Network A and Network B (see Figure 1). This is the simplest internet possible.

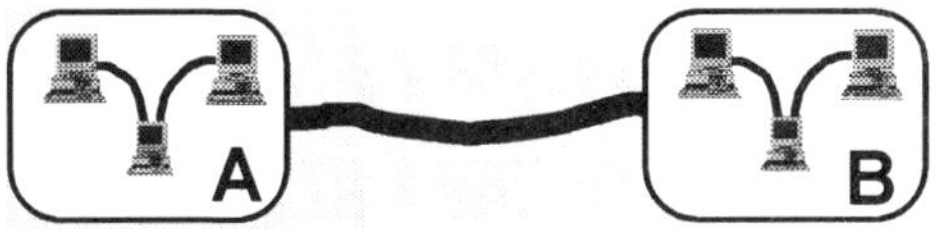

Figure 1 A basic internet

More networks can be connected, but in the simplest form of an internet, they all must be directly connected to each other (see Figure 2). Notice that each network, labeled Networks A, B, C and D, has a direct connection to every other network on this internet.

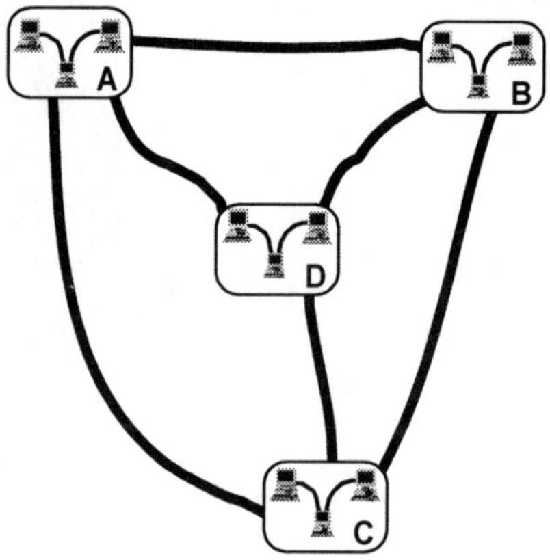

Figure 2 Directly connected internet

It's easy to see that directly connecting each computer would limit the size and area that an internet could cover. Linking them in series would reduce the number of lines (see Figure 3) but Network A is not connected to Network D. For A and D to exchange information, the middle networks, labeled Networks B and C, must act as relays for the outerlying networks.

Networks that act as relays include devices called routers. In Figure 4, for example, Network B and Network E are not directly connected, so they can communicate only via the routers in intermediary networks. If Network A has a router, then data traffic could be routed from Network B through Network A to Network E. If Network A does not have routing capability, but Network C and Network D do, then Network B still could communicate with Network E through Networks C and D. Routers are what makes the global Internet possible.

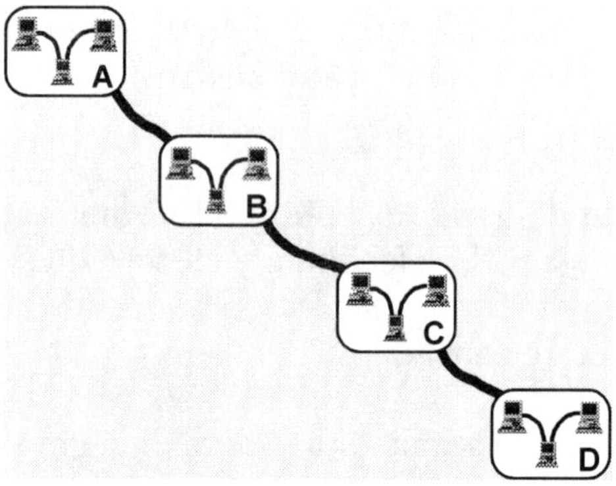

Figure 3 Linear internet

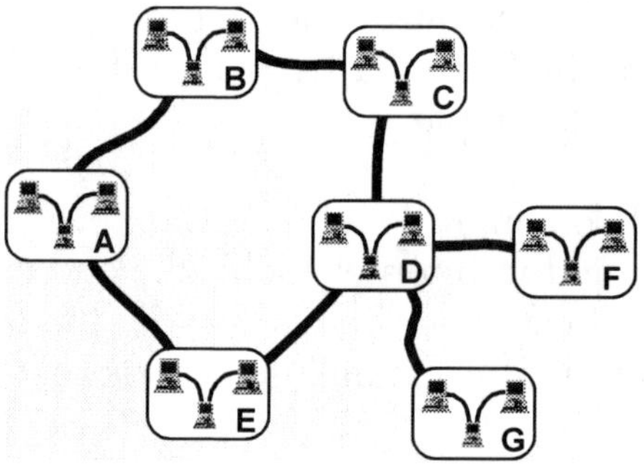

Figure 4 Small internet with routers

The Internet

Imagine if one of the above-depicted network models grew to connect millions of computers around the world. That's the capital "I" Internet—the master of all internets—and it has become practically a living entity.

No one knows how many networks the Internet connects. The number of computers connected via the Internet increases daily, approximately doubling every six months. Some Internet gurus predict that the number of Internet users could reach 100 million by 1998 and could reach 500 million by 2001.

Or, those figures could be off by a large margin in either direction. The bottom line is that the Internet is a vast, global entity of, literally, countless computers, networks, routers and data lines. If you really want to know the latest estimates, check out some of the addresses listed at the end of this chapter.

How the Internet got started

The Internet started at the U.S. Department of Defense (DoD). In the Cold War era, the DoD needed to create a research network to link computers in universities, research labs and government centers all across the country. The DoD donated a lot of money to universities and helped universities get connected to each other.

The DoD, therefore, accidentally did us all a wonderful favor. They planted the seed for the Internet by sponsoring the development of the basic "genetic-coding"—called network protocols—and then they set it free. From this early research sprang the TCP/IP network protocols (Transmission Control Protocol/Internet Protocol) that handle the global data transfers that race across today's Internet. The government's hands-off approach worked in your favor because it left the Internet to grow without the burdens and restraints of being accountable to an office of bureaucrats.

The Internet was designed and built in a totally free environment by the people who knew best how to build it. It's so vast and uses such a varied collection of computers and connections that it can't be destroyed without destroying the nerve centers of every developed nation. And that was the DoD's plan, illustrated by this quotation from RFC1462 that says the Internet was born "...trying to connect together a U.S. Defense Department network called the ARPANET and various other radio and satellite networks. The ARPANET was an experimental network designed to support military research—in particular, research about how to build networks that could withstand partial outages (like bomb attacks) and still function."

So, while the U.S. Government was the parent, no group ever has controlled the Internet. And now it's too big for anyone to even try to control it.

Why the Internet is so popular

Personal computers have been consumer products for more than 20 years, since the Apple II launched the PC revolution in 1974. During that time, most people have avoided computers completely. Many of those who use PCs do so because they're expected to use PCs at work—even though many users would be happy to never touch another PC. So why is it, after so much avoidance, that everyone seems to be racing to get on-line?

> "A human being is a part of the whole, called by us 'Universe,' a part limited in time and space. We experience ourselves, our thoughts and our feelings as something separated from the rest—a kind of optical delusion of our consciousness. This delusion is a kind of prison for us, restricting us to our personal desires and to affection for a few persons nearest to us.
>
> Our task must be to free ourselves from this prison by widening our circle of compassion to embrace all living creatures and the whole of nature in its beauty."
>
> **Albert Einstein**

Einstein understood that one day we would, collectively, begin to see through this optical delusion of separateness. The Internet is the first tangible evidence that humankind can truly be interconnected and can widen "our circle of compassion to embrace all living creatures." Cyberspace is the planetary space from where we finally can see beyond the limitations of our personal desires and realize the vast benefits to global unity.

There's really no control?

That's right!

Practically speaking, of course, no complex system would function smoothly without some central coordination. But coordination is not control. The Internet's central coordination is provided by the Internet Architecture Board (IAB) that *ratifies* the communications standards on the Internet.

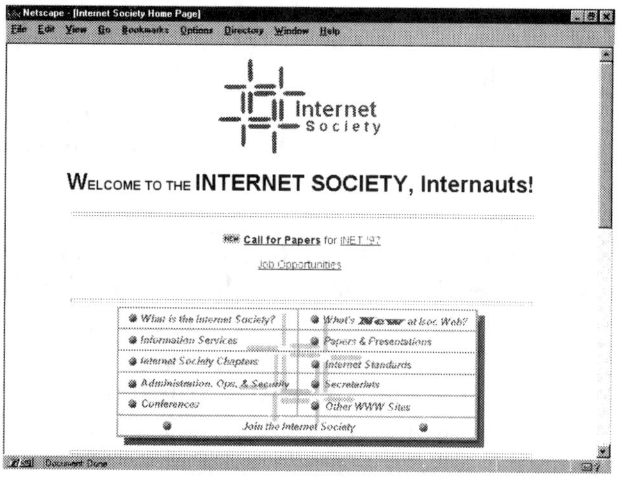

Figure 5 The ISOC home page

The IAB heads a group of volunteers called the Internet Society (ISOC) that fosters the Internet and promotes Internet usage. The ISOC is based in Reston, Virginia, has branch groups around the world and hosts an annual, global conference (see Figure 5). The ISOC's first president, Dr. Vinton Cerf, is the co-creator of the basic programming codes—called TCP/IP (Transmission Control Protocol/Internet Protocol)—that you will use as you "surf" through cyberspace.

Another group of volunteers—no more groups after this, we promise—called the Internet Engineering Task Force (IETF) develops standards and resolves Internet technical and operational issues. The IETF functions as a public forum that organizes workgroups that explore ways to keep the Internet abreast of technology changes.

How you got invited

During the Internet's first 20 years or so, the people who were building and using it did not allow any commercial or personal usage. Its construction had been funded by a vast conglomeration of organizations and was used primarily for technical communications between those who built it.

The first major step toward you being invited to the cyberspace party occurred in the late 1980s when the National Science Foundation (NSF) established its own network, the NSFNET, to connect five supercomputers that it owned. The NSF realized that these supercomputers had the potential to be a national treasure if they were inter-connected and made available to other computer systems across the U.S. Wisely, the NSF set up a national network modeled after the existing Internet. This provided regular Internet connections and access across the U.S.

Cyberspace

Cyberspace has become a generic term that represents the total universe of all interconnected computers. The term was created by science fiction author William Gibson. In Gibson's books, cyberspace is a computer network called "The Matrix." His books foretell of a cold and forbidding future that suffers from too many people and too many computers. Mere fiction, right?

The dissolution of the Communist Party in the Soviet Union triggered some vast changes in the lifestyles of former Soviet citizens. But the collapse of the Soviet Union has had a far-reaching impact on us all and the Internet may be a highly visible sign of the sweeping, global changes that have followed.

With the Cold War threat gone, the defense-related purposes of the Internet all but evaporated. Blessedly for all of humankind, the people who held the reins of this potential military machine recognized its value as a tool for the growth of global peace and international harmony. Commercial Internet traffic no longer was considered to be unacceptable or inappropriate usage and restrictions on Internet connection requirements were lifted.

Commercial On-line Services

Where do commercial on-line services—such as CompuServe, America On Line (AOL) and Prodigy—fit into the Internet? You most likely have been bombarded by their advertising hype touting their Internet service. Many people ask me, "Isn't AOL the Internet?" Not exactly.

AOL is a self-contained on-line service that only recently connected itself to the Internet. Your Erol's system is connected directly to the Internet, so Erol's users don't need AOL for Internet service.

Let us illustrate.

Back in the 1960s there was a television series called *Route 66* in which two guys cruised the country on a perpetual road-trip in a Corvette convertible. Now, many years later, the Route 66 TV series has become a good metaphor for the Internet:

The Internet is to on-line services what Route 66 is to Disney World.

You can enter the gate at Disney's theme park and pick up a nice, colorful map of what to do, read a schedule of events, and easily locate safe places to eat. The restrooms are clean and there's not a gum wrapper in sight.

But a road trip on Route 66 in a Corvette convertible is entirely a different experience. Where do you go next? What will happen next? What will you see next? No one knows, but that's the fun part.

We realized that just jumping onto a cyberspace version of Route 66 might be a bit overwhelming. That's why we created the Erol's Home Page for your Internet service. Erol's brings you a sense of order without restricting you as some on-line services do.

By the way, Route 66 itself is on the Web. In fact, it's an incredibly detailed and well-done site. Believe it or not, however, the site was built and is maintained by Swa Frantzen, who lives in *Belgium*. The site begins with the full map of Route 66 and permits you to click on segments to zoom in to evermore detailed maps and eventually to zoom down to photos taken along the way. Get your own kicks on Route 66 by visiting *http://route66.netvision.be*, you don't even need a Corvette.

Who is the Internet?

You are. And so are your friends. And so is your Erol's Internet service.

And *where* is the Internet? It's your computer, every other computer connected to the Internet, plus millions of miles of copper wire, fiber optic cable, microwave channels and satellite links. It's similar to the air you breathe; no one owns it or controls it and it's everywhere.

Isn't it wonderful that the Internet, with its roots tied to the DoD, has now become a thriving, open system? It seems to fulfill an ancient prophesy that said, "They will beat their swords into plowshares and their spears into pruning hooks." Well, that's a bit of a stretch because they were virtual swords and they've become virtual plowshares, but now it's yours. So jump into your virtual Corvette, hit the gas and enjoy an exciting road trip!

What's out there for me?

You have probably heard a lot lately about the Internet. Most of what you've heard is about one aspect of the Internet that's called the World Wide Web. You'll often see it written in shorthand—Web, WWW and W3. There are several other aspects to the Internet, but the importance of the others is waning rapidly. But here's a short rundown of each, beginning with the Web.

World Wide Web (Web)

As with many inventions, the World Wide Web has become more than anyone ever dreamed. The Internet created the basic connections to join us all into a single interrelated system, but the Web merged the old Internet with modern graphics, colorful screens, sound and animation. The Web made the Internet user-friendly by employing technology called *hypertext*. Hypertext, as used on the Web, makes the Internet almost universally accessible because you can access information with simple mouse clicks instead of arcane computer commands.

Jargon Cutter

World Wide Web - An Internet-based system, created at the CERN laboratory in switzerland in 1991, that lets you access documents that are linked together with the Hypertext Markup Language (HTML). It's called a Web because all of its documents are woven together into what is essentially a single system, even though it's made up of documents from millions of sources.

When information is written in hypertext, key words and graphic images can be highlighted and linked to related text. The reader merely clicks on a highlighted word to jump to the linked, related text.

Think of the end of an article in an encyclopedia that has a listing of "Related Topics." How many times have you actually dragged out all the additional volumes that would be required to see those related topics? How about never?

But in a hypertext encyclopedia (CD-ROM encyclopedias use hypertext), you simply click on the titles of the related topics to jump to the follow-on article. How many times will you actually click on a hypertext link to see a related topic? How about constantly? Hypertext is a charismatic attraction—it's an electronic black hole that can pull you ever deeper into interesting areas in cyberspace—and that attraction is why you may have heard so much about the Web.

E-Mail

The bulk of Internet traffic is electronic mail (e-mail). E-mail enables you to swap messages with anyone on the Internet anywhere in the world. The best part is that e-mail is free through your Erol's Internet service—there are no distance-based or per-message charges for e-mail. A few on-line services still charge a per message rate, but you don't have to worry about that. E-mail will completely change the way you conduct much of your communication.

We've included a full chapter on Internet e-mail in Phase 2. It's got plenty of Step-by-Step exercises that will help you master the Eudora e-mail software that came with your Erol's subscription.

Newsgroups

Newsgroups—sometimes referred to as the Usenet—are electronic discussion forums. Newsgroups are akin to community bulletin boards upon which people can post notices, but they serve the global community and have no formal membership requirements—anyone on the Internet can read and post messages. No one can accurately count their number, but we've counted as many as 26,318 public newsgroups. There also are private newsgroups but counting them would be impossible.

You'll also be using your Netscape software to access Internet newsgroups. There's a full chapter on newsgroups in Phase 2.

FTP (File Transfer Protocol)

The title pretty much explains its usage—you can use the File Transfer Protocol (FTP) to transfer computer files between your computer and other computers on the Internet. You will use this mostly to transfer files into your computer from larger computer systems (download or receive), though you also can transfer files from your computer to others (upload or send). What can you get using FTP? Just about anything you can imagine that can be stored on a computer: software, documents, spreadsheets, maps, photos, a copy of the Constitution, audio sound clips and even video clips. The Internet has thousands of FTP sites and millions of files.

Perhaps you'll use the FTP directly sometime, but you will encounter it primarily as a hidden part of the Web. You can use your Web browser to access FTP sites and to download files, but you cannot upload files with your Web browser. You'll find a full chapter on FTP, including Step-by-Step exercises, in Phase 2.

Mailing Lists

Here's a terrific tool to stay informed up-to-the-minute on a vast array of topics. The best feature about getting information from this system is that—unlike most of the Internet—it comes to you. Instead of providing a repository of information that can be searched and downloaded, mailing lists send automated e-mail to users who subscribe to electronic publications.

When you subscribe to most mailing lists, you join an informal, electronic community. The core of any mailing list is a software application called a *list server* that runs the list. When any member sends a message to the mailing list (actually to the designated list server), that message is redistributed to all members of the group. In a large group with lots of traffic, the In box in your e-mail application can fill in a few hours.

Some mailing lists are *moderated*, which means that someone reads the incoming messages and decides which ones to redistribute to the entire group. Depending on your point of view, you'll regard the moderator either as a meddling censor or as a thankless saint doing you an enormous favor.

Gopher

A team of computer folks at the University of Minnesota developed in 1991 a system that enables Internet users to "go fer" stuff all over cyberspace. Can it be merely coincidence, then, that the mascot of the University of Minnesota is a gopher? The name certainly fits because this electronic rodent can burrow all over the Internet to find information you want.

Once the mainstay of surfing the Net, most people now use Gopher only when it pops up on the Web. There are some Web-based Gopher searching tools, but it's not likely that you'll need any of them. Sometimes a regular Web site—especially at universities and libraries—will take you to a Gopher page. The Web browser we've included with your Erol's service handles Gopher pages so well that you may hardly notice you're not actually viewing a hypertext document.

Golden Oldies

In the Introduction to this book, we told you that many aspects of the Internet already have become passé. That doesn't mean they're old—it just means that life in cyberspace moves pretty fast and yesterday's hot technology is today's "Remember when..." The vinyl records of the Internet are Veronica, Archie, Jughead, Finger, Telnet and WAIS. This book won't cover any of these, but wait until you've gotten deeply involved with the Web to see if you are crying, "More!"

Information that until recently only was available through these golden oldies is rapidly migrating to the Web. Depending on your field of interest, you may need some of these temporarily. You, however, should be able to find everything you want without leaving the Erol's system or the Netscape Web browser. Since almost all of your Internet work will involve the Web, let's close your Internet tour by returning to the topic of the World Wide Web.

Web principles

While the Web is vast and it may seem complicated, the Web's underlying principles are surprisingly simple. The task of implementing those simple principles across a dizzying array of incompatible computer systems, however, has not been simple. Our hats are off to the talented people who invented and created the Web. It required a lot of detailed planning and work, but the core principles remain simple.

The Web is built around computer documents. That is basically it. Using any Web browser on the Web basically resembles loading documents into your word processor. As you most likely are aware, your Windows word processor can display embedded graphic images and play embedded sound files. So can the Netscape Navigator. The Netscape Navigator just can't edit the files it loads. So, you can think of your Web browser as a "read-only" word processor.

Why use a read-only word processor?

You'd have little use for a read-only word processor if all you ever loaded in it were files from your own computer. But what if you could connect your read-only word processor to a remote computer that held documents that contained information you could use? You might be interested in loading some of those files even if you couldn't edit them—especially if you could print them and save them so that you could edit them in your word processor.

Inside Info

The Netscape Navigator has a "Gold" version that is not a true "read-only" application. Navigator Gold allows users to edit Web documents and create their own HTML pages. The read-only principle remains the same, however, because even with Navigator Gold, you can't change the files on the original Web server.

Then we could connect your read-only word processor to thousands of remote computers—located all over the planet—that held millions of documents that contained just about every type of information you can imagine. Then we'll give you a wide variety of search tools to help you pinpoint information you need from among the millions of available documents.

Then we could include in these documents graphic images, photographs, sound files, video clips and forms that let you submit applications and make credit card purchases. Then, we could cross-link all of these millions of documents so that when you locate a document that contains some information you want, it could link you to other documents on related topics merely by clicking a mouse. We'll call these links "hypertext" because they hyper-accelerate your ability to find what you need from among millions of pages of text.

Finally, we could give you the ability to put your own information on this system so that anyone connected to it could find your information by topical index or by a keyword search and give you the ability to cross-link your information to other documents on related topics. If this sounds valuable to you, then you'll find the Web to be an exciting tool that will revolutionize the way you think about the world.

Hypertext

If you are becoming confused by the term "hypertext," don't be dismayed. It's not your fault that hypertext isn't hypertext anymore.

The term was created as a definition for a word or phrase within a text document that provides a link to other text documents. In an electronic encyclopedia, for example, you merely click on any of the "Related Topics" and you see the related article—that's hypertext.

Your first exposure to using hypertext, however, might be to click on a graphic image that jumps to another graphic image. Or you might click on a graphic image that downloads a sound file. "Why," you might ask, "is a button called *hypertext*?"

Sorry about the confusion. But a long, long time ago—way back in 1991—no one had any idea that hypertext would become what it is today. Obviously the people who coined the term hypertext were better computer programmers than seers. That's not a complaint, though, because no one saw this coming. If the term were to be coined today, it might be called "hyperlink."

The bottom line is that hypertext is on-screen magic. It is revolutionizing communication. You'll be able to click on words, buttons or graphic images and be swept off to any region within cyberspace that the author wanted you to see—other documents, images, sound clips, video clips, forms, software and tables of data. And you easily will be able to create your own hyperlinked documents, thus being able to jump your readers off to any region within cyberspace that you'd like them to see.

We all are one

We all want to be connected—it's a natural part of human nature because, truly, "We all are one." The hyperlinks on the World Wide Web are rapidly creating a physical manifestation of our longing for unity—to become one.

> "In a real sense all life is inter-related. All persons are caught in an inescapable network of mutuality, tied in a single garment of destiny. Whatever affects one directly, affects all indirectly... I can never be what I ought to be until you are what you ought to be, and you can never be what you ought to be until I am what I ought to be. This is the inter-related structure of reality."
>
> **Martin Luther King, Jr.**

King probably wasn't thinking of the Internet when he wrote about the "network of mutuality," but it's possible—the Internet had been born. Whether or not he knew it then, today we have an unsurpassed network of mutuality that will have joined together everyone on this planet by the end of 1996. As this book is written, the World Bank is completing its Web presence in Africa, the last populated continent to get Internet connectivity. Thus, global Internet service soon will be in place and the planet will be able to act as a unit.

The World Wide Web has given us the ability to transform humanity into a single living organism. Think of it on a personal level first, then on a planetary level.

If you get a splinter in your finger, your whole body rallies to help the tiny area that's affected. Similarly, the World Wide Web has given us the ability to direct our energies toward even tiny areas that need the help of the entire system. And, such an intense focus will help us all because it will prevent small problems from festering into much larger ones that could harm the global population.

For example, if we all had had the benefit of "splinter-like" communication when the HIV virus first was discovered in monkeys, there likely would be no global epidemic today. Unfortunately, the parts of humanity that had the ability to stop the problem while it was only a splinter did not feel a oneness with such a small affliction. We still were suffering under the delusion that we all are separate. But the Web can help us prevent future "splinters" in the body of humanity from festering into serious, harmful problems. We hope that as you learn to use the Web, you'll bear in mind its unprecedented ability to join us as we always have been meant to be joined.

Erol's Internet access

And where, might you ask, does Erol's fit into the Internet? Well, we are connected to the Internet through high-speed cables that deliver Internet information to our facility at blazing speed. Our service is something extra—and no one is better equipped to bring it to you. It's all about a technical term called "bandwidth."

Jargon Cutter

Bandwidth - A term that represents the amount of data that can flow through an electronic cable. You could equate it to the size of a pipe in a water system. The larger the pipe, the more water, the larger the bandwidth, the more data. Internet bandwidth is expressed in bits per second. Data can flow no faster than the slowest section of bandwidth through which it passes.

If you use a 14.4kbps modem, it may be the weakest link in the chain of electronics that brings Internet service into your computer. Think of a 14.4kbps modem as an especially narrow section of road. Most of the Internet has sufficient bandwidth, but a slow modem will mask the speed potential because data must go the last few feet of its journey through a narrow passage.

Today, however, your system no longer has to be the weak link in the chain. Erol's has an enormous bandwidth capacity—thousands of times faster than telephone modems. In fact, your Erol's service can dish out information to you much faster than most of the Internet can deliver it. That means we've got lots of bandwidth to spare and you can experience our faster service by upgrading your phone line and modem to Integrated Digital Services Network (ISDN) service.

Jargon Cutter

ISDN - Integrated Digital Services Network is digital service from your local telephone company. ISDN lines have two channels, each with a capacity to carry data at up to 64Kbps. They can be bonded to produce 128Kbps Internet access speed, or you can use only one 64K channel and use the other channel for voice calls or faxes *while* you're orbiting in cyberspace!

Does this also mean that everything you do on the Internet with ISDN will be blazing fast? No, not at all. Your Erol's system gets its Internet traffic via a wide highway and then it delivers it to you via a wide highway, but much of the Internet still suffers from serious bandwidth limitations. If a Web site you visit has a slower Internet connection than yours, you'll receive data from it no faster than it can send data. So, sometimes the weakest link is the Web sites you visit. The speed at which data loads into your system depends on the speed of every Internet connection between your computer and every Web site you contact.

Until ISDN Internet service made its debut in your community, only very large Internet service providers or very large companies could afford to get high-speed service from the telephone company. But recent cuts in ISDN service pricing have made this special high-speed service quite affordable. For more information on how you can enjoy maximum Internet speed at home, call our sales office at 703-321-8000.

Orbiting in Cyberspace

The Internet changes too rapidly to pin down in one book. Because of this, we include at the end of each chapter a collection of Internet resources that will help you with the chapter you've just read. We call these collections "Orbiting in Cyberspace." The resources in them include a lot of valuable Internet sites that will keep you abreast of the rapidly-changing world of the Internet.

The Internet Society
http://www.isoc.org

The Internet Society (ISOC) is the non-governmental, international organization for global cooperation and coordination for the Internet and its internetworking technologies and applications. Its members, both individual and organizational, have a common goal of maintaining the viability and the global scaling of the Internet.

For individual membership: membership@isoc.org
For organization membership: organization-membership@isoc.org
Fax: 703-648-9887
Voice: 703-648-9888 (or 800-468-9507 in the USA only)
Mail: 12020 Sunrise Valley Drive, Suite 270
Reston, Virginia, 22091, USA.

Useless Web pages
http://www.primus.com/staff/paulp/useless.html

There's more to the Web than education, value, business and commercialism. Need a break? Then check out "America's Funniest Home Hypermedia." This site has been rated by Wired magazine as "A waste of electrons." But don't confuse this with "bad Web pages." Useless isn't necessarily bad, it's just useless. Sometimes that means you'll see some very good Web pages—depending on your point of view and sense of humor. Be forewarned, though: this page can lead you into the deepest, darkest side of the Web. Sit back and waste some electrons, Internet bandwidth and time.

The Smiley FAQ
http://www.newbie.net/JumpStations/SmileyFAQ.html

Let me quote the opening text of this page, "Because you can't see the person who is sending you electronic mail you are sometimes uncertain whether they are serious or just joking with you. About 14 years ago, Scott Fahlman, of Carnegie Mellon University, devised a scheme for encoding and conveying one's feelings as small text glyphs to overcome this frustration." These glyphs are called "smileys" and this page includes a listing of the most commonly used smileys and their definitions.

Cyber Course
http://www.newbie.net/CyberCourse

Here's a permanent, on-going training site on the Web, designed especially for new Internet users (newbies). It's an extremely well-done treasure trove of information and it's free. It includes a section called "Cyber Course" and another called "Newbie Newz." The course has several sections that can walk you through learning Internet basics. The Newbie Newz is a mailing list that will help you learn about the Internet.

Computer Literacy Bookshops home page
http://www.clbooks.com

Here's a Web page that was designed with functionality, not glitz, as the highest priority. It serves its purpose well and you won't waste time browsing through unnecessary graphics. Use their search feature to locate books by topic or by author. You even can use this page to order Internet books for your friends and colleagues who aren't lucky enough to have the Internet book that came with your Erol's service.

Internet joke book
http://www.clarinet.com:80/inetjoke.html

The Internet is more than boring computers, networks and computer nerds. It has its funny moments. Check out this page to order an Internet joke book—although you might need to be a computer nerd to get the jokes. It's edited by Brad Templeton, the founder and editor of the ClariNet Communications Corporation, publisher of the Internet's first electronic newspaper. If going on-line has made you a bit edgy, see if you can use it to find something to laugh about out there in cyberspace.

Dear Emily Postnews
http://www.clarinet.com:80/brad/emily.html

Another Brad Templeton creation. This guy is very versatile. He also has a feature on his Web site called the Top 10 Copyright Myths, excellent reading if you plan to publish on the Web. It's everything you always wanted to know about netiquette, but were afraid you already knew. You do, but this puts it in a humorous perspective and is far more interesting than reading a guilt-oriented plea to be kind to your neighbors.

Boardwatch Magazine
http://www.boardwatch.com

Originally a magazine for the Bulletin Board System (BBS) community, Boardwatch magazine (see Figure 6) now covers the Internet and commercial on-line services as well. This Web site has the full text of back issues, dating back to October 1994. The articles deal with trends, legal and social issues and technology. Luckily, they avoid much of the hype that plagues a lot of Internet sites. It's a great site if you want to know all of the latest Internet developments.

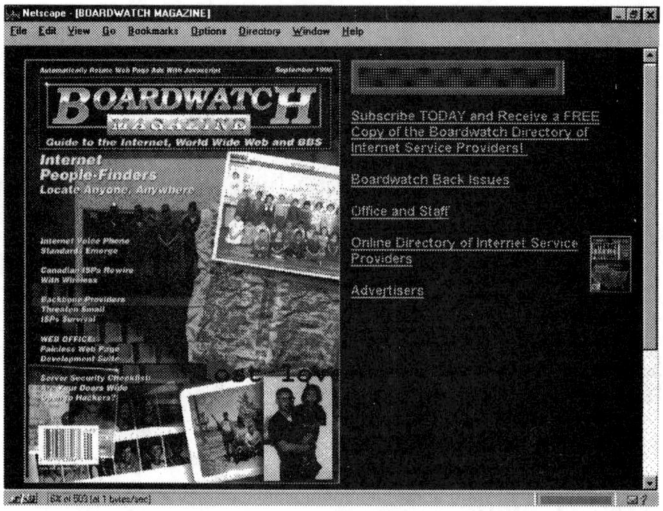

Figure 6 An Internet staple: Boardwatch Magazine

3

Rules of the Road: Netiquette

Every land has its own language and culture. Cyberspace has both of those, plus a whole new psychological demeanor. It's a good thing, too, because the Internet itself consists of computers and a few million humming, blinking electrical boxes that would be too cold, ugly and boring for humans to tolerate. In this chapter, we're going to help you understand all three aspects of the land of cyberspace: language, culture and psychological demeanor. This discussion introduces yet another bit of Internet jargon: netiquette—Internet etiquette.

Proper netiquette—the special rules of Internet social consideration—will improve the quality of your relationships and smooth the complicated process of communication. The detached nature of Internet communication presents some serious limitations to expression and understanding that require special care.

Sociologists say that between 70 percent to 90 percent of human communication is conveyed through body language and tone of voice—only 10 percent to 30 percent is conveyed through words.

Mailed letters have expressive abilities because you can communicate a lot with your choice of paper, letterhead design, how the envelope is addressed, font size and style, your signature, plus embellishments such as color, bold, italics, pictures, charts and even enclosures. The telephone at least lets you use tone of voice and pauses, but its role in both business and personal communication is waning. Thus, much of your communication is at risk of becoming impersonal because the Internet reduces our messages to nothing but plain text.

New communication tools

Since few traditional communication tools convey across the Internet, we'll show you some replacements. These tools include examples of popular "emoticons"—icons that emulate emotions—that can prevent misunderstandings by letting people experience the emotional context behind the text on the screen.

We also will give you some tips on writing for the Internet. The timbre of language is different from written business or personal letters of the past and that results in more misunderstandings. Our "Electronic elements of style" section later in this chapter can spare your fingers a few keystrokes because rules of grammar are less rigid and time-saving acronyms abound. We'll give you enough tools so that you'll be able to understand the ones you read and quickly shed the status of "Newbie."

Flaming words

We present these tools because misunderstandings abound on the Internet. The result often is something called a flame war—the Internet equivalent of a shouting match. The heated messages that are flung back and forth in a flame war are called flames. Sending flames is called flaming.

When you eventually encounter a flame war—we hope only as an observer of someone else's battle—be prepared to witness a return to the grade school playground. No, it's worse than that. Grade school kids have better things to do than to devote as much time to getting in the last word as some Internet users spend. Flame wars are a tremendous waste of Internet resources and totally unnecessary.

Apologies R painless

Often, good netiquette on the part of either correspondent will stop a flame war before it starts. You can do your part to keep the peace in cyberspace. If something you send or post earns a hostile reply message, instead of firing back the first barb that comes to mind, perhaps you could reread your original message.

Did you leave open the possibility for an alternate interpretation? Remember that if the other person *feels* they've been flamed then there's no question about it—they have been flamed. Even if you're completely perplexed by their interpretation, the best course is to acknowledge the results and accept responsibility for the harm.

The Bright Side

Here's a high note in case reading all of these negative things about communicating in cyberspace is making you jittery. Not being able to see the other person has its benefits. There are countless excellent relationships on the Internet between people who wouldn't engage each other in person. In cyberspace, bigots can't be biased. Age and gender barriers don't exist. Accents don't impede comprehension. And no one will criticize what you're wearing.

When you feel that the impersonal realm of cyberspace has cost you the good will of a relationship, think of how many relationships have been created that never would have blossomed F2F (face to face).

You will step on a few toes in any crowd, and in cyberspace newsgroups, for example, you can stomp on a lot of them fast. When you do, you'll do yourself a favor to simply reply with something like, "Sorry. Your reply showed me that I hit a sensitive spot. I didn't phrase it carefully at all. Will you accept my apology and can you accept a rephrased version of what I meant to convey?"

It's amazing, though, how a few people never can apologize or accept responsibility for their actions even across the anonymous reaches of cyberspace. The Internet gives you the ability to insult thousands—perhaps millions—of people at the speed of light. The good news, though, is that it also gives you a fast and almost painless way to apologize and make amends—and doing so is excellent netiquette.

Let it be

Finally, consider the other side of the flame war alliance: Help prevent flame wars by being slow to come to a boil.

Few people send intentional insults, so someone may be taken aback if you blast off an immediate, flaming retort. They may feel that you have thrown the first punch and blast you back when you were certain you'd receive a humble apology. So you nail them for being so stupid as to think that you flamed them and—voilà—a flame war has been launched.

The Internet may well trample your feelings if you are sensitive to every perceived wrong. Instead of being quick on the flamethrower trigger, give the benefit of the doubt to your e-mailing friends, family and business colleagues by assuming the best of their intentions and let most things slide.

There's one other good reason to let things slide. Some newsgroups are haunted by "trollers," people who troll through the Internet fishing for a flame war. Their motives, often politically-based, are to start flame wars that will disrupt communications and distract other users from accomplishing their planned goals. As with most activities, when you're on the Internet, stay focused. Ask yourself if responding to flames will help you accomplish your goals. If not, then avoid the distraction, disruption and wasted time of a flame war. If, however, your goals are to "scream" at people, then go ahead and jump into the fray—but remember, some trollers may be laughing that they tricked you into wasting time on a contrived fight.

Business netiquette

Practicing good netiquette is even more important for you if you have a home-based business. A private flame war is annoying, but a business-related flame war—even between just two individuals—can tarnish the reputation of your entire organization. Countless programs—called "sniffers"—roam the Internet and sample text in message traffic and alert people to read messages that contain "interesting" words. Any sensitive topic might be considered interesting by someone who owns a sniffer—and they'll be excited that their sniffer made a catch. Anything you say in Internet e-mail could be on the front page of The Washington Post or your local paper tomorrow.

Your trusty old telephone creates fewer opportunities for misunderstanding because you can hear each other's tone of voice. Tone of voice works to head-off trouble from both ends of a conversation. You may hear words that might have sounded offensive in a transcript of the call, but on the phone you don't take offense because the tone of voice clearly signals a light-hearted context. Conversely, if you accidentally offend someone on the phone, you can sense by a change in their tone of voice that you've touched a sensitive area. You have time to recover.

The Internet brings to you the burden of double-trouble: not only does it make you more easily misunderstood, it leaves documented proof of what you say that can span the globe in a few minutes. So, not only can your communication quickly insult vast reaches of humanity, it can create evidence for a lawsuit. And remember that the U.S. has more than twice as many lawyers as the rest of the world combined!

Spam

Practicing good netiquette will do more than create good relations, it can keep you from being thrown off the Internet. Sending spam—the act is called spamming—is a sure-fire shortcut to getting your Internet plug pulled. Spam is universally hated and you surely will join the crowd when you first see it. So what is spam?

The Hormel Company, who for years have produced the commercial meat product Spam, are not happy that their trade name has been appropriated by the Internet community and used in a negative context. Nonetheless, on the Net, "spam" (lowercase) refers to a message or document that nobody wants. The Internet usage actually comes from a Monty Python comedy bit in which every item on a restaurant menu was made of Spam.

Most often spam refers to grossly inappropriate usage of newsgroups. It comes from entrepreneurs who ridiculously believe that they've got the hottest product or service ever created and that the entire world will thank them for instantly telling every one of us about it. And it seems that they usually have a title similar to, "$$$ MAKE REAL MONEY FAST $$$." So the spammer writes a tome of breathless hype and then posts it to a vast array of unrelated newsgroups, often hundreds of them and sometimes thousands.

First, advertising on newsgroups generally is not considered to be good netiquette. So the spam annoys people who logged onto the newsgroup for some news on their favorite topic. Second, in the groups where ads are considered to be appropriate, the ads you see are related to the newsgroup's topic, they are well-written and they convey exactly the type of information that the group's readers are seeking—which is **not** spam!

People who spam are likely to have their messages canceled from the Internet and may find *themselves* canceled from the Internet. Some spammers cry that this infringes on their free speech rights, but the U.S. 1st Amendment doesn't cover disturbing the peace. People have a right to express their opinions in the proper forum, but society doesn't tolerate screaming and bombarding everyone with the same message—neither does the Internet. Gross offenders usually are reported to their Internet providers and find their Internet account quickly canceled.

With all that said, would you believe that there is a light side to spam? As much as people rail against how much time is wasted by this uninvited intrusion, they've devoted plenty of computing power to discussing spam as well as laughing about spam. Visit the Web site at *http://www.ip.net/BL/blacklist.html#spam,* where you'll find hypertext links to a tasty menu of spam.

To reduce your Newbie status, you definitely can benefit from learning the rules of the electronic road that make up the rest of this chapter. Let's start with some handy acronyms. These widely-accepted Internet shortcuts can save you typing time and help convey what you really mean to say.

Electronic elements of style

So here, in alphabetical order is a glossary of helpful and well-known Internet acronyms.

AND	Any Day Now
AFAIK	As Far As I Know
B4N	Bye for Now
BBS	Bulletin Board System
BL	Belly Laughing!
BTA	But Then Again
BTDT	Been There, Done That
BTW	By The Way
CUL	See You Later
CUL8R	See You Later
DTP	Desktop Publishing
F2F	Face to Face
FAQ	Frequently Asked Questions
FB	Flame Bait
FLAME OFF	Off limits for flaming
FLAME ON	Normal flaming rules restored
FUD	Fear, Uncertainty and Doubt
FWIW	For What It's Worth
FYI	For Your Information
<G>	Grin
GAL	Get A Life
GIGO	Garbage In, Garbage Out
GIWIST	Gee, I Wish I'd Said That
GMTA	Great Minds Think Alike
IAC	In Any Case
IC	I See
IDTT	I'll Drink To That
IME	In My Experience
IMO	In My Opinion
IMHO	In My Humble Opinion
IOW	In Other Words
IRL	In Real Life
JIC	Just In Case
LOL	Laughing Out Loud
OTOH	On The Other Hand
::POOF::	I'm gone
POV	Point Of View
PTB	Powers That Be
RE	Regarding
SYSOP	System Operator
TAFN	That's All For Now
TIA	Thanks In Advance
TNTL	Trying Not To Laugh
WRT	With Regard To

Emoticon lexicon

The Internet has embraced a shorthand language called *emoticons* or *smileys* that help remedy its inability to convey tone of voice. The name smiley comes from the first emoticon, which was a little smiley-face. :-) Smileys since have evolved well beyond their simple origin and now convey a wide range of emotions.

These little electronic writing aids are so widely used that entire books have been written about them. If you want to keep a more complete reference guide by your computer, check your local computer book store for an emoticon book—they have more smileys than you can use. Or is that *should* use? Smileys are not widely used, so if you use a smiley that is found only in emoticon books, will it convey anything other than a confused, "What?"

Here's a brief listing of some of the most widely understood emoticons. The key to understanding them lies in your perspective: look at them sideways.

Positive emotions

:-)	The original smiley, conveys friendliness or kidding
:->	A surprised smiley
:-D	Delighted smiley
:'-)	Tears of joy
:-}	Sarcastic grin
:-]	Goofy grin
:-x	Kiss
[]	Hug

Negative emotions

:-(	Frown, sadness
:-P	Sticking out your tongue
%-(	Confused and sad
:-O	Shocked or screaming
>:-|	Frowning
>:-<	Frowning and very angry
:-<	Dejected
:-C	Very unhappy
:'-(	Crying
:-{}	Blabbermouth who won't shut up

Mixed emotions, etc.

:-\	Mixed feelings leaning toward happy
:-/	Mixed feelings leaning toward sad
:-|	Neutral
:-J	Tongue in cheek
:-@	Screaming out loud
:-$	Put your money where your mouth is
'-)	Wink

Miscellaneous netiquette

Here, in no particular order, we'll close this chapter with a short collection of general netiquette that can help us all.

Use mixed case

PLEASE DON'T EVER POST OR MAIL ANYTHING IN ALL CAPS. IT'S ANNOYING TO READ, ISN'T IT?

All caps definitely rate as poor netiquette; it's the equivalent of screaming all the time and is harder to read than normal mixed case text. Save the all caps for an occasional SPECIAL EMPHASIS when needed unless you want the whole message to be ignored.

Bold, italics and underlining

Most likely your e-mail message window won't accept any of the standard font attributes such as bold, italics and underlining. Even if it does, expect the codes to be scrambled for your readers. Keep an eye out for changes in this area because they're coming fast. Expect to soon be able to send fully formatted e-mail messages with bold, italics, underlining and a selection of fonts, perhaps all of your installed Windows True Type fonts! For now, however, if your reader needs a document with all the formatting codes intact, then create a document in your word processor and attach the file to a short e-mail message.

Nonetheless, some typing standards have emerged on the Internet that enable you to use regular characters to represent both underlining and italics. You'll find underlining represented by bracketing a text string with underscore characters, perhaps using it to emphasize something _that is really important_. Similarly, asterisks are used to bracket text that should be italicized such as a book title, *Gone With The Wind.*

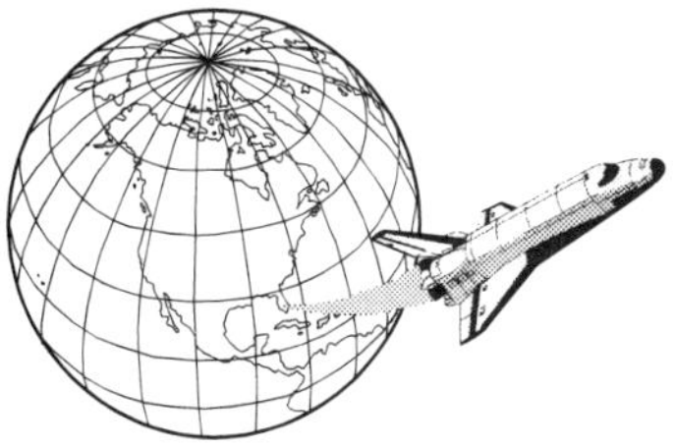

ORBITING IN CYBERSPACE

Guidelines for conduct on and use of the Internet

http://www.isoc.org/proceedings/conduct/cerf-Aug-draft.html

An Internet publication in which Dr. Vincent G. Cerf, President, Internet Society discusses constructive models of Internet conduct both by those who use the system and by those who provide its services. Dr. Cerf co-authored the foundational computer coding of the Internet known as TCP/IP (Transfer Control Protocol/Internet Protocol).

Everything you wanted to know about netiquette
http://www.clarinet.com:80/brad/emily.html

This URL will get you to Brad Templeton's "Dear Emily Postnews." Brad boasts that Emily is the "foremost authority on proper net behavior, who gives her advice on how to act on the net." This is some terrific and fun reading, yet it will give you a lot of good tips on netiquette—at least you'll know a lot of things *not* to do when posting to newsgroups.

Arlene Rinaldi's Netiquette home page
http://www.fau.edu/rinaldi/netiquette.html

This site includes a lot of Internet netiquette tips and guidelines. It includes links to many other Internet sites on the same topic. Also, as you browse through Arlene's site, you'll encounter information on subscribing to many mailing lists that cover a variety of Internet topics.

The Netiquette© Cybertoon
http://carbon.concom.com/~dmenter/Netiquette/

Prerelease_Netiquette_homepge

Netiquette© is a comic about diverse electronic life on the Internet that gives the Net the opportunity to make fun of itself by examining the Internet point of view. Its creator, David G. Menter, says he hopes to provide daily "netisodes©" and is in the process of accumulating enough panels to provide a little breathing room to ensure that his comic can feature a daily original.

4

Safety Check: Money and Security

Money makes the cyber-world go 'round, just as it does it the real world. But why not? These days money is mostly just electronic energy zipping around between people and financial institutions, so the Internet is a natural tool for some of that zipping. We will need money in the cyberspace world, just as in the real world, especially as the distinctions between the two merge. This chapter deals with cyberspace money issues. You'll find a mixture here, however, of security issues and financial issues, because on the Internet—as in real life—the two are closely related.

The key to making on-line financial transactions possible has been the development of technology that keeps messages secure while they fly through cyberspace—sort of like electronic lock boxes. But there are other uses for secure technology than protecting just financial transactions.

Use Your Own Judgment

These are heady times on the Web as stock prices for Internet-related stocks have made everybody think that cyberspace is the gold rush of the new millenium. But just how are we going to get all that gold out in cyberspace back to earth when everything is only 1s and 0s in computer code? The whole area of interactive commerce is still in its experimental phase and new approaches are emerging daily. The technology for secure transactions—the ability for you to electronically transfer funds out of your bank to a seller of goods, or to use your credit card to make a purchase on-line—contains some risk at the moment.

Erol's, therefore, does not endorse any existing methodology for electronic commerce nor does it guarantee the security of any transaction that may pass through its system. While Erol's takes all reasonable precautions to protect the integrity of its system, it assumes no liability for financial transactions that may occur between Erol's users and others. The following sites are provided for your information only.

By using security documents, merchants of all sizes now can use the Internet to conduct electronic commerce transactions anywhere in the world via the Web. A few examples of what's being done with secure documents:

- Cyberspace retailers can sell everything from computer software to astrology reports to flowers.
- Financial merchants can offer on-line banking and stock trades on-line or can accept credit card applications.
- Internet travel services can let customers make their own reservations and buy airline tickets.
- Non-profit organizations can accept membership applications on-line.
- Publishers can offer subscriptions to on-line versions of their publications.

These security measures are not restricted to financial transactions, of course. Many other uses are appearing on the Internet:

- Circulating confidential business marketing plans, product announcements and private personnel information.
- Survey data and customer questionnaires can be collected because organizations can protect the privacy of its Web users by using secure documents.
- Geographically diverse organizations can exchange sensitive company financial data, market reports, research data and new product ideas and designs.

But that's enough digression—the main focus here is on money issues. We'll begin with income by giving you an overview of how money moves around in cyberspace. Then we'll cover some expense issues that will help you plan and implement a Web site for personal use, for a home office or for work.

The truth about credit card purchases

The security of making credit card purchases is a major topic of concern among new Internet users. Most people are reluctant to use their credit card for Internet purchases. Most of these fears are unfounded and are based on some over-blown anecdotes that people have read or heard about Internet credit card security risks.

Most likely you, too, have read some bad news about Internet credit card security. Credit card transactions are but one aspect of exchanging funds on the Internet. There are many other options, but credit card transactions are easy to understand and they're related to something we all know and they've been a hot topic in the press.

If you give someone a credit card number on the Internet, you can't be sure where the information will travel and who might copy it while it's en route. Because conventional data transfer on the Internet isn't encrypted, an experienced computer hacker might create a program that grabs and saves for later analysis any data that looks like #### #### #### #### ##/##, the sequence usually used for credit card numbers. The hacker then could build a database of credit cards numbers and, supposedly, use them to buy things or fence the numbers to professional credit card thieves. But credit card security problems didn't originate on the Internet.

Unsafe at any speed

Unfortunately, the Internet isn't the only place where you can't be sure where your credit card information will travel and who might copy the information. Internet credit card number theft certainly is possible, and occurs occasionally, but it's no more of a threat than any other credit card transaction and is safer than most.

Consider other credit card transactions and you'll realize that there are plenty of easy ways for people to collect and sell credit card numbers without needing the technical expertise, the tools and the access required to hack the Internet. When you make a mail-order purchase or even hand your credit card to a waiter, you are risking theft by people who need far fewer skills than experienced computer professionals. It's far more likely that you'll be the victim of traditional credit card fraud than someone will intercept an Internet purchase you might make.

Internet technology actually makes credit card transactions safer than handing your card to a waiter. The basic technology is called "public-key cryptography," the foundation of "secure" Web documents. Secure documents are encrypted, which means they are scrambled by the sender and unscrambled by the receiver. A secure document can't be read without a "key" that is used during the unscrambling process.

Inside Info

For more information about public-key cryptography, visit the Web site of the Internet security masters at www.rsa.com. They created the Secure Sockets Layer (SSL) encryption technology that's used by your Netscape Navigator.

Figure 1 A secure URL

When you access a secure Web document, your Web browser may warn you before that document is transferred to your system. This may only occur on the first secure document you encounter because the warning will include an option to stop all such warnings in the future. If you mark the option as checked, you'll not see a warning on future secure documents, but you can change back at any time by changing your preferences settings. Whenever you accept a secure document with a public key, the site certificate is added to your browser's certificate list.

It may seem dangerous to deactivate the automatic secure document warning feature, but there are several other ways to recognize a secure document. With or without a warning you will see two other clues that tell you you're viewing a secure document:

- The status bar will display a padlock.
- The document's URL automatically changes from "*http://*" to "*https://*" even if you entered it manually without adding the "s" on the end (see Figure 1).

Public-key cryptography scrambles numbers and other personal or corporate data before it's sent, then enables the receiver to unscramble the original information. New technology planned by credit card companies will let buyers pay by credit card without merchants ever knowing the buyer's card number.

Sniffers and snoopers

Have you ever wondered how Internet hackers break can break into a system?

One simple technique is to obtain the login ID and password of a system administrator. But that's secure information, isn't it? So, how could a hacker get it? You may be surprised how often hackers use inside sources who sell computer security information. The rampant waves of corporate downsizing that is sweeping the U.S. has bred a whole generation of employees who do not hold a high degree of loyalty to large corporations. Selling a key login ID and a password may bring a disgruntled employee the "severance pay" he or she believes is fair compensation for being dumped.

Or, a hacker may use sniffers or snoopers to find passwords that can get them inside a system where they might find a system administrator's password.

Jargon Cutter

Sniffers and snoopers - Internet programs that monitor Internet traffic looking for data that they suspect might contain login IDs or passwords used to log onto targeted systems. They're automatic and work around the clock, saving Internet messages for a hacker to browse through at his convenience.

When a user logs in to a remote host, his or her login ID and password travel across the Internet unencrypted. Most e-mail also can be monitored and a sniffer or snooper that has targeted your Internet traffic can pick out login IDs from e-mail. If you e-mail a password to a colleague or a business associate, you may also be inviting in a host of hackers. If you ever have to let someone else know your password, it's safest to use something other than Internet e-mail.

Spoofing

Hackers can pretend to be a trusted user, by changing their host login IP address to match a user's. They then force their data to take a particular path through the Internet using "source routing," and having the last link in the route be the trusted user's system. Data sent back to the trusted user's host is then sent on to the hacker's system. Such masquerades as well as using bogus e-mail messages are called "spoofing."

Jargon Cutter

IP Address - Every computer on the Internet has a unique number called an IP address. An IP address is something like a telephone number. This number travels with e-mail and other Internet traffic to keep everything going to the right places—-that's the good news. The bad news is that hackers can slip in fake IP addresses to make mail appear it's from another source.

Thus, even if you receive a direct e-mailed request from someone you trust, you have to consider that the message could be a spoof. Before you e-mail sensitive data, at the very least, be certain that the trusted individual actually sent the message. For maximum Internet security never send any sensitive data without encryption.

Collecting tolls on the information highway

The real challenge to the Internet and the information age is how to get very small payments to creators of intellectual property without making everyone on the information superhighway run through countless electronic toll booths. It can be done and we'll discuss later some emerging technology that will make possible very small payments (micropayments).

One toll-collecting method would be to employ advertising as in other electronic media. This is a rapidly growing phenomenon. You'll see Web pages sprinkled with logos that advertise "site sponsors" who help the site owner cover the costs of maintaining a database, newsletter or a search engine. In exchange, the sponsors get to place a link on the site—often a graphic image of their logo—so that visitors can quickly get information on the sponsor's product.

If you maintain a Web site, you may be able to help finance your Internet costs by selling space to sponsors. And you may be able to increase traffic at your site by sponsoring well-done, related sites that already have high traffic. Site sponsoring could be a quick way to draw attention to a new home-based business you've just begun.

Another option is to dispense Internet cash that can be collected in small amounts any time you get a piece of information. Internet cash also has the benefit of being able to keep all transactions private. When paying by Internet cash, even the merchant you pay may not know who made the purchase. Some early companies that offer on-line payment plans are:

- First Virtual
  (*www.fv.com*)
- DigiCash
  (*www.digicash.com*)
- Cybercash (see Figure 2)
  (*www.cybercash.com*)
- ATS
  (*www.versanet.com*).

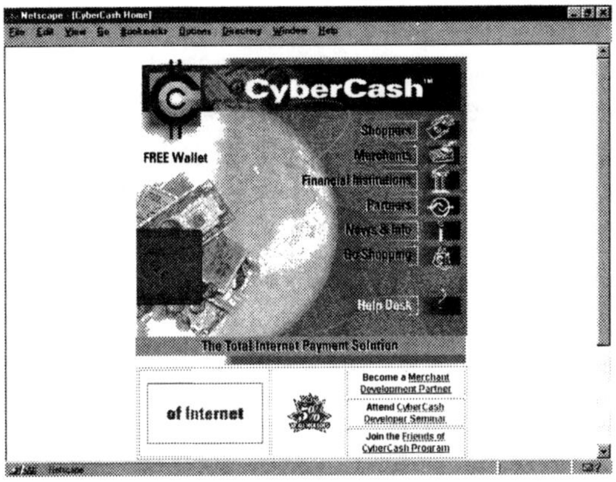

Figure 2 CyberCash's Security Internet Payment Service (SIPS)

The other side of the privacy coin

Privacy cuts two ways, though. Criminals are eager for new ways to hide and launder income from illegal activities. Terrorists want to eliminate money trails that can lead authorities to them or their sponsors. The U.S. Government is exploring ways to monitor transactions, but Internet privacy systems—especially secure data-encryption and digital cash—would make their mission much more difficult. No one knows how this conflict will play out, or whether an acceptable compromise can be found between Big Brother and anarchy. Meanwhile, as the government ponders options, the

Internet is rapidly creating its own monetary system—let's learn more about this phenomenon.

Inside Info

You might be surprised to find that the U.S. Government is interested in Internet security, and that some security technology faces import restrictions. If you intend to use international commerce transactions via the Internet, then you'll need a security system that's certified for export outside the United States and Canada.

Internet commerce systems

Many potential merchants are anxious to sell information, search services, software and audio or video clips on the Internet. When these merchants begin to sell on the Internet, they'll find an eager cadre of potential clients and customers. But turning those into paying clients and customers is going to take some consumer education because today most things on the Internet are free. Under the present system, owners of intellectual property have little incentive to make their valuable "information goods" accessible through the Web. This will improve as Internet collection systems become more secure, reliable and inexpensive.

Free Internet products abound today because Internet commerce is only a small percentage of sales for most companies that distribute products via the Internet. As the balance shifts in favor of the Internet, companies will be less able to subsidize their Internet service sales with traditional sales.

For example, let's look at the cost of obtaining an upgraded software driver for a printer. For years we all expected to be charged a few dollars to cover the company's cost of producing and mailing a diskette that contained the updated files. Today, however, you can download updated files free directly from a company's Web site. But this can't continue. Companies bear some distribution costs even when they use the Internet for file updates. The good news is that they will be able to cover their Internet distribution costs for far less than it costs to cover mail distribution of diskettes. Few of us would mind being charged fifty cents or a dollar for instant delivery of a file update. But for now, there is a gap in what buyers expect to pay and what sellers need to charge.

Countless entrepreneurial groups are developing Internet commerce mechanisms that will bridge this gap between sellers and buyers by creating a common and inexpensive Internet marketplace. Let's consider some of the features that these groups may employ in the commerce systems that are being developed.

Micropayments

The Internet marketplace will explode when it is able to support *micropayments*. Micropayments will enable merchants to profitably sell information for as little as 10 cents. But for *micromerchants* to flourish, the Internet needs to offer extremely low cost accounting and billing. Transaction costs need to be as little as one cent for a 10-cent item—now you'll be able to sell your best jokes or even family recipes.

Internet commerce systems that support micropayments will enhance the quality and variety of information products sold and bought on the Web. Those selling the information—even micromerchants selling a single page of information—will receive fair compensation for their products and will be able to remain in business.

Inside Info

To learn more about how micropayments may impact your life, check out the Web site of Dr. Brad J. Cox, Ph.D. at *www.virtualschool.edu/mon/TTEF.html.* Brad's a professor at George Mason University in Fairfax, Virginia and this site is the home page for his book *Superdistribution: Objects as Property on the Electronic Frontier* (Addison-Wesley, 1995).

Security

Internet commerce systems have to provide secure transactions for both your family's needs and your business' needs. When you sell products via the Internet, you'll need assurance that hackers cannot sniff through your e-mail for passwords that will enable them to download products without paying. We all want assurances that our credit card information will remain a private matter.

In client/server systems such as the Internet, transaction security is a two-way street. Both your system (the client) and the merchant's system (server) must use software that includes security features. Your Web browser has built-in security features already, so you already have the required software. This means that, in effect, Internet security is now a one-way street, with the responsibility falling to the merchant to create a secure service that uses your Web browser's security features.

Certified delivery

Another Internet commerce requirement is for "certified delivery" of on-line transactions. Certified delivery protects both sellers and buyers, especially when the product's value is time-sensitive. The seller needs to be able to prove that the buyer got the product on-time, while the product had the value for which the buyer paid. Sellers also need to know when they transmit their information that they will get paid.

The same system also gives buyers assurance that they will not be charged if some system problem prevents delivery. Buyers do not want to be charged just because the seller's system transmitted the information. This requires an information exchange between seller and buyer that verifies that a delivery can be accomplished and that payment can be made. The seller's system will transmit electronic products only after the availability of a valid payment is confirmed. At the same time, certified delivery also means that you are charged only when the information is actually received. It's a tricky "Catch 22" situation, but system developers have created programs that protect both sides of the seller-to-buyer partnership.

Automated flexible pricing

Few businesses charge the same price for the same product to all buyers. Because a lot of factors can affect pricing, a merchant's Internet commerce services might need to offer discounts and handle premium-pricing. Here are some pricing factors that some advanced Internet commerce systems can handle:

- ❖ Prepaid, subscription-type sales that track your balance of available funds, sending information to you without charge if you have a balance and requiring additional payments if you've depleted your balance.

- ❖ Discounts—perhaps even free copies—if you are a member of a site license group that has paid a flat rate.

- Volume discounts if you're a member of a pre-registered consumer group, user group or government agency.
- Volume discounts if you're a single buyer who is a frequent customer.
- Premium surcharges for purchases made during peak-hour access and discounts for off-peak access.
- Time-sensitive charges that could invoke a premium for information downloaded today, discount that same information tomorrow and perhaps offer it to you next week as a free sample.
- Price quotations for when you are shopping, but not ready to buy. The best systems can store quotations with your database record so there won't be price confusion when you return to complete the sale.

A typical commerce group

Let's look in-depth at a company that describes itself as a business model for a commerce server. The NetBill project has teamed with strategic business partners, Visa International and Mellon Bank Corporation. NetBill research, however, is funded in part by a grant from the National Science Foundation (NSF). While NetBill has a growing full-time and part-time staff—drawn mainly from the ranks of Carnegie Mellon University (CMU)—much of its development has been completed by students in project courses taken as part of CMU's graduate program in Information Networking.

Inside Info

The National Science Foundation (NSF) has been funding Internet development for a long time. NetBill is another example of how they've helped us all enjoy the incredible power of the Internet. Now they're helping to make it more secure.

A commerce server is a set of standards and the software that implements those standards so buyers can pay merchants on-line. A typical commerce group—such as NetBill—maintains commerce servers that link you and the organizations with which you'll conduct Internet business. These links not only handle the actual financial transaction, but they certify the delivery of both product and payment. NetBill's project group handles both sides of certified delivery (see Figure 3).

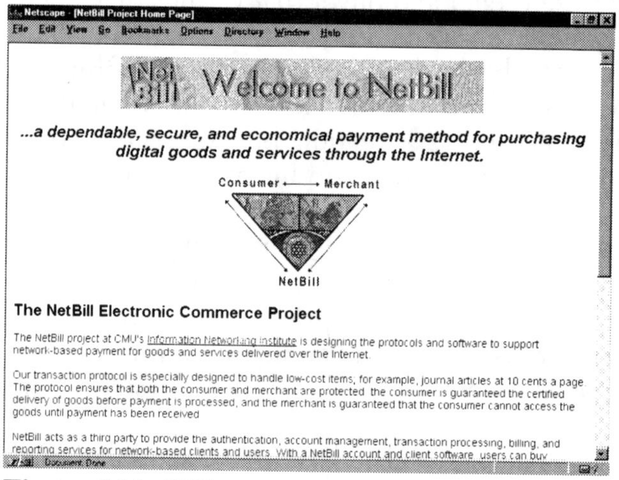

Figure 3 NetBill commerce server project

NetBill uses a financial transaction protocol that supports flexible pricing and can calculate customized quotes for individual buyers and handle pricing approvals. It uses digital signature technology to provide account security on both sides of transactions.

Buyers can sign orders digitally using a key that is never revealed to the merchant, so eavesdroppers cannot intercept credit card numbers and approval authorizations.

The Ins-and-Outs of a Commerce Server Transaction

When a buyer requests an electronic product from a merchant, the buyer's client software sends a digitally-verified purchase request to the merchant's server. The electronic product is transmitted to the buyer in an encrypted format. Encryption transforms data into a format that is unreadable by anyone without a secret decryption key that will "unlock" the information and restore it to a readable format.

The merchant's information server computes a cryptographic checksum—a series of arithmetic operations that detect whether a file has been damaged or modified—on the encrypted message. After transmitting the product to the buyer, the merchant's server then sends an electronic payment order (EPO). At this point, the buyer has the goods—but does not have the key required to decrypt the goods—and the buyer has not yet been charged.

The buyer's system calculates a checksum and sends a reply to the merchant's server. When the server receives the EPO reply it compares its checksum against the one computed by the client library. If the checksums match, the server knows that the buyer received the encrypted goods without error.

After this verification, the merchant creates a digitally-verified invoice that includes the price, the checksum and the decryption key for the product. The merchant sends both the EPO and the invoice to a commerce server, which verifies that the product identifiers, prices and checksums all match.

The commerce server debits the buyer's account (which was pre-funded) and credits the merchant's account, logs the transaction and saves a copy of the decryption key. It then sends the merchant a digitally-verified message with either an approval code, or an error code if the transaction failed.

Finally, the merchant forwards the commerce server's reply and the decryption key to the buyer's client software, which enables the buyer's software to decrypt the information product.

This probably sounds ridiculously complicated, but computers handle the whole process in a few seconds.

Multiple users and accounts

NetBill supports "many-to-many" relationships between consumers and accounts. This means that a single corporate or academic account may authorize many users to charge against it and obtain special pricing. Also, individual consumers may maintain multiple personal accounts. One user on every multiple-user account must be designated as the account owner, and someone must be designated as the account administrator. An authorized administrator can use a standard Web browser to open an account, view and change an account profile, authorize funds transfers into the account and view current statements of account transactions and balances. Account information checks by administrators are handled as regular financial transactions to ensure authentication and security.

Account creation is one of the largest costs associated with traditional credit card and bank accounts. The automatic account creation features of commerce servers helps to limit costs for both consumers and merchants. Low-cost account creation is going to be a key contributor toward developing widespread micropayment systems.

Account types

A commerce account currently comes in two basic flavors:

- Debit model (pre-paid);
- Credit model (post-paid).

In the debit model—used by DigiCash and Cybercash, for example—buyers must deposit into a commerce account sufficient funds to cover anticipated purchases. Buyers first would deposit real money (via check or credit card) with DigiCash or Cybercash and then go surf the net with electronic money.

In the credit model—patterned after traditional credit card vendors—transactions are accumulated and billed to the buyer's commerce account at the end of a billing period. These accounts, again like credit cards, have a pre-established dollar limit for each buyer. Both models give both merchants and consumers instant on-line access to transaction status and statement activity.

Other uses for commerce servers

So far, we've focused only on the sale and purchase of electronic goods and information. But there are plenty of non-electronic products to sell, and a good commerce model will support the purchase of traditional goods and services. Let's consider a few possibilities:

- Ticketing for entertainment events and for airline reservations. Airlines are setting the stage for this as they develop ticketless flights. Your ticket might be no more than a confirmation—printed from a Web page—with a code number that agents would match with their computer when you check in.
- Utility payments, such as for electric bills, phone service, gas bills, tax payments and perhaps even lottery sales.
- Products that currently are sold via traditional mail order catalogs.
- Contributions to charitable organizations or political campaigns.
- On-line video and audio, although at the present time, this conflicts with the safeguards in certified delivery.
- Software application rental. Software could incorporate the client library in any application. Periodically, the software would ask users to approve another purchase to get the next month's activity or "issue" of new software.

While many of the information exchanges on the Internet may continue to be provided by merchants for free, commerce systems will increase the incentive of creators and producers of information goods to supply more and better products. And we all benefit from the improved quality and increased quantity of new goods available via the Internet.

Summary of money issues

Never rely, however, on a single source for security or commerce information for your business. Be sure to cross-check information you read on the Web and get second opinions from professionals you interview.

The Netscape Navigator chapter in Phase 2 explains the details of handling secure Web documents, including Step-by-Step guidelines to ensure that your Web browser is configured the way you want.

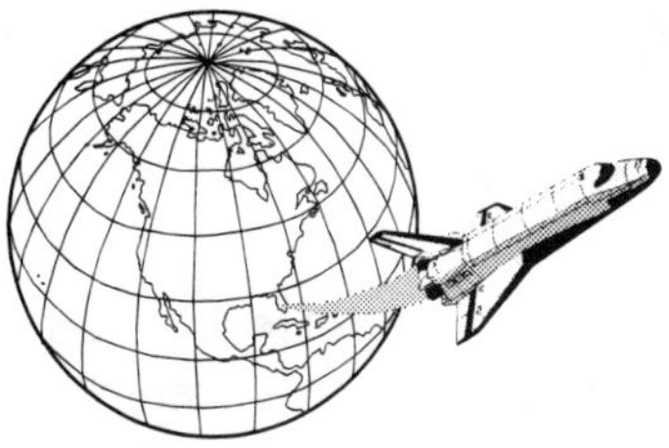

ORBITING IN CYBERSPACE

Network Money: The Future of On-Line Banking & Commerce
http://nearnet.gnn.com/gnn/meta/finance/feat/emoney.home.html

This page is a feature of the GNN Personal Finance Center and has a lot of links to Web sites that deal with Internet money issues. A few choice examples are "An Introduction to Electronic Commerce" by Jason Solinsky and an article by Arnold Kling, entitled "Banking on the Internet." These suggest that micropayments hold a tremendous potential to reduce unwanted junk mail and newsgroup pollution.

Network Money Sites on the Internet
http://nearnet.gnn.com/gnn/meta/finance/feat/links.html

The sites here will help you learn more about the development of Internet commerce systems. It's an annotated collection of links to the most interesting electronic commerce sites on the Net. In addition to some of the services mentioned in this chapter, you'll find links to experimental money-related sites and discussion of Internet crytography in general.

Miscellaneous Web business sites
http://www.owi.com/netvalue

Here's a list of miscellaneous, interesting Internet business sites that you can visit to see how they handle money transactions. This site is the home of Net.Value, The Web Strategy Forum. Instead of searching for specific businesses, you'll select by category, such as Small Business, Consulting Services, Electronic Markets, Virtual Catalogs, etc. There is definitely some inspiration lurking around on this site to fire up your creative engine.

Digital Cash
http://www.digicash.com

Digital Cash (DigiCash) has created a new monetary system for transferring money via the Internet (see Figure 4). DigiCash vendors accept payments from customers in the form of "ecash" money. To use this service, you first will have to transfer some actual cash from your bank into ecash at DigiCash. With this account established, you then can shop Internet vendors who accept ecash. This system has more advantages for the vendor than for you. But some businesses that have suffered collection problems like the security because when you buy something your ecash goes straight into their bank. It's good for you because you don't have to worry about transmitting your credit card number all over the globe.

Figure 4 DigiCash is the home of ecash, a currency for cyberspace

CyberCash
http://www.cybercash.com

CyberCash offers consumers, banks and merchants the Secure Internet Payment Service (SIPS™). SIPS protects credit card numbers used for shopping on the Web and lets merchants safely process Internet credit card transactions. In 1996, SIPS began to let consumers use their own money for Internet payments. Check out this Web site for details on how you can use their system. CyberCash encryption software has been approved for worldwide export by the U.S. Government.

NetBill
http://www.ini.cmu.edu/netbill

Here's the Web site for Carnegie-Mellon's NetBill commerce server project that we profiled earlier in this chapter. NetBill's research is funded in part by a grant from the National Science Foundation (NSF), one of the founders of the Internet.

Open Market commercial sites index
http://www.directory.net

Open Market, Incorporated develops and markets software, services and custom solutions that facilitate electronic commerce on the Web. Open Market applies both advanced technology and a business perspective to the expansion of business into an electronic marketplace. They offer solutions that address the needs of small companies and global businesses alike (see Figure 5).

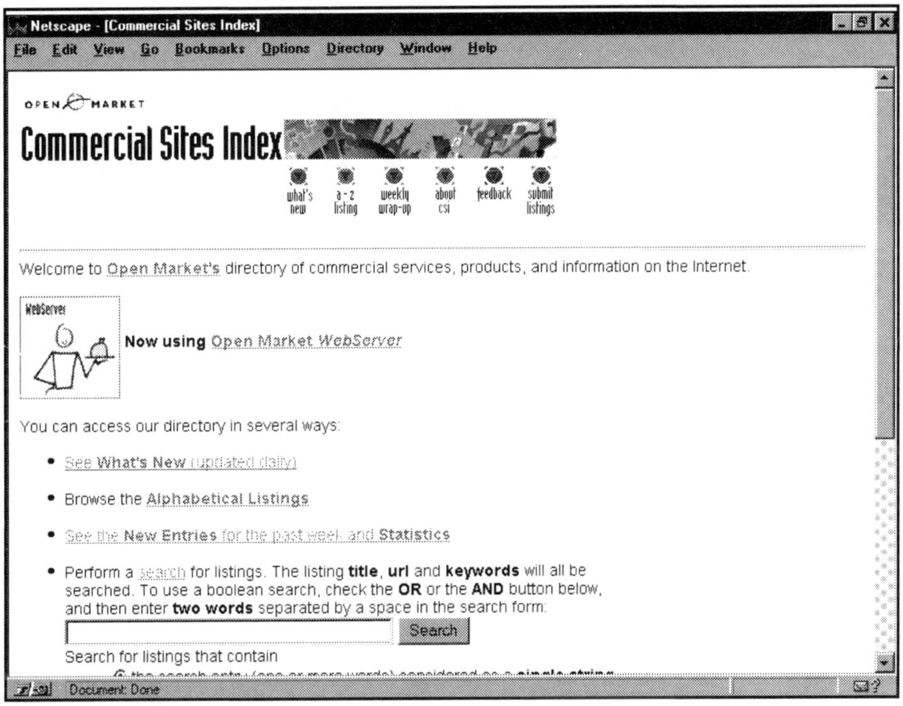

Figure 5 An index to commercial sites all over the world

Jargon Cutter

FAQs file - A file of Frequently-Asked-Questions that serves as something of a help file. The theory is that most of the questions you'll ask about an Internet service or feature have already been asked. Rather than repeat the answers about a million times, many Internet sites provide a file of the most frequently asked questions.

GoSite

http://www.direct.net

GoSite is a full-service Web service provider. They will walk you through the entire process of establishing, building and maintaining a Web site. All of their service is SSL encrypted. GoSite has 24-hour-a-day telephone support, but then you'll find other Web providers, especially Erol's, to be far less costly than GoSite. GoSite, however, offers a lot of other services that are options at many providers. And some users might need to hire consultants to do the work that GoSite includes with its basic service. If you need CGI scripts or other complicated features on your Web site, and you have no idea how to proceed, GoSite will handle the entire process after you tell them what you want.

Jargon Cutter

CGI - An acronym for Common Gateway Interface, a method that UNIX Web servers use to permit interaction between users and programs on the server. The most common usage is with fill-in forms on Web pages. You may have used one of these if you have ever entered your name and address in a Web reply form.

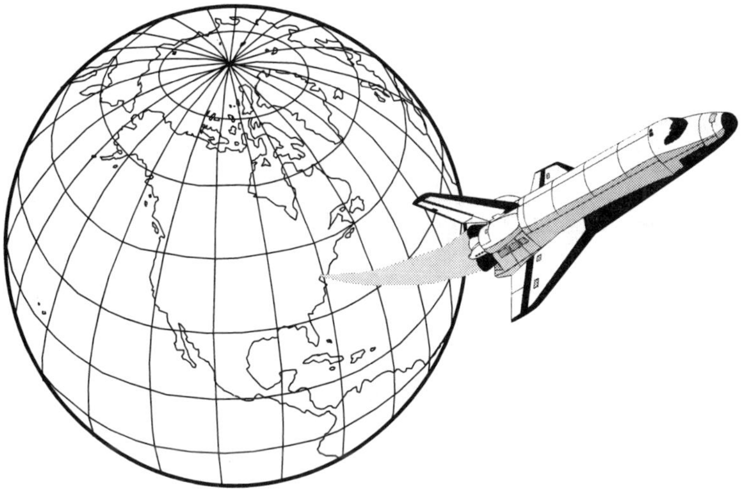

Phase 2

Phase 2: The Launch

Congratulations on finishing ground school. You've completed Phase 1 and you certainly know enough now to actually head out into cyberspace—and that's where we're taking you next.

These chapters feature hands-on exercises that we call "Step-By-Step," because they literally walk you through the different topics one step at a time. We'd like to lay a little groundwork for this chapter before you start.

Each Step-By-Step exercise starts with a Goal, so you'll know what we're going to achieve. Every step begins with a checkmark. Many of the steps have brief messages after them that clarify either the step you just performed or let you know if you need the next step or if you should skip it.

Inside Info

We've written the exercises with some assumptions about your basic skills in Windows, so here's a little test. If terms such as dialog box, scroll bar, radio button, menu, double-click, or right-click, sound unfamiliar to you, then read the Windows Primer in the appendix before you tackle the exercises.

So, if you're comfortable with basic Windows commands, let's get started. Here's what you'll get in the chapters in Phase 2:

- **Chapter 5** introduces basic Web surfing techniques and teaches you how to use **Netscape Navigator** as a powerful information tool. Netscape Navigator is a software application that's called a Web browser. The name is perfect because you'll use it to navigate the Web.

- **Chapter 6** expands on the basics presented in the previous chapter and shows you some **advanced features** of the Netscape Navigator. You'll learn about using the Netscape Navigator to play audio and video clips over the Internet. And you'll learn about the exciting developments in animation and interactive features that are quickly bringing the Internet to life.

- **Chapter 7** covers Internet **electronic mail** (e-mail). E-mail has absolutely revolutionized global communications and most likely will revolutionize your personal communications. This is hard to comprehend at first, but you can send as many messages as you want—anywhere in the world—and it won't cost you anything above your basic Internet service charge!

- **Chapter 8** shows you how to use one of the most popular areas of the Internet: **newsgroups**. Newsgroups are akin to community bulletin boards, but they're electronic and the community is the planet. They're organized by topics and the topics are organized into larger categories. Now, are you sitting down? Okay. This may be hard to believe, but on the day we wrote this, we found 26,318 Internet newsgroups! There ought to be a topic in there somewhere that interests you, and we'll show you how to find it.

5

Countdown: Netscape Basics

Most of the time you spend on the Internet you'll be surfing the World Wide Web. It's an awesome experience and there seems to be, literally, no end to how much you can see and do on the Web. This chapter will give you an overview of how to surf the Web with a software application called a "Web browser." And this chapter includes a lot of hands-on work that we call "Step-By-Step" exercises.

For your Web browser we've chosen Netscape Navigator 3.0. You may have heard of other browsers, but there's no reason to use anything else. Even if you don't use Netscape, though, much of this will be beneficial anyway because you're going to get a lot of concepts that apply to all Web browsers.

Why did we choose Netscape Navigator? Netscape has a wealth of "extensions" that have been added to the normal Web browser functions—many of which are not yet supported by other Web browsers. These extensions increase its ability to bring you exciting, user-friendly Web pages. Today, millions of people are navigating the Web with Netscape Navigator because it's a fabulous Web browser.

We also selected Netscape Navigator because it works seamlessly with Usenet newsgroups. You'll see in the last chapter in Phase 2 that Netscape newsgroups reader will bring you the power of the Usenet with little new to learn.

Inside Info

The "Bookmarks" feature in Netscape Navigator enables you to store the addresses of Web sites so you can return to them without having to type in the URL manually each time. Your Bookmarks file soon will be quite valuable to you, so we recommend that you back it up—you might label a floppy disk "Bookmarks" and regularly copy the Bookmarks file from your hard disk to the floppy.

You'll soon discover that the basics of using Netscape Navigator are in many ways very much like using Windows itself. But we want you to progress beyond the browsing basics and the exercises in this chapter will transform you into an efficient, productive power-user of Netscape Navigator. Okay, that's enough background for now—let's begin the Step-By-Step exercises.

Inside Info

Each Step-By-Step exercise starts with a Goal, so you'll know your mission. Every step begins with a checkmark. Many of the steps have brief messages after them that clarify either the step you just performed or let you know if you need the next step or if you should skip it. If you come across a Windows term you don't know, check out the Windows Primer in this book's appendix (see page 265).

Let's go surfing

We'll begin with the simplest Web process of all: visiting a site on the World Wide Web. You have probably done a little surfing already, but just in case you've never visited a Web site, this will show you how.

STEP-BY-STEP

GOAL: Learn to visit a site on the World Wide Web

✔ Start Netscape Navigator.

✔ Press **CTRL+L** to open a Web Location.

This dialog box lets you open either a site on the World Wide Web or a file on your local hard drive or network.

✔ Type *www.whitehouse.gov*, then press **ENTER**.

This is the home of the White House in Washington. It's one of the most popular sites on the World Wide Web.

✔ Press **PAGE DOWN** to scroll down through the page, or use your mouse on the scroll bar on the right side of the screen.

✔ Press **PAGE UP** to scroll back up to the top of the page, or use your mouse.

The words that appear in underlined blue text are the hypertext links that you read about in Phase 1. Just click on any of them to see where they take you.

That's all there is to it. From now on, anytime you see a Web address, just press **CTRL+L**, type the address, press **ENTER** and voilá, you can go anywhere in the world in seconds and then just keep clicking on those underlined hypertext links.

✔ Press **CTRL+L**, type *www.switchboard.com*, then press **ENTER**.

Believe this or not, Switchboard is a national white pages phone book. This is a valuable Web site. Test it out while you're here by entering your own name and city, then telling it to look you up. Try a couple of long lost friends or relatives.

✔ Press **CTRL+L**, type *www.unitedmedia.com/comics*, then press **ENTER**.

From here, you can click on the graphic of the Dilbert comic strip. That will jump you to the Dilbert Web page—just a sample of some of the fun things you can do and see on the Web.

✔ Press **CTRL+L**, type *www.pathfinder.com/twep*, then press **ENTER**.

This is the home of the Pathfinder Electronic Publishing Web site. It's a rich resource of Web sites that covers a wide variety of topics.

Inside Info

Did you wonder why we left off the "http://" in front of the Web addresses? You've always seen it there, right? And you've always diligently typed it in, right? Well, save yourself the agony. Netscape is smart enough to figure out that you want a Web site. So, just leave it out as we've done and simplify your surfing.

Netscape Navigator help menu

Netscape Navigator itself has a pretty good selection of on-line resources built in. You'll find them under the **Help** menu at the top of the screen. With this menu up there, you'll never have to hunt for *something* to do with Netscape. Let's check out the current items under that menu.

STEP-BY-STEP

GOAL: Learn what's on Netscape Navigator Help menu

✔ Click **Help, How to Get Support.**

This is the official Netscape support center. Be sure to start here if you've got any technical questions about using Netscape Navigator.

✔ Click **Help, Frequently Asked Questions.**

Before you waste a bunch of time trying to track down your Web questions, check this page—they may already have an answer for you.

✔ Click on the link for **The Unofficial Netscape FAQ**

You can use normal keystrokes to scroll up and down through this page to see topics about Netscape, but we'll practice this in the next exercise.

Exploring one Web document

When you view a page on the Web, the process that puts it there is similar to when you open a document in a word processor. Thus "Web pages" are pages in opened documents that are available via the Web. While Web surfing is akin to viewing documents in a word processor, you can't edit them—Web documents are read-only.

Besides being read-only, Netscape differs from your word processor in another important way: It can open documents from computers all over the world. Your word processor only opens documents that are on your hard drive your network. But Netscape can communicate over the Internet with TCP/IP (Transmission Control Protocol/Internet Protocol). Don't worry about what TCP/IP means, though. The magic works invisibly to pull in documents from anywhere on the Internet.

Surfing one Web page

So, Web pages are no more than computer documents. Okay, sure, they're usually spiffed up with color and graphics. And, increasingly, they also include sound, video or even animation. But the basic principle remains the same: the Web is just a network system that loads documents into a reader called a Web browser.

Inside Info

Here's an important concept: Web documents don't really have "pages" as do documents in your word processor. Web documents are continuous, like a scroll. When you go to another "page" you're actually getting another document or jumping to another spot on the current scroll.

Since Web pages are no more than documents, let's review some shortcuts to moving around within a single Web document because you'll need to be as efficient at surfing individual Web documents as you are at surfing the entire Web.

STEP-BY-STEP

GOAL: Learn to surf one Web page

- ✔ Press **DOWN ARROW** to scroll down through the last Web page.
- ✔ Press **UP ARROW** to scroll up through this document.
- ✔ Use your mouse on the scroll bar on the right of the screen.

  Use the arrow at the top or the bottom to scroll up or down. Or, grab the elevator button (square box) on the scroll bar and drag it up or down to more quickly scroll long distances.
- ✔ Press **CTRL+END** to jump to the bottom of this document.
- ✔ Press **CTRL+HOME** to jump to the top of this document.
- ✔ Press **PG DN** a couple of times.
- ✔ Press **PG UP** a couple of times.

  Remember these keystrokes throughout all of your Web surfing. When your computer is pushing the limits, using the mouse places a strain on your Windows resources. If the mouse acts sluggish or skittery, try using these keystrokes instead. Besides, the keystrokes are faster anyway.

Marking your trails

It's easy to wander off into cyberspace and get yourself lost. You'll be jumping from one hypertext link to another, ever more deeply probing the depths of cyberspace and then you'll decide you want to return to a screen you saw earlier. But you'll have no idea how to find it again because you never actually saw or typed the URL—it was just the result of choosing one of the dozens of hypertext jumps you've made. All you've got is a memory of how the screen looked, and now you want to see it again.

Jargon Cutter

URL - Just in case you've missed it earlier, a URL is a Uniform Resource Locator. It's somewhat equivalent to having the telephone number of someone you want to call. URLs specify the type of resource first (http, ftp, or gopher), followed by a colon and two slashes (://) and then the actual name of the resource.

Fortunately, Netscape folks experienced this lost feeling enough times that they created some tools that you can use to mark your trail through cyberspace. Some are permanent markers and some just track where you've been today. Let's see how Netscape Navigator can help you quickly return to screens you've seen before.

Back and forward

The simplest trail-marking features are Back and Forward. Netscape Navigator includes several methods to activate these two features. So, how many of these methods do you need to remember? Just the ones you like! Try them all, then don't worry about the rest.

STEP-BY-STEP

GOAL: Activate the Back and Forward features

- ✔ Click the button at the top of the screen that's labeled **Back.**

This jumps back to the previously-viewed page. It pops up quickly because Netscape stores pages temporarily so they don't have to be downloaded again.

- ✔ Click the **Forward** button.
- ✔ Press **ALT+LEFT ARROW**.

  This is the keystroke equivalent of the **Back** button. If you'll press the **ALT** key with the thumb on your right hand you can activate the left or right arrow keys with your little finger and quickly jump back and forth through Web pages.
- ✔ Press **ALT+RIGHT ARROW**.
- ✔ Click **Go, Back** to surf using the menus.
- ✔ Click **Go, Forward**.
- ✔ Right-click the page, then click **Back** to see even *another* way to go back.
- ✔ Right-click the page, then click **Forward** to go forward again.

View history

If the document to which you want to return is a long way back, these techniques may become tedious navigation tools, although you can jump back very rapidly using the **ALT+LEFT ARROW** keystroke. Still, there are more direct routes back to pages you have previously viewed—without having to revisit everything else along the way. Let's practice using them now.

STEP-BY-STEP

GOAL: Use Netscape Navigator History to find previous pages

- ✔ Click **Go** to see the most recent pages.

  They're at the bottom of the menu with numbers next to them.
- ✔ Double-click on any page you want to see again.

  Naturally this list won't record many pages, it only shows the site titles, and it's cleared every time you exit Netscape, but there are other methods.
- ✔ Click **Go, Open History Folder**.

  This list includes the full name of the site as well as the title.
- ✔ Double-click on any site on the list to jump directly to it.

  Once you've activated the History Folder, it remains open, so you don't have to click on the menu again to see other sites on the list.
- ✔ Double-click on any other site on the list to jump directly to it.

  There is an alternative to double-clicking, so let's see that now.
- ✔ Click on any other site, then click **Go to**.

  You can see by this menu that you also can add a site on this list to your Bookmark list.

Netscape Navigator caching

When you use the commands you just learned, you may notice that the screens load more quickly than they did originally. That's because Netscape stores downloaded screens (called "caching" in computer talk—pronounced "cashing" in people talk) so that it doesn't have to download them from the Internet again if you decide to return.

The larger the cache size, the more screens Netscape can hold and the faster your system will respond to Back and Forward.

The default cache size is set in Netscape Navigator is a compromise to accommodate computers that have little free memory. Hard disk prices have dropped dramatically and you may now have more free disk space *after* installing all of your applications than you used to have when your hard drive was empty. If so, you can increase the cache size to improve speed by following these steps:

STEP-BY-STEP

GOAL: Learn to adjust Netscape Navigator's cache size

- ✔ Click **Options, Network Preferences.**
- ✔ Click on the **Cache** tab.
- ✔ Double-click in the **Memory Cache** text entry box.

  Experiment with different sizes, depending on the amount of total RAM in your system and on the number of applications you plan to have open at any one time. Start by allocating 25% of your total RAM to the cache.
- ✔ Double-click in the **Disk Cache** text entry box.

  The maximum allowable size for this entry is 32000. If you enter a number higher than that, the setting will be changed to zero.
- ✔ Change the **Disk Cache Directory** if you'd like the cache stored on another hard drive or in a special directory.
- ✔ Click **OK** to save the settings.

Switching applications

What if you need to use another application while you're surfing? Remember that Windows has full multi-tasking ability—it can perform more than one function at a time. This means that you don't have to keep track of where you left off on the Web if you need to use another application for a while. Instead, you can switch to another application then come right back to Netscape and pick up where you left off. Everything will be preserved, including your cache and history. Here are two time-saving techniques to keep in mind when you're surfing the Net.

You can switch to other open Windows applications by cycling through them with the **ALT+TAB** key or by clicking on the Taskbar to select any currently running applications. This is particularly valuable when you hit a Web site during peak hours that uses extensive graphics. You can **ALT+TAB** to another application and get a little work done or write a letter while Netscape Navigator continues to download. For example, you could jump to Eudora and compose an e-mail message. It's not much, but at least you can save a little time instead of watching the hourglass.

Run multiple Netscape Navigator sessions

Here's another little treat that will solve some problems of having too many sites to see: You can open multiple Netscape sessions. This certainly is not a solution to bandwidth problems, but it permits you to see two Web pages at the same time—or three Web pages, or more!

When you create multiple Netscape sessions, each occurrence is a separate Windows task that will appear on the Taskbar. You'll then be able to switch between them using **ALT+TAB** or clicking on the different sessions on the Taskbar. The title of each open Web site will appear on the **ALT+TAB** dialog box or on the button on the Taskbar. Follow these steps to open an additional Netscape window (see Figure 1).

STEP-BY-STEP

GOAL: Learn to open multiple Netscape windows

✔ Click **File, New Web Browser** or press **CTRL+N**.

This opens a new Netscape window and you might still see the first session in the background. You can set each of them to different URLs. If you can see both sessions, you can use your mouse to switch back and forth, if not, you can switch between them with **ALT+TAB**. Perform the next step **only** if the current window is not already maximized.

✔ Double-click in the title bar of the new Netscape window.

Activate the Taskbar to see them both. The icons are the same, but the title of the current pages appears in square brackets after the word "Netscape."

✔ Click on the first Netscape session you had open.

✔ Press **ALT+TAB** once to return to the new Netscape window.

Note that this menu also lists in square brackets the name of each window's current document.

✔ Press **ALT+TAB** once again to return to the first window.

✔ Press **ALT+TAB** once to return to the new Netscape window.

Of course you don't have to run these windows maximized. You might want to use the Restore command (the middle icon in the upper-right corner) and then size them so that you can see both Web pages at the same time, perhaps to compare two Web sites.

✔ Click **File, Close** to close the new Web browser.

Notice that this closes only the current window. Closing the new one will not affect the first Netscape Navigator window.

Inside Info

You're not limited to opening Web sites *only* in one Web browser. If you've got Windows 95, you also have the Microsoft Internet Explorer. You can open a Web site in Netscape and then start the Internet Explorer and see how the same site looks in two different browsers. Or you can load different sites into each browser. And, you can run multiple sessions of either browser.

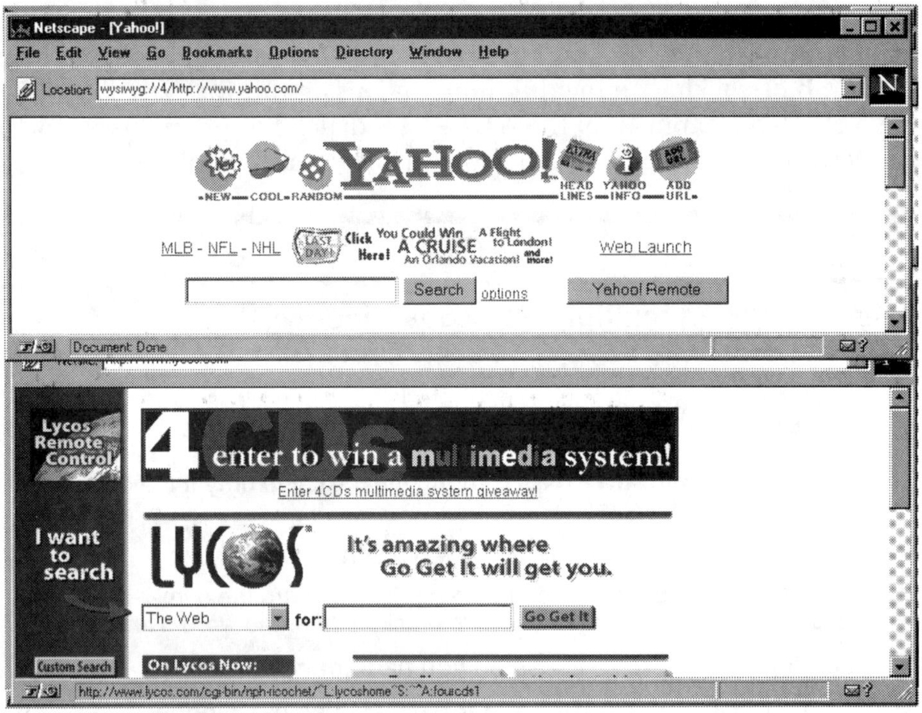

Figure 1 Double your surfing—double your fun!

Creating some on-screen elbow-room

Most Web pages are too large to fit into Netscape Navigator main screen all at once, including the one you've been using so far. Usually, then, you'll need to scroll the screen to see everything available, but you'll still want to see as much as possible at one time. In this next exercise, we'll have you maximize your viewing space by eliminating some unnecessary screen clutter.

STEP-BY-STEP

GOAL: Maximize your Netscape Navigator viewing area

✔ Click **Help, Handbook.**

Notice how this document appears on-screen, especially note how little of the document you can see at one time. Scroll through this document using your **UP ARROW** or **DOWN ARROW** keys or your mouse. Now let's improve your view.

If your Netscape Navigator doesn't already fill the screen, double-click the title bar to maximize the browsing window.

✔ Click **Options, Show Directory Buttons**.

This eliminates one unnecessary row of buttons—these buttons are really for the convenience of Netscape marketing department—and you still have access to all of the sites represented by these buttons by clicking on **Directory**.

✔ Click **Options, Show Toolbar**.

This eliminates the Toolbar and really opens up the screen (see Figure 2). You don't need the Toolbar. The buttons all have equivalent keystrokes, mouse commands or menu choices, detailed later.

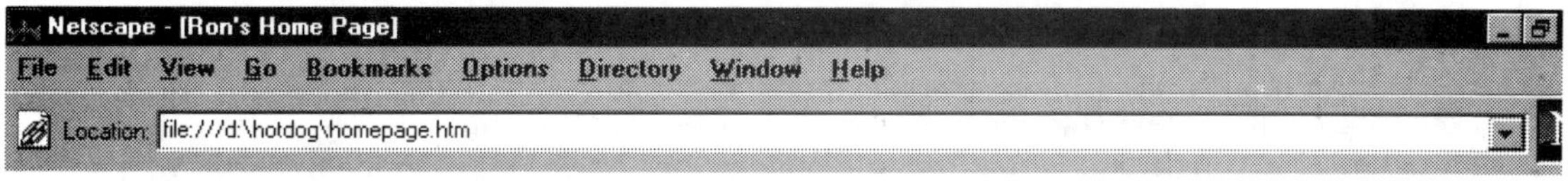

Figure 2 Compact Netscape header for maximum viewing area

Once you've eliminated the Toolbar, you'll enjoy the increased viewing area. We don't recommend eliminating the **Address** bar because it's a crucial navigation tool that you most likely will prefer to keep. The next table lists simple keystrokes and right mouse button replacements for the buttons you have just hidden from view.

Toolbar Button	Replacement Command
Back	**ALT+LEFT ARROW** or **Go, Back** Goes back to the previous Web site you visited.
Forward	**ALT+RIGHT ARROW** or **Go, Forward** Goes forward after you've used the Back command.
Home	Click **Go, Home** Jumps to your designated home page.
Reload	**CTRL+R** or **View, Reload** Forces the current page to download from the Internet again—highly useful for incomplete images or for Java applets (see the next chapter) that get stuck.
Location	**CTRL+L** or **File, Open Location...** Opens a Web site
Print	**CTRL+P** or **File, Print...** Prints the current Web page
Find	**CTRL+F** or **Edit, Find...** Searches the *current Web page* for keywords you enter.
Save	**CTRL+S** or **File, Save As...** Saves the current Web page on your local system.
Stop	**ESCAPE** or **Go, Stop Loading** Stops loading a page that's taking too long to load, if you get tired of waiting.

Finding what you need on the Web

So much information is available on the Web that all the power that's built into Netscape Navigator would be nearly useless if it weren't for the existence of a wide variety of Web search engines. The result is that you have a vast array of fast, powerful and comprehensive search engines that will help you locate nearly any topic in cyberspace. Web search engines are one of the primary reasons that the Web has become so popular, so let's learn some of the basics now. There's a whole chapter on search engines in the next Phase.

Inside Info

Search engines - Software applications that help you find information within computer information files are called search engines. They have two basic functions. The first is to run through the information files word-by-word and build an index of the words it finds—much like the index in the back of this book. The second function is a user interface that accepts keyword input that the search engine uses to locate your search request.

Netscape's Web search engine

You've got some Web searching ability built into the menu system of Netscape Navigator. Try clicking on **Directory, Internet Search** to see Netscape search page. Type in a keyword that interests you and click the button to submit your search.

In the Orbiting in Cyberspace section at the end of this chapter you'll get URLs and summaries for other Web search engines—and more in the search engine chapter. You most likely will add an array of search engine URLs to your Favorites Folders so you always will have them handy to answer your research demands. Search engines are just about the most valuable resource on the Internet.

Use Netscape Find command

Many of the hypertext Web pages that you'll view include jumps to other spots in the same document. These jumps don't load a new page, they just scroll through the current page and find a mark, called a "target." You'll be able to tell if you've jumped to a target within the same page because the URL will not change except for the very end, onto which will be appended a pound sign (#) and the target name.

But what you want to read might not have a targeted link, forcing you to do a lot of scrolling to find a particular phrase or keyword. Fortunately, Netscape Navigator lets you search the full text of the current Web document with the Find feature that we'll practice next. For this exercise, let's say you want to find all references to "ISDN" within an Internet glossary.

Step-By-Step

GOAL: Learn to use Netscape Navigator Find feature

- ✔ Press **CTRL+L**
- ✔ Type *www.familypcfun.com/glossary.htm* and press **ENTER**.
- ✔ Press **CTRL+F** or click on **Edit, Find**.

  This is a trick. The next step won't actually work. But it will fail due to a common problem that we want you to see it in action.
- ✔ Type *ISDN* and press **ENTER** to jump to that phrase.

  See, it didn't find anything did it? What's going on? It's the frames, that's what. Right now the active frame is the one at the top of the screen and that page doesn't have the word ISDN on it.

  Any time you try to search a frame-based Web site, be sure that you activate the correct frame. Let's do that now and then try again.
- ✔ Click your mouse in the bottom frame, but not on the "Home Page" button.
- ✔ Click **Find Next** to try it again.

This time, the first occurrence of "ISDN" will be highlighted. This only finds text within this specific document—it doesn't search the Web itself. It's not even searching other documents that are on the same Web site.

You can continue to click **Find Next** to jump to other occurrences of the word. Eventually it will tell you it's through.

✔ Click **Cancel** to terminate the search.

Using the information you find

Finding information for a school report, tracking down an important business lead, picking up a tip or an idea are all exciting things to accomplish on the Web. Finding some obscure material you've been seeking can be a huge relief. Discovering exciting information on the Web that you never knew existed is exhilarating. But once you find something, you need to know how to transfer it elsewhere within your system so that you have it in a useful format. There are numerous options and you will probably use them all depending on the information you've found and how you plan to use the information later.

Copying and pasting Web pages

Probably the quickest and simplest option for transferring Web text is with the clipboard and the Copy and Paste commands. If you can see the information on your screen, you usually can paste it into your word processor. After the transfer, you can reshape and reformat the text, embellish it with nice fonts and print it as part of a larger document. Let's try an exercise to illustrate this principle.

STEP-BY-STEP

GOAL: Learn to transfer Web text into your word processor

✔ Find your word processor icon and start the program.

If you don't have a word processor, you can use the Windows Notepad, Write or WordPad.

✔ Use **ALT+TAB** to cycle back to Netscape.

✔ Drag your mouse to highlight the ISDN listing you found in the last exercise.

✔ Press **CTRL+C** to Copy it to the Windows clipboard.

Or, you can click **Edit, Copy**.

✔ Use **ALT+TAB** to cycle back to your word processor.

✔ Press **CTRL+V** to Paste the copied text into a blank document.

You now could return to Netscape and grab more text from the last document you accessed or pull in more text from any Web document in the world!

You won't be able to grab all of the text you read on the Web because some text actually is part of a graphic image. In those cases, you won't be able to grab the text you want by simply dragging your mouse over it. You'll know it's not regular text characters because as you drag your mouse, the text will not highlight.

Inside Info

Netscape Navigator has a command that will automatically select all of the text on a Web page. You can press **CTRL+A** or click **Edit, Select All**. Then use the normal Windows **CTRL+C** command to copy the selected text to the clipboard.

Printing in Netscape Navigator

If you only need to read a Web document and you don't need to use it in your word processor, you can use Netscape to print the document directly. This is a quick way to get a hard copy of Web information, but this method is inflexible because you can't control or reformat the printed copy.

When you print the document directly, you'll get all of the graphics as you see them on the screen. And, Netscape Navigator offers optional embellishments for printed Web pages that include headers and footers with name, date and URL. We'll show you these printing setup options later.

The print function is great for information such as airline schedules and data tables, when you need a quick hard copy or when you need the graphics as well as the text. And remember, the Web is rich in color, too, so if you've got a color printer you'll be able to enjoy hard copy printouts of Web pages.

Step-By-Step

GOAL: Learn to print a Web document

- ✔ Click **File, Page Setup...**

  The best settings for **Page Options**, at the top-left, will depend upon the printer you're using, so we'll let you experiment with those. The same applies to the **Margins** settings.

- ✔ Set **Margins** as desired.
- ✔ Check options under **Header** to change them as desired.
- ✔ Check options under **Footer** to change them as desired.
- ✔ Click **OK** to save the setup.

  If you'd like to see the results of your changes *before* you commit to a paper printout, you can click **File, Print Preview** and make sure you're getting the effects you want. Print Preview lets you zoom in and out, switch to a two-page mode and page through the document.

- ✔ Press **CTRL+P** or click **File, Print...** to see the printer dialog box.
- ✔ Set the page range and the number of copies as desired.
- ✔ Click **OK** to print the current Web page.

  If you don't have a printer ready right now, you can click **Cancel** to end this exercise without printing.

Saving Web documents

You can use Netscape to save Web pages, but if you're not careful the file will be saved with all of the hypertext markup language (HTML) codes. If that happens, you'll need to clean out the HTML codes to get down to only the text you need. Fortunately, there is a Netscape Navigator option that cleans the HTML codes from the document as it saves.

STEP-BY-STEP

GOAL: Learn to save a Web document

- ✔ Click **File, Save As File...**

  Netscape lets you enter a name for the page. If you skip the next step, the file will be saved in HTML format—the language of the Web. That's wonderful if you're learning to create your own Web pages and want to see all the codes that made this page possible. But if you just want the text itself, do the next step.

- ✔ Click on the **Save as Type** drop list.
- ✔ Change to **Plain Text (*.txt)**.

  You don't have to actually use the *txt* extension—the document will be saved as plain text even if you keep the *htm* extension as long as the file type has been set correctly with this drop list.

- ✔ Use the normal **Save As** folder tools to set the desired path.

  Put this document in a directory that you use for word processing because you'll open it later in this exercise. Please write down or remember the directory.

- ✔ Click **OK** to save the document.
- ✔ Use **ALT+TAB** to switch to your word processor.

  If your word processor is not running, start it now.

- ✔ Click **File, Open...** or press **CTRL+O**.

  Navigate to the saved Web document and double-click on it to open it and display the conversion dialog box.

  WordPerfect for Windows only: (see Figure 3)

- ✔ Click the drop-list arrow to get a list of formats.
- ✔ Select **HTML** and click **OK**.
- ✔ Click **File, Save** or press **CTRL+S** then click **OK**.

  Microsoft Word for Windows:

- ✔ Click **File, Save** or press **CTRL+S**.

At this point, the document you had in Netscape has now been saved in the format of your word processor. If you didn't switch to plain-text you'll see a lot of HTML codes. If you don't want the codes, you can clean up the file manually, or you can return to Netscape and save the page again in the plain-text format.

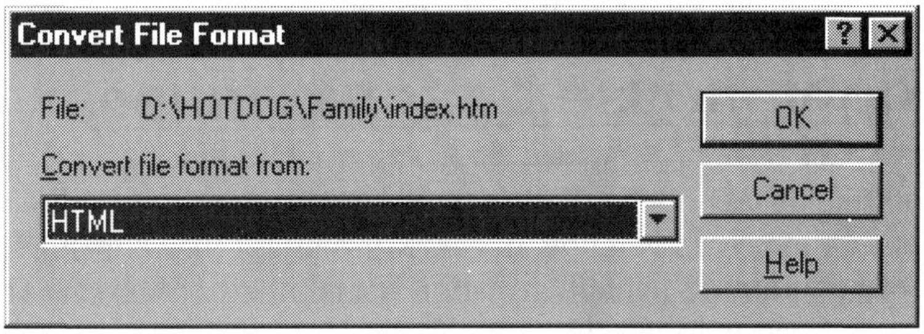

Figure 3 HTML files import into your word processor

Saving images

The last method you have for capturing Internet information is to save graphics files, and Netscape makes this easy. All you have to do is click your right mouse button on any Web graphic and choose the correct save option. Let's do it.

STEP-BY-STEP

GOAL: Learn to save a Web page graphic image

✔ Click **Go**, then click on the glossary listing.

As a reminder, it's at *www.familypcfun.com/glossary.htm.*

✔ Click the right mouse button over the *Family PC Fun* logo at the top.

✔ Click **Save Picture As...**

Select a directory in which to save it.

✔ Click **OK**.

The image has been saved in the Graphics Interchange Format (compressed graphic images). At the time this book was written, Microsoft Word could not handle .GIF or .JPEG files directly, so you cannot open this in Word without converting it first with a graphics utility application. Corel WordPerfect 7 will handle both file types for importing and exporting, and it enables you to draw original images and save them in either format.

Getting the Latest Netscape Navigator

We want to make sure you're using the latest version of Netscape Navigator, so you'll be able to download upgrades from Netscape Web site. Check periodically so you'll know when a new version is available. All you have to do is click on **Directory, Netscape's Home** and you'll be able to read about the current version and follow the links to download an upgrade, if one is available.

Netscape almost always has a Beta test version of the next generation of Netscape Navigator. We can't recommend that you download these, because you can get technical support only for the latest, final-release version of Netscape Navigator. We've found that the Beta versions generally work fine, so you might want to experiment even if you can't get technical support.

Jargon Cutter

Beta test version - A version of a software product that has passed the initial in-company testing phase (Alpha test) and is ready to be tested by actual users, but is not considered reliable enough to release as a final product. Technical support is not available for Beta test versions. Once the Beta testing bugs have been fixed, the product is released as a full version.

Right mouse button bonuses

If you used the right mouse button in the last exercise when you saved a graphic, then you may have noticed that the menu had several other shortcuts. We'll run through one of them with you now in case you missed them or didn't save a graphic. To see these commands actually function, you'll need a Web page that has a graphic image. Let's continue to use the same Web page.

Copy a link location

Netscape also uses the right mouse button to let you copy the URL of a hypertext link into your Windows clipboard. You then may use **ALT+TAB** to cycle to your word processor and paste in the URL. As you've seen, some URLs are a real mess to retype, so this method may save you a lot of time, aggravation and mistakes.

STEP-BY-STEP

GOAL: Save a link location to the Windows clipboard

✔ Start with the glossary page used earlier.

✔ Place the mouse over the **Home Page** link, but don't click.

Read the link's URL on the status line at the bottom of the screen. You don't want to type that, do you?

✔ Click the right mouse button and click **Copy Link Location**.

The URL is now in the clipboard. You can switch to another application with **ALT+TAB**, then press **CTRL+V** to paste it.

If you click on **Copy Image Location** on this menu, the URL of the image itself will go in the clipboard instead of the URL to which the image is pointing.

Reload the current document

Remember that if you use the Back command to cycle to a document you've already seen, you'll be getting a cached copy and Netscape won't pull in a new copy from the Internet. Sometimes you'll need to force Netscape to pull in a document from the Internet again. Why? Here are a few examples:

- To update a live-action video camera, such as a traffic watch system. If you check traffic and then surf for half an hour, then go back to the site, you'll just get the old picture. Reload would pull in the latest view.
- To update a stock report or a sports score. Again, you'll just see the old numbers when you return to the page.
- To fix a Java applet that's locked up with an "exception" error. Reloading the page will get it going again.
- To thwart those little Internet gremlins that sometimes—for completely unknown reasons—keep a page from loading correctly the first time you hit it. In fact, sometimes you'll get a message that the address is invalid, but a simple reload command will load it correctly the second time.

Here's how to refresh a page in Netscape Navigator:

STEP-BY-STEP

GOAL: Learn how to force a page to reload from the Internet

✔ Use your History to return to the Internet glossary we used earlier.

✔ Click **View, Reload** or press **CTRL+R**.

These commands refresh all pages on the entire screen. Sometimes, though, you only need to refresh the page in a single frame. Let's try that now.

✔ Click in the bottom frame.

✔ Click **View, Reload Frame**.

Bookmarks

Netscape Bookmarks let you save Web locations so you can easily return to them without having to write them down. Bookmarks create a permanent file that saves the URL of any Internet document and assigns it a plain-language name. You can pop up your Bookmark List any time and quickly jump to all of your favorite sites.

We'll show you four different Bookmark features: 1) adding Bookmarks, 2) editing Bookmarks, 3) modifying and arranging the Bookmark List itself and 4) turning the Bookmark List into your own personal "home page."

Adding bookmarks

There are two ways to add personal Bookmarks in Netscape. The first is so easy you don't even need a hands-on exercise to learn it. Whenever you see a site for which you want easy access, simply press **CTRL+D** for the "Add Bookmark" command. Using the mouse, the steps are: click **Bookmarks, Add Bookmark**. The current URL is added to the Bookmark list under the main folder unless you've specified another folder to be your default. We'll show you later how to move Bookmarks to any category.

You also can add Bookmarks directly to the list. This has the advantage of enabling you to enter Bookmarks for sites you've yet to visit or to add Bookmarks to a selected category. Let's try it now.

Step-By-Step

GOAL: Add a Bookmark directly to the listing

- ✔ Press **CTRL+B** or click **Window, Bookmarks**
- ✔ Click on the top folder on the list.
- ✔ Click **Item, Insert Folder...**
- ✔ Type *Practice* and click **OK**.

  This creates a new folder under the main folder.
- ✔ Click on the folder "Practice."
- ✔ Click **Item, Insert Bookmark...**
- ✔ Type *Internet Glossary* and press **TAB** to jump to **Location (URL)**.
- ✔ Type *http://familypcfun.com/glossary.htm* and click **OK**.
- ✔ Click on the folder "Practice."
- ✔ Click **Item, Insert Bookmark...**
- ✔ Type *Lycos* and press **TAB** to jump to **Location (URL)**.
- ✔ Type *http://www.lycos.com* and click **OK**.
- ✔ Click **Item, Insert Bookmark...**
- ✔ Type *Yellow Pages* and press **TAB** to jump to **Location (URL)**.
- ✔ Type *http://www.yellow.com* and click **OK**.
- ✔ Click on the top folder on the list.
- ✔ Click **Item, Insert Folder...**

- ✔ Type *Internet Resources* and click **OK**.

  This creates another new folder.
- ✔ Click on the top folder on the list.
- ✔ Click **Item, Insert Header...**
- ✔ Type *Directories* and click **OK**.

  You can continue the lesson now by adding folders for your own categories. Here are a few more suggested headings that you could create now:

  - Search Resources
  - Reference Resources
  - Corporations
  - Universities
  - Miscellaneous

Now that you've set up all of these folders, we'll give you two exercises that will let you check out your Bookmarks and sort your Bookmarks for quicker reference.

STEP-BY-STEP

GOAL: Check Bookmark URLs

- ✔ Click **Bookmarks, Go to Bookmarks**.
- ✔ Click **File, What's New?**
- ✔ Click **Start Checking** to have Netscape verify your Bookmarks.

  If you only want to check out some of your Bookmarks, select the ones you want to check before starting the check. To do that, hold down either **CTRL** key as you click so you can select multiple links.

Netscape will sort your Bookmarks to make the listings easier to locate. Follow these steps to sort your Bookmark list.

STEP-BY-STEP

GOAL: Learn how to sort Bookmarks

- ✔ Click on the top folder.
- ✔ Click **Item, Sort Bookmarks**.

  If this command is disabled, you're not on the top folder. If you're not then scroll through the list and highlight the top folder, then repeat the command.

To place a new Bookmark in a category other than the default, you first must add it to the list under the default. Then you can press **CTRL+B** to open the Bookmark List and then drag and drop the new Bookmark onto the desired category. But you can change the default category, to which new Bookmarks are added, at any time. This enables you to quickly add Bookmarks on the fly while you're surfing, and then go back later and organize them into more logical folders. Follow these steps:

STEP-BY-STEP

GOAL: Learn to specify a default Bookmark category

- ✔ Click on the folder of the category you want to be the default.
- ✔ Click **Item, Set to New Bookmarks Folder**.

  You can make a folder called "New" and make that folder your default. That way you'll know where all of your new Bookmarks are so you can easily find them and move them later to their proper folders.
- ✔ Press **ALT+F4** to return to Netscape.

  From now on, all of the Bookmarks you add with **CTRL+D** will go to this category.

Editing existing bookmarks

Sometimes a URL for which you've created a Bookmark will change or you'll get some new information about a Bookmark site that you'd like to add to the description. Netscape makes Bookmark editing a snap.

There's a bonus associated with this procedure. When editing a Bookmark, you also will see the date it was added and the last date it was visited. Sometimes, then, you might want to start this process just to see that information even if you do not need to edit the link information.

STEP-BY-STEP

GOAL: Learn to edit a Bookmark

- ✔ Click on any existing Bookmark.
- ✔ Click the right mouse button, click **Properties**.
- ✔ Make any necessary changes, then click **OK**.

  Note the two dates near the bottom of the dialog box.

Modifying bookmarks

The order of the folders and the document references under each folder can be rearranged at any time simply by dragging any entry either to a new folder or to a new location under the same folder.

STEP-BY-STEP

GOAL: Modify the bookmark listing

- ✔ Drag and drop "Internet Glossary" onto the "Internet Resources" folder.
- ✔ Click on "Internet Resources."
- ✔ Click **Item, Insert Bookmark**.
- ✔ Type *Yahoo*, then press **TAB**.
- ✔ Type *http://www.yahoo.com*, then press **ENTER**.
- ✔ Drag and drop "Yellow Pages" onto the "Directories" folder.

✔ Click on the folder "Practice."

✔ Press **DELETE** or by clicking on **Edit, Delete** to delete it.

Now that you've rearranged everything, let's sort your Bookmarks.

✔ Click on the top folder.

✔ Click **Item, Sort Bookmarks.**

✔ Click the exit button or press **ALT+F4** to exit Netscape Bookmarks window.

There are several ways to use your Bookmark List to surf the Internet. Here's a summary:

- Press **CTRL+B** and double-click the item on the list.
- Click **Bookmarks, Go to Bookmarks...** and double-click the item on the list.
- Click **Bookmarks** and click on the drop-down menu or sub-menu of Bookmarks.
- Press **ALT+B**, then use **DOWN ARROW** to highlight the link you want, then press **ENTER**.

Selecting the menu folder

While you were editing your Bookmarks, you may have found a feature that lets you control which folder Netscape uses to build the drop-down menu mentioned in the last bullet above. Here's a Hands-On exercise that will illustrate how to use this handy, organizing feature.

STEP-BY-STEP

GOAL: Learn to set the drop-menu folder

✔ Press **ALT+B** and stop.

This keystroke has activated the Bookmarks drop-menu. Note that, by default, this menu begins with your main folder. The only folders you see here are the ones directly off this main folder. If an entry here has links under it, you'll see a triangle next to its name and you can see the links by highlighting their parent folder. Let's do that.

✔ Press **DOWN ARROW** until you highlight "Internet Resources."

You now can see the links under this folder.

✔ Press **G** to **Go to Bookmarks.**

✔ Click on the "Internet Resources" folder.

✔ Click **Item, Set to Bookmark Menu Folder.**

✔ Press **ALT+F4** to close the Bookmark window.

✔ Press **ALT+B** to see the Bookmark drop-menu.

Now the only items you see on this menu are the ones under the "Internet Resources" folder. This feature may not make a lot of sense right now, with so few links and folders, but when you've got hundreds of links you might want to change the menu folder for a while to more easily activate links in a focused category. But you eventually will want to restore your main folder as the menu folder. Let's do that now to finish this exercise.

✔ Press **G** to **Go to Bookmarks.**

- ✔ Click on the main folder at the top of the list.
- ✔ Click **Item, Set to Bookmark Menu Folder**.
- ✔ Press **ALT+F4** to close the Bookmark window.
- ✔ Press **ALT+B** to see the Bookmark drop-menu.

  Note that right now, the first two items on this list are the only ones that have underlined letters. That means that you can activate these items with keystrokes. You could press A for Add Bookmark or G for Go to Bookmarks. Now I'll show you how to set up your own underlined letters so you can activate your actual links with keystrokes.
- ✔ Press **G** for **Go to Bookmarks**.

  Stop here and go on to the next exercise.

Setting up ALT letters

We'll use the opened Bookmark window now to edit your Bookmarks so that you'll be able to activate some of them with keystrokes. You most likely will have far more Bookmarks than just the 26 letters of the alphabet, but you can single out your most frequently-used Bookmarks and set them up for speedy access.

STEP-BY-STEP

GOAL: Learn to set ALT letters on your Bookmark menu

- ✔ Click on "Internet Resources."
- ✔ Click the right mouse button, click **Properties**.
- ✔ Press **HOME** to move to the beginning of the entry.
- ✔ Type *&* and press **ENTER**.

  When you place an ampersand in front of a letter on a link's name, that letter will be underlined on the Bookmark menu. You do not have to use the first letter. Let's continue.
- ✔ Click on "Internet Glossary."
- ✔ Click the right mouse button, click **Properties**.
- ✔ Press **CTRL+LEFT ARROW** to move to the beginning of "Glossary."
- ✔ Type *&* and press **ENTER**.
- ✔ Click on "Yahoo!"
- ✔ Click the right mouse button, click **Properties**.
- ✔ Press **HOME** to move to the beginning of the entry.
- ✔ Type *&* and press **ENTER**.
- ✔ Press **ALT+F4** to close the Bookmark window.
- ✔ Press **ALT+B** to activate the Bookmark menu.
- ✔ Press **ALT+I** to activate "Internet Resources."
- ✔ Press **ALT+G** to go to "Internet Glossary."

Saving your bookmarks

Your Bookmark file may become one of your most valuable computer assets. It may contain links to crucial business partners from around the world, so you'll want to protect it.

Netscape keeps this valuable resource in its program directory. Many people do not regularly run a backup of their program directories. If your Netscape program directory isn't backed up frequently then you could lose valuable information.

Periodically copy your bookmark file to a floppy or to a directory on your PC or your network that is included in regular backup sessions. Don't trust this to chance—your Bookmark file may be one of your most treasured information resources—protect this important file.

Bookmark summary

As you've now seen, Bookmarks are an important feature of Netscape because they will speed your work by enabling you to save any URL you find on the Internet. Please note that the Bookmarks are not limited to saving URLs of Web documents. You can use a Bookmark to save the URL of anything on the Internet: FTP sites, Gopher sites, and newsgroups. You even can create links to local HTML documents on your organization's own network server and create an "Intranet" effect even if your organization doesn't have an Intranet.

Jargon Cutter

Intranet - An internal Web that runs on your organization's own network. The documents on an Intranet usually are kept private and are not accessible on the World Wide Web, although they could be. An Intranet is a powerful productivity-enhancing tool that is sweeping through organizations of all sizes. In fact, I've written an entire book on Intranets, *Building and Managing the Corporate Intranet* (Ronald L. Wagner and Eric Engelmann, McGraw-Hill, 1996).

Creating your own "home page"

When you start Netscape, it automatically loads your default "home page." Your home page can be any site on the Internet or any hypertext document on your own system, even if you are using a stand-alone PC. If you installed Netscape from an Erol's installation disk, the Erol's home page will be your default home page.

If you haven't modified Netscape since you installed it, you probably still have our Web page set to be your home page. We've got a lot of valuable resources for you, but we understand that you may want to turn your Bookmark file into a tailored home page that presents your most frequently-visited Web sites. Here's how:

STEP-BY-STEP

GOAL: Turn the Bookmark file into your home page

- ✔ Click **Options, General Preferences...**
- ✔ Click on the **Appearance** tab.
- ✔ Under **Browser Starts With:**, check **Home Page Location**.
- ✔ Click in the text entry box immediately below this button.

✔ Type *file:///c:\netscape\bookmark.htm* and click **OK**.

The path to this file may be different on your system. Also, note that there are *three* slashes after the colon.

Now every time you start Netscape your Bookmark List will be loaded. The folders will show up as bolded headings and each entry will show up as a hypertext jump. If you place your mouse—without clicking it—over a highlighted jump, you can read the URL in the status bar at the bottom of the screen. Any descriptions you manually entered on your Bookmark List will show up as regular text under its associated hypertext jump entry.

File Transfer Protocol (FTP)

Netscape Navigator lets you load more than Web documents from the Internet. It also retrieves Gopher information and downloads files via the FTP.

Don't worry about Gopher. In the first place, you won't see much of it. And, you're most likely to encounter it while surfing a Web page that includes a Gopher link. If you click on a Gopher link, Netscape will handle the Gopher page almost as if it were a Web page. You'll hardly notice a difference, except that the page will appear as just a plain listing. We're not going to give you a Step-By-Step exercise on Gopher because the Gopher sites are disappearing from the Internet so rapidly that there's a very good chance you wouldn't be able to access the example we used.

FTP is another story. It's not disappearing from the Internet and you very well could use it regularly to update system drivers or software. You might even use it to download word processing documents, large image files, sound files, video files, spreadsheets and database files. NASA uses FTP to make available thousands of images from space—some of the most popular files on the Internet.

When you need to download something via the FTP, you definitely will know you're not working with a Web page. And, you'll have to take some steps to get the file saved on your system. But don't worry, it's not difficult and we'll give you an example for practice. We'll show you how to get an update to your Netscape by directly using the FTP instead of going the normal Netscape Web page route because it's often faster.

STEP-BY-STEP

GOAL: Learn to use the File Transfer Protocol (FTP)

✔ Start Netscape Navigator.

✔ Press **CTRL+L**

✔ Type*ftp12.netscape.com*, then press **ENTER** (see Figure 4).

Patience on your part is a valuable FTP asset. Expect problems. This step may fail, giving you an error message that Netscape couldn't open the site. If so, try it again and again. Many FTP sites have extremely high traffic loads and FTP servers will reject new users if capacity has been reached. So you must try and try again until you catch an opening—don't just try again later, keep after it continuously in one session.

✔ Click on **navigator**.

✔ Click on **3.0**.

✔ Click on **windows**.

✔ Click on **README.txt**.

This file will explain which version you need to download for your system. Of course you may already have the latest version.

✔ Click on the file you want to download.

Patience, patience. Keep trying. After you finally get it, specify the directory and save the file to your hard drive.

✔ Select a target directory.

You should create a new directory for all new programs. Use File Manager or the Windows Explorer to create a directory under your netscape directory called "install," then point the Save As dialog to this new install directory.

✔ Click **Save**, then wait for the download to complete.

When the process is complete, you may be asked a security question about whether or not you want to allow this action to save something on your hard drive. Since this is Netscape's home you can say yes. But be careful at other sites—say yes only to sites that you trust not to try to sneak a virus into your system.

After the download is complete, the file will be saved to your system and you can run it and install the latest Netscape Navigator or, just delete it and do these steps again with a file you do want to install.

Inside Info

FTP is a faster method than the Web page for downloading Netscape files. There are currently 13 FTP servers, numbered **ftp1** through **ftp12**, and **ftp20**. Do not use **ftp1**, but you can use any of the other 12. Just substitute **2-12** or **20** when you use the steps above. Remember, you can create a Bookmark for a FTP URL just as well as for a Web URL.

WS_FTP

Netscape Navigator offers only limited FTP functions—it doesn't offer you much control over the files, or over your system. And it doesn't keep you well-informed about the status of the download. For full FTP control, you'll need dedicated FTP software. The best one on the Internet today is called WS_FTP (see Figure 4). It's freeware, which means that it is actually *free*—you can download WS_FTP and use this excellent application at no cost.

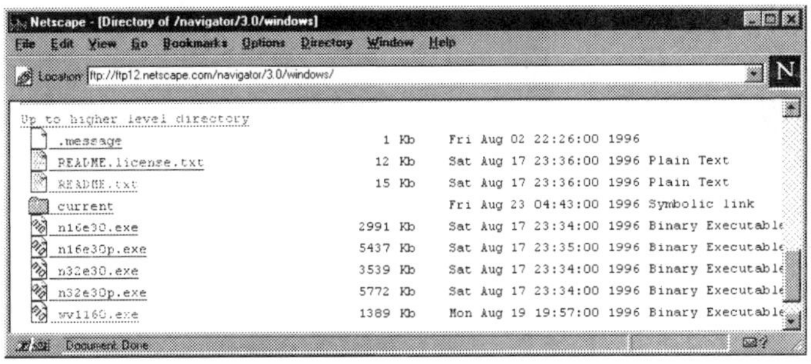

Figure 4 Netscape Navigator FTP page

You can use Netscape Navigator to download the WS_FTP application by going to *www.ipswitch.com*. From there, you'll have to browse around to find the download link. You can download WS_FTP LE (Limited Edition) free, and you can get the Pro version for a small registration fee. After you install WS_FTP, you're not likely to use Netscape Navigator for FTP functions. But if you expect to have limited FTP needs, then there's no reason to take up hard drive space with a separate application.

Inside Info

Downloading an installation program into a main program directory can result in a confused mess of co-mingled files. **Before** you download any installation program, create a new directory (call it "Install") below the program's main directory and then download the installation program into that directory. Then when you run the actual installation, tell it to install the files into the main program directory. This technique will always keep your installation files separated from their programs, avoiding confusion and clutter.

Advanced Netscape Navigator features

Now that we've covered the technical aspects of using Netscape Navigator to navigate around in cyberspace, you've seen all the basic Internet tools that you'll need. We've postponed any discussion of advanced topics such as using Java, audio files or video files until the advanced chapter, which follows this one. They're cool to watch and you'll probably enjoy most of them, but you don't *need* them so you can skip the next chapter for now. So, if your main interest is basic Web surfing, then you're ready to begin using Netscape now. You can launch yourself straight into cyberspace in Phase 3 and save the next chapter for later.

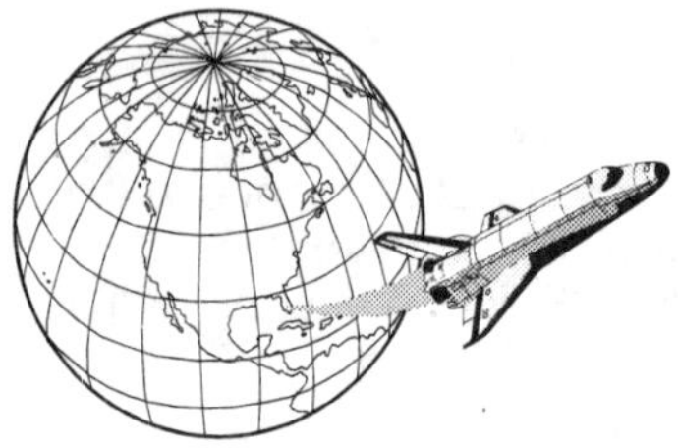

ORBITING IN CYBERSPACE

WWW FAQ
http://www.boutell.com/faq

With so much cyberspace to surf, where do you start? Start here. This on-line Frequently Asked Questions (FAQ) site is an excellent site for new Web users. Most of the other sites listed here are information-searching resources, so you might want to try this site first to get a better overview of what's out there waiting for you in cyberspace.

Truly awesome Web stuff
http://www.clark.net/pub/journalism/awesome.html

The URL listed above is not the same as the URL listed in the Step-By-Step exercise earlier in this chapter. This is a generic address that gets you into the site. "The glory and the grandeur of the Internet all on one site," is their claim-to-fame. They've got the "Truly Awesome" list (last count: 30 sites) and the merely "Awesome" list (last count: 101 sites). Be sure and check out the latest update at this address. From here, you can spend your entire life surfing the Web—of course you will still be farther behind than you are today, but at least you will have a fun trip.

All-In-One Internet search
http://www.albany.net/allinone

Awesome! That word applies to this site as well. It's the most comprehensive research tool on the Internet today—of course, by the time you read this, who knows! It's a compilation of various forms-based search tools found on the Internet that have been combined to form a consistent interface and create a convenient "all-in-one" search engine. If you can't find it through this site, it isn't worth finding.

Point Communications Top 5%
http://www.pointcom.com

These folks scour the Web searching for the most valuable sites (see Figure 5). They award their logo to the winners, then list them by category so you can find the best sites quickly and easily. In addition to listing top Web sites, they have Internet news, general news, hot topics and even politics. Be sure to put this site on your Bookmark and check it often to help you stay abreast of the latest Web developments.

Figure 5 Pointcom - The Top 5%

Open Text Web Index
http://www.opentext.com

An excellent search site that provides both simple and compound search strings (see Figure 6). Click on "Open Text Web Index" to get to their "Simple search" engine. This site also enables you to search the Web in languages besides English: Deutsche, Français, Italiano, Nihongo. Check the options you want, enter a keyword or phrase and click on **Search**. You also can select more detailed searches using the optional hypertext links to **Power Search** and **Weighted Search**. Like other search engines, Open Text is growing rapidly as they index tens of thousands of Web pages per day.

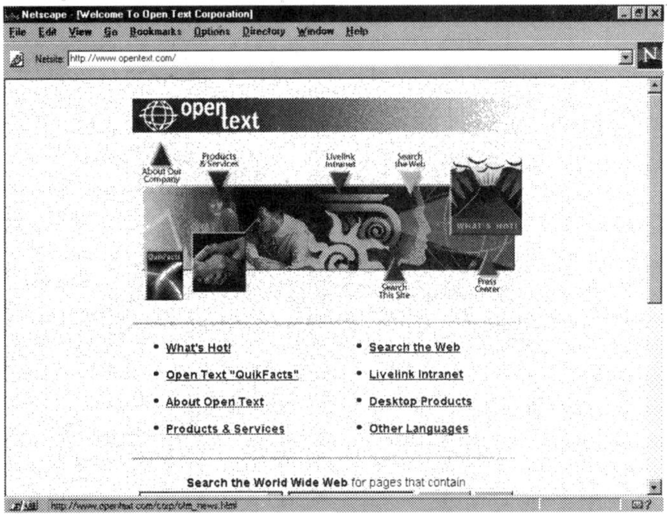

Figure 6 OpenText - multi-lingual Web searching

Yahoo! directory
http://www.yahoo.com

This is a staple Web search engine. It's got just about everything you could want. The search mode is based upon your browsing through hypertext-linked tables of contents to find topics that appear to match your area of interest. It's got plenty of competition now, but it was among the pioneers and deserves a look simply because of the huge number of people who learned from the early work that Yahoo! did.

Lycos
http://www.lycos.com

This Internet search tool was created by Carnegie Mellon University, in Pittsburgh, and is one of the most popular sites on the Internet. It's based upon a vast index of keywords that it has pulled from HTTP, Gopher and FTP files all over the Internet. At the beginning of July, 1996, Lycos had indexed 47.8 million documents. Go see how many pages it's indexed today.

The Lycos index searches document titles, headings, links and keywords to build a reference against which you can search the Internet. You find topics by entering a keyword or a string of keywords that Lycos compares against its index. The results of the search are reported to you with a score based upon how many of your keywords it finds, the number of occurrences and how far into the document the words are found.

Whole Internet Catalog
http://gnn.com/gnn/GNNhome.html

Here's a rich source of additional Web material. Click on "The Whole Internet Catalog" link on their graphic. You also will discover "Virtual Places" and tips on building your own Web pages.

6

Booster Rocket: Netscape Advanced

The hills may be alive with the *Sound of Music*, but the Web is alive with the sound of on-line music. And, since actions speak louder than words, you can forget about writer's block and begin expressing yourself through your own Web site, complete with video clips, live-camera video and animated action.

This is an exciting chapter that will show you how to use your Netscape Navigator to play audio, video and animation. All of these features are still pretty primitive, but the core technology is in place and it's advancing at the speed of light. Prepare to be thrilled at the sights and sounds you're going to pull in from all over the world.

This chapter is an overview of the major Web special features that you'll see as you cruise the Net. Here's the menu for the delightful treats that await you:

- ❖ Java, the Web's own programming language;
- ❖ Audio, sound clips and real-time;
- ❖ Video, clips and live-action;
- ❖ Virtual reality, a whole new world.

Java

Java is an object-oriented programming language developed in the 1990s at Sun Microsystems, Inc. It was developed there by a team headed by James Gosling and was intended for the microprocessors in small appliances. With this focus in mind, Java had to work on a wide variety of processors and it needed excellent safeguards against locking up the processor. After all, you've become accustomed to your PC locking up occasionally, but how would you reboot your dishwasher?

While the Sun team developed Java, the World Wide Web grew up around them. Along the way, someone realized that the same characteristics that made Java perfect for appliance processors also made it perfect for the Web. The two technologies were married and introduced to the world in May, 1995. Java will be a major factor in the Internet changing the way we all work, play and live.

What's In A Name?

Contrary to rumors, Java does NOT stand for "Just Another Vague Acronym." Java originally was named Oak in honor of a large tree outside James Gosling's window. Trademark considerations forced the team to come up with a new product name. That's a tough task in today's crowded markets, but Java hit the spot.

What's the difference between Java and HotJava? Java is the programming language. HotJava is Sun's Java-compatible Web browser. At first HotJava was the only Java browser available, but HotJava never really caught on because soon after Java became available, Netscape agreed to make its Navigator browser Java-compatible. Once Microsoft added Java-compatibility to its Internet Explorer, that pretty much sealed Java as *the* Internet programming language.

Two other factors have spurred Java's incredible rise in fortune. First, Java resembles the highly popular C and C++ programming languages used by most programming professionals. So, most programmers learn it easily and can adapt existing code. And, it's more forgiving than C or C++, so debugging is simplified and novices can pick it up more quickly. Experienced C programmers will appreciate Java's relative ease of use. These factors combined will bring millions of Java applets onto the Web.

Jargon Cutter

Applet - Java programs are called applets because they depend in part on code that's embedded into your Web browser. Without that code a Java program would be useless, so they're just called applets instead of applications.

Sample Java input script

Many popular Java applets are written to receive input from a script file. This means that a lot of people will be able to add Java applets to their site without knowing anything about programming. They'll be able to write a script from scratch, or perhaps modify a sample script that the programmer included with the applet.

For an example of what Java looks like behind the scenes, here's a small block of HTML codes (see listing below) that shows the commands that tell Netscape to run the code stored on the server's Web site. It plays a scrolling LED sign that carries a running message similar to the sign on the side of the Goodyear blimp.

```
<applet code="LED/LED.class" width=320 height=60>
<param name=script value="Scripts/FamilyPC.led">
<param name=font value="Fonts/default.font">
<param name=spacewidth value="3">
<param name=bordercolor value="100,130,130">
<param name=border value="3">
</applet>
```

Once the Java code is loaded on the server and these lines are imbedded into the HTML codes on the Web page, the sign will display. The Web page author doesn't need to be a programmer, because the only thing that must be tailored is the text file that's referenced on the second line—that file contains the words that scroll. You can see it in action at *www.FamilyPCfun.com*.

So What?

Think about your Web site visitors if you decide to add Java to your site, and be realistic. Someday, Java will run easily on all systems, but today it can strain slower systems and annoy Web surfers. People with 486-based PCs, or slower, may not see the cool show you planned.

There are several other considerations to keep in mind:

- Java is not yet enabled in 16-bit versions of Web browsers. This means that users with Windows 3.x will not see your little marvel anyway.
- Many visitors will have non-Java browsers.
- The Java code takes extra time to download even for those users with Java-compatible browsers. Will your visitors agree that your Java application was worth the time they had to wait to get it?

Don't abandon your Java plans, however, because Java will be a major factor in the Internet revolutionizing our lives, but just not in the next year or two. Until then, make sure that your use of Java has a higher purpose than making you feel good about your site.

How you can use Java

There are practically no limits to what can be done with Java. You're going to see an explosion of Java applets on the market that will enable Web developers to do almost anything you can imagine. The resources listed in the Orbiting in Cyberspace section of this chapter contain links to a lot of Java-powered sites, so there's plenty to see.

Before Java, the only programming you were likely to encounter on the Web was CGI (Common Gateway Interface) programs that ran on the Web server. You may have seen CGI in action if you have filled in an information form and sent it to the company that was hosting the site.

CGI works only on a two-way street—user actions must interact with the Web server. This increases Internet bandwidth demands and server load because CGI programs must go back and forth to verify user input. A busy site could cause user delays as the server goes into overload keeping up with the programming commands forced on it by many users activating CGI scripts.

Java, on the other hand, is more of a one-way street. Of course Java must load its code onto your computer before it can begin working, but once it's on your system, it can perform data verification tests within your browser. Thus, it uses the server only when the task is ready to send back. This enables Web sites to provide better service and handle more traffic because the workload is shared with every visitor's computer.

Banish Programming Forever

If you don't care which is easier, CGI or Java, because you have zero interest in learning either one, there are alternatives. You can create interactive brochures and databases on the Web without having to learn either CGI or Java, thanks to user-friendly applications that let you work in an intuitive environment. Then, when you're done, these new applications handle the Web technical stuff. These new applications are simple enough that a Web site even for your home-based business can sport some advanced features.

Interactive brochures and catalogs

Made by AMT Learning Solutions, Interactive Brochure lets you easily create interactive multimedia presentations that can work over the Web. And a companion product, Interactive Catalog, lets you set up an on-line catalog from which users can order directly. Combine this with a commerce server and you've created an inexpensive on-line sales outlet.

Interactive Brochure has an expanded version that creates interactive training sessions. It includes a testing, scoring and reporting system that can handle all functions on-line, including gathering scoring information from any computer in the world.

For more information, contact AMT Learning Solutions at *www.amtcorp.com*, or e-mail a request to *amtsales@amtcorp.com*.

askSam

askSam is the famous free-form database that led Federal prosecutors to break open the Iran-Contra case. No human mind or ordinary database had been able to piece together the facts that prosecutors suspected could lead to filing charges. Once the information was entered into askSam, the big picture came into focus. A free-form database can deal with information that doesn't fit into traditional database fields.

Now, you can create an on-line askSam database that users can interact with from anywhere in the world. You can organize data that users input from the Web, or you can let users search through your database to retrieve information. Sam doesn't care how much you dump in, he'll be able to index it and give you exactly what you want when you want it. It's a perfect solution for archives of e-mail or Usenet newsgroup articles. Visit the Web page at *www.asksam.com* for more information.

CGI isn't dead and will probably be around for years. But Java will quickly replace many of its functions, especially for all the new people coming onto the Net who don't know—and don't want to know—anything about CGI.

Here is a list of some Java functions that already are in use on the Web:

- Clickable image maps;
- User friendly link buttons;
- Active and interactive site navigation help;
- Scrolling messages to present hot topics;

- Sound and video players that activate automatically;
- Automated visitor reply-and-response forms;
- Calculators tailored for a specific use;
- Spreadsheets that present tailored financial data.

JavaScript

JavaScript is a simplified version of Java that you may want to investigate if all this talk of programming is giving you the jitters. You can find a lot of valuable JavaScript examples that you can use without programming knowledge. This isn't the same thing as the use of a script that was demonstrated earlier. That was a script that fed parameters to a Java applet, JavaScript is another programming language.

JavaScript complements Java by bringing the useful properties of Java applets to less-experienced authors. JavaScript is a descendant of smaller, dynamically-typed languages such as dBASE. These scripting languages bring programming capability to a broader set of users because of their simpler syntax, specialized built-in functionality and minimal requirements for object creation.

The next feature is something that works well with Java: on-line audio. Before Java, Web authors needed to create links on Web pages so that visitors could click and download an audio file. But Java enables Web authors to automatically play an audio file—a welcome message or a musical fanfare—when the page loads into a Java-compatible browser.

On-line Audio

On-line audio works by converting sound into digital information and storing that information in audio computer files. These files then can be transferred across the Internet and can be played on a wide variety of operating systems and computer platforms. You will soon see that sound files come in a lot of different formats and that each of these formats uses a proprietary compression scheme to reduce the size of the saved sound files they produce. File compression is crucial to the spread of Internet audio because sound files require very large file sizes in relation to the length of the sound clip. Don't be surprised to watch sound files grab 11K of disk space for every second of sound.

The use of on-line audio is increasing rapidly. Unfortunately, there isn't a uniform standard for digital audio formats, though the field is narrowing. Here are the more common types you'll encounter in a Windows environment:

- .WAV files (common SoundBlaster-type audio files);
- .AU files (common Internet audio files);
- .RA files (Real Audio files, best for voice only).

Wave audio

Wave is the native sound format for Microsoft Windows systems. The short musical segments you hear sprucing up your Windows activities are wave files. The wave format is the least efficient of the three listed here, requiring approximately 50 percent larger files than .AU sound files. It's main advantage lies in the huge number of wave files that are available—including lots of public domain clips. And, if you find a wave clip that you want to use, you can convert it to the efficient Sun format, .AU.

Sun audio

One of the most popular Internet sound file formats is the .AU format, also called the uLaw, NeXT, or Sun Audio format. This format can be used on most of the machines on the Internet that are equipped to play sound. It also produces reasonably small files that consume little bandwidth to transfer. It's a nice balance between audio quality and required transfer time. It definitely has sufficient audio quality for the typical sound clips you might offer, pretty much matching wave.

Real Audio

Real Audio is the name of a company that developed the .RA standard (see Figure 1). It's become popular on the Internet because of its extremely small bandwidth demands. In fact, with a good connection, even a 28.8kbps modem can play .RA sound clips in real time. Of course, this won't be a concern for you if you use Erol's speedy ISDN Internet access.

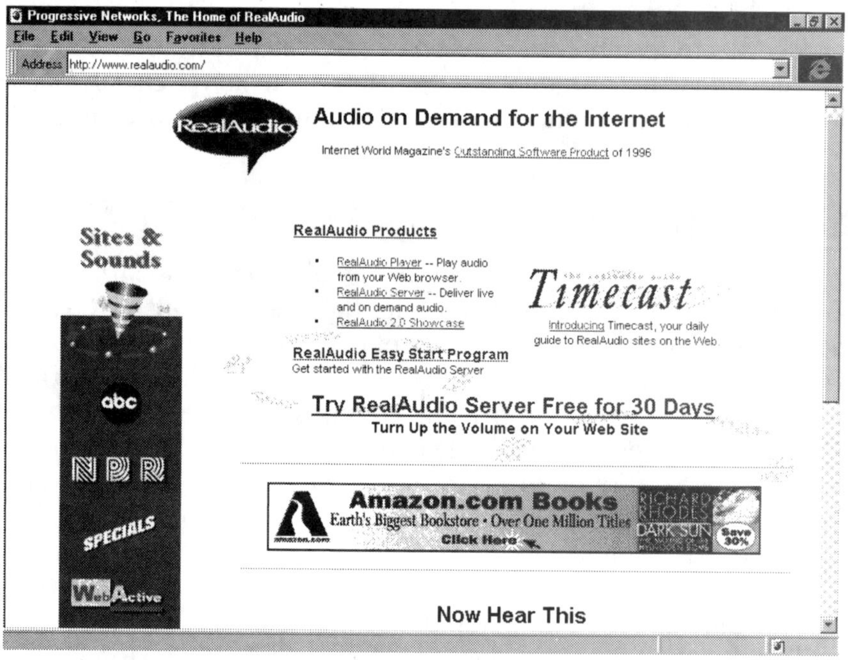

Figure 1 Real Audio - permitting Web surfers with slow modems to hear audio

Netscape Navigator cannot play sound files by itself. Instead, it hands off the files to other applications, such as the built-in Windows Sound Recorder. There are many players available and you can download them yourself on the Web. Some players are dedicated to playing only a single type, while others can play a variety of sound files. Whichever you choose, you'll have to set it up under your Netscape options.

If you don't have a special audio player configured, then Netscape Navigator will use the default Windows sound player—which includes the ability to save a sound file to disk. But the default Windows player won't handle Real Audio .RA files, so you'll need the .RA sound player. Once the sound player is installed for that type of file, however, Netscape Navigator will handle future files of that type automatically.

Check out Real Audio's Web site at *www.realaudio.com* to download the latest version of the .RA player. And if you plan to develop a Web site, check out their links to Web sites that use Real Audio so you can get some ideas on how to use it yourself. When you've completed the download, you'll need to run the installation.

Differences In File Formats

If you're going to offer audio on your site, before choosing a file format carefully consider your visitors and what you're delivering with the audio files. There are dramatic differences in file sizes and resulting download times. We did a comparison test to illustrate the real-life differences. It uses a clip from *Hollywood Online* (profiled later) that offers sound clips in multiple formats.

Bandwidth comparisons

The clip tested was from a scene in the film "American President," starring Michael Douglas and Charlie Sheen. The clip is 5.71 seconds long and goes like this:

Michael Douglas: "She didn't say anything about me?"
Charlie Sheen: "Well, no sir, but I can pass her a note before study hall."

Here's a comparison chart of the test:

Format	Size	Comments
.RA	5K	Music barely audible, voices not clear
.AU	44K	Music clear, voices excellent
.WAV	62K	Music clear, voices excellent

Even though you might not notice a difference in formats if you use Erol's ISDN Internet service, keep in mind that your visitors may have slow modems.

Other formats

If you're having trouble finding a player for an Internet audio format, check out the site at *www.geocities.com/Hollywood/1158/sndutils.html*. If you offer sound on your site, you can link your Web page to this site so visitors can get a sound player—it includes non-IBM-compatible players as well.

Recorded audio

The use of recorded audio is increasing rapidly on the Internet. You can expect this growth to accelerate now that Java applets enable Web authors to embed automated sound into Web pages. Whether or not you automate their playing, sound files can be a nice addition to many types of Web sites.

You are probably only a few dollars away from having all the equipment you need to record a message and put it on your Web site. For example, Windows 95 includes an application with recording capability—just add a microphone and you've got a home recording studio.

Your PC's sound card has a microphone input jack on it, next to the jack into which your speakers are plugged. Inexpensive microphones are now available at all large computer stores and electronics outlets. Make sure your microphone has the micro-plug and not a standard 1/4" plug.

So, assuming you've got a sound card, speakers and a microphone, here's how to record an audio file:

STEP-BY-STEP

GOAL: Learn to record using Windows 95

- ✔ Click the **Start** button.
- ✔ Click **Programs, Accessories, Multimedia, Sound Recorder**.

  Get ready with your microphone before the next step.
- ✔ Click the red **Record** button.
- ✔ Say, "One small step for multimedia... one giant leap for me."
- ✔ Click the square **Stop** button.
- ✔ Click the right-arrow **Play** button.
- ✔ Click **File, Save** to save the file to disk.
- ✔ Type *smalstep.wav* and click on **Save**.
- ✔ Press **ALT+F4** to close the sound recorder.

You now have recorded and saved a wave sound file that you can use on a Web site. If you'd like a more sophisticated recorder, be sure to visit the GoldWave site at *web.cs.mun.ca/~chris3/goldwave* and get its latest version (see Figure 2). It's a full-featured, professional-quality digital sound recorder.

GoldWave supports many file formats (.WAV, .AU, .IFF, .VOC, .SND, .MAT, .AIFF, and raw data) and can convert to or from these formats. It also has all kinds of editing and mixing controls, such as: distortion, Doppler, mechanize, echo, filter, offset, pan, volume shaping, invert, resample, and transpose.

Jargon Cutter

Doppler, mechanize, etc. - Writing about GoldWave certainly generates a lot of jargon, doesn't it? These are terms for sound effects that you can apply to your sound files. So, instead of settling for just the basic recording, you can tweak your voice or music with a wide variety of sound effects. Mechanize, for example, will make you sound like a robot—a fun effect for your Web site!

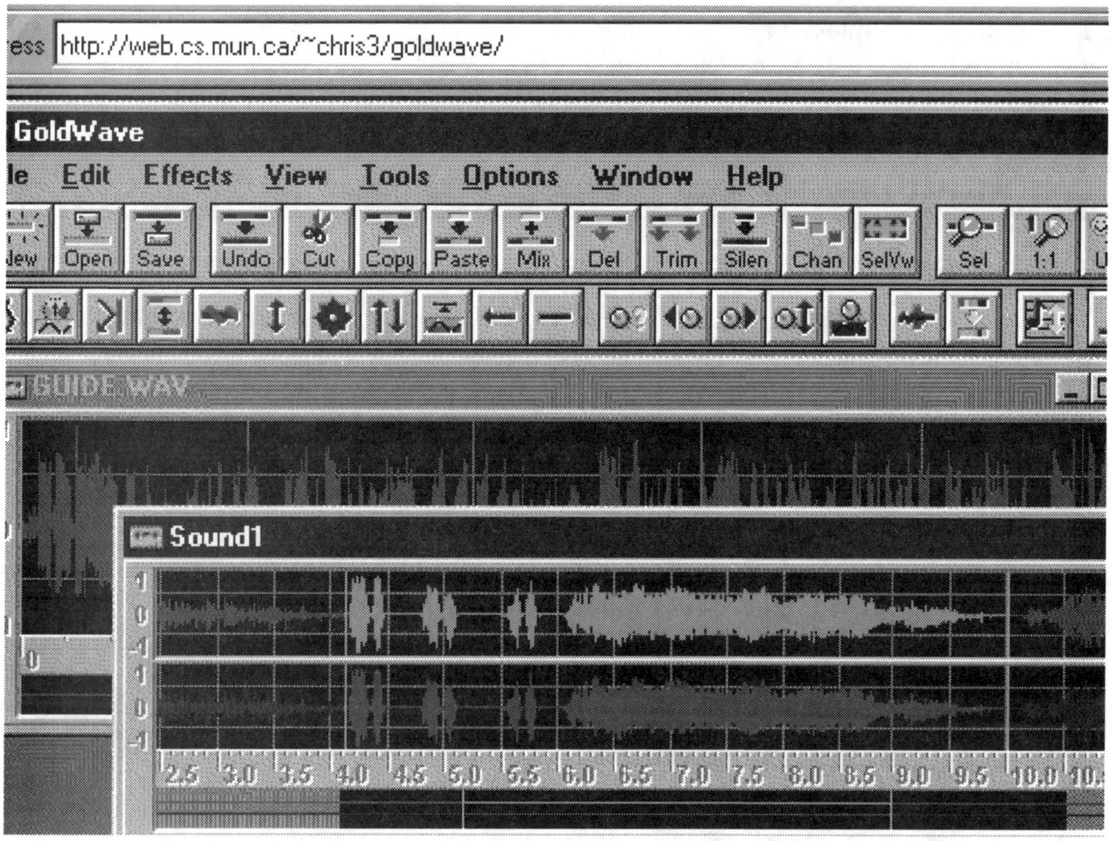

Figure 2 GoldWave - a versatile sound player that handles nearly any format

Downloading audio

Once you've recorded an audio clip, you may wonder how you get it on your Web site so that users can download it and play it. The user side is a cinch if their browser is configured to play audio files. Your side also is easy because you reference the audio file with normal HTML codes, as if it were a Web page or a graphic image. Here's a sample of HTML coding that would let visitors play the file you recorded in the last Hands-On exercise:

<A HREF="sound/smalstep.wav">My First Clip</A>

In addition to modifying your Web page, you would need to make a new directory on your server for your sound files and transfer the *smalstep.wav* file to that directory. Future visitors to your site would see My First Clip as a normal, underlined hyper-jump. If they click on it and their browser is configured to handle a wave file, the file would download and play automatically. If their browser was not configured for wave audio, it would ask what to do with the file. At that point, the visitor either could save it to disk for later play, or select an audio player.

Inside Info

Many Java applets these days permit Web sites to have background sound that will play a sound file in the background while you view a Web page—if, of course, your computer has a sound card and speakers.

To see more examples of on-line audio clips, visit Hollywood Online Sound Bites at *www.hollywood.com/movies/sound.html* (see Figure 3) and have a ball. Careful, though! Don't try this at work—it's way too much fun! And—as if it's not enough fun by itself—this site has links to other sound Internet sources.

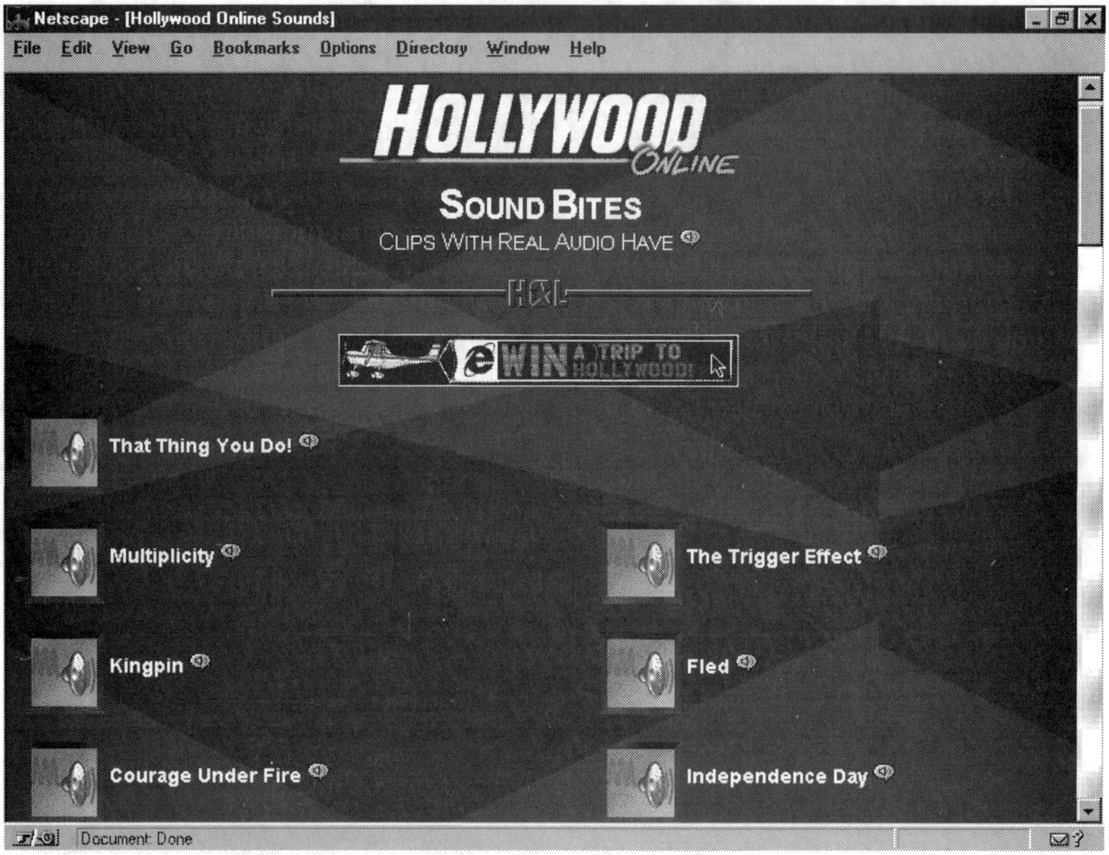

Figure 3 Hollywood Sound Bites - sample your favorite flicks

Real-time audio

How could we include so much about audio on the Internet without mentioning that you can use the Internet as a voice telephone? It doesn't exactly fit in here, but it's a related topic and an incredible Internet function.

Just in case you haven't heard already, you can use the Internet as a telephone to talk to anyone in the world without incurring any additional long-distance charges (see Figure 4). Most people simply don't comprehend it—or believe it—the first time they hear about Internet phone service, but it's true. After all, the Internet runs on phone lines, mostly maintained by MCI and Sprint who started out in the long-distance business.

Internet phone service has a lot of room for improvement, but if you do any international business or if you've got friends in other countries, you probably won't care about the limitations. One problem with Internet phone service is that you can't just call someone, or "ring them up." Both parties need the right software, the right hardware, and Internet service, and both will have to be on-line at the same time. Another problem is poor audio quality, but it's not bad and quality will improve rapidly.

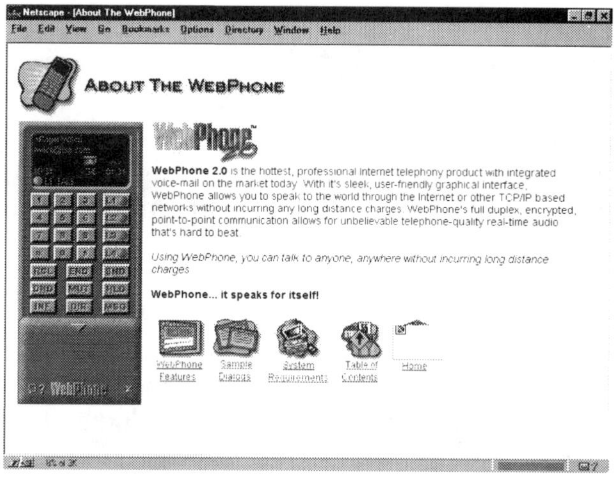

Figure 4 WebPhone - free calls anywhere in the world!

To learn how to use the Internet as a phone, check out the WebPhone site at: *www.netspeak.com*. This site includes Internet phone software and details on using the system (see Figure 5). You can download a free version of WebPhone for test purposes, but it's limited to 3-minute calls and a very short directory listing. The paid, commercial version removes the limitations and lets you make unlimited calls anywhere in the world.

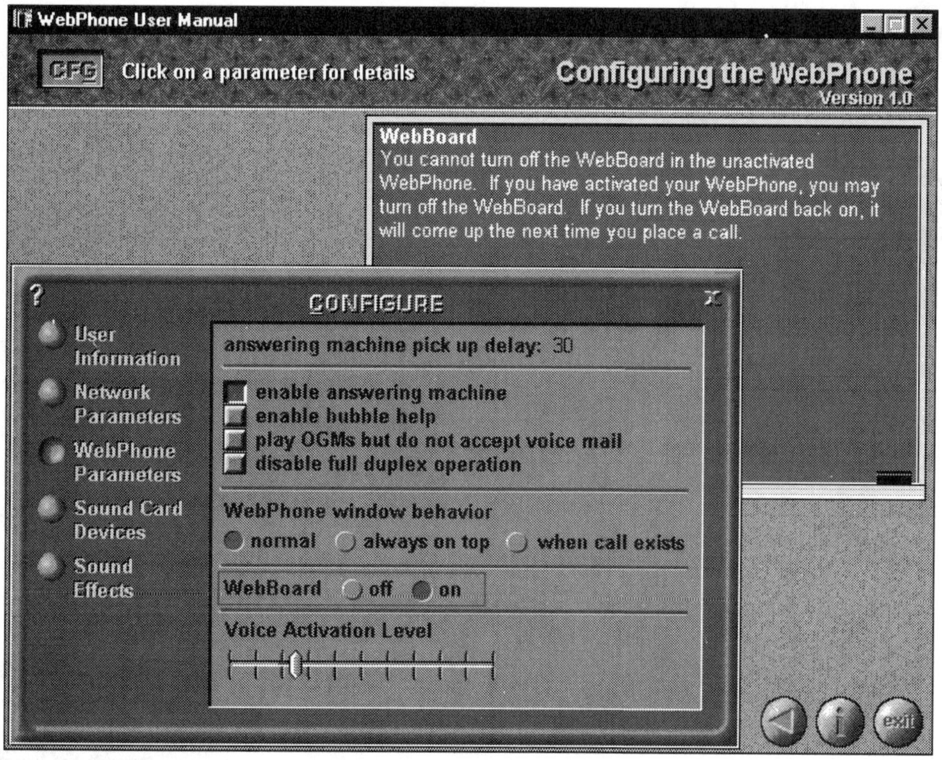

Figure 5 WebPhone - on-line manual

Finally, if you'll do a Yahoo! search for the phrase "Internet phone," you'll be inundated with listings. As this book was written it resulted in 125 hits—see how many you get today!

On-line Video

Digital video standards have been quickly adopted by the Internet, and in particular, by the World Wide Web. Because video fits so well with the expectations we have all developed for graphic displays on the Web, you'll see a rapid increase in Web video. Currently there are three formats commonly used by PCs for video on the Web: MPEG, .MOV files, and .AVI files.

MPEG

The MPEG (Moving Pictures Experts Group) is a group of people who meet under the auspices of the ISO (International Standards Organization) to generate standards for the compression of digital video and audio. The MPEG conducts about four one-week meetings each year. Between meetings members work on topics discussed at the meetings.

Specifically, the MPEG defines a compression standard that reduces the storage space needed by digital video. The compression standard ensures that, much like video cassette standards, we all can use each other's digital video files. The technical details, however, are not defined. That's left to individual vendors and that is where proprietary advantage is obtained, even though MPEG is a publicly available standard.

Jargon Cutter

The MPEG video files that are used on the Internet have a file extension of either .MPEG or .MPG. The MPEG core technology used in these files includes many different patents from different companies and individuals worldwide. Since the MPEG committee only sets the technical standards without dealing with patents and intellectual property issues, there are differences in the performance of video files from one vendor to the next, even though they use the same file extension.

Quicktime

Quicktime video files sometimes have a file extension of .QT, but most often you'll see the .MOV extension. Some video sources will give you a choice of formats. A good example, again, is *Hollywood Online* (see Figure 6) that was used for the sound sources. You'll find a wide assortment of video clips there as well. The Windows file formats listed there are .AVI and .MOV, so you'll need a Quicktime video player for the .MOV files.

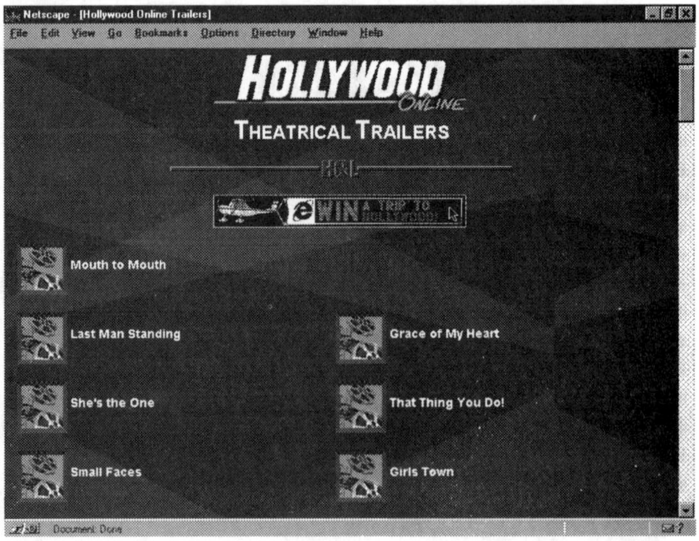

Figure 6 Hollywood - trailer videos

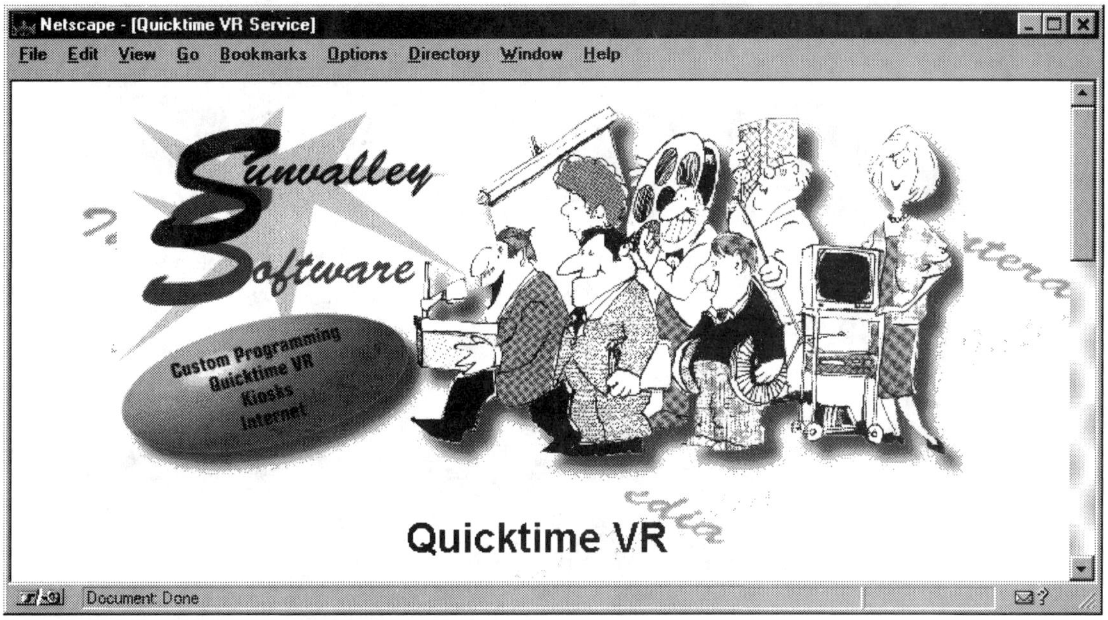

Figure 7 Sunvalley Software - home of the Quicktime player

The Quicktime helper application installs the same way as the MPEG player used in the next exercise. To get a Quicktime (QTVR) player, visit the Sunvalley Software site at *www.kwanza.com/~embleton/service.html* (see Figure 7) and click on the link for downloads to get the Apple Quicktime player, then download it and install it. Don't worry about the "Apple" in there if you don't have a Mac because it also comes in a Windows variety.

After the Quicktime files are on your system, complete the Hands-On exercise listed under the MPEG heading below, but change it for Quicktime. The Quicktime application can be added to Netscape. If you want more information about digital multimedia files, check out the following sidebar. From it you can learn more details, find more sources and keep up with the latest industry changes such as player upgrades. If you've seen enough technical details for now, then skip ahead to learn how to configure your Netscape Navigator to play video.

Multimedia File Formats on The Web

For more coverage on these topics, visit: *ac.dal.ca/~dong/contents.html*, maintained by Allison Zhang (see Figure 8). Our thanks go to Allison for creating such an informative site and sharing it with all of us on the Web. Her home page is entitled, "Multimedia File Formats on the Internet: A Beginner's Guide for PC Users." Check out the Table of Contents to see all the topics offered. She also maintains a helpful FAQ file that can be a ready reference source as you learn Web multimedia.

Figure 8 Allison Zhang's multimedia FAQs file

Configuring Netscape to play video

If your installation of Netscape Navigator does not include support for playing videos, you can use this Step-By-Step exercise to configure it to use an MPEG player. If you don't already have one on your hard drive, check out the following sidebar for sites from which you can download a file that will install the latest version of an MPEG player application on your system. Once the application is installed, you can complete this exercise.

Step-By-Step

GOAL: Install an MPEG player in Netscape Navigator

- ✔ Start Netscape Navigator.
- ✔ Click **Options, General Preferences**.
- ✔ Click the **Helpers** tab.
- ✔ Highlight **video/mpeg**.
- ✔ Click **Launch the Application**.
- ✔ Type *mpeg,mpg,mpe,mpv,vbs,mpegv* in **File Extensions**.
- ✔ Click on **Browse**, then locate the MPEG player you've installed.
- ✔ Click **Open, OK**.

Video Player Source

If you want an MPEG player, you need to update your current player, or you want to include a video clip on your Web site, here's a good source. If you use this source on your Web site, be sure to give obvious instructions to your visitors on how to obtain and install a video player. Here are two sources you can use for the MPEG player:

> *ftp.cic.net/pub/Software/pc/www/viewer/mpegw32h.zip*
> *ftp.ncsa.uiuc.edu/Web/Mosaic/Windows/viewers/mpegw32h.zip*
>
> The file is about 640k bytes, so it won't take long to download via Erol's fast service. If either of these doesn't work for you, just go to a search engine such as Yahoo! and search on the keywords "MPEG player."

Video conferencing

The Internet is exploding with real-time video technology. Already, you can conduct video conferencing and check weather and traffic. The 1980s brought us the great business revolutions of the fax machine, but the 1990s is the decade of video conferencing. By the end of this decade, it will a common business tool.

Figure 9 CU-SeeMe - have a world-wide family dinner, but no food fights

In fact, video conferencing will probably be a common household appliance. Just imagine Thanksgiving Day dinner in front of a large, wall-mounted, flat-screen monitor. You'll be able to enjoy a family meal with relatives and friends from all over the country, all over the world, actually. You'll be able to do everything but pass the cranberry sauce. And don't be surprised if the next decade brings you a technical solution for that limitation—3-D e-mail!

For a taste of video conferencing, check out the Cornell University CU-SeeMe project (see Figure 9). They've done lots of Internet video development and they're sharing their results on the Web site at: *cu-seeme.cornell.edu*. What you'll see there will appear a little primitive by the standards of cable television. The key to using video conferencing lies in seeing the possibilities that are demonstrated at this site.

Real-time video

Many major cities around the world now have multiple live-action weather cameras linked to the Internet. There's something powerfully charismatic about being able to see a live-action shot of a city anywhere in the world. You may see it as mind-broadening, graphic evidence that we all are one—everyone on the planet.

Figure 10 Live video - the next best thing

On-line camera images sap a lot of Internet bandwidth, and even then they deliver small, fuzzy pictures. And, they only update once every minute or two. But remember the little black-and-white television sets of the 1950s and consider the pace at which electronic advancements are racing into our future. Before long you'll be able to adorn your office wall with a real-time, wall-sized, stereo-sound shot of Niagara Falls (see Figure 10). For more scenic views from around the U.S., check out the Weather Cam site at *cirrus.sprl.umich.edu/wxnet/wxcam.html* and pick your favorite spot.

What's next after on-line video cameras? Virtual reality, where you can stay at home and make yourself *think* you're going over the falls in a barrel—or, doing just about anything else you can imagine!

Virtual reality

The next generation of Intel micro-processors, the Pentium Pro, includes built-in support for Web sites that use the Virtual Reality Markup Language (VRML). What can VRML do on the Internet? Don't be surprised if you soon can stroll through a grocery store on-screen, click on the items you want and have them delivered to your door faster than you can fight traffic and wait in line to get them yourself.

But at first you're going to see a lot of "gee whiz" virtual reality gimmicks designed to show off the technology. That's normal, though. After all, there was a time when the Wright Brothers flew down city streets in Washington, D.C. just to show off their new technology. After the "Wright Brothers Effect" wears off of VRML, it could be the best thing that happened to our time-pressed society since the airplane.

To see VRML in action, visit *www.intel.com/procs/ppro/intro/index.htm*. This site features some VRML tours of Pentium Pro applications. But you won't be able to view these tours in 3-D virtual reality without a Live3D player.

For all of its potential, virtual reality definitely is *future* cyberspace reality. The Internet can't spare the required bandwidth and few users have enough PC power. Besides, VRML programming is too complicated for the average HTML author. So, expect to see it only on sites where its use truly makes sense. If you want to learn more, visit the site of a VRML book *www.mcp.com/general/news7/vrml2.HTML*.

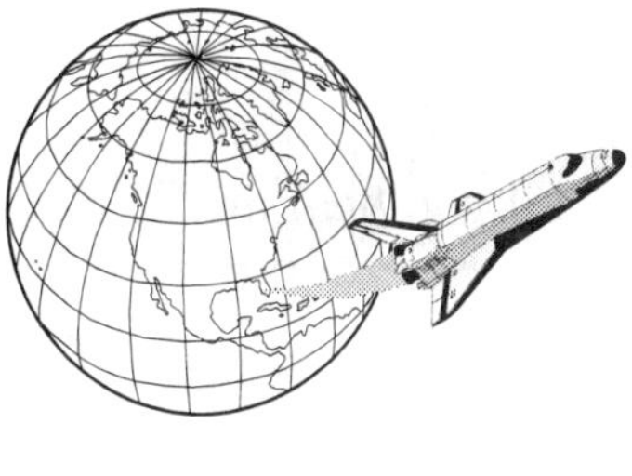

Orbiting in Cyberspace

Hooked on Java
http://java.sun.com/hooked

This is the home of the book *Hooked on Java* (see Figure 11). You'll find supplements to the book, including bug reports, updates and new applets that aren't on the book's CD-ROM disk. If you don't already have the book, this site is an excellent source for Java samples. And even if you do have it, you can find other Java resources here as well as stay in touch with the latest developments from the Java team at Sun Micro-Systems.

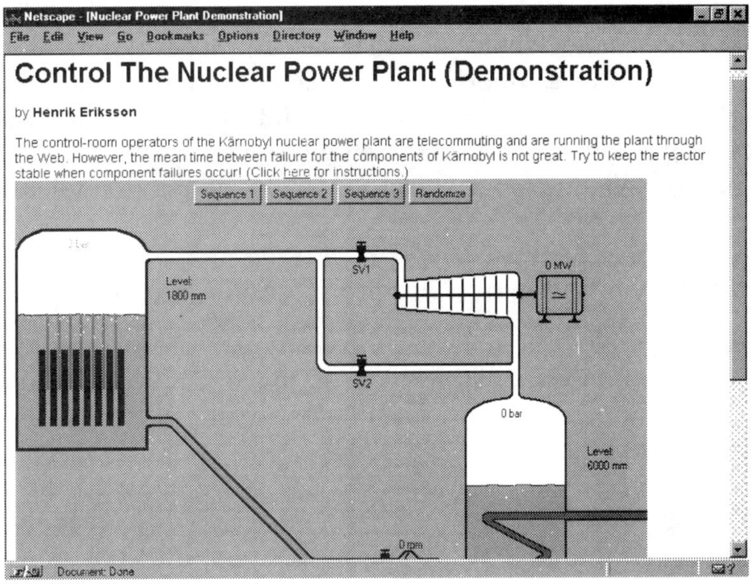

Figure 11 Hooked on Java - create your own Java effects

Gamelan Java applet collection
http://www.gamelan.com

This site features a vast array of Java examples, instructions, references, sources and applets. It's a very well-done, user-friendly site that gives you easy access to its resources by using the frames feature. It's a rich resource for Java applets. They also maintain a JavaScript site at: *www.gamelan.com/Gamelan.javascript.html*.

Belle Systems Java resources
http://www.belle.dk

Here's Bjarne Jensen's Java home page in Denmark. Bjarne maintains a well-tested list of Java links that should be able to guide you to some sites that will give you a good start with Java. This site shows off a lot of the possibilities of the Net, such as: extensive use of the HTML language, Java Prestel emulator, Java Telnet emulator, and links (Java, magazines, graphics, HTML and ISDN). These features, plus his big joke collection, add up to several pages that you should see for yourself.

Java newsgroup
news:comp.lang.java

Newsgroups are not a good source for reference material. You might, however, be able to use this one to get an answer to a specific question. And if you hear any rumors of new Java developments, you could start checking this newsgroup regularly to follow the discussions.

Teach Yourself Java in 21 Days
http://www.lne.com:80/Web/Books/Java

If you're interested in learning more about working with Java, *Teach Yourself Java in 21 Days* is the first complete hands-on tutorial guide for working with the Java language. It also includes class libraries to create applets for Web pages and full-fledged applications. *Teach Yourself Java* covers the Beta and 1.0 Java API and contains complete information about most aspects of Java development including the language itself, the Abstract Window Toolkit class libraries, sounds and animation techniques, and technical details about packages, interfaces and the Java virtual machine. It comes with a CD-ROM that includes the complete Java development release for Unix and Windows NT/95 platforms, plus all the examples from the book.

Hollywood Online
http://www.hollywood.com/movies/video.html

This site is a lot of fun. Its huge collection of photos, sound bites and video clips comes from the latest Hollywood hit movies and you'll hardly find a richer source for photos, sound and videos. The photos are available in .GIF and .JPEG. Sound is available in four formats: .AU, .WAV, .RA and Macintosh. Videos are available in two formats: .MOV and .AVI. This site is a preview of what the Web one day will bring us: full-length, on-line videos, with instant access. It's a primitive preview, but your Erol's Internet access speed will help you to use on-line movies—and ISDN service will make it even better. Once the rest of the Internet has caught up with your level of speed, this site might replace your video store membership card.

EARchives
http://www.geocities.com/Hollywood/1158/earchive.html

The audio clips on this site are taken from popular movies and television shows (see Figure 12). All files are in .WAV format. Most were recorded at 11KHz mono, but all files have been digitally reprocessed to enhance quality. Use these files to attach your favorite sounds or sayings to Windows events, objects or dialog boxes, using sound utilities like Icon Hear-It or the Windows Sound System. The collection increases constantly, so check back often and enjoy! Be sure to read the chapter in this book on copyright issues before offering these clips on your Web site.

Figure 12 EARchives - a cyber-treasure of sound clips

7

Earth-to-Cyberspace: E-Mail

Internet electronic mail (e-mail) is a powerful, revolutionary communication tool. The world is rapidly becoming a global community and e-mail is the perfect answer to communicating in this emerging, global environment. World-wide, overnight package delivery and fax machines certainly had a major impact on communications, but faxing even a short message overseas is quite costly. Internet e-mail has turbocharged the emergence of a global community by drastically reducing the cost of international communication—you pay the same, flat, monthly rate, no matter how many e-mail messages you send or how far they go.

In this chapter, you'll learn how to use this exciting Internet tool. A key lesson in this chapter will be helping you see Internet mail as more than a substitute for the standard letter or fax. E-mail today is still in a rudimentary form but fast-moving improvements in technology will soon enable e-mail to handle document formatting codes. You won't be using e-mail just because it saves postage. No, sometimes, you would use e-mail even if it cost more than first-class postage or a long-distance call. But the joy is that all of its amazing abilities don't cost you any extra.

In this chapter we will use graphic, screen images and sample messages to show you the basics of Internet e-mail. And, since Internet mail is not perfect, we also will show you what happens to e-mail between here and there, why mail sometimes gets lost and how to protect yourself.

The First International E-Mail Message

In September, 1973, the U.S. Government's ARPANET (an international network project launched by the U.S. Department of Defense in 1969) held a conference to set up a temporary computer link via satellite from Los Angeles to Brighton, England. This link was used for an international experiment in data packet transmission between computers.

Len Kleinrock, a computer scientist at UCLA, had attended the conference in Brighton, but returned home a day before the conference ended. As he unpacked, he noticed that he had left behind his electric razor. Knowing that the link was still operating, Kleinrock logged on and linked to his friend Larry Roberts in England. Kleinrock asked Roberts to retrieve his razor and Roberts replied, "Sure. No problem."

Roberts asked Danny Cohen, a mutual friend, to return the razor to Kleinrock. The razor arrived the next day and *voilá*, electronic mail was an instant hit.

Inside Info

If you skipped the netiquette chapter, you'll benefit by going back and reading it before you complete this chapter. E-mail has its own social order and Internet communication will go more smoothly and be more effective for you if you follow common netiquette guidelines.

The Eudora e-mail application

For the Step-By-Step exercises in this chapter, we'll use the Eudora e-mail application that's included with your Erol's installation package (see Figure 1). Eudora is from Qualcomm, Inc. and it is the most powerful and popular Internet e-mail application available today. It's rich in advanced features that can help you organize your mail and increase your productivity. And, along the way, we'll present a host of helpful information that will show you what's going on behind the scenes. Don't worry, we're not going to get technical on you; it will just be an overview that will help the whole Internet e-mail process make more sense.

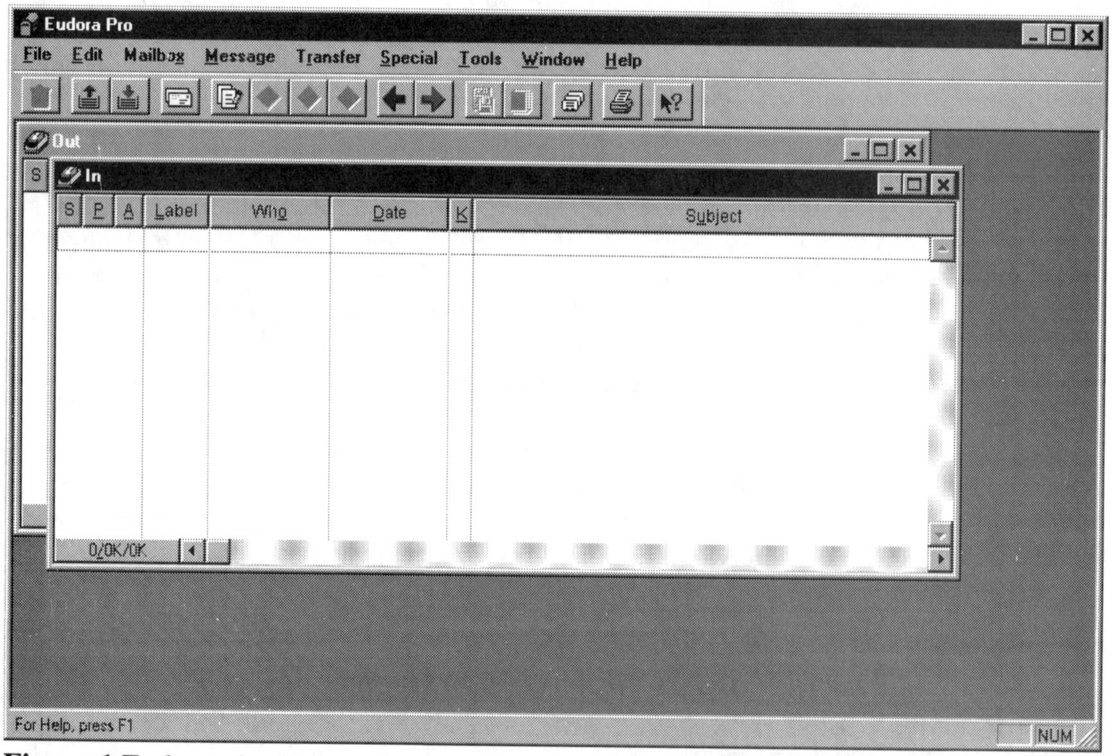

Figure 1 Eudora - basic screen

Nearly all Internet e-mail applications provide the same basic services but with different user interfaces. Here are the basic services that we'll cover, using Eudora as the model:

- ❖ Send—Compose, edit and send messages.
- ❖ Read—Check mail, open In box and read messages.
- ❖ Response options—Reply to, forward or redirect received messages.
- ❖ Attachments—Include computer files that "tag along" with messages.
- ❖ Housekeeping—Delete messages, create tailored mailboxes and transfer messages between mailboxes.
- ❖ Signature files—Create a block of text that is automatically attached to the end of all messages you send.
- ❖ Address book—Create a list of frequently used e-mail addresses and assign a plain-language nickname.
- ❖ Multiple recipients—Send Carbon Copies (CC) and Blind Copies (BC) of messages.
- ❖ Print—Print the contents of any e-mail message.
- ❖ Save—Save the contents of any e-mail message for inclusion in other documents.

Eudora has all of these features, and more. For example, with Eudora, you can filter incoming messages so that they are placed automatically into targeted mailboxes. And, there are some advanced features designed mostly for the business user. We recommend that you master the basic features, then see if you need more capability.

E-Mail Addresses

Most likely you already have seen Internet e-mail addresses. In case you're wondering how to decipher the codes, we'll help you with a typical example:

isatest@internet.com

The special symbol in an Internet address (@) is called the "AT" symbol. To pronounce this e-mail address, you would say "isatest AT internet DOT com." And it's actually pretty much what it sounds like. The user "isatest" is "at" the Internet location called "internet dot com." The part of the address before the @ is the user and the part after the @ is the user's Internet domain name.

What does the "com" represent? It's called the *first level domain* and identifies the broad category of the user's cyberspace domain. The first level domain gives you an idea of the type of organization in which the user is based. There are six commonly used first-level domains in the U.S.:

com	commercial	**edu**	educational
gov	government only	**mil**	military only
net	networks	**org**	organizations

Outside the U.S., other countries have their own first level domain name. These are too numerous to list here, but some common ones you'll see are:

ca	Canada	**de**	Germany
fr	France	**uk**	United Kingdom

Internet addresses are used backwards, from right to left. Each step up the chain narrows down the path to the user. Let's examine an example:

jsmith@library.utulsa.edu

Starting with the right segment, "edu," you see that this domain is an educational institution. The next step up is "utulsa" which represents the University of Tulsa. Those two together are called the second-level domain. The next step indicates the library server within the utulsa second-level domain. Finally, the user, "jsmith" AT "library.utulsa.edu" is pinpointed. Later in this chapter we'll tell you how the Internet uses these plain-language addresses and how to get one tailored to use your own domain name.

Send e-mail

The first thing we'll do with your Eudora will be to send a practice message to yourself that we'll use in later lessons. But before you *send* your first e-mail message, you've got to *compose* one. So, we'll walk you through all three basic phases of e-mail: composing a new message, editing it and then sending it.

Before you create your first message, we need to make sure that your copy of Eudora is set up to hold messages in a send "queue" instead of sending them instantly as each message is created. Holding messages in a queue lets you connect only once and send them all at the same time. Let's make sure your Eudora will queue messages.

STEP-BY-STEP

GOAL: Verify your Eudora set up options

✔ Click **Tools, Options**.

✔ Scroll down to the **Sending Mail** option on the category list.

✔ Make sure the **Immediate Send** box is NOT checked.

With this box unchecked, messages are held in a delivery queue so you can send them all at once. Otherwise, you'll have to be connected to Erol's the entire time you're composing multiple e-mail messages. While we give you unlimited connect time, our servers monitor usage and will disconnect you during long periods of inactivity—a process called 'timing out." So, unchecking this option will spare you the need to reconnect after being timed out.

✔ Click **OK**.

Creating a new message

Here's a Step-By-Step exercise that will walk you through the basics of creating an e-mail message. Eudora is going to work through your Erol's TCP/IP connection, which gives it the ability to communicate with any other computer in the world that's connected to the Internet. But, you don't need to be connected yet—we'll tell you when it's time to connect.

STEP-BY-STEP

GOAL: Learn to compose an e-mail message

- ✔ Start the Eudora e-mail application.
- ✔ Click **Message, New Message** or press **CTRL+N**.

  The insertion point is flashing on the **To:** line.
- ✔ Type your own Internet e-mail address.
- ✔ Press **TAB** to move the insertion point to the **Subject:** line of the message.
- ✔ Type *E-Mail Exercise 1*.
- ✔ Press **TAB** three times to move the insertion point to the body of the message.
- ✔ Type a salutation then press **ENTER** twice.

  Press **ENTER** only to end a paragraph or for blank lines. Let Eudora handle the word-wrapping automatically as your word processor does.
- ✔ Type a message, then press **ENTER** twice.
- ✔ Type a closing.

Edit a message

You easily can edit your message anytime before you send it. Use the normal editing commands that you use with your favorite word processor. Here's a quick summary of some of the most useful keys:

- ❖ Cut (**CTRL+X**), Copy (**CTRL+C**), and Paste (**CTRL+V**)
- ❖ Top of document (**CTRL+HOME**), bottom of document (**CTRL+END**)
- ❖ Word right or word left (**CTRL+RIGHT ARROW/LEFT ARROW**)
- ❖ Check spelling (**CTRL+6**) or click **Edit, Check Spelling**.

Remember that you can size a window by dragging its borders. Touch the borders in any corner with the mouse to get a diagonal mouse arrow so you can drag both horizontally and vertically with one move. Resizing the window may help you compose your message (see Figure 2). The message can automatically include your tailored signature block at the bottom of each new message. You won't see it on this screen, but later in this chapter, we'll show you how to change your signature as well as how to set up an alternate signature, or even stop the signature from being included.

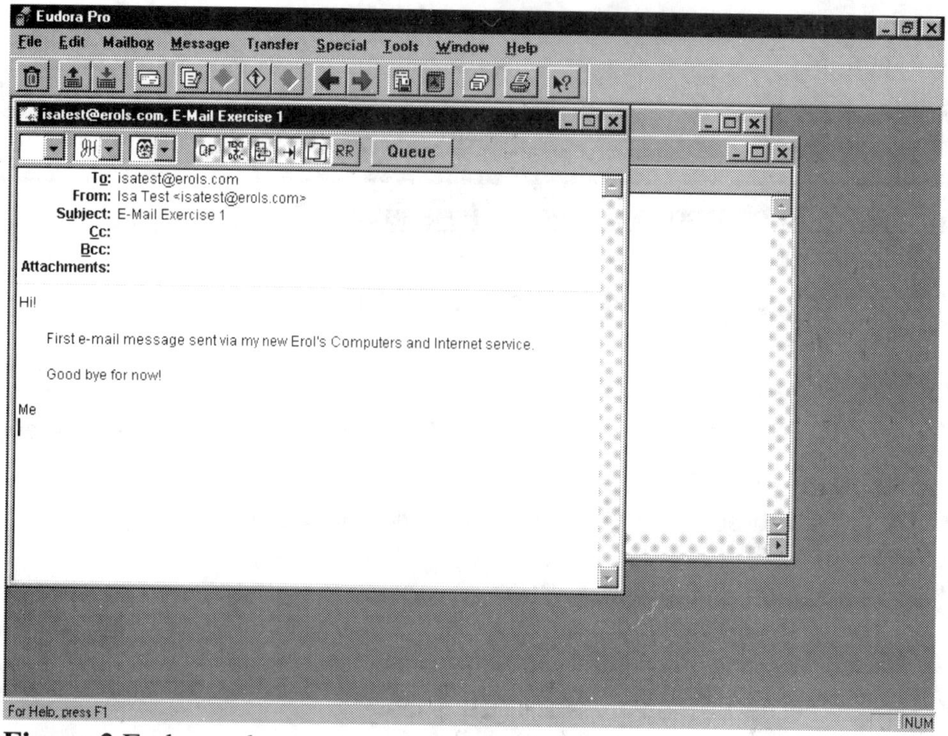

Figure 2 Eudora - the create message window

Send a message

Now let's spell check and then send the message you just created.

STEP-BY-STEP

GOAL: Configure and use your spell checker and send e-mail

✔ Click **Edit, Check Spelling** or press **CTRL+6** to check spelling.

✔ Click **Options** and check the options you want, then click **OK**.

If the spell checker has found any misspelled words, it has stopped, highlighted the word and perhaps offered suggested corrections. You'll choose the action from the list on the right side of the dialog box. If the highlighted word is one that you expect to see repeatedly, click **Add** to add it to Eudora's dictionary. Go ahead now and complete the spell checking operation.

✔ Click **OK**, if necessary, when the spell checker is finished.

✔ Click **Queue**, or click **Message, Queue for Delivery**, or press **CTRL+E**.

The Queue button is the last button at the top-right of the message window, just below the message window's title bar. When you click on **Queue**, your message is ready to be sent as soon as you're connected to Erol's. Normally, you might create several other e-mail messages, then connect to Erol's, then send all of them at the same time. But for now, this is your only message to send.

✔ Connect to **Erol's**.

When you're logged on to our service, use **ALT+TAB** to return to Eudora.

✔ Click **File, Send Queued Messages** or press **CTRL+T**.

Watch the progress bar to verify the message is sent.

This e-mail message has now been launched on its journey through cyberspace. Your Internet post office knows how to forward the message to the next computer in the delivery chain, as does each computer along the chain. Eventually—usually within a few seconds—the message has found the recipient's mail server and is stored on a hard drive, waiting for them to check their mail.

Inside Info

Just as with real mail—affectionately called "snail mail" in cyberspace—there's no way to predict how quickly your message will reach its destination. It may be seconds. But then, it may be days, if there are problems along the way. Normally, however, if your message doesn't go through right away, you'll get a returned mail notification so you'll know the message didn't arrive. You can try sending again immediately, but sometimes the return message will tell you how long to wait.

How Do I Lookup Someone's E-Mail Address?

Someday you will be able to find almost anyone on the Internet. But that day hasn't yet come. The Internet today is like an early rural telephone system. If you've grown accustomed to instant directory telephone assistance and you are using a CD-ROM telephone book that can locate nearly anyone in the country, Internet directory services may be a disappointment.

Today, CD-ROM directories are your best bet for tracking down an old friend, an old sweetheart or a long-lost business associate. Once you look them up and telephone them, of course, you can ask for their e-mail address and stay in touch with them free—no matter where in the world they've moved.

But what e-mail address lookup resources are available on the Internet today? Check out some of our Internet directory references in this chapter's Orbiting in Cyberspace section. We also will point you to the Internet Yellow Pages, an early implementation of a true Internet directory service.

Currently, information is only available for individuals who are registered with these directories. Other Internet lookup tools are experiencing explosive growth, so look well beyond what you read in this book.

What about people who are searching for your e-mail address? Help your friends, family, clients, customers and associates find you by registering yourself in as many directory services as you can find. It will take a bit of work, but if you begin with the resources listed at the end of this chapter, you'll increase your chances of being found. You might as well let us all know how to find you!

Read messages

Before you can read any e-mail messages, you must get them from your mail server by checking your mail. After you've checked your e-mail, you can read messages at any time and then perform a wide variety of follow-up actions. In this section we'll cover receiving, opening and reading messages, as well as basic reply actions.

Jargon Cutter

Mail Server - A computer at an Internet service provider that acts as a 24-hour-a-day cyberspace post office. All mail transactions are processed by this computer. It sends out-going messages across the Internet and it holds incoming messages until retrieved at the user's convenience.

Receive, open and read messages

After starting Eudora you'll need to activate the Check Mail function. Depending on how you set your options, you may not need to check mail manually. But, even if your setup checks mail for you, we'll show you here how to check mail manually anytime you need an immediate update.

STEP-BY-STEP

GOAL: Learn to check mail

- ✔ Start Eudora.
- ✔ Click the **Check Mail** button, or click **File, Check Mail** or press **CTRL+M**.

  Your mail will be checked immediately and any messages you've received will be placed in the **In** box. If you performed the previous exercise, you should have at least one message right now. If not, check again later.
- ✔ Click **Mailbox, In** or press **CTRL+I**.
- ✔ Double-click on **E-Mail Exercise 1** to open a message window.

  You can scroll through the message with your mouse or with **Page Up** and **Page Down**. If you have received more messages, you can jump directly to the next message on the list by clicking the red right-arrow on the toolbar. Once you move beyond the first message on the list, you can scroll through your previous messages with the blue left-arrow on the toolbar.

What Happens Between Here and There?

Your e-mail messages do not traverse the Internet in a straight line or even as a single unit. Messages are broken up into digital units called *packets*. Your mail server then performs some very fast magic on the packets that will carry the pieces of your e-mail.

Your mail server begins by checking its own directory of Internet addresses to see if it knows how to get your message to the destination address. If you've e-mailed before to this addressee, your mail server knows the address and the message begins its journey. If not, then your mail server hasn't a clue about how to locate the addressee and must ask for help.

When a mail server does not know an addressee's location, it contacts the InterNIC domain name registry system (the InterNIC is based in Reston, Virginia) and uses their directory. The InterNIC is the central location for all domain names. Thus, they can translate into computer-coded numbers your addressee's e-mail address. Your mail server will store that number for future reference so it won't need to waste resources going back to the InterNIC if you transmit to the same addressee again.

Once the plain-language address you typed has been converted into a computer-coded address that the Internet understands, your e-mail can be sent. Messages are broken up into packets and each packet is tagged with the address as well as being numbered so they can be reassembled.

The Transmission Control Protocol/Internet Protocol (TCP/IP) that the Internet uses to handle traffic always finds the quickest route for each packet. Each packet could, theoretically, take a different route to its destination, though this is unlikely. Once the packets arrive at the destination, they are reassembled by the recipient's mail server and saved as a single computer file.

Reply options

Naturally, you'll want to reply to most of the e-mail you receive. That's why the Internet is so busy—everyone is replying to everyone else in an ever-increasing cascade of e-mail messages. But quick replies are part of the value of the Internet, so let's learn how to reply and how to use some of the options. We'll cover replying, forwarding, redirecting and requesting a return receipt.

Inside Info

Messages might look poorly formatted when you read them—this happens when there's not enough room in your mail window for a full line to fit across. Remember that you can resize windows. Normal appearance will be restored by making the window slightly wider, or you can maximize the window for a full-screen view.

What's This Gibberish At The Top of My Messages?

The top of your e-mail may contain several lines of text before the actual message. These extra lines are just above the body of the message and they identify the sender, give the date of the message plus its subject, and show the priority that the sender assigned to the message. But there's more.

You can click on the **BLAH, BLAH, BLAH** button to see even more details about your message. All the extra text you see now—it's sometimes called "cruft"—traces the path the message followed to reach you. With the aid of an expert, it can help sort out problems you might have with an undeliverable message. Fortunately, Eudora filters the cruft for you automatically, so you can now click **BLAH, BLAH, BLAH** again and keep it that way.

Inside Info

Now that you've seen that messages have a priority, you might be tempted to make all of your messages "high priority" so they'll get through faster. The priority rating on a message, however, is simply an internal note between you and the other person—-it has no affect on the speed at which the message will arrive.

Reply to a message

Eudora simplifes the task of replying to a current e-mail message by automatically addressing the new message to the sender and entering your address. It also includes the original subject and adds a "Re:" in front of it (see Figure 3). The "Re:" lets the original sender know that this a reply to a previous message. If you use the message sorting options in Eudora, the "Re:" portion of the subject is ignored so that the reply messages will be sorted next to their corresponding originals.

You'll see at the top of window the date and time of the original message, followed by the actual text of the message—indented with angle-brackets—and then the sender's signature block. You'll be able to blend your reply into the original message. This makes it easy for the sender to follow your reply comments in context with the original. It's definitely different from replying to a traditional snail mail letter. Let's perform another Step-By-Step exercise now to learn how to reply.

Inside Info

Eudora can paste text from your clipboard with an angle bracket at the beginning of each line so that it will look like copied text. This is especially useful if you're copying text between messages, so you don't have to manually insert angle brackets. To use this special paste feature, click **Edit, Paste As Quotation.**

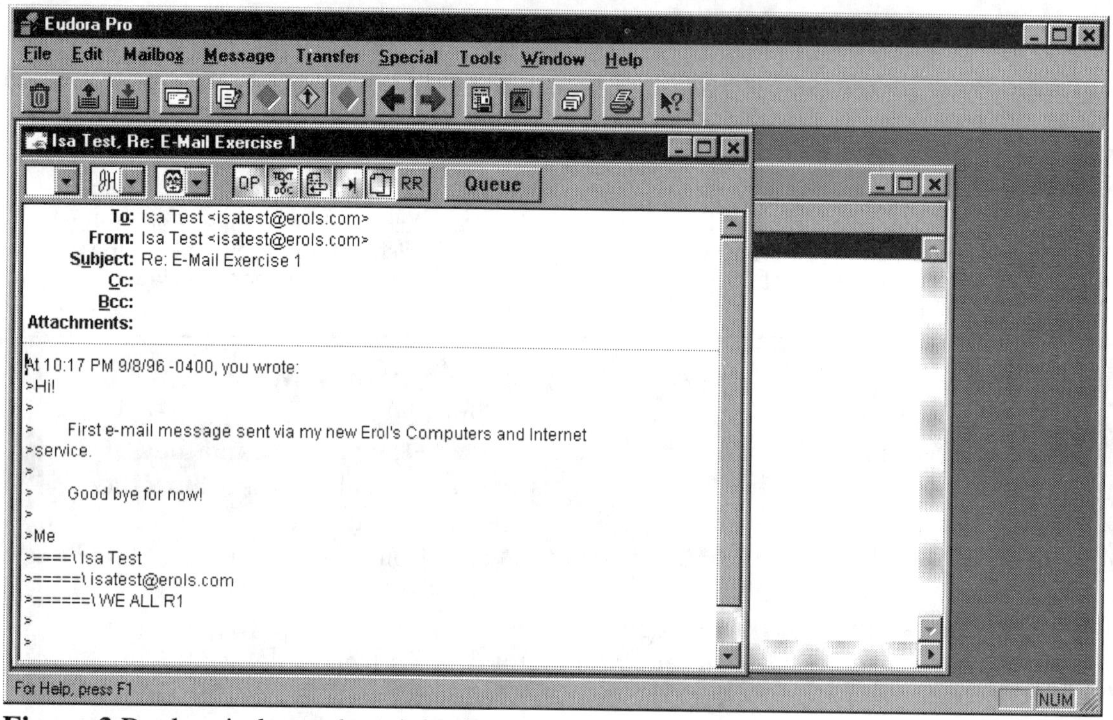

Figure 3 Reply window - the original message is automatically included

Step-By-Step

GOAL: Learn to reply to an e-mail message

✔ Click **Message, Reply** or press **CTRL+R** to open a reply window.

You also can click on the 180° reverse-arrow icon immediately under the menu word "Message." The original message is copied into this window with angle-brackets (>) at the beginning of each line. You can use your mouse to make the box wider or taller for easier editing.

✔ Review the **To:**, **From:** and **Subject:** lines.

✔ Use your mouse to select any text you want to cut away then press **DELETE** or **CTRL+X** to delete it.

Don't return the entire contents of the original message to your sender unless it's very short. Sending back long sections of original text is annoying to the original author. Leave just enough text to provide a context for your reply comments.

✔ Add blank lines between sections of the reduced message.

✔ Type your responses to each topic in turn (see Figure 4).

✔ Click **Queue.**

If you're not still connected to Erol's, then reconnect before the next step.

✔ Click **File, Send Queued Messages** or press **CTRL+T** to send.

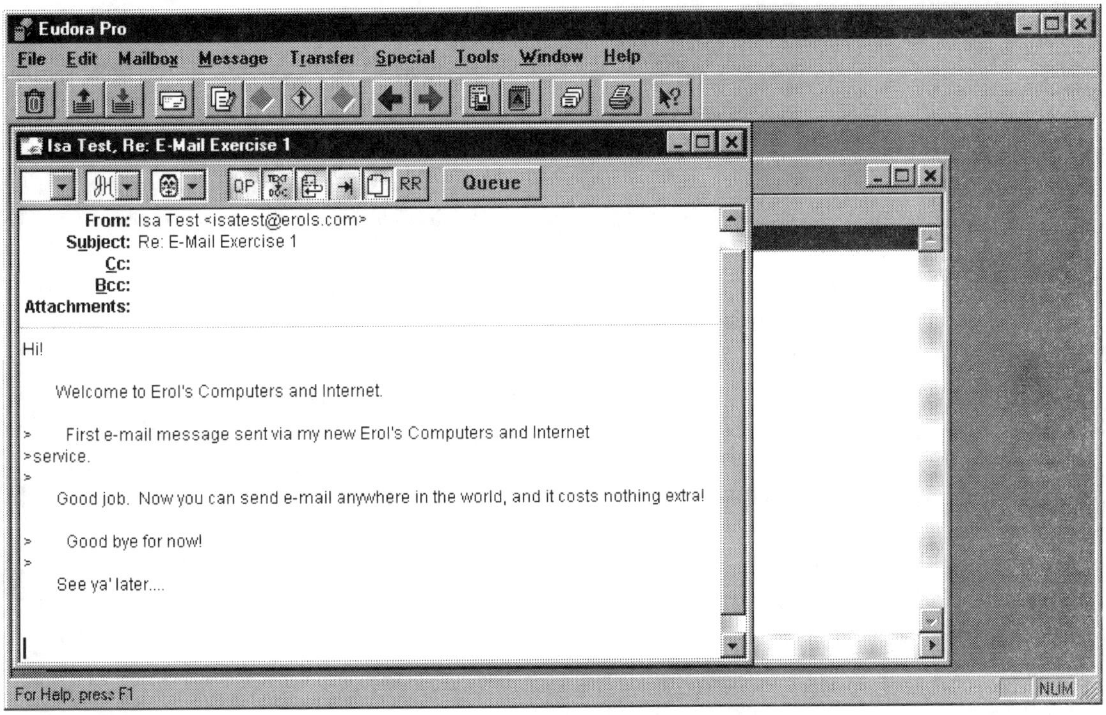

Figure 4 Reply window - after you've entered your responses

Frequently Asked E-Mail Questions

What if my addressee's computer isn't running right now?

Internet e-mail does not pass directly between the computers of its sender and its recipient. E-mail goes through a routing process similar to that of a regular, mailed letter. Instead of being handled by a series of people, however, e-mail is handled by a series of computers across the Internet until it ends up at the local post office—the mail server—of the recipient. Mail server computers run 24 hours a day so they can receive mail continuously. Your computer doesn't need to be running for you to receive e-mail any more than you need to be present at your local post office when a letter for you arrives on a mail truck.

E-mail is like regular mail that goes to a general delivery address: E-mail remains at the post office—saved on your mail server—until you go to get it. But you can pick up your e-mail without leaving home, and at any time, any day.

E-mail software uses the Internet to ask the mail server if it's holding any mail for the recipient. If the mail server has any messages, it transfers them to the In box of your e-mail application where the mail can be read.

All those computers—can anyone else read my messages?

Yes, they can. Internet e-mail is not secure at all. This doesn't mean that anyone *will* read your mail. Do you imagine that a lot of postal workers read postcards that travel via regular mail? And what harm would be done anyway, even if someone did read it? Well, that depends on what you're saying, doesn't it! If you need to send secure messages, be sure to read the chapter on security.

How often should I check my mail?

You probably will check e-mail much more frequently than the postal carrier brings regular mail, but don't overdo it. An informal poll we took for this book revealed that some users spend up to two hours a day reading and responding to Internet e-mail. If you're expecting an important message, you would check more frequently, of course. Otherwise, a couple of times a day is customary.

Is there a limit to the size of an e-mail message?

Generally, the maximum file size allowed for Internet e-mail is 2 megabytes. If you're sending text files, that's enough to hold three or four full-length books. Graphics, sound files and video files, however, can easily exceed the limit. If you need to send files larger than 2 megabytes, we can set up an FTP site for you. You can put up files of nearly any size, then send e-mail to the recipient with the URL, directory and filename so they can download the file via FTP when it's convenient for them and *after* they've determined they have enough free disk space on their computer.

Forward a message

You may want to forward some messages to another recipient. Perhaps if the message didn't interest you, but you know a friend would want to read it, you could forward it to her or him. The entire original message will be transferred. You probably should leave it intact so they new recipients can read the same message you read. Sometimes, however, you might edit the message or add a comment of your own.

STEP-BY-STEP

GOAL: Learn to forward an e-mail message

- ✔ Double-click on **E-Mail Exercise 1** to open a message window.
- ✔ Click **Message, Forward**.

  You can also click on the straight-arrow icon immediately under the menu word "Message."
- ✔ Type the new recipient's address.
- ✔ Review the **From:** and **Subject:** lines.

  Your name has been inserted as the sender, so the forwarded message will appear to the recipient to have come from you.
- ✔ Enter the addressee's information in the **To:** line.
- ✔ Press **TAB** until you reach the body of the message if you want to make any changes or additions to the text, then make the changes.
- ✔ Click **Queue**.
- ✔ Click **File, Send Queued Messages**.

Request a return receipt

The out-going message window has a button that you can use to request return receipts for messages you send. This is not yet a reliable system because many mail servers lack automatic response capability and will not respond with a return receipt. If you'd like to try it anyway, click the **R R** button to say that you want to be notified when the message is safely on the recipient's mail server.

Attachments

Any computer file can be sent along with an e-mail message as an "attachment." Attachments ride along across the Internet with e-mail messages and enable you to send word processing documents, spreadsheets, programs, configuration files, full-color drawings, photographs, charts and graphs, sound clips and video clips. The recipient gets the e-mail message in his or her normal In box and the attachment file or files are transferred into a "download" directory.

Attachments are easy to include and greatly expand the value of e-mail. Attachments can be a lot of fun. For example, you could attach a scanned, digitized photo to an e-mail message you send to a friend or family member.

First, let's create a special download directory, so that you'll be able to find all the files that you receive as attachments.

STEP-BY-STEP

GOAL: Set up a download directory for e-mail attachments

- ✔ Start the Windows 3.1 File Manager or the Windows 95 Explorer.
- ✔ Create a directory on your hard drive called *c:\download.*
- ✔ Return to Eudora with **ALT+TAB**.

  This will keep the File Manager or Explorer open for use in a later exercise.
- ✔ Click **Tools, Options**, then click on the **Attachments** category.
- ✔ Click **MIME** under **Encoding Method**.
- ✔ Click the bar under **Attachment Directory**.
- ✔ Navigate to *c:\download*, click **Use Directory**, then click **OK**.

MIME file attachments

The best format for sending attachments is the MIME (Multipurpose Internet Mail Extensions) option. With the MIME option, you can send any computer file, which means you can send a WordPerfect file to a friend or associate and the file will contain every font, graphic image, table and formatting command. If the recipient has the same version of WordPerfect, they'll see the file exactly as you created it. Let's learn to send an attachment, then learn to open an attachment you've received.

STEP-BY-STEP

GOAL: Learn how to include an attachment with e-mail

- ✔ Start a new message to yourself by clicking **Message, New Message** or by pressing **CTRL+N**.
- ✔ Type your own address on the **To:** line and press **TAB** once.
- ✔ Type *E-Mail Exercise 2* and press **TAB** three times.
- ✔ Type in the body of the message *Practice e-mail with attachment.*
- ✔ Click **Message, Attach File** or press **CTRL+H**.

- ✔ Double-click on the **c:** folder to go to your root directory.
- ✔ Click on **autoexec.bat**, then click on **OK**.

  The file name and path will appear on the **Attachments** line at the bottom of the message header. You can repeat the last three steps and include multiple files with a single e-mail message.
- ✔ Click **Queue**.
- ✔ Click **File, Send Queued Messages** or press **CTRL+T**.

The e-mail message will now be delivered via normal channels, but it will include the file you specified as an attachment. You might notice a slight increase in the time it takes for a message to be sent if the attached file is relatively small. But, if you send a very large file, such as a graphic image, a program or an audio/video clip, you can expect a longer delay. Keep in mind the limit of two megabytes per e-mail message, including the attachments.

Transmission Times

Transmitting a normal e-mail message does not place a major burden on Internet bandwidth. The transmission time is almost insignificant and no one has to wait and watch the file download anyway because mail is delivered to mailboxes even when the user isn't logged onto his or her mail server.

Attachments, however, bring the possibility of significant transmission time because you can include nearly any computer file. Still, even moderate-size graphics images won't encounter a noticeable delay in transmission. Nonetheless, quite a lot of Internet bandwidth is being squandered these days by people attaching huge graphics images to e-mail just to show a picture to a friend.

Therefore, regardless of Internet bandwidth issues, before you attach a large file, you may want to verify that your recipient has enough free hard disk space to store the files you plan to send as e-mail attachments.

Receiving an attachment

Your mail server now should have received the attachment practice document and we can retrieve it. Use the same steps outlined earlier because attachments do not require any special efforts on the part of the recipient. Retrieve it now.

The e-mail message itself will be in your normal In box and you'll see the attachment listed after you double-click on the message to open it.

So now let's look at the copy of your autoexec file. What happens in this next exercise, however, depends on how your system is set up. We'll assume that you created and specified the directory as we showed you in a previous Step-By-Step exercise.

Step-By-Step

GOAL: Verify the download of an attachment file

- ✔ Double-click the message with the attachment to open it.

  You'll see that the message includes an attachment.

✔ Use **ALT+TAB** to return to the File Manager or Explorer.

✔ Navigate to **c:\download**.

If you're still on this directory from the earlier exercise, you might have to refresh the display to see the new file. With File Manager, you can do this by clicking on any other directory, then returning to the download directory. With Explorer, you can click **View, Refresh**.

✔ Highlight **autoexec.bat** and press **Delete**.

Attachments always create complete copies of all original files, so this is an exact copy of your autoexec.bat file. Your original file is never transmitted.

WinZip

Even though you've got a fast connection to the Internet through your Erol's service, most of the Internet still struggles with serious speed problems. And you won't be immune to those problems because Internet speed is like a chain—it's no better than its weakest link.

If you want to send large files as attachments to e-mail, you'll help everyone on the Internet if you'll compress your files so that they require less Internet bandwidth. File compression reduces the wasted space inside files so that they become smaller. They're not usable in their compressed form, but once they're uncompressed, they're perfectly restored.

The compression process is called "zipping" and the uncompressing process is called "unzipping." Zipping a file produces a second, smaller version—leaving the original completely intact on your system—that is anywhere from 10% to 90% smaller than the original. That could save a lot of Internet bandwidth.

You can download a nice utility called WinZip that will give you a highly user-friendly way in which to compress and uncompress files. The Windows 3.x version attaches to your File Manager and is very easy to use. But even better is the Windows 95 version that becomes a part of the Explorer so you can compress files with a simple drag-and-drop operation.

WinZip is available on-line as shareware at *www.winzip.com*. After you install WinZip, register it via e-mail.

The next time you need to give someone a large file as an e-mail attachment, zip it up before you send it. Of course, they'll need an unzip program but if they don't have one you can tell them about the Web site where you got your copy.

Housekeeping features

We've completed the coverage of the basic e-mail features. We'll now give you some bonuses that will make your life easier. We won't cover everything—there's a wealth of Eudora features that can help you if you have specialized needs. What we'll include next, however, are "advanced basics" that nearly everyone can use.

Delete messages

You will soon have a plethora of messages stored in your Eudora In box. The list of messages in your In box and Out box can quickly grow to unmanageable lengths. Fortunately, deleting messages from *any* Eudora folder is easy.

As a safeguard, Eudora does not actually delete your messages when you use the normal delete function. Instead, deleted messages are transferred into a separate folder called "Trash." When a message is deleted from the Trash folder, then it is truly gone, but you must take specific action to delete messages from Trash. Or, you can configure Eudora to empty the Trash every time you exit the application.

STEP-BY-STEP

GOAL: Learn to delete messages

- ✔ Click the **In box** to open it.

  Or click **Mailbox, In** or press **CTRL+I**.
- ✔ Highlight **E-Mail Exercise 1**.
- ✔ Click on **Message, Delete** or press **CTRL+D**.

  Or click on the Trash icon.
- ✔ Click the **Out box** to open it.
- ✔ Highlight **E-Mail Exercise 1**.
- ✔ Press **CTRL+D**.
- ✔ Click **Mailbox, Trash** to open it.

  These messages may be deleted when you exit, depending on the option you've set. Let's set Eudora to automatically empty the Trash upon exiting.
- ✔ Click **Tools, Options**, scroll to the **Miscellaneous** category.
- ✔ Check **Empty Trash when exiting** and click **OK**.

  You can manually delete a message from Trash right now and it will be gone immediately rather than waiting to exit. If you'd like to practice this, highlight a message in Trash and click **Message, Delete** or press **CTRL+D**. You also can empty the Trash without opening it by clicking **Special, Empty Trash**.

Inside Info

There are several other interesting options under the **Miscellaneous** category. For example, you can set up Eudora to give you an audible notification when it receives an e-mail message. This is a good idea if you've programmed Eudora to check mail for you automatically. To set an audible notification, click **Tools, Options** and then check **Play a sound** under the **Getting Attention** category.

Create tailored folders

Eudora includes only three basic folders: In, Out and Trash. This is a somewhat limited organizing system and most likely you will soon need additional folders and mailboxes. So, we'll explain the basic concepts and show you how to create all you need. Let's make a new folder and mailboxes now.

STEP-BY-STEP

GOAL: Create a new mailbox

- ✔ Click **Mailbox, New**.
- ✔ Type *Test*, check **Make it a folder**, then click **OK**.
- ✔ Type *Test - In* and click **OK**.

This has created a new folder *and* one new mailbox within that folder.

✔ Click **Mailbox, Test, New**

✔ Type *Test - Out* and click **OK**.

As you think of folders to create, keep in mind that you can set up filters for Eudora to use to automatically transfer messages into folders. For example, you could name a folder after your best friend, create an In and Out box under that folder, and then tell Eudora to place all messages from your friend into the friend's In mailbox and all messages to that friend in the friend's Out mailbox.

Transfer messages between mailboxes

After you've created a new tailored mailbox you may already have messages that need to be moved into it. Let's learn to do that now by transferring one of our test messages into the Test folder.

STEP-BY-STEP

GOAL: Learn to transfer messages between folders

✔ Click **Messages, In** to open it.

✔ Click on **E-Mail Exercise 2**.

For now, we only have this one message to move, but if you wanted to move several messages at once, you can highlight as many as you like before you perform the next step. All highlighted messages will be moved.

✔ Click **Transfer**, or click the **Test - In** folder to move the message.

There's no limit to the number of times a message can be moved, so you can always move them back to the original mailbox or to any other mailbox.

Inside Info

You may notice in Windows that you can only select one item on a list at a time. But there are several techniques that let you select multiple items on a list. To select a series of items, you can drag the mouse across them, or click on the first item in the series, then hold down **SHIFT** while clicking on the last item. You can select a random assortment of items from the list by holding down a **CTRL** key while you click.

Signature block

One valuable time-saving feature in your Eudora mail application is the automatic signature block. Eudora actually lets you have two separate ones so you can tailor your closing message. Let's learn now how to create a signature block.

STEP-BY-STEP

GOAL: Learn to create a signature block

✔ Click **Tools, Signature** (see Figure 5).

✔ Type a signature block.

Common netiquette is to keep your signature block to about four lines, perhaps five if you truly need the space. Scrolling through some of the obnoxiously long signature blocks that you'll encounter will surely inspire you to keep yours short.

Normally people do not include phone numbers, only e-mail addresses. A fax number could be included as well as your Web site URL if you have one.

- ✔ Close the window when finished.
- ✔ Click **Yes** to save the changes.

You can cancel the use of your signature block for any one message by simply changing the signature icon on the message box to say **None**. Of course you also can create an alternate signature block for special occasions. For example, you may want to include your phone number with some messages.

- ✔ Click **Tools, Alternate Signature**.
- ✔ Enter a signature block with your telephone number.
- ✔ Close the window when finished.
- ✔ Click **Yes** to save the changes.

Figure 5 Eudora signature block

Address book

Eudora calls its address book "Nicknames." You'll want to start your own list of e-mail addresses right away so you'll have a place to store important addresses and a tool to speed your handling of daily e-mail duties. We'll guide you through creating one nickname and then show you a quick method for using them.

Create a nickname

The next exercise will create a sample nickname. You can delete it later.

STEP-BY-STEP

GOAL: Learn to create a nickname

- ✔ Click **Window, Nicknames** or press **CTRL+L**.
- ✔ Click **New**.
- ✔ Type *Bloggs - Joe*, check **Put on the recipient list**.

Eudora automatically will alphabetize your list, so you probably will want to type the last name first, but you *cannot* use commas. We use a hyphen between first and last names.

Nicknames that you put on the "recipient list" appear on Eudora's main menu for quick access. Note that this nickname is going into the "Main Nicknames" file and that you can create and maintain several different nickname files.

- ✔ Click **OK**.
- ✔ Type *test@erols.com*
- ✔ Click in the **Notes** box and type *Practice Nickname*
- ✔ Double-click the menu control box to close the window.
- ✔ Click **Yes** to save the changes.

Inside Info

The **Address(es)** list under nicknames permits up to 64k bytes of text. That's enough room for more than 2,000 addresses. If you don't want to manage so many names in this little window, you could maintain them in a database until you're ready to send, have the database output a list into your word processor in plain ASCII, use the Windows clipboard to Copy the list, go to Eudora, delete the current list and then Paste the new list into the **Address(es)** window.

Using the address book

You now have saved your first nickname. Names on the recipient list will pop up on the menu items **New Message To, Reply To, Forward To**, and for **Redirect To**. Even if you don't put a nickname on the recipient list, you can still access the name quickly by pressing **CTRL+L**. Let's use the nickname list to quickly create an e-mail message to Joe Bloggs.

STEP-BY-STEP

GOAL: Learn to use the nickname list and to delete nicknames

- ✔ Click **Message, New Message To, Bloggs - Joe**

  That's it! You now are set to complete and send the message. Note, however, that you can see only the nickname "Bloggs - Joe" on the **To:** line instead of the actual e-mail address. We will now show you how to get the actual address on the **To:** line instead of the nickname.
- ✔ Cancel this message by double-clicking the menu control box.
- ✔ Press **CTRL+L** for the nickname list.
- ✔ Click on **Bloggs - Joe**, then hold down **SHIFT** while clicking **To:**.

  Note that you now see the actual address. Let's finish this exercise by removing Joe Bloggs from your nickname list.
- ✔ Cancel this message by double-clicking the menu control box.
- ✔ Press **CTRL+L** for the nickname list.
- ✔ Click on **Bloggs - Joe**, then click on **Remove**.
- ✔ Double-click the menu control box and click **Yes** to save changes.

Multiple recipients

Any e-mail message you send can have multiple recipients. They simply will be listed in the **To:** text box below the address button. Just keep adding as many as you need. If you choose to use the address book to enter multiple **To:** entries (or for multiple carbon copies or for multiple blind copies) you simply hold down **CTRL** to highlight multiple nicknames before clicking on **To:**. When you use this method for multiple addresses, Eudora automatically inserts all selected names.

Carbon copies

You may send a carbon copy of any e-mail message by changing the **To:** drop-list to **Cc:** and entering the recipient's address on the usual line. Carbon copies are copies of your message that are sent to additional recipients who are not prime recipients of your message. If you use the address book, highlight the name and then click on **Cc:** instead of **To:**, then click **OK**.

Blind copies

The blind copy function is similar to the carbon copy function except that the prime recipient will not know that additional copies were sent. If you use the address book, highlight the name and then click on **Bc:** instead of **To:**, then click **OK**.

Print messages

You easily can print any e-mail message with Eudora. Eudora also lets you change print options. Let's run through the printing steps now.

STEP-BY-STEP

GOAL: Learn to print a message

- ✔ Click **In** and highlight **E-Mail Exercise 2**.
- ✔ Click **File, Print...**

  Make sure you have a printer on-line and available before completing the remaining steps, or just read them instead. Also, before the next step, be sure you've selected the correct printer, if you have more than one.
- ✔ Click **Print**.

  If you know you've got the correct printer selected, you can take a shortcut by clicking the printer icon on the toolbar.

Save messages

First of all, you need to know that Eudora saves all of your e-mail messages on your hard drive or network. You don't have to take any special action to save them in their normal folders. Messages can be saved to a separate disk file, however, so that they're more easily accessible for editing in your word processor. The saved messages are formatted as basic ASCII text.

STEP-BY-STEP

GOAL: Learn to save an e-mail message

- ✔ Use the message window that was opened in the last exercise.
- ✔ Click **File, Save As...**
- ✔ Select a directory in which to save the message.
- ✔ Enter a filename.
- ✔ Check **Guess Paragraphs**.

With this checked, Eudora will break up the message into paragraphs and save them so that they will wrap in your word processor. If it's NOT checked, then the saved message will have a hard return at the end of every line.

- ✔ Check **Include Headers** if you want to save the full message information.
- ✔ Click **Save**, or click **Cancel** if you don't want to actually save this message.

Thanks for sticking with us through these exercises and have fun with this hot cyberspace communications tool. Be sure to check out the Orbiting in Cyberspace section for Web addresses that will help you learn even more.

ORBITING IN CYBERSPACE

World Wide Yellow Pages
http://www.yellow.com

Here's an easy-to-remember URL that may find its way onto millions of browser bookmark lists (see Figure 6). You can use this page to search for a wide range of businesses with a Web presence. It's incomplete today, but is expanding rapidly. World Wide Yellow Pages is a commercial, for-profit venture and is a trademark of Home Pages, Inc.

Figure 6 World Wide Web Yellow Pages directory

Four11 directory services
http://www.four11.com

Here's a Web page with links to several good directory services. Of course, the main feature is the Four11 Internet Mail Directory itself (see Figure 7). It's also got listings for Internet Web telephone addresses. This is a commercial service of the SLED Corporation, but they provide free basic listings for all Internet users as well as free searches. Of course they hope you'll sign up for their premium services.

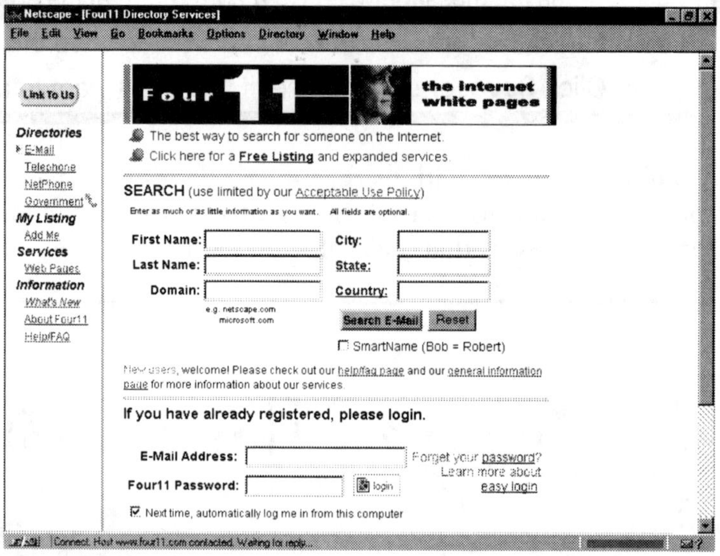

Figure 7 Four 11 Internet e-mail directory

InterNIC directory and database services
http://www.internic.net/ds/dspg01.html

Your primary use of this site most likely will be its "InterNIC Directory Services" (white pages). It's one of the most comprehensive e-mail address locations that you'll find. This page also features the "InterNIC Database Services" (public databases) and an area entitled "Additional Internet Resource Information."

Directory of directories
http://www.internic.net/ds/dspg01.html

The InterNIC Directory of Directories is an index of references that will link you to resources, products and services all over the Internet. The links on this page include descriptions of available Internet resources. The Directory of Directories is compiled by InterNIC Directory and Database Services (e-mail at: *admin@ds.internic.net*). This work is in conjunction with the National Science Foundation (NSF). Neither of the parties assumes any responsibility for the accuracy of the directory listings.

Signature file ideas
http://www.brandonu.ca/~ennsnr/Tags/

You'll read a lot of witty aphorisms in e-mail and newsgroup signature block. You will also read a lot of silliness. You'll find some examples of both if you check out this site and its more than 11,000 one-liners. Enjoy yourself, but remember the generally-accepted "4-line-limit" on signature files.

8

A Global Community: Newsgroups

Newsgroups are global, electronic "bulletin boards," and each newsgroup serves as a central location for messages on one targeted topic. Related messages are "posted" in each newsgroup and anyone who looks at a newsgroup will see all the messages that have been posted to that group by other users. Theoretically anyone can access any newsgroup from anywhere in the world.

All of the Internet newsgroups, collectively, are called the Usenet and they are booming at an unprecedented growth rate. What's the attraction? Through newsgroups, everyone on the Internet can have a say in any topic that interests him or her and can read what others have to say on the subject. Because users can post questions to an entire group and get answers from all over the world, newsgroups have enhanced our sense of living in a global community. Through newsgroups, the Internet truly delivers "something for everybody."

There are thousands of newsgroups, and tracking them all would be a huge task. Actually, it would be impossible. Fortunately, your system includes the Netscape newsreader that enables you to select—from the master list of all the groups on the Erol's system—only the groups you choose to view on your computer.

The process of selecting newsgroups to view is called subscribing, although your system always has full access to all newsgroups. That probably sounds confusing right now, so we'll put it another way: Subscribing and unsubscribing to newsgroups uses a process that is handled internally by your Netscape newsreader. You cannot control the number or the subject matter of the groups that Erol's sends you, but you can control the groups that are displayed on your computer.

Jargon Cutter

News server - A computer at an Internet provider that receives all of the Usenet newsgroups and makes them available via an Internet connection. Both the news server and your system use the Network News Transfer Protocol (NNTP) that enables all types of computers to enjoy access to all of the newsgroups.

Any time that you decide to see a newsgroup to which you don't subscribe, you can subscribe and see the group's postings. You don't have to wait for a subscription to arrive because all of the groups remain available to you all the time and you control the ones you see. Similarly, if you unsubscribe to a group, your newsreader merely stops displaying that newsgroups's postings and that group remains available for resubscription.

How Many Newsgroups Are There?

How many can you stand?

As we researched this book, we found exactly 26,318 public newsgroups. A week later, there were 26,368—then we stopped checking! How many will you find? Well, there's no way to tell. It varies by system and we've only been counting the public newsgroups—it would be impossible to count them all because there are thousands of private newsgroups.

How many do you need? Erol's subscribes to all of the major, well-known newsgroups available today—and we're adding new ones all the time. If you learn of a newsgroup that is not available to you, contact Erol's technical support and request that the group be added.

Jargon Cutter

Private newsgroups - Many organizations start their own newsgroup and restrict usage to people within the organization. These newsgroups can be used to coordinate projects and to exchange ideas between offices scattered all over the world. We'll have more information on starting a newsgroup later in this chapter.

Remember, if a newsgroup is available to you on your news server, then subscribing merely means that Netscape automatically checks that group for new messages when you start your newsreader. We'll cover the actual steps to subscribe later, because we're first going to show you how to get the master list of all newsgroups and how to read a single newsgroup message.

Getting started

Before you can read newsgroups, you'll have to download the master list of newsgroups that your news server provides. We'll give you a Step-By-Step exercise that will download the list and then another that will show you how to read the messages within the newsgroups that are on the list.

You'll find three basic components to the Netscape news module: the menus, the toolbar and the message windows. If you've never opened your Netscape news reader, the master list will be very short and only will contain the names of the lists that Netscape provides as a default. Normally this is just a single group for new users that's called *news.announce.newusers*. Don't worry, you'll soon see more newsgroups on your list than you could ever use, so let's go get them now.

The first Step-By-Step newsgroups exercise will make sure your Netscape is configured correctly and then download the list of newsgroups that are on the Erol's news server. But first, you'll need to start your Netscape Web Browser.

STEP-BY-STEP

GOAL: Learn to browse your newsgroups list

✔ Click **Options, Mail and News Preferences**, then click the **Server** tab.

✔ Enter *news.erols.com* in the **News (NNTP) Server** text entry box.

✔ Click the **Identity** tab and verify the entries are correct.

✔ Click **OK** to save the changes.

✔ Click **Window, Netscape News**.

✔ Click **Options, Show All Newsgroups**.

If you've never before connected to Erol's newsserver, this step will take a long time as it downloads the titles of more than 26,000 newsgroups.

✔ Scroll down to **alt.*** and click the **+** sign next to the folder.

Listings that end with an asterisk lead to sub-topics. Clicking on a sub-topic expands the listing to increasingly specific levels. Some headers, such as **alt.***, have a lot of sub-topics and can require additional time to download.

✔ Click on **alt.quotations**.

You'll now see the number of messages available in this group, and in the right window, you'll see the actual messages posted in this group.

✔ Click on any message in the right window to read it.

You'll now see something in all three windows. The list of available groups is in the upper-left, the current group's messages are in the upper-right and the text of the current message is displayed in the bottom (see Figure 1).

✔ To subscribe to this group, click the **Checkbox** after the group's name.

Go ahead and subscribe for now because you can unsubscribe any time.

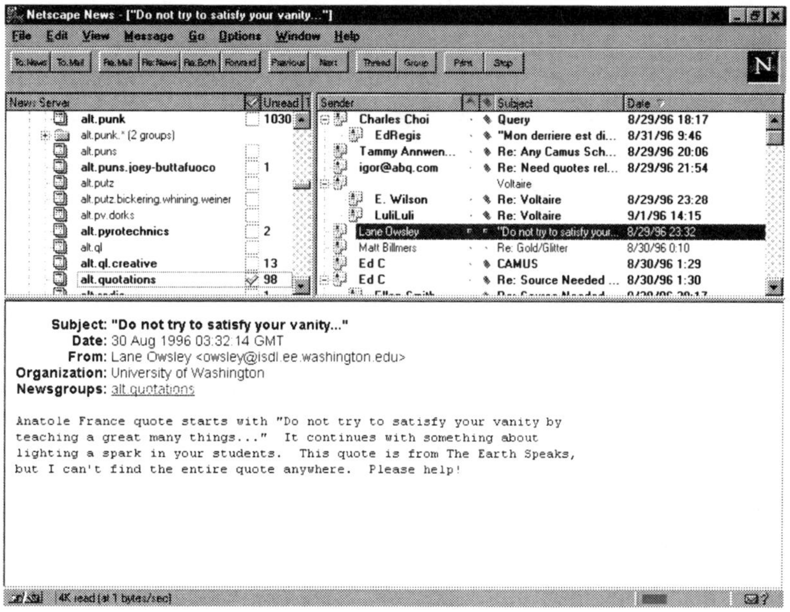

Figure 1 Netscape news reader with groups and messages

Once you've subscribed to one or more groups, Netscape News will check those groups for new messages each time it starts. The results will be listed and you then can select any of the groups within which you want to read messages.

You can change the maximum number of messages you can see in any one group. To change yours, click **Options, Mail and News Preferences**, click the **Servers** tab, then change the **Get:** number under **News** and click **OK**.

Popular Usenet Newsgroups

Erol's has nearly the most complete selection of Internet newsgroups possible. An international Internet rating organization recently ranked Erol's as second in the world. If you previously used another Internet provider, you may have had fewer than half the number we provide to you now.

But you can't use them all because a lot of newsgroups that appear up in our extensive master list are empty. In fact, if you randomly browse through newsgroups to which you've never subscribed, you may see that about one newsgroup in three is empty. Nonetheless, there are thousands of active newsgroups. Here's a list of a few of the major categories:

Category	**Topics**
alt	Alternative topics that don't fit under other major topics. These can get pretty far-out and include messages on any topic—in other words, not everything in *alt* is suitable for all ages or all tastes!
biz	Business discussions, advertisements and postings of new products and services.
comp	Computer-related topics.
misc	Miscellaneous topics, but none as far out as alt.
rec	Recreational topics; you won't believe what some people consider to be recreation—here's something for everyone.
sci	Science topics.
soc	Social topics with an international flavor, as well as covering religions.
talk	Not enough talk radio stations for you? At least you can get through to this one.

This is just a brief orientation into some of the most popular main categories. Some of these categories have thousands of subtopics.

Message threads

The indented articles that appear under an article are related articles that are replies to the original. If someone replies to a reply, that article will be shown indented yet another level, etc. This hierarchical listing system creates a *thread*—a focused series of related messages. Threads help you easily track a newsgroup discussion.

The plus and minus signs in front of the thread folders can be used to expand or compress any thread. Also, note that you can adjust the vertical bar between the two upper windows to permit you to see more of either side. This can help if you're zeroing in on the threads in a single newsgroup. And, you can adjust the horizontal bar to see more threads at once, though you'll reduce the size of the message window.

Inside Info

If you'd rather not even see the full list of newsgroups on your list, click on **Options, Show Subscribed Newsgroups**. This will reduce your screen clutter and make navigating through the remaining lists a little cleaner. You can always return to the full listing by clicking **Options, Show All Newsgroups**.

Subscribing and unsubscribing

Since the list of newsgroups that you downloaded is very long, you'll appreciate the subscribe feature because it will limit your view to only those newsgroups you choose. We had you quickly subscribed to one in the previous exercise, but we want to show you how to go back and subscribe (or unsubscribe) to other groups. Both are simple processes as you'll see in the next Step-By-Step exercise.

Step-By-Step

GOAL: Learn to subscribe or unsubscribe to newsgroups

- ✔ Click **Options, Show All Newsgroups**.

  This ensures you can see the full list.
- ✔ Highlight a group in the left window, then check the group's check box.
- ✔ Click **Options, Show Subscribed Newsgroups**.

  You'll now see only groups to which you've subscribed. Now, let's unsubscribe from this newly-subscribed group and then refresh the list.
- ✔ Highlight the newsgroup to which you just subscribed.
- ✔ Uncheck the group's check box.

  Notice that the group remains on your list.
- ✔ Click **Options, Show All Newsgroups**.
- ✔ Click **Options, Show Subscribed Newsgroups**.

  This will recreate your subscribed groups without the group you just cut.

Start Your Own Usenet Newsgroup

Can't find a newsgroup for your favorite topic? Are you kidding? Well, if not, there is a newsgroup for you! A group called *news.announce.newgroups* contains posts of announcements of either the creation of new newsgroups or the consideration of proposed newsgroups. Newsgroups are created after a successful "call for votes" (CFV), which begins with a posting to this newsgroup. Also, calls for discussions, vote results, and creation notices should be posted here as well. Post a CFV to *announce-newgroups@uunet.uu.net*. Follow-ups will be redirected to *news.groups*.

Post only *after* reading about the process by checking out these sources:

- ❖ "How to Create a New Usenet Newsgroup," found in *news.admin.misc*, *news.announce.newgroups*, *news.announce.newusers*, *news.answers*, or in *news.groups*;
- ❖ "Usenet Newsgroup Creation Companion," found in *news.announce.newusers*, *news.answers*, or *news.groups*.

- ❖ "So You Want to Create an Alt Newsgroup?" found in *alt.config*, *alt.answers*, or *news.answers*.

What if my idea isn't accepted?

You can find services that bring you newsgroups that have been deemed "unnecessary" or "of too little use to store on corporate news servers." How many? Well, one service brings you 13,000 "reject" newsgroups. For details, e-mail to *ccaputo@alt.net*. Perhaps this service will suffice if your own newsgroup proposal doesn't succeed.

Sorting messages

Tracking articles within a newsgroup may be a real challenge because some groups will have thousands of active messages. Fortunately, Netscape includes a few tricks to help you find messages quickly. In the right window, you can click on the header bar to change the sort order of the displayed messages (see Figure 2).

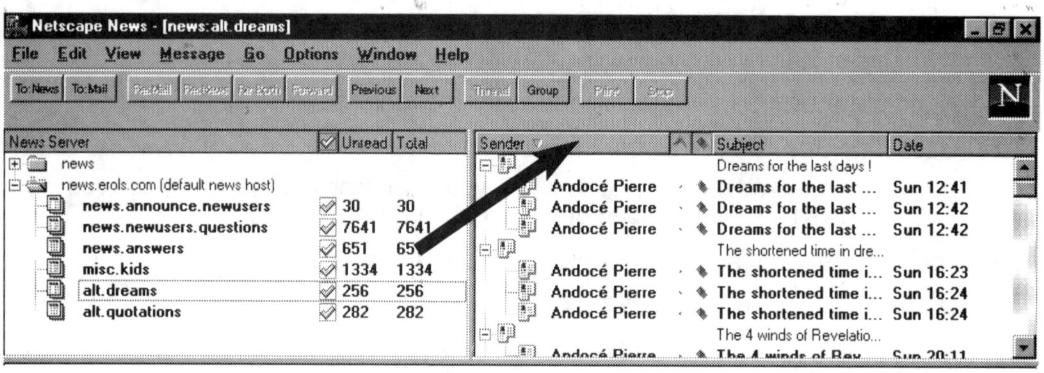

Figure 2 Netscape lets you sort messages by Sender, Subject or Date

Thus, if you click on **Sender**, the messages will be alphabetized by sender name. This sorts by first name first, but it's still useful once you know the name of a particular sender and you want to group together all of that person's messages. Clicking on **Subject** will alphabetize the messages by title. The default is to sort by date, which you can restore by clicking on the **Date** bar.

Replying

Often, reading an article will inspire you to jump in and share your views. If so, join the crowd, because we all get the same urge—newsgroups clearly demonstrate the natural human desire to have the last word. Replies are what keep the Usenet alive and humming. There are two ways to reply to an article:

- ❖ Post a follow-up article that everyone in the world can see. Of course, that's only if everyone in world browses through this newsgroup, but at least it's there for anyone who wants to read it. Be careful what you post!

- ❖ Mail a reply directly to the author of the article you're reading and keep it between the two of you. This is a good choice either when you have a focused reply that would not interest general readers in the group or when you prefer to keep the reply private—well, as private as e-mail can be, anyway.

Inside Info

You can view detailed information about any message by viewing the message and then clicking **Options, Show Headers, All**. This gives you all kinds of details about the message's origin and the path it took across the Internet to your system.

The next exercise will show you both of the ways that you can reply to a newsgroup article. You should have an article on-screen from the last exercise. From there, we'll go to the reply function.

STEP-BY-STEP

GOAL: Learn how to post a reply to a newsgroup

- ✔ Click **alt.quotations** to see the articles.
- ✔ Click an article on the list.
- ✔ Click the **Re: News** button or click **Message, Post Reply** (see Figure 3).

  The original message text will be included by default, but this is optional. Usually you can cut out most of it, leaving only enough so that your reply will make sense to other readers. Often, you can break up the article into chunks and insert immediately after each piece a reply that is tailored to that section of the original. Be sure to remove the original poster's signature file.
- ✔ Type your reply.
- ✔ Click **Send** to post the article to this newsgroup or click **File, Close, Yes** or the **Close** button, then **Yes** to return to the reader.

  This process sends the reply to the entire newsgroup.

GOAL: Learn how to e-mail a reply to the original article author

- ✔ Click the **Re: Mail** button or click **Message, Mail Reply** or press **CTRL+R**.

  Often, this is the best reply method, but many people clog up an entire newsgroup with personal replies that would best have been sent directly.
- ✔ Type your reply.
- ✔ Click **Send** or click **File, Close, Yes** or click **Close, Yes** to return to the reader without sending this reply.

  This posts a private message only to the original poster.

Inside Info

You can use *both* reply methods at the same time, which will send your reply to the newsgroup as well as directly to the original poster. This might seem redundant, but the original poster might not check the newsgroup regularly and could miss your reply. A direct e-mail reply will ensure that he or she sees your reply quickly.

You are not limited to replying only to the original group or to the original poster. When the message dialog box appears, you can manually add any other newsgroups to the original newsgroup. And, if you're sending a private reply, you can enter the e-mail addresses of several people on the same line as the original poster. Or, you can enter additional e-mail addresses on the **Cc:** line of the message so that other users will get a copy of your message.

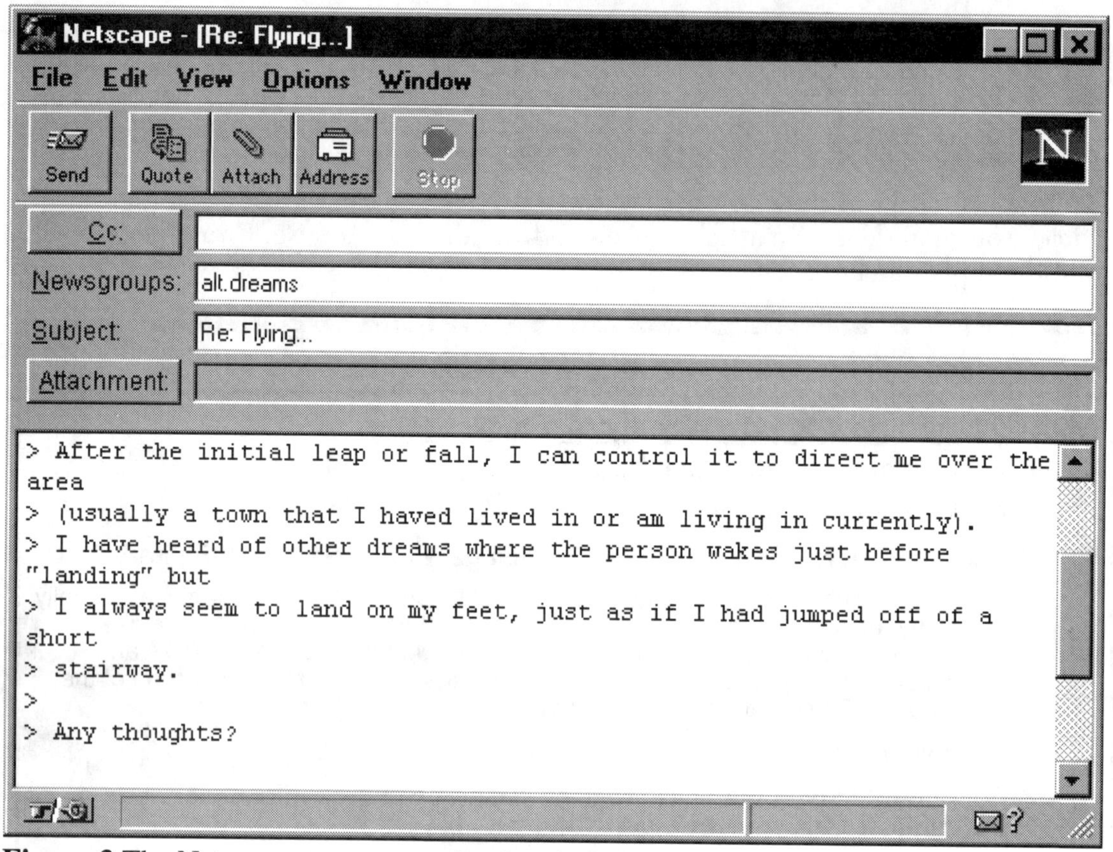

Figure 3 The Netscape newsgroups Reply window

Posting an original newsgroup article

Sometimes you'll want to post an original idea to a newsgroup. Or, perhaps, you may have a question that you believe someone in the group might be able to answer. In either case, you'll want to create and post an original article for the newsgroup. It's basically the same as posting a follow-up, with one major exception that's important to remember: *The subject line will be blank and you'll need to fill it in manually!*

STEP-BY-STEP

GOAL: Learn how to post an original newsgroup article

- ✔ Return to the list of articles in the **alt.quotations** groups.
- ✔ Click the **To: News** button to create an original message (see Figure 4).
- ✔ Type *your own subject.*

  Leaving the subject line blank is a good way to get some of those flames you read about in the netiquette chapter!
- ✔ Press **TAB** to move the insertion point into the message body.
- ✔ Type the body of your message.
- ✔ Click **Send** to post the article to this newsgroup or click **File, Close, Yes** or the **Close** button, then **Yes** to return to the reader.
- ✔ Click **File, Close** to close the newsreader and return to your Netscape Web browser, or click **File, Exit** to exit Netscape completely.

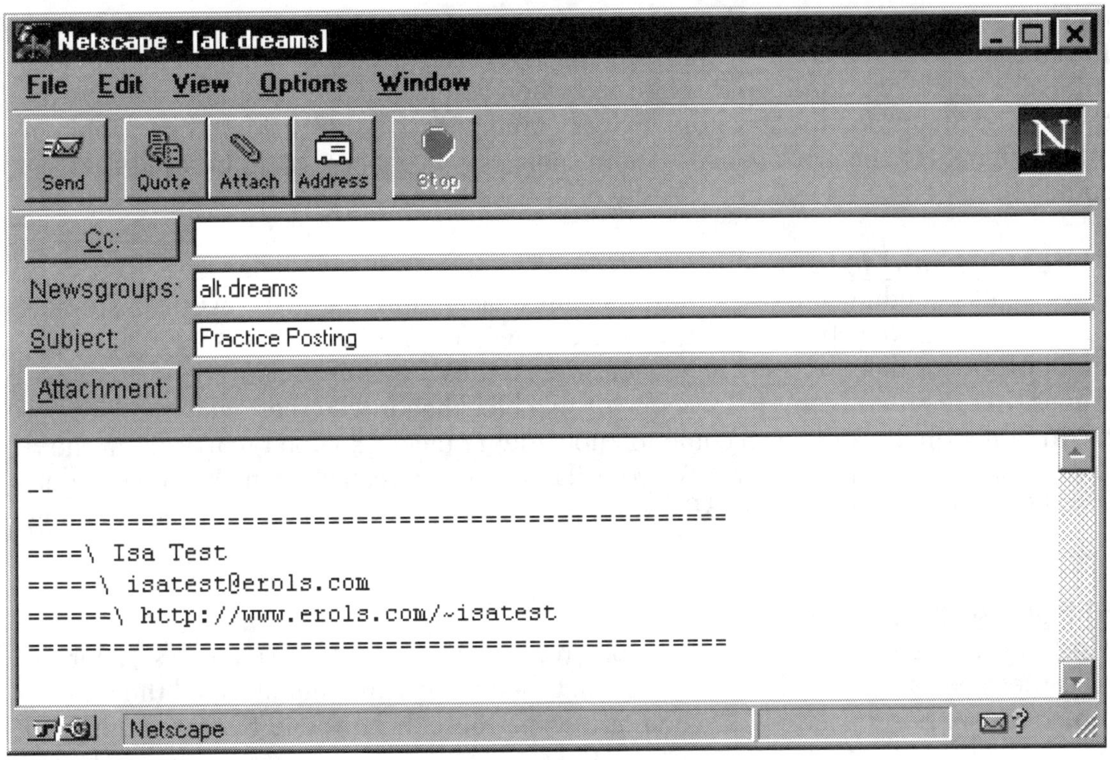

Figure 4 Create a new newsgroup article with Netscape news

Nine Keys to Newsgroup Success

There's much more to newsgroups than knowing the technical steps that you've learned. When you use newsgroups, you're jumping into a global realm that can reach anyone in the world. They are powerful communication tools that deserve a lot of respect, courtesy, discretion and common sense. These nine keys will help you to improve our global cyberspace community and to boost their potential value to you and your organization.

1) Get the FAQ

Many newsgroups have a FAQ (Frequently Asked Questions) file. Look for it or ask for it. Many questions you'll ask as a newbie to a group will already have been asked repeatedly. The established users of the newsgroup are tired of browsing through posts that ask the same old questions. Get the FAQs and *read* the FAQs before you get flamed for asking the group a "dumb newbie" question.

2) Lurk around first

Newsgroups can get quite personal and develop a timbre of their own. Each is slightly different. Until you've sampled that timbre, you don't know what might be considered offensive, rude or stupid. The proper term for sampling a newsgroup is "lurking." You know the kind of people who don't lurk: the same ones who butt into your verbal conversations. If you post to a newsgroup where you've never lurked, don't be surprised if you quickly get flamed.

3) Remember the global community

Lurking will help you abide by this principle. Newsgroups likely will have members from all over the world. Keep this in mind when you post. For example, if you live in the United States don't refer to the U.S. as "America." That's considered by people in other Americas to be arrogant. Also, ethnic and regional jokes will at best fall flat, could be misconstrued and might easily offend thousands of your fellow Interneters.

4) Forgive and forget

If you read something annoying, offensive, misplaced, misguided or just plain stupid, your best course of action is to forget it and move on. The Internet has enough bandwidth problems that it doesn't need electronic tennis matches of flames and counter-flames. Every group seems to have one or two blockheads who seem never to have heard of netiquette and you'll come to know them quickly, so don't worry about the occasional accidental offender. Save your flames for the really bad guys. Or, consider e-mailing a chronic repeater's ISP—you may get his account canceled, which flaming will never do.

5) Follow the threads

Most interesting newsgroup articles evoke replies. And your Netscape newsreader links these posts together into "threads" that follow the same theme. Read the entire thread before posting a reply. Several others may already have said the same thing. No one will appreciate reading your belated opinion that parrots what's already been said. Reading the whole thread also relates to the previous key—forgive and forget. If a post really has you steamed, you can count on it annoying others as well and they probably already have done plenty of flaming for you.

6) Short and sweet

Remember an ancient adage on writing that says, "I'm sorry this is so long... I didn't have time to make it short." We've got two tips for keeping your posts short.

First, keep them short. This actually takes longer than simply spewing forth every word on a topic that comes to mind. But the time you spend will be multiplied many times over by happy newsgroup members who, in appreciation of your courtesy, may actually read your post and may even reply.

Second, don't make them long. You will soon tire of wading through replies in newsgroups in which the respondent copied the entire text from the original post—which you just read—then tacked on only the clever reply, "I agree." People can follow threads! You need not copy any more of a post than a brief contextual reminder. Sure, it takes time to delete chunks of a post that don't need to be repeated, but the time you spend will be rewarded.

7) Put it where it belongs

Stick to the subject. Usually you can tell by the title, but make sure you're in the right place by lurking and reading the FAQ file. Post only when you're certain you're writing to the right audience. Posting to the wrong newsgroup wastes resources.

If you accidentally post to the wrong group, just forget about it. Similarly, if you see an accidental post, ignore it. One of the most annoying events in newsgroups often begins when someone accidentally posts to the wrong group, then six people post to say how stupid this person is, then the person posts again to say to ignore the first post, which draws several more flames about brain size and family lineage, to which the original poster apologizes, then the apology draws a string of posts commenting on what a stupid waste of resources this whole event has been. Twenty messages can cascade out of a single errant post. Post correctly and remember to forgive and forget when others slip—perhaps they'll do the same for you.

8) Remember you're invisible

No one can see you smile on the Internet. No one can hear you chuckle. No one can see your tongue in your cheek. If you joke, don't assume that everyone understands that you're joking. Remember the global community. Jokes or twisted humor on newsgroups rarely come across as funny. If you must make a crack about something, at least use one of the emoticons we've listed in the netiquette chapter so that everyone will know that you *meant* it to be a joke. They still may not *get* the joke, but perhaps they'll understand you were *trying* to be funny and you won't get flamed.

9) Use e-mail when appropriate

Newsgroups are an excellent place to get answers to tricky or obscure questions. If you've read the FAQ file, lurked in the background for a while and followed all the threads, but still have a question—that's the time to post. But if the answer is not going to be of general use to the group, ask for replies by e-mail and make sure your e-mail address is included in your signature file at the end of your post. (It's supposed to be in the header, but a backup is a good idea.) Conversely, if you want to send a personal reply to a posted question, then use e-mail and spare everyone in the group the clutter of unnecessary, personal messages.

Infomagnets

New newsgroups are appearing at an ever-increasing clip and existing groups are garnering new members faster than ever. Keeping up with all of the traffic is, quite literally, impossible—the wealth of information they offer can seem to be more of a burden than a blessing. With so many public newsgroups, you can't even read the subject lines for each day's new messages. In other words, browsing through newsgroups isn't for everyone.

Perhaps you'll prefer a computerized news magnet—called an infomagnet—that filters through on-line news resources and brings you the news you can use. For example, you can subscribe to a tailored news service that will send you articles after it finds the ones you want.

ClariNet news services

ClariNet e.News is an electronic newspaper that delivers professional news and information directly to your computer. It sends live news (including technology-related wire stories), timely computer industry news, syndicated columns and features, financial information, stock quotes and more.

You can receive, upon request, a free sample of selected articles that are posted to the Usenet newsgroup *biz.clarinet.sample*. If you want more information, contact ClariNet for a targeted sample of the news topics you want to track. If that isn't enough, they'll give you a free, two-week trial with no obligation.

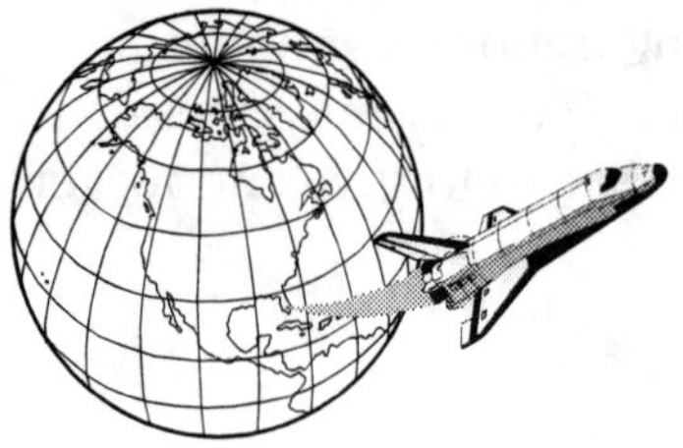

Orbiting in Cyberspace

Usenet FAQ
http://www.cis.ohio-state.edu/hypertext/faq/usenet/FAQ-List.html

This Web site contains a list of all of the Usenet FAQ documents found in the newsgroup *news.answers*. This FAQs listing is alphabetized by topic as much as possible. Many of the FAQs in this list are presented in the same format as they appear in the newsgroup, while others have been enhanced and split into additional documents. A few of the documents are provided in hypertext and there is a limited search capability. Search capability is available for the newsgroup names, archive names, subjects and keywords.

Dejanews
http://www.dejanews.com

DejaNews is a World Wide Web search engine for Usenet newsgroups. Even though it's a Web site, DejaNews has archived millions of Usenet postings. You can enter keywords and DejaNews will build a list for you of articles from its archives that contain those keywords. The basic searching service is powerful, but you're likely to find *too many* articles. You can narrow your search and increase your chances of finding exactly what you want by clicking on the *Power Search* icon. For even more control, click on the "Create a Query Filter" link so you can filter the search by newsgroup, date range and author.

Farcast
http://www.farcast.com

Farcast™ is an alternative to newsgroups. It's an agent-based, personal news and information service. Farcast lets you browse and search its collection of news, press releases, reference material and stock quotes. The service is available interactively 24-hours-a-day, or you can contract with Farcast to automatically send you news articles from a wide range of topics. You can also create your own information robots (they call them "Droids") that will search thousands of articles daily to retrieve news that interests you. Farcast uses your regular e-mail account so you are ready to begin using it today without any special software or equipment. Farcast offers its complete service for a reasonable, flat-rate fee, and they offer a free ten-day trial.

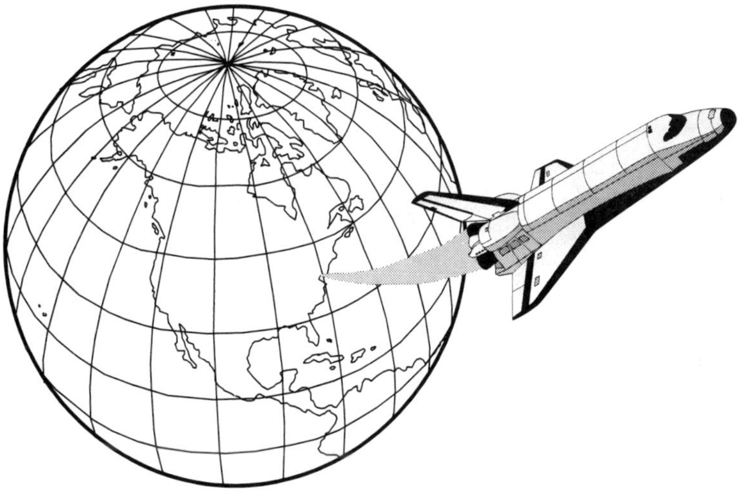

Phase 3

Phase 3: Cyberspace

Now that you've learned how to use the basic tools, we want to show you some valuable things you can accomplish on the Web. We've included chapters that help you find specific information and do on-line research in major libraries all over the world. You'll also learn about how governments are getting into cyberspace and how you can interact with them. Then we'll close Phase 3 with business tips.

Consider these chapters to be just the start of your Web surfing. No book could contain it all! The Web is growing daily, but that's the beauty of the whole system. There's so much out there in cyberspace that everyone can have it his or her own way. And, if you don't find what you want today, just check back later.

As you use these chapters, keep in mind the Bookmarks feature that you learned about in the Netscape Navigator chapter. Be sure to mark sites to which you plan to return. And a final reminder before you jump into all the Web sites in these chapters—remember that Netscape is also a valuable resource for locating on-line information. You're lucky because you're not limited to the standard Web sites—in addition to everything that everyone else has, you have Erol's!

- **Chapter 9** presents a starter-set of **cool Web sites** so you can do some fun surfing right away. After a while you'll have plenty of your own favorite Web sites, but until then, these ought to keep you busy.

- **Chapter 10** is about a Web feature called **search engines**. Search engines are Internet tools that search the World Wide Web for information you want to find—and it's a good thing they do. With all the information on the Web today, the proverbial *needle in a haystack* would be easy to find by comparison.

- **Chapter 11** uses a completely different approach to help you find information via the Web. It features on-line **bookstores, libraries, encyclopedias** and other reference sources. You can tap into some vast resources right from the computer in your own home. We think you'll be astounded at what you can find using the sites we present here.

- **Chapter 12** shows you how to access **government** services via the Web. Have you ever tried to track down a copy of your birth certificate? It just about took you forever, right? Well, now the Web can zip you directly to your hometown records. Only a few government agencies are truly set up to do business across the Web, but that's changing rapidly and you'll be ready when they are.

- **Chapter 13** presents an array of **business tips**. You'll see how to manage home finances and investments and you'll get tips on buying and selling businesses and on small business marketing. We even show you how to proceed if you'd like to buy or sell a home on the Web.

9

What to See First: Cool Web Sites

Since you've subscribed to the Erol's Internet service, you've most likely heard about many amazing, exciting, interesting and enjoyable things that you can see and do on the Internet. Most of what you've heard about are things that you can see and do on the World Wide Web. As you learned in the Quick Tour chapter, there's more to the Internet than just the World Wide Web. Realistically, however, the Web is where you'll spend most of your time and find the best things to see and do.

But the Web is so vast that it's difficult to know where to begin. So we're going to give you some starting points. These aren't things that we endorse or support, they've just been selected to give you an overview of what's out there on the Web. The rest of the chapters in Phase 3 will present Web sites by category and will help you understand how to use some of them for your work or play.

Once you get started, you'll quickly develop your own set of favorites. Then, you'll find that browsing those favorites will lead to more, and to more, and to... well, let's just say that we give you our best wishes for an enjoyable cyberspace adventure.

Inside Info

If you skipped the Netscape Navigator lesson, you'd benefit from reading it before you jump into this chapter. At least read about the Bookmarks so you'll know how to record your favorite Web sites when you see things to which you want to return. And, there are plenty of other good tips in that chapter that will make your cyber-surfing more enjoyable and more productive.

Sampler

We'll begin by presenting a light and lively sampler of selected Web sites. We selected these first three sites because they'll be interesting to most people and because they show off what the Web can bring you. And some of them show off the advanced features of the Netscape Navigator Web browser.

Smithsonian

The Smithsonian Institution has been around for more than 150 years and they've chronicled the world's technological progress. Now they're even using the latest in technology to report to you about technology—and much, much more (see Figure 1). Yes, the venerable Smithsonian Institution has taken the leap into cyberspace.

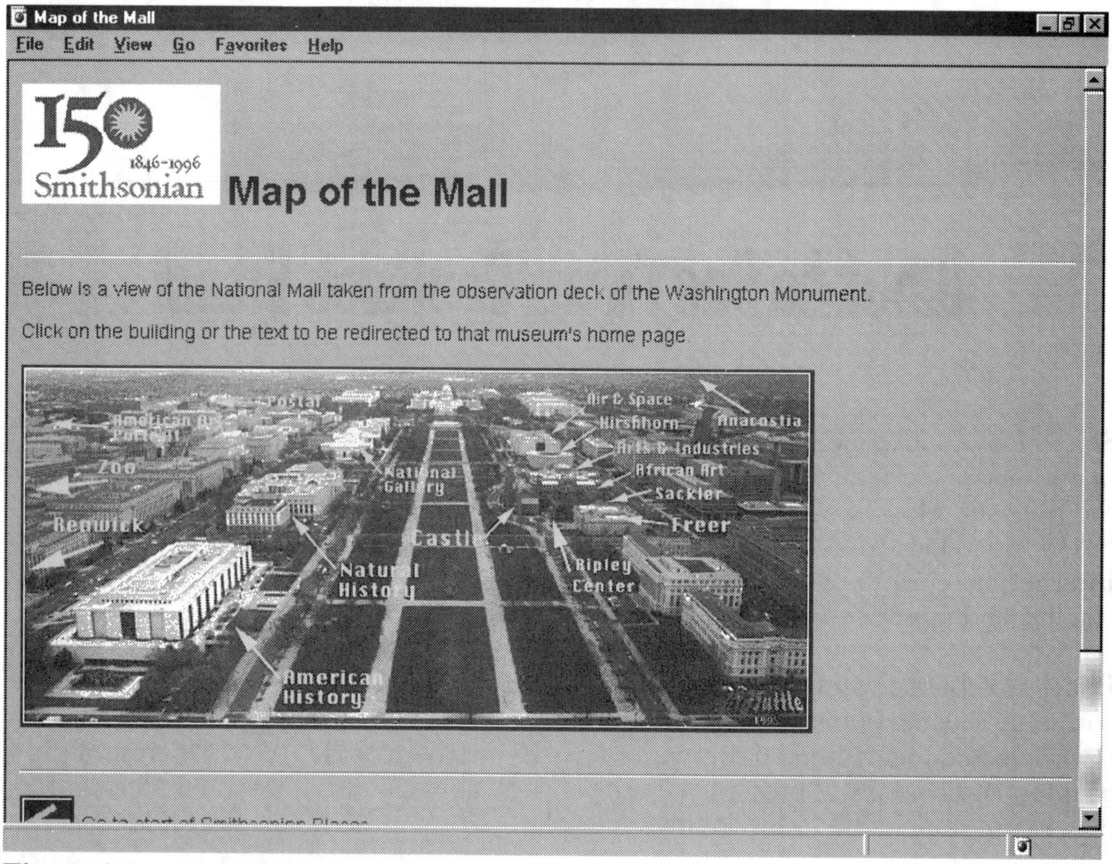

Figure 1 Smithsonian Institution - A great place to introduce yourself to the Internet

Since we've already given you the chapter on how to use your Netscape Navigator Web browser, we'll assume in this chapter that you know how to load a Web site. So, we'll just give you the URL of these sites and leave it to you to get there. This one is located at: *www.si.edu/organiza/mallmap.htm*.

This opening page is a user-friendly example of a clickable map graphic. You'll see that all of the major attractions on the Mall in Washington are labeled. When you decide what you want to see, you can click on the label or on the building to jump to the associated Web site.

If there were nothing else on the Web, you could almost justify having an Internet connection for this Mall map alone. It makes a terrific addition to your Bookmarks. Once you've marked it you can come back for research projects, school reports, general curiosity or just for something to do on a rainy day.

NASA

NASA really has the space angle covered—real outer space and now cyberspace. They've got one of the most popular sites on the Internet. This, too, is a good example of a clickable map (see Figure 2). You can select a general topic and then surf off into a wealth of cascading sites that cover everything NASA does. To get started, jump to *www.nasa.gov* and then jump right in to whatever looks like fun.

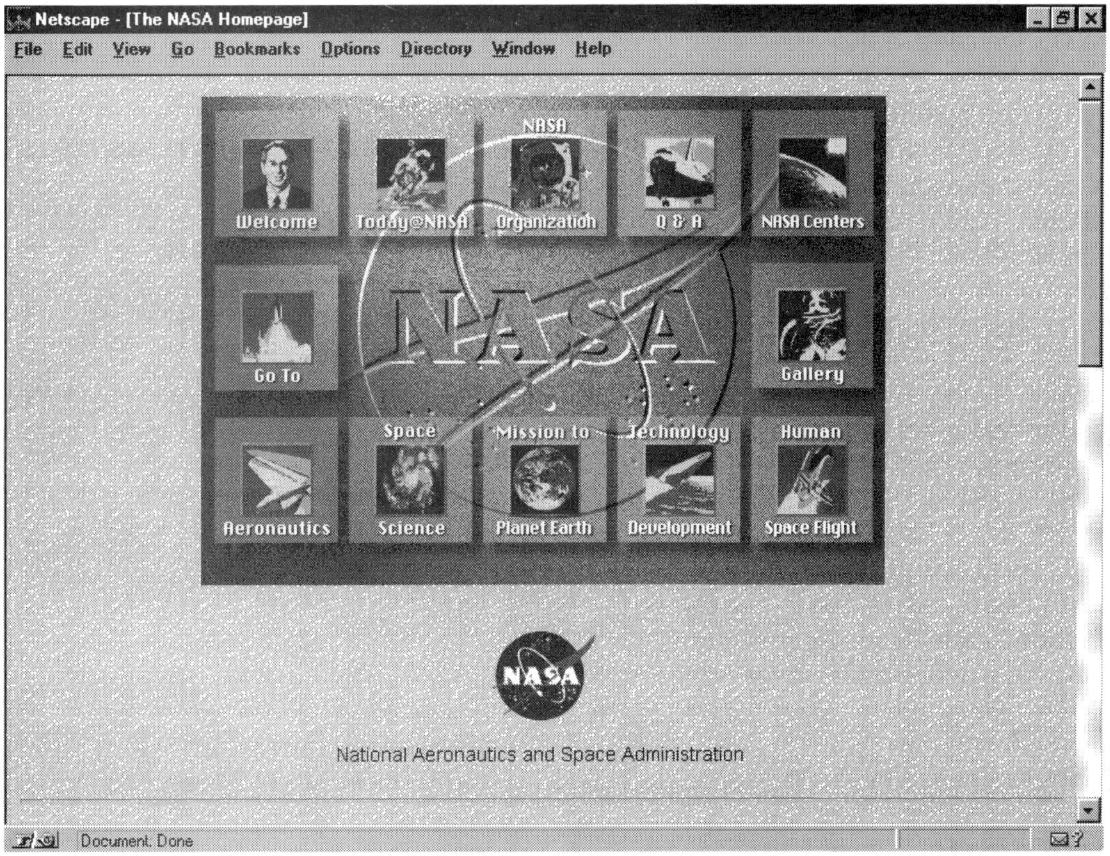

Figure 2 NASA - cyberspace is fun, but this shows you the real thing

A really fun way to start is by clicking on the "Human Space Flight" button. After that you can click on the "Space Flight" link and find a vast stores of information and images from space. Want to know about the next Shuttle flight? No problem, they're scheduled well in advance. So far in advance that you can even read about the Shuttle Atlantis' mission that's scheduled for launch on January 18, 2001! And you thought - *2001: A Space Odyssey* was only a movie!

If you've got a color printer, you might enjoy downloading color images of the patches worn by the astronauts on each mission as well as loads and loads of images taken during the missions. They've even got complete biographies of all the astronauts that you can print—in full color, of course.

Inside Info

The Smithsonian and the NASA sites are easy to use because of their user-friendly, clickable graphics images. Most Web surfers, however, find these sites to be annoying because the graphics require so long to load. But with Erol's ISDN service, you can use graphics-intensive interfaces such as these without dreading long download times. And, both sites are rich in images you can download. For example, NASA regularly presents spectacular, up-to-date images from its missions. These images are very large, however, which means that the download time is too long for many Web surfers, but you can download almost anything you want in a reasonable amount of time.

Star Trek Holodeck 3

Now that we've started down the space travel path, how about some fictional space exploration? Okay, then let's beam over to the Star Trek Holodeck 3, which will bring you some impressive sights and sounds. The fun starts with the fanfare sound track on the home page (see Figure 3) and then takes off from there. You won't find a much better use of Web graphics anywhere in cyberspace.

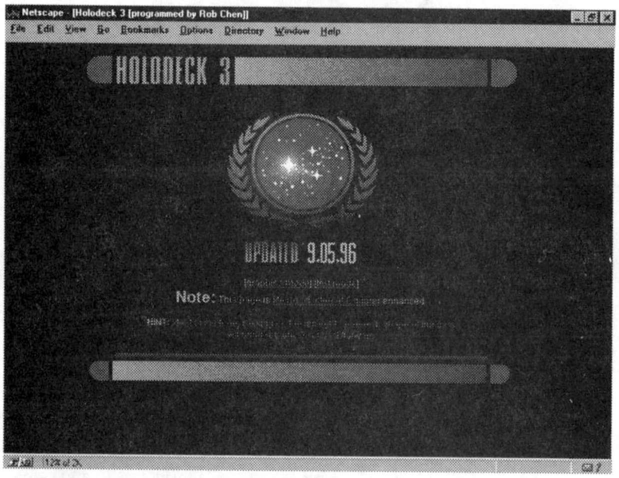

Figure 3 Star Trek Holodeck 3

We hope that your computer includes a sound card and speakers. The Internet is rapidly becoming a full multimedia experience and this site is a good demonstration of what's coming. In other words, if you think this is cool... things are only getting better. Even if you're not a Star Trek fan, visit *www.starbase21.com/holodeck3/index.html* to at least get a glimpse of what a fun Web site can do as well as what your Netscape can do.

MapQuest

Space travel—whether fictional or real—is very exciting and a lot of fun, but it's time to get Scotty to beam us back down to Earth now. Where will you go once you land back here? Anywhere you like if you start with MapQuest (see Figure 4) at *www.mapquest.com*.

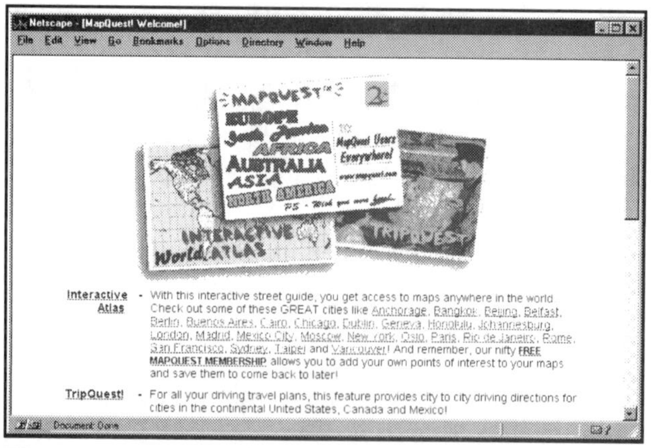

Figure 4 Map Quest - anywhere on Earth

This site gives you some insight into the problems that Web authors face in developing sites to look good on a wide variety of computers. For example, in Phase 4 of this book, you'll learn in the Web publishing chapter about the problems of writing for different screen resolutions in Windows. The MapQuest site solves this by letting you select a Web page tailored to your screen. If you don't know which choice to select when you see the menu of screen options, you can skip over to the chapter on Web publishing and read about Windows screen resolutions.

Inside Info

Save this site in your Bookmarks for the next time you take a cross-country road trip. Before you leave, visit this site, click on the "Trip Quest" link and enter the starting city and the destination city. Within seconds, you'll get a complete set of directions that you can print and take along. It can give you directions between more than 150,000 cities and towns in the U.S., Canada and Mexico!

Perhaps the best part about this site is that it gives you a fabulous introduction into the world of the ActiveX capabilities of your Netscape Navigator. Using this site will be like running an application on your computer as if you had bought it and installed it on your system. It's a lot of fun. This is definitely something that would be a lot less enjoyable experience without your high-speed Erol's Internet service!

Jargon Cutter

ActiveX - New technology that merges the power of your computer with the Internet. ActiveX takes the Internet beyond static text and picture documents to give you a new generation of active, exciting and useful experiences. ActiveX lets Web developers build applications that offer enhanced functionality and productivity beyond basic HTML document sharing.

Games & Programs

The Internet has launched a revolution in the software industry. The industry has always been plagued with distribution problems. Traditional retailing methods—such as stores with boxed products on a shelf—have not applied well to selling software. It's sort of the equivalent of selling apples in shrink-wrapped boxes; you've got to pay for it without seeing it and you know that it began to spoil the moment it was boxed.

The Internet has solved many of the software industry's distribution problems. First, the products don't have to be sealed in shrink-wrapped boxes and shipped to stores to sit on shelves where they age. Instead, the Internet lets you go straight to the orchard, wander through the trees to see what you want and then pluck the freshest one and use it immediately.

Another benefit to cyber-software is that you can obtain upgrades on-line as well. Instead of waiting for an upgrade to come to your store, you can have it almost instantly. And, software companies that use the Internet for distribution have incentives to upgrade more often than when the products went through stores because the upgrade doesn't make obsolete all their existing stock.

Shareware

The Internet also has been a fabulous boon for the *shareware* industry. Shareware is software that you get to "try-before-you-buy." That means you can download it, install it and test it free. If you like the software and plan to use it, then you're expected to register with the author and pay a registration fee. It's a cool deal for you because you don't have to pay for software until you know that it works for you. And the shareware distribution system is so inexpensive that authors can offer software at very low prices.

Some shareware lets you download a full, working version right at the beginning. This means that they're really trusting the honor system because if you never contact them to pay, they'll never know the difference. We really encourage you to take the time to register because it's in everybody's interest to keep a steady flow of top-flight shareware on the Internet. Many shareware products, however, have "time-bombs" that will disable them after a trial period, which is usually 30 days. After the trial period, you can contact the author, pay a registration fee and get a code that will bring the software back to life.

One of the best shareware sources in the world is the C/NET Web site. Check them out by visiting *www.shareware.com* (see Figure 5). As this book was being written, they had 210,000 shareware titles and the number grows steadily.

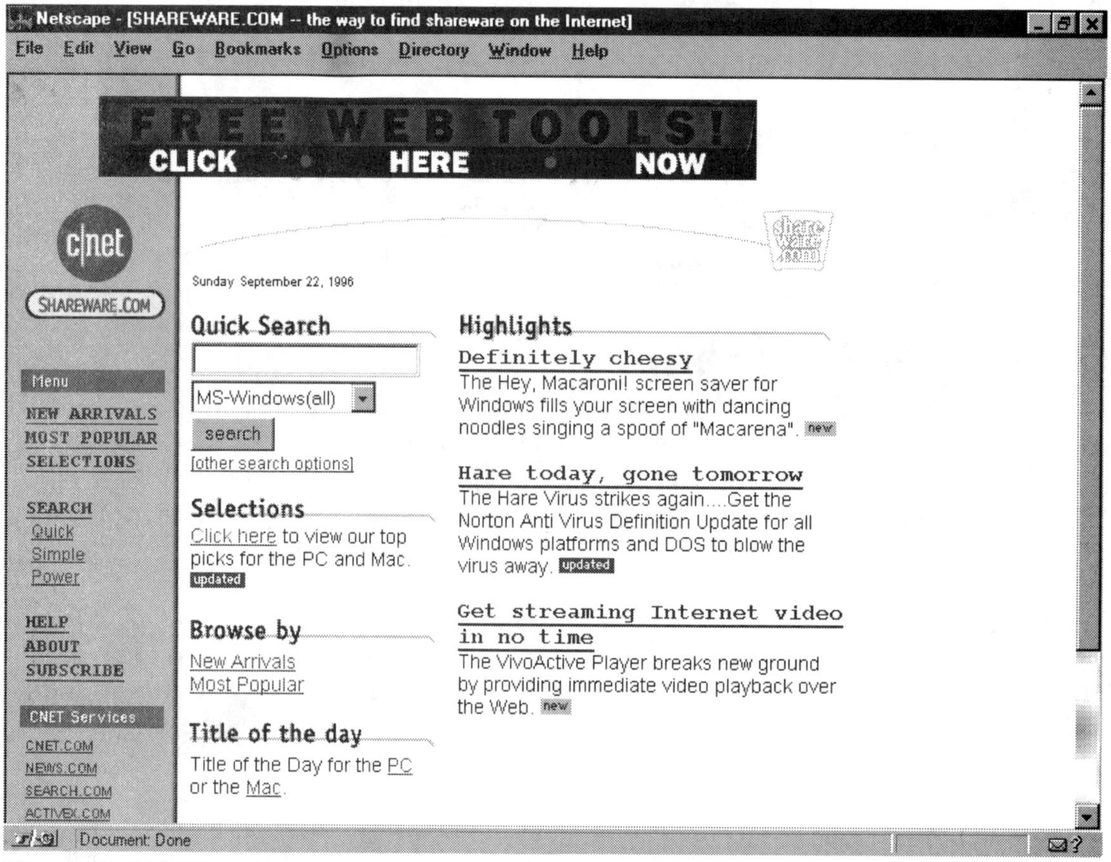

Figure 5 C/NET - More shareware than you can imagine!

This site will let you casually browse through the categories and titles and it lets you jump straight to an application by entering a keyword search. If you can't decide where to start, why not just select the "Title of the Day" and be surprised! This Web site is an excellent Bookmarks candidate because it can bail you out at those times when you need some software *today*!

Kids Shareware

Our previous selection certainly has enough shareware for everybody, but if you're looking for shareware for kids and don't want to tackle 210,000 titles, then try this site at *www.gamesdomain.com/tigger* (see Figure 6).

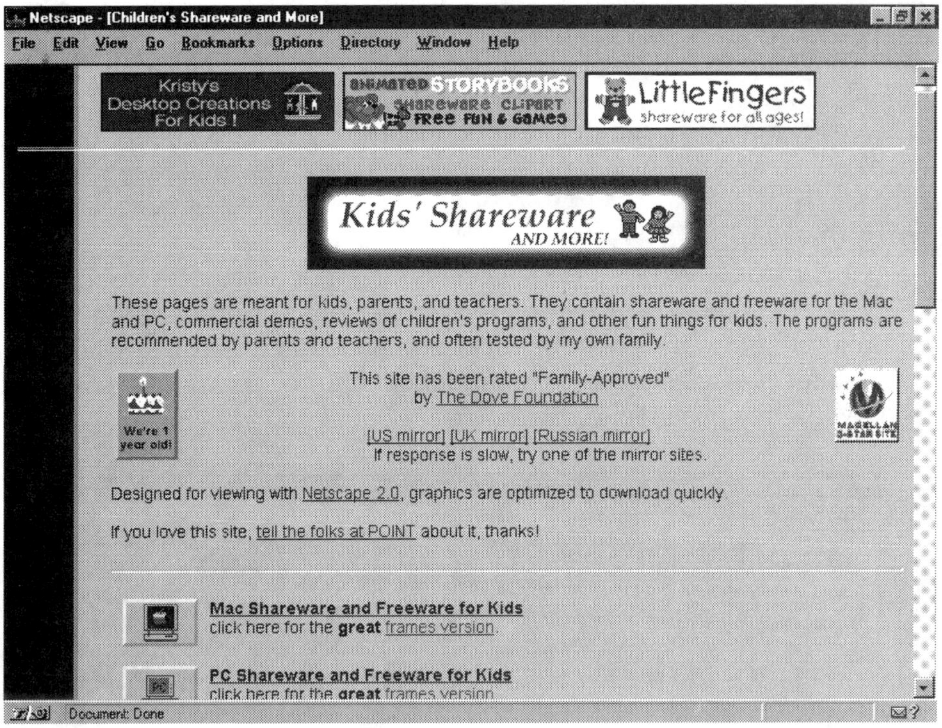

Figure 6 Kids' Shareware - For kids of all ages

At this site, you'll start by selecting a major category, such as "PC Shareware and Freeware for Kids" or "Commercial Demos." If you select the shareware links be sure to click on the "frames version" link because it's a very user-friendly interface. The page you get after you select the frames version (see Figure 7) is a likely candidate for your Bookmarks because you'll then be able to bypass the normal home page and jump straight to the frames page.

On the frames version, you can still get to the commercial demos by clicking on the "Demos" button. This a great resource for cyber-parents because they can evaluate software for their kids *before* they buy it at a store. It's not quite shareware, but it's better than a shrink-wrapped box on a store shelf. Cyber-parents will also find the reviews to be valuable. And it even includes the best reviews you can find on kids' software—the favorite software of the author's own kids!

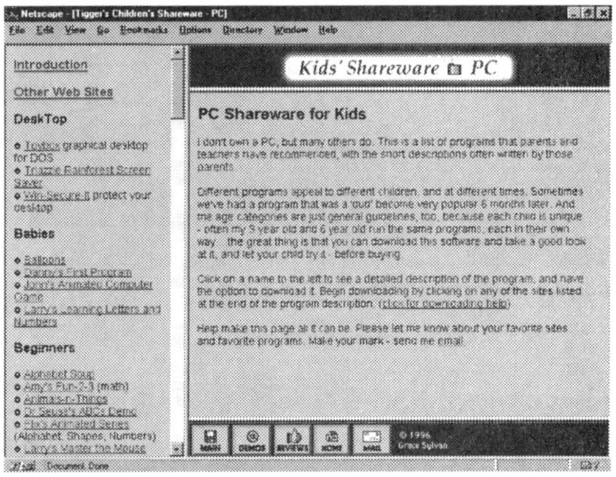

Figure 7 User-friendly frames version

Families

Okay, since we've started on the family idea, we won't stop now. Families have become a major force on the Internet. There are Web sites for just about every aspect of families and family life that you can imagine.

In this section, you'll discover organizations that scour the Internet looking for safe, wholesome family fun. You'll learn about software companies that can help you monitor your family's Internet usage and restrict certain types of content. And you'll find sites that serve as centers for family-oriented material. You'll even learn how to get a place in cyberspace for your own family—or even for you personally.

The Dove Organization

As you browse the Web looking at family sites, you might notice the seal of approval from The Dove Foundation (see Figure 8). They're a non-profit organization that encourages and promotes the creation, production and distribution of wholesome family entertainment. To learn what's behind that "Family Approved" seal, you can visit Dove's Web site at *www.dove.org*.

Figure 8 The Dove Foundation - Family approved Web sites

There's more here than just cyberspace help, too. Be sure to scroll down past this home page to the graphic image of their links. You then can click on any category that interests you.

In addition to helping you find wholesome Internet sites, the Dove Foundation has a rating list of more than 1,500 family-approved movies. This service is tied in with a video sales service they offer as well as a Children's Hospital movie channel. Their movie channel provides wholesome, uplifting movies to patients in every children's hospital in the U.S. and to their families staying in neighboring Ronald McDonald Houses. This entertainment is free to the patient and is shown on a dedicated channel on the TV in their rooms.

White House for Kids

One of the most popular attractions on the Internet is the famous White House Web site. If you haven't seen it, be sure to pay them a visit at *www.whitehouse.gov*. But few people who visit the White House Web site know that they've got a separate White House for Kids site at *www.whitehouse.gov/WH/kids/html/home.html*

That may be a long URL for kids to type, but you can put it in your Bookmarks and the kids can visit the White House with a mouse click. They'll be treated to a very kid-friendly interface (see Figure 9) that most kids can handle on their own. Of course parents will find plenty of interesting things to see and do here along with the kids, so browsing through it should be a nice family activity.

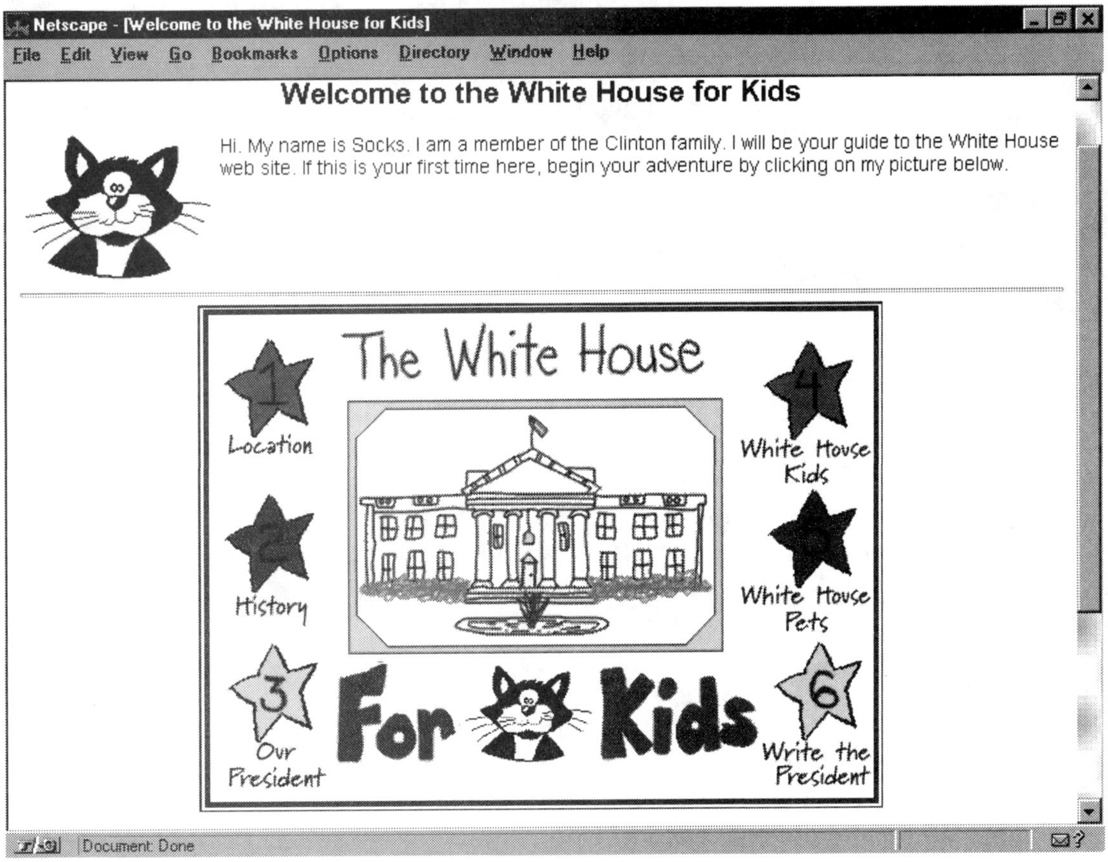

Figure 9 The White House for Kids - A special tour

The CyberMom

The Internet not only has sites just for kids, but it also has sites just for parents. Almost any modern-day mom with Internet service will enjoy the activities, news, chat rooms and reading material at *www.thecybermom.com* (see Figure 10).

The Web site is organized as a house with virtual rooms. You can run all over the house jumping from room-to-room—pretty much the way the kids do when they're home. But in this house you'll never trip over toys on the stairs! For starters, you can visit the virtual bedroom and go to the virtual night stand where you'll find reviews of some non-virtual books—that means *real* books.

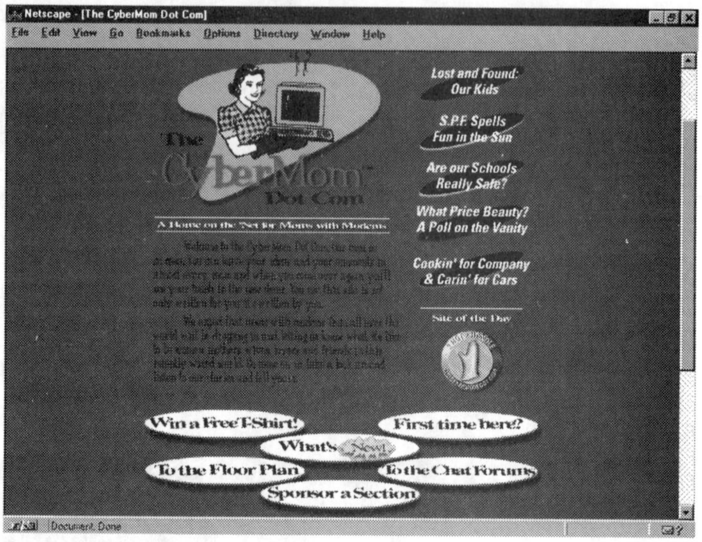

Figure 10 The CyberMom - Come on in and relax with some on-line friends

The Play Room includes reviews of children's movies, books and software. The Back Yard is a place to share gardening tips and the Kitchen is a wonderful exchange for recipes and cooking tips. And, throughout the house, you'll see coffee cup icons that link to related chat rooms in which you can discuss "mom" issues with other on-line women.

The CyberMom also is a good place for frequent visits because they have regular, on-going polls in which you can participate and share your own views. The site also features a selected Web site of the day that will give you an ever-expanding overview of other interesting information on the Web. If you save this site to your Bookmarks, be sure that you use the name *www.thecybermom.com* (remember the "the" at the beginning.)

Family PC Fun

Here's a Web site that blends the old with the new. Family PC Fun is a Sunday comic strip that helps families find fun things to do together on the Internet. The thinking behind it is that computers have separated families because people tend to use computers alone. But Family PC Fun creates shared cyber-experiences. To see what all the fun is about, visit *www.FamilyPCfun.com* (see Figure 11).

Family PC Fun is a good resource for parental guidance on kids in cyberspace. It also includes links to many other family sites, including family newsgroups. Each week, they have a new Featured Family that showcases one of the top Web sites created jointly by a family. Take a look at what other families are putting on-line and then submit your own family's site—maybe your name will be in the Sunday comics!

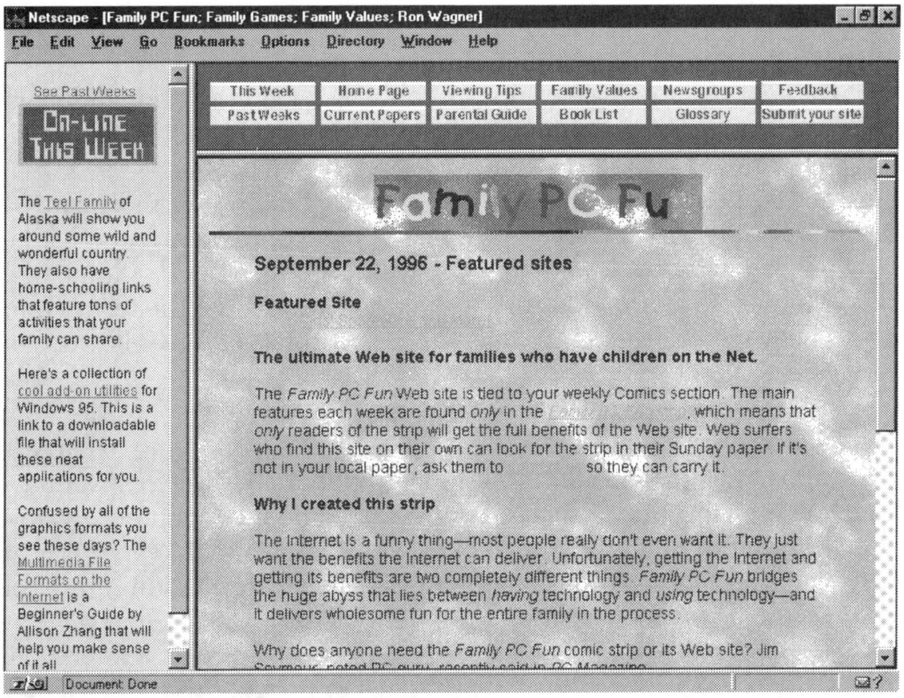

Figure 11 Family PC Fun - shared cyberspace fun and activities

Family PC Fun has some nice bonuses, too. For example, it includes valuable pointers for configuring your Windows and your Web browser for maximum viewing enjoyment. And it has perhaps the most user-friendly Internet glossary of terms.

Families in Yahoo!

If you want to create a family Web site, here's another place where you can find examples from other families. Of course, the list here hasn't been screened as it has with the Family PC Fun Featured Family sites, so be prepared for just about anything!

Once you've launched your family into cyberspace orbit, be sure to submit it to Yahoo! so other families can find your site. Submitting your site is very easy. Once you've got your URL, just visit the Yahoo! family page by jumping to *www.yahoo.com* and then going to Entertainment:People:Families. When you get to that page, click on the Submit button and follow the instructions.

Within a few weeks of submitting your family's Web site, anyone on the Internet will be able to go to Yahoo! and find you just by entering your name. On page 156, we'll show you some services that can automate the indexing process.

New Frontiers

The Internet has opened a communications channel that permits each of us to find something interesting, something valuable or something special. Any topic that can be imagined can now have a Web site and reach the world. A whole new frontier of information has opened up for highly-specialized and narrowly-focused topics. We'll close this chapter with a glimpse at three examples, just to give you an idea of what's out there on the cutting edge of originality.

Breathing Space

Before they were 24, your grandparents probably had acquired enough knowledge or training to make a good living their entire lives. Such a deal is not available to you.

The volume of new knowledge disseminated in every field is enormous and easily exceeds anyone's ability to keep pace. As a result, everyone today fears that he/she is increasingly under-informed despite absorbing an unprecedented volume of information. The volume of information that spewed forth to spawn the term "Information Age" is dwarfed by what's happening today. The Information Age—if it was ever here—is long dead.

You now live in the Over-Information Age and the Internet is going to carry it into your life faster than ever. The Internet is going to put at your fingertips more information than you ever imagined existed. You will become more acutely aware of an ever-increasing number of topics and areas in which you cannot keep up. Fortunately, you need not become a victim of the Over-Information Age—you can now have some Breathing Space (see Figure 12) by visiting *www.brespace.com*.

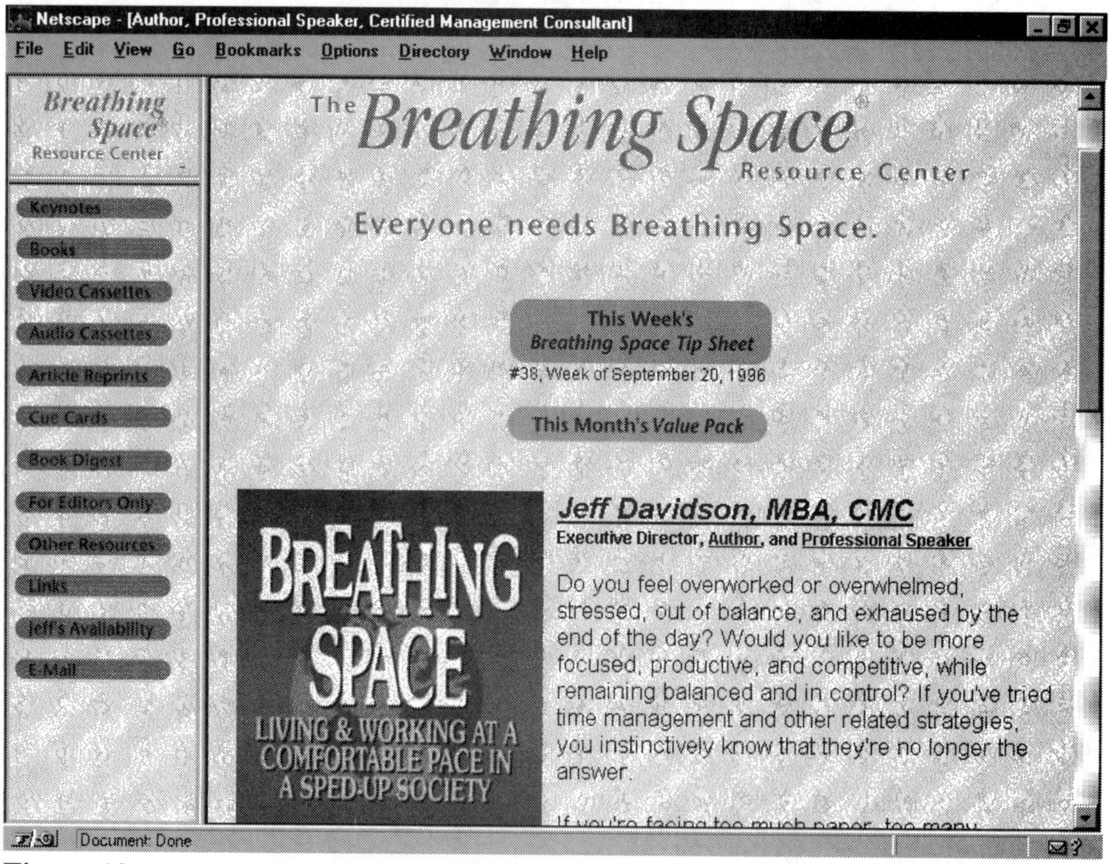

Figure 12 Breathing Space - Take a respite from the Over-Information crunch

The material on this Web site is derived from a variety of resources produced by Jeff Davidson, the Executive Director of the Breathing Space Institute. Jeff is a popular speaker and the author of *Breathing Space: Living and Working at a Comfortable Pace in a Sped-up Society* (MasterMedia).

Intentional Communities

After reading about the Breathing Space principles, this may be exactly the site you need. It's devoted to the "intentional communities" that are springing up all over the world (see Figure 13). The idea behind an intentional community is that most of us live in communities that have more or less just "happened," but intentional communities are built from the ground up with a specific purpose. For example, some of the purposes they list are: ecovillages, co-housing, land trusts, communes, student co-ops, urban housing cooperatives and other related projects and dreams.

If you're interested in learning more, go visit the Web site at *www.well.com/user/cmty*. Only a couple of years ago, communities such as these were impractical because most peoples' livelihood depended on the business concentration found in large cities. But the Internet has created the possibility of earning a living anywhere in the world. Demographic studies have noted a shift in living patterns in the U.S. The result has been a slowing of growth and sometimes even a decline in the populations of large cities, with a corresponding growth in the populations of smaller towns and new, intentional communities.

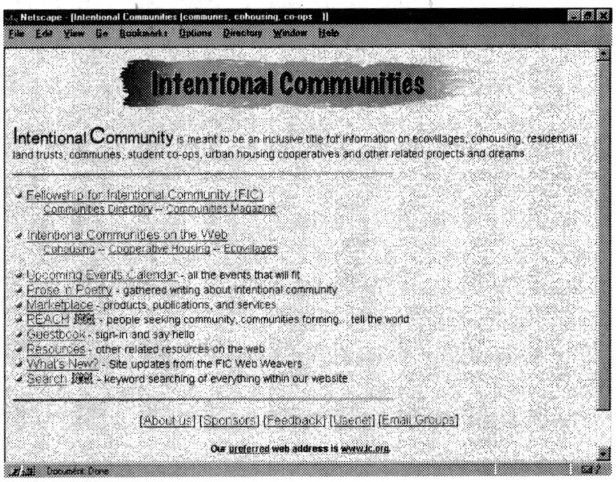

Figure 13 Intentional Communities - The solution to finding Breathing Space?

The Starbuck Net

We'll close now with a Web site that lets you go even farther than a new community. At the Starbuck Net, there are no limits. Not even the sky! The Starbuck Net Web site is at *www.starbuck.net* (see Figure 14). It's been created by Dr. Henry Reed, one of the world's leading experts on dream research. We're not talking about clinical dream laboratories here, though. Henry was a pioneer in the earliest dream labs at Princeton University, but abandoned the formal academic research to pursue a practical, hands-on approach to dreams.

So, while you'll see some advanced Web features, this site isn't about technology. It's a rich repository of dream research, dreams, and a lot of other topics that are reaching out into new frontiers for humankind. It surely fits in, then, with all the changes we're experiencing as the world's social paradigms change almost weekly.

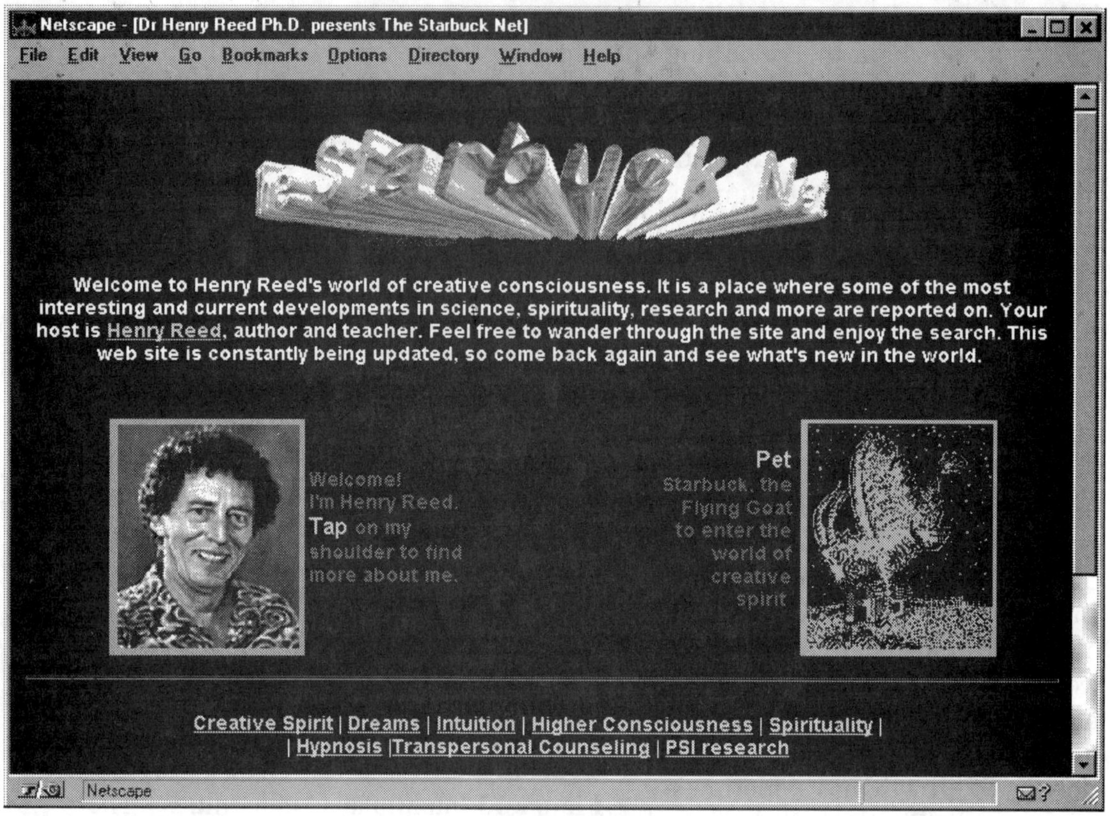

Figure 14 The Starbuck Net - The place of your dreams... literally

The Internet, of course, is a major factor in all of these changes. We hope you've enjoyed our brief overview of these examples of interesting Web sites. There's more out there than you can imagine, and we know you didn't get Erol's Internet service to see Web sites that someone else selects for you. Fortunately, the Internet itself has tools that help you locate exactly what you want from the mass of over-information. Move on with us now to the next chapter and we'll show you how to find what you want, when you want it.

10

Finding Your Way: Internet Searches

We wanted to start this chapter by telling you that the Web was growing like... but, what? We couldn't think of a metaphor to describe it because nothing has ever grown like the Web. Then we got it: the Web *is* the metaphor. Someday, we might say that something else is growing like the Web. But for now, *nothing* has ever grown like the Web since the Big Bang. Hey, that's it: "the Web is the Big Bang of cyberspace!"

Just as the Big Bang created too many stars to count, the Web has created too many documents to count. Fortunately, you're not going to need to count Web documents because a major part of the Web explosion has been Web searching services that can help you find the *stars* in cyberspace.

These Web searching services are called search engines and before long we might not even be able to count their number. The reasons for their phenomenal growth is no surprise because people are drawn to sites that deliver value and Web search engines are the most valuable sites on the Web.

Without search engines the Web would be like a phone system that had neither telephone books nor directory assistance—you would only be able to use a site if someone gave you its location. But with search engines you can locate Web documents based on keywords or topics that interest you. They're like a phone book, directory assistance, library card files and Sherlock Holmes all rolled into one.

Search engine principles

Web search engines are almost too powerful for their own good—or for your own good. You are unlikely to ever have a problem finding *something* on a given topic, but you may have a lot of trouble sifting through what you find to get *something you need*. There are tricks to using the search engines that will greatly enhance your success at locating targeted information.

We'll look first at how Web search engines work. Then we'll move on to some searching tricks that will hone the accuracy of the searches you perform. Next, we'll give you some tips on helping your clients, customers and prospects find your site. Then we'll close with an overview of some of the best search engines on the Web.

Inside Info

Metasearch - Web sites that are made up of links to a wide variety of Web search engines. Some of them are no more than a collection of search engine links and some are actually interactive and will simultaneously submit your search request to several Web searching services. See page 163 for more on metasearch.

How search engines work

All search engines are based on computer-indexed information. Using a variety of methods, search engine developers gather information from around the Web and then store it and index it. Web search engines use two different, basic approaches that enable you to locate the information they have indexed.

One approach presents a list of categories. These categories are broken down first by major topic and then each major topic is broken down into an increasingly detailed hierarchy of subtopics. The search service lets you browse through its topical index to see the Web documents it has stored. Of course you have to guess the category under which your information might be located. Since there are no standards for dividing information into categories, you might have difficulty guessing the category under which the site's managers stored the information you want.

The second approach lets you perform a keyword search on the engine's indexed documents. This means that the search engine will give you a list of documents that contain a keyword, or keywords, that you specified. Since keyword searches don't rely on categories, they produce documents from a wide variety of topics—many of which may have nothing to do with the information you were seeking. Keyword searches are based on *boolean logic*.

Boolean Logic

Boolean logic is a mathematical system consisting of a set of elements and operators that specify relationships between the individual elements. The system was devised in 1854 by the Irish mathematician George Boole. Internet search engines use three important Boolean operators: AND, OR and NOT.

These operators are important tools for you in using search engines because they can be used to widen searches or narrow searches to get the results you need. We'll illustrate their use with the three words, "hot air balloon."

Using AND

If you wanted to find hot air balloon sites on the Web, you actually need to search for documents that contain all three words "hot" and "air" and "balloon." Otherwise your search would produce a huge list of documents that contained any one of those words. The words could be entered as "hot AND air AND balloon" but most sites assume the AND operator if you don't specify anything between words. In other words, a space is an AND operator. Some search engines use a "+" symbol instead of the word AND.

Using OR

Since AND is the default for most sites, if you actually wanted to find pages that had any one of those words, you would have to enter "hot OR air OR balloon." But stand back if you do because the list might melt down your PC. You'd be getting every indexed document that contained the word "hot" or that contained the word "air" or that contained the word "balloon." Can you imagine the number?

Using NOT

The NOT operator can be used to eliminate pages that contain a certain word. For example, if you searched for "hot AND air NOT balloon" you would get just the "hot air" Congressional sites in Washington because all of the "hot air" sites that also contained the word "balloon" would be eliminated.

Read the directions

For the best search success, you need to know the default Boolean operator for the engine you're using. For example, if you enter *hot air balloon*, most sites use AND between the words, thus giving the highest priority to documents that contain all three words. But some will treat each word separately unless you use *hot AND air AND balloon*. And others might require you to enter the words in quotation marks, *"hot air balloon."* There's no substitute for reading the directions to be sure of the rules and the tricks. In fact, many of the engines, such as Lycos, jump you to a user-friendly screen that can greatly increase your search accuracy with little extra effort.

Improving your search success

In addition to using Boolean logic in your searches, some search engines let you specify wildcards, similar to the wildcards you use in DOS filenames. For example, you could use "hot air balloon*" to find "hot air balloon," "hot air balloons," and "hot air ballooning." That's a very simple example, but wildcards can spell the difference between quick success and nagging frustration if you aren't sure how to spell a word.

Jargon Cutter

Wildcards - Symbols that can substitute for other characters. The asterisk (*) usually represents zero or more characters and the question mark (?) usually represents a single character.

Wildcards can also be valuable in searching for someone by name. For example, if you were trying to find Peter A. Russell, the author of the book *The Global Brain*, you could search for "Pete* Russell" to find strings that begin with "Pete," have any number of characters in between (including zero) and that end with "Russell."

Another tool is the substring search. A substring is a portion of text that's contained within a longer string. Fortunately, most search engines automatically look for substrings. In the Peter Russell example, looking for "Pete Russell" would find pages with "Peter" and "Russell" because "Pete" is a substring of "Peter."

A few sites allow "natural language" searches. These are convenient and require the least thought, but then again, the results they produce may be less accurate. An example of a natural language search could be "I want to find all of the sites that talk about hot air balloons." The search engine would use a pre-programmed set of rules to eliminate the words it found to be extraneous and then search on the remaining words. You can't be sure, however, which words will be stripped and which will be included in the search.

Helping others find your page

If you create your own Web site, which we'll show you how to do in a later chapter, it's important to tailor your Web pages so that others can more easily find your site when they're using a search engine. You can find lots of examples of what *not* to do. One lousy example is making the title of your Web page "Welcome to Our Home Page!" But that's a perfect title if you want to attract visitors who've gone hunting for "Welcome" or "Home Page."

Create an accurate title

The title of your Web page doesn't have to be pretty. It's only going to show up in the title bar at the top of your browser's screen. The words in the title are going to be indexed into the search engines. But many Web sites waste the power of the title by using something nondescript. If you create a Web page—especially if it's for a home-based business or for your family—be sure to include a good selection of keywords that other people might use if they wanted to find something that you've included on your site. You've got only about a dozen words or so, so use them wisely.

Submitting Your Own Site

There are two ways to submit your own URLs to search engines so other people can find your site. First, you can physically go around to every search engine with which you want to be listed and look for their submission link. Second, you can visit a comprehensive submission Web site that handles multiple submissions to most of the Web's best-known search engines.

Each method has its own edge. The advantage of using a submission service is obvious: you use a one-stop, time-saving site that minimizes your workload. The advantage to doing it yourself is more subtle: you get to be more careful that your site is indexed in the best category and that your listing is consistent with the pattern of other listings on that service.

We suggest that you try one or two manually to get the idea of how your listing looks after it's been indexed. You may be surprised by the keywords that are featured or by the title. You can't control the search engine, but you can control your pages. If you're not happy with the early results, delete the experimental listings, edit your Web pages, then resubmit and check the results after they have been indexed. After a few of these experiments you'll have a better idea of whether to do the rest of them yourself or use a consolidated service. In either case, you'll have refined the indexing ability of your pages.

Submit It!

This is a completely free submission service, supported by paid advertising, that handles all of the major search engines. You can visit it at *www.submit-it.com* (see Figure 1). While you're there, you can test their metasearch engine.

> **The PostMaster**
> Try the PostMaster at *www.netcreations.com/postmaster*, another submission service. Before completing the lengthy submission form, be sure to read the FAQ file. This is intended to be a fee-based service, though they do allow some "Try Before You Buy" experimenting. But if you don't follow their terms when you post your free submission, they say they'll bill you for the full fee.

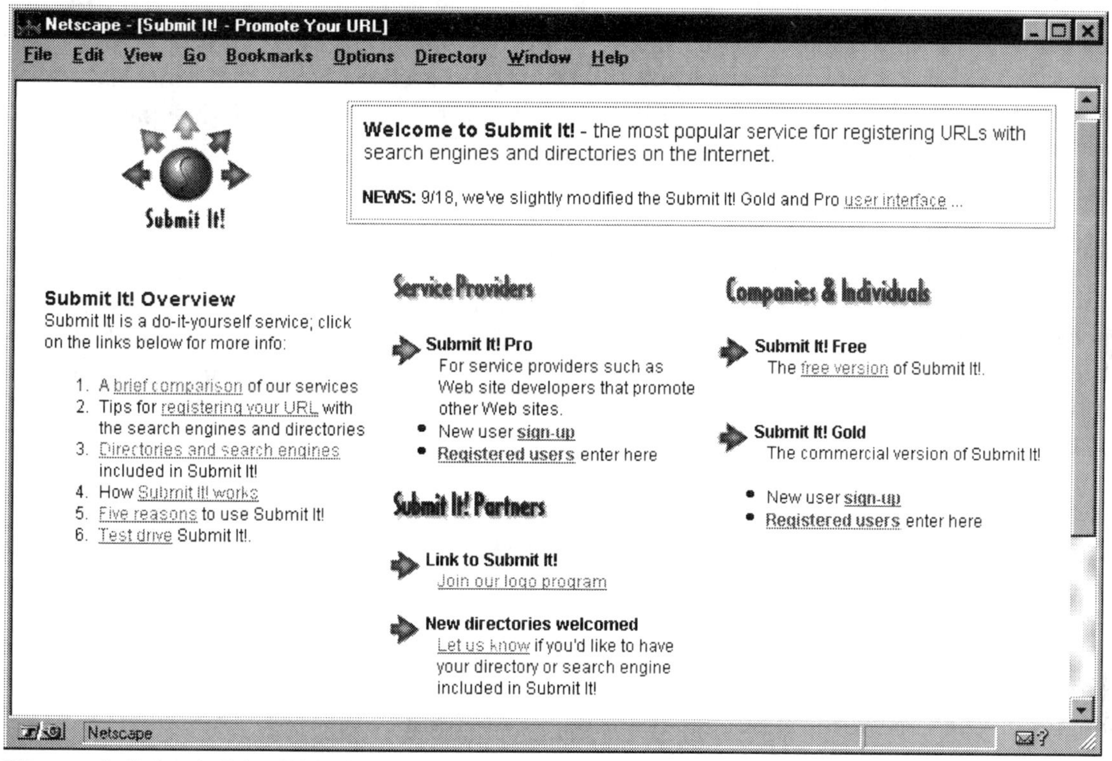

Figure 1 Submit It! will help you get your own Web site noticed on the Web

Keywords

Make sure that your Web site has some appropriate keywords near the top of the home page. Some search engines score documents by the location of the keywords. If a keyword is found high in your home page, that word will generate a higher score than if the same word were buried deep within some linked sub-documents on your site.

Choose categories carefully

Finally, one important key to successfully being found can lie in going into each site individually to submit your page. By browsing the site thoroughly you can learn the most appropriate heading under which to place your site's URL. And you can learn if the engine allows you to submit multiple headings. Yahoo! is an excellent example. It allows you to list under multiple headings and it's got so many headings that you have to be careful to choose the ones you expect your visitors to try.

Web search engines

There are two categories of Web search services: free and commercial. Consider using both types when you're searching as well as when you're submitting your own pages for indexing. While commercial services charge for performing searches, neither type usually charges you to submit your site for indexing.

The free services are much like broadcast television networks. Most of them include paid advertising (like NBC or Fox) and some of them are public services (like PBS stations) that are funded by corporations or universities. And, as with broadcast television, you can ignore the ads and use only the search tools. The commercial services are much like premium cable channels and come in two varieties: pay-per-search and monthly subscription.

Free search services

The Web's free search services come in two basic categories: search engines and metasearch services. The search engines are actual indexing computer systems that seek out data on the Web, index it, catalog it and serve it up to users as requested. A metasearch search service taps into multiple search engines so your query will check a broader range of sources. First we'll cover a few popular search engines and then profile one metasearch service.

Yahoo!

If you've read *Gulliver's Travels*, you've got to wonder why anyone would name themselves after the despicable Yahoos that Gulliver encountered, especially since this Yahoo! is so delightful (see Figure 2). Yahoo! offers two searching options on its home page. You can use a keyword search or you can browse through its listing by category.

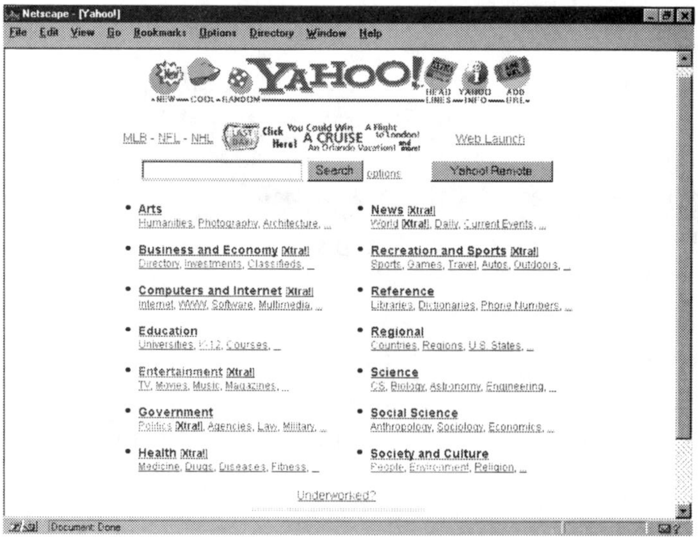

Figure 2 One of the busiest Web sites in the world

Keyword searches are the best choice when you've got some sites in mind, such as "hot air balloon races." But those sites would be difficult to find if you browsed under headings. Under which heading would you expect to find hot air balloon races?

On the other hand, you might want to find pages that deal with a general topic, such as politics. If you performed a keyword search for "politics" you'd get every indexed page that contained that word. That would be gross overwhelm. But worse, it's entirely possible for an important article about politics to *not* contain the word politics.

Fortunately, Yahoo! gives you both options right up front. But there's more. The top of the Yahoo! page has links to pages that give you "New," "Cool" and "Headlines." These links will help you skip past the old stuff. And if you're just bored some night and want to read something about anything, you can spend the evening sipping Jolt Cola, eating Twinkies and clicking on links under the "Random" link. Good luck!

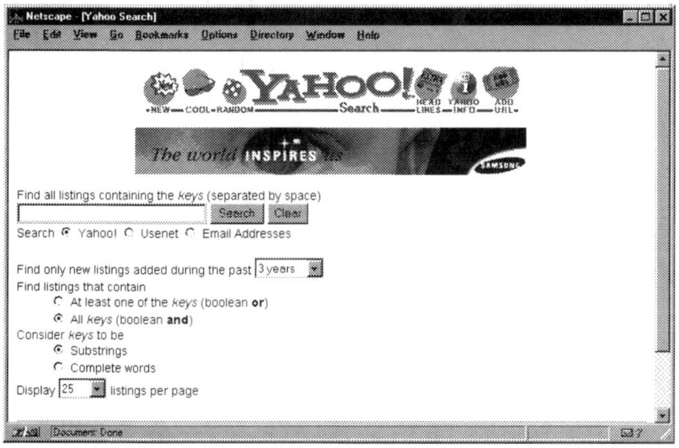

Figure 3 Yahoo! search options page

Yahoo! also has a special page that lets you refine your search request (see Figure 3). Unfortunately, the path to this special page changes periodically. For a while there was a link called "Options" right next to the text entry box. As this book was written, that link had been replaced with another cool link, outlined below, and the "Options" button was gone. You can always get to the options help by clicking on "Search" with the text entry box blank. Yahoo! will display a link entitled "More..." that leads to a screen with the "Options" link next to the "Search" button.

This page gives you the ability to choose between searching either the Web or newsgroups for your keywords. You also can specify to use the OR operator and force a search for whole words instead of substrings. The bottom of each Yahoo! page also has links to other popular Web search engines. If you click on those links Yahoo! automatically enters your last search request and takes you to the new search engine's home page.

DejaNews

DejaNews is a search engine for Usenet newsgroups. Even though it's a Web site, DejaNews has archived millions of Usenet postings. And it's even become a link within Yahoo! from which you can jump directly to DejaNews, or you can click on DejaNews after performing a normal Yahoo! search and apply your latest search criteria to a newsgroup search. DejaNews builds a list for you of articles it pulls from its archives.

Yahoo! Remote

Yahoo! offers a special feature that, so far, is unique among search engines. It's called "Yahoo! Remote" and it's a miniature version of your Web browser that contains only the Yahoo! search engine (see Figure 4). Once you activate Yahoo! Remote, it stays in a separate window that can float around on top of the screen of any application. For example, you could place it on top of WordPerfect for Windows so that you could see a document and Yahoo! Remote at the same time. This might make it easier for you to search for keywords in the document you're writing. With Yahoo! Remote active, you can switch between Remote and any other application using **ALT+TAB**.

Finally, don't overlook the "Add URL" button at the top of the Yahoo! main screen. You can use it to add your own Web site to Yahoo! so that other Web surfers can find you.

Figure 4 Yahoo! Remote

The key to adding a URL is first to navigate to a category that is a logical choice for your own home page before you click on the link. When you're in the right place, clicking on it will start the Yahoo! procedure to add your page to that Yahoo! category. But be patient, because you can expect a delay of one to three weeks before your links appear under the category.

Lycos

What is it with these search engine names? After Yahoo!, you get to see another service named after a rather unpleasant creature, Lycos, named for some wild jungle spider. The tie-in to the Web probably made sense at some late night session. Oh well, a Lycos by any other name will still search as fast (see Figure 5).

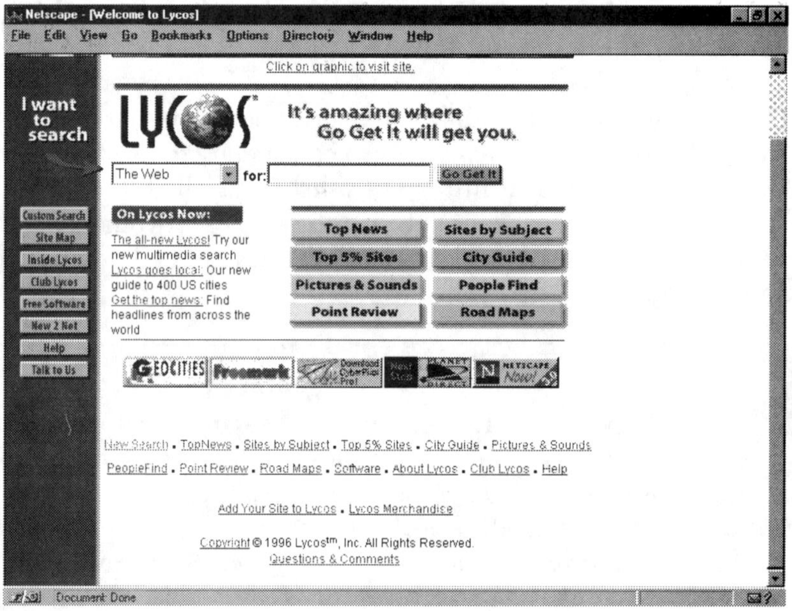

Figure 5 Find more than you'll ever need with the Lycos search engine

Lycos has a limited set of categories on its home page as well as the keyword search entry box. Lycos displays search results quite differently from Yahoo! It lists all documents that contain *any* or *all* of your keywords. In effect, it gives you both an AND search and an OR search.

The AND results are presented first and include a score that's derived from how and where those words appear within the listed page. The highest score would go to a document in which all three keywords were present near the top of the document. The score drops as the words get more separated and farther into the document. Of course the score also drops on documents that contain only *some* or *one* of your keywords.

In addition to keyword searches, Lycos lets you search the Web by subject. To use this feature, click on the "Sites by Subject" button on the Lycos home page. But if you plan to use this feature regularly, you might want to set the URL as a Bookmark so you can jump directly to it, instead of having to visit the normal Lycos home page first. The direct URL is: *a2z.lycos.com* (see Figure 6).

Figure 6

OpenText

OpenText has perhaps the most user-friendly main screen of any of the services. Its catalog is not as extensive as some of the larger services, but you nonetheless may achieve better overall results because of its interface (see Figure 7). For example, some searches in the OpenText service list nothing more than references it finds in the Yahoo! index. Still, it's a good service, so let's look at how those optional drop lists can help you:

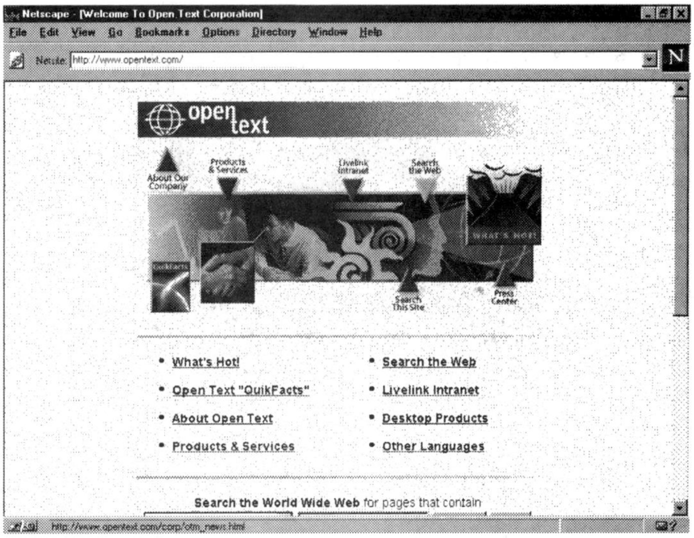

Figure 7 OpenText, home of the Livelink spider

- ❖ Search for your keywords anywhere in the document, or within the summary, the title, the first heading or the URL;
- ❖ Narrow the search with AND, OR, BUT NOT, NEAR or FOLLOWED BY.

You are supposed to enter only one word or phrase per text entry box and then separate multiple words or phrases with the drop-list operators. If you're looking for a phrase you must enclose all of the words in quotation marks. OpenText also is the name of the company behind this site. They produce Web software such as Livelink Spider, the Web crawler software behind the OpenText free Internet search service.

AltaVista

At the beginning of this chapter, we said that nothing has ever grown like the World Wide Web—the Web is now a metaphor for other fast-growing things. We've included this search engine (*www.altavista.digital.com*) because its appearance confirms our statement about the Web's astonishing growth (see Figure 8).

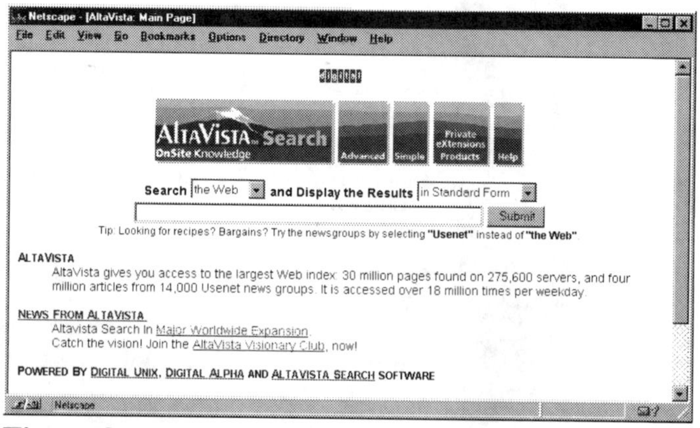

Figure 8 Part of the Big Bang of cyberspace

Digital Research Labs in Palo Alto, California began the AltaVista project in the summer of 1995. After two months of internal testing, they had produced an index consisting of the full text of more than 16 million pages. They made the site public on December 15, 1995. Within three weeks, AltaVista was servicing more than two million search requests per day. Within two months it was receiving more than five million daily search requests on its index of more than 21 million pages—an incredible total of ten billion words!

Behind The Scenes

Have you ever wondered what kind of computers it takes to handle more than five million search requests per day and to store ten billion words in more than 21 million document pages? Here's a summary of the equipment that's working behind the scenes when you ask AltaVista to help you out:

- AlphaStation 250 4/266, 256 MB memory, 4 GB disk. Two AlphaStations handle all external traffic to the site and run a custom, multi-threaded Web server that sends queries to the Web indexer and News indexer.
- AlphaServer 8400 5/300, 10 processors, 6 GB memory, 210 GB RAID 5 disk. Two of these—the most powerful computers ever built by Digital—handle Web indexing and the query engine. The Alta Vista Web index is larger than 30 gigabytes, but most requests take less than a second.
- AlphaStation 250 4/266, 196 MB memory, 13 GB disk. This machine indexes newsgroups. This is an extremely busy machine because of the furious pace at which new articles appear and old articles expire.
- AlphaStation 400 4/233, 160 MB memory, 24 GB RAID 5 disks. This machine maintains a news spool for the news indexer and serves the news articles via http to users who want to read Usenet news.

- DEC 3000/900 Alpha Workstation, 1 GB memory, 30 GB RAID 5 disk. The super-spider runs from this machine, fetching pages from the Web and sending them to the Web indexer.

Oh, don't be so impressed. In a few years, your kids will be using PCs bigger, better and faster than these and they won't believe that back in "the old days" the entire Web could be indexed on one of these puny little things.

The AltaVista engine has some powerful Boolean logic capability built-in. And they even give you a sample of how to write it. For example, they say that to find a bedtime story you could enter: "fairy tale" +frog -dragon. That means that you're looking for documents that contain the *phrase* "fairy tale" and that also contain the *word* "frog," but that *do not* contain the *word* "dragon."

All-In-One

All-In-One search is a metasearch service. It doesn't actually perform the search, but passes off your query to any one of a long list of actual search engines. This is a wonderful feature for checking the broadest possible set of resources. There are several on the Web, but we've chosen this one because it's highly-rated and the way they've broken down the categories gives it a user-friendly interface (see Figure 9). It's located at *www.albany.net/allinone*.

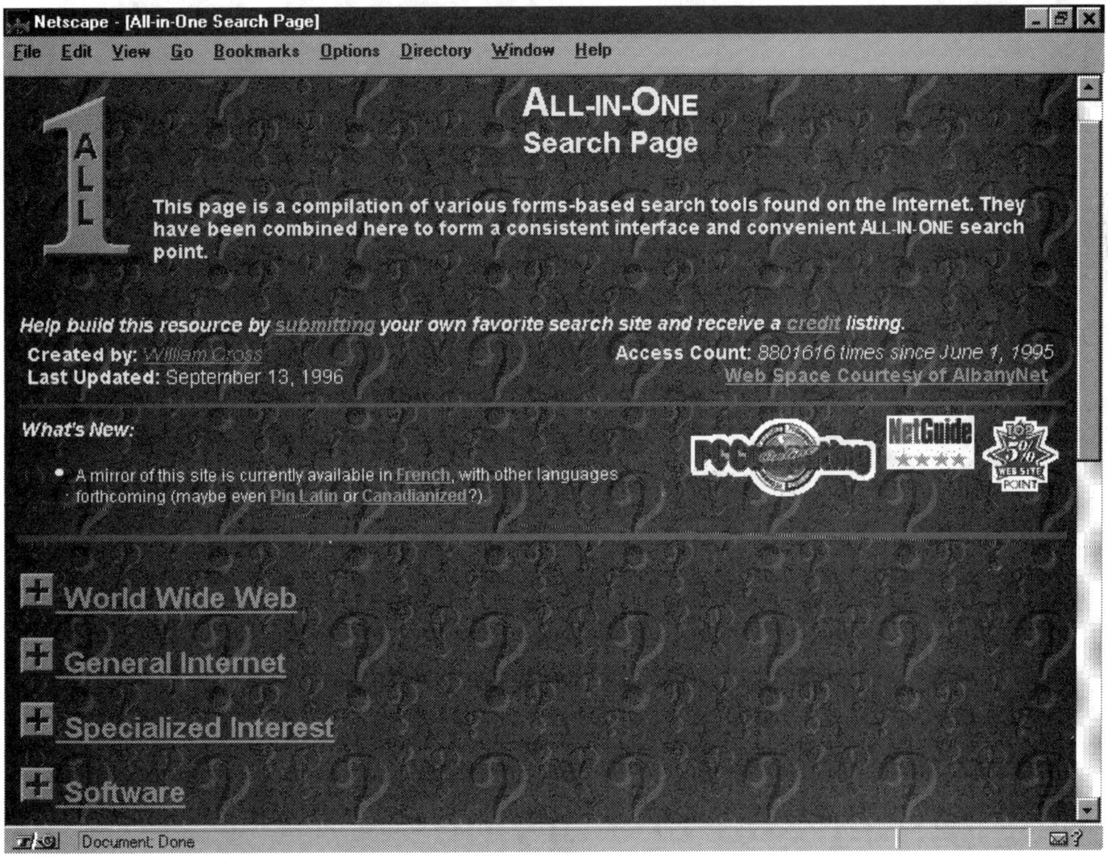

Figure 9 Try an Internet metasearch engine

As you can see in this screen shot, All-In-One lists major search topics such as World Wide Web, General Interest and Specialized Interest. Beyond this page lie options to search these categories: Software, People, News/Weather, Publications/Literature, Technical Reports, Documentation, Desk Reference and Other Interesting Searches/Services.

All-In-One's ease of use lies in the "plus" signs that precede each heading. When you click on a plus sign, the heading's category expands and all of the related searching services under it are displayed (see Figure 10). In this example, the World Wide Web plus sign was clicked. On this screen, you can fill in your query and click the Search button. All-In-One will then submit your search to that service. Clicking on a minus sign will collapse the category back down to just a heading.

We'll close this section on free search services with a reminder to browse through the Orbiting in Cyberspace section at the end of this chapter. It can lead you to many more sites, including other metasearch sites such as C/Net's site at *www.search.com*, which is a large collection of Web searching services.

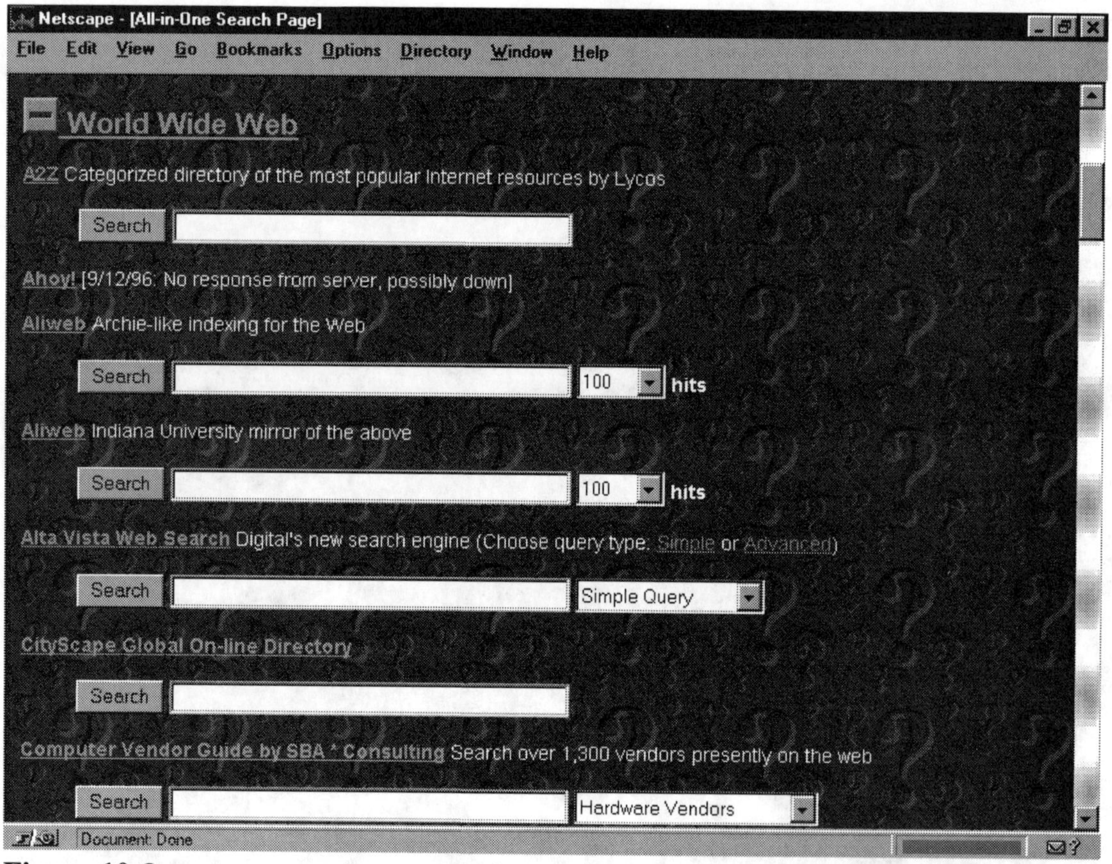

Figure 10 One screen—and more search engines than you'll ever need

Commercial search services

We've included two commercial services because each offers a completely different approach to searching for information. The first, NLightN, is a super-set indexer that dwarfs even the large search engines such as Lycos. The second is the famous encyclopedia Britannica, but now in an on-line version. Both sites charge a usage fee, but Britannica sticks to its own internal information while NLightN includes references from all over cyberspace.

NLightN

If you need in-depth research instead of "hits" on a free search list, then try the most comprehensive information on the Internet: NLightN at *www.nlightn.com* (see Figure 11). It's touted as, "...the Web's largest library of meaningful information. It is the fast and easy way to find anything you want to know."

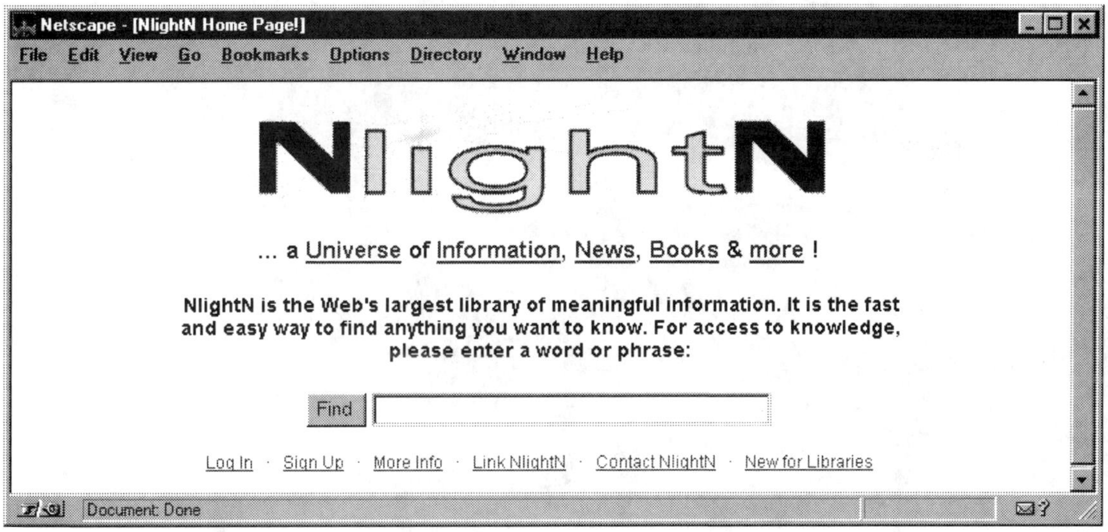

Figure 11 Lycos is just a small subset to the massive NLightN information service

If you think Lycos is comprehensive, prepare to be dazzled—or overwhelmed. NLightN is so vast that Lycos is a subset and provides only about five percent of the information resources that NLightN has indexed. In other words, the NLightN index lets you search a universal index that's 20 times as large as Lycos! It includes 10 million books; 1 million dissertations; 1 million patents; hundreds of thousands of wire service records from more than 20 wire services; tens of millions of journal articles; book, movie and audio-visual reviews; informal and formal searches of the full-text of encyclopedias, dictionaries and standard reference works.

NLightN is a fee-based service and you'll have to sign up for a membership. Pricing is transaction-based, rather than per-minute, with charges as low as ten cents. You'll pay only for information you request when you click on a BUY or ORDER button. NLightN content providers set the price and that price is always shown, so you know the cost before you spend any money.

The resources listed represent the best reference sources in the world, such as: Library of Congress, National Library of Medicine, British Library, Cambridge Scientific Abstracts, ABI/INFORM, SPORT Database, Merriam-Webster, Film Literature Index, Magazine Articles Summary, Reader's Guide to Periodic Literature, U.S. Patents, Dissertation Abstracts and many others. In addition to archived information, NLightN provides full-text indexing of newswire services, including Knight-Ridder, PR Newswire, Sports Wire and Investment Wire.

Britannica Online

Britannica Online brings a venerable reference source out of the libraries and onto your computer screen (see Figure 12). It's priced a bit steep—actually by today's Web standards, it's priced in the stratosphere. But this is an extensive, highly-respected reference work that lets you cut and paste the articles you find and download the pictures. Plus you won't have to pack a huge multi-volume encyclopedia set when you move, and it will never go out of date.

Figure 12 A research classic, now available on-line, anywhere in the world

This service is offered for home, business or academic use. The annual subscription price for home use is US $150 per year, plus a one-time, non-refundable registration fee of US $25. The annual subscription price for business use is US $300 per year, plus a one-time, non-refundable registration fee of US $50, for *each* single user. The single-user academic fee is US $120 per year with no registration fee. Site licenses are available for multi-user corporate and academic environments, but you'll have to inquire via this site for rates.

Britannica Online offers a free 7-day trial period that will give you a temporary login ID and a password. Just visit the home page at *www.eb.com* and complete the instructions. Be careful that you don't accidentally sign up for the full service because the registration fees are non-refundable! Signing up is a two-step process that only takes a couple of minutes:

- ❖ First, click on Step 1, complete the form and submit it. They will e-mail you a validation code that will be in your mailbox in a minute or two.
- ❖ Get the code from the e-mail message, return to your Netscape Navigator, then complete Step 2. You only need the validation code once, but you *must* carefully record the user name they assign and remember your password.

After this, you'll have full access to the entire site. You'll have to spend some time with it during this short trail period to see if it's worth the resources you can locate.

Commentary on Web searching

Browsing through the Britannica Online site can be an interesting illustration of the diversity of the Web. There is definitely an eclectic mish-mash of information on the Web. For example, let's discuss searching both Britannica and Lycos for "Carl Jung" to compare the findings. Naturally Britannica Online has excellent references, ten of them, in fact. And they are informative and well-written.

But then you can jump over to Lycos and search the Web for references to the most famous native of Switzerland. The differences are startling. Where Britannica had found ten nice, clean articles, Lycos pulled from cyberspace a dazzling array of Web pages that included all kinds of information about Jung. None were as clean as the Britannica listings, but does that necessarily make Britannica better? It's certainly a personal judgement, but, many people miss the wild variations in style, content, color, layout and opinions. Of course Britannica Online has truly authoritative articles written by experts in their field—but the experts aren't always the best ones to explain something, are they?

Contrasted against the cleanliness of Britannica Online, the sight of all of those un-tamed and diverse Web links might remind you of the line in My Fair Lady when Rex Harrison sings, "I've grown accustomed to her face." You may soon find that you've grown accustomed to the face of the Web.

Okay, that's enough philosophy. Let's continue our exploration of Web resources by shifting gears in the next chapter to look at cyberspace business and financial services.

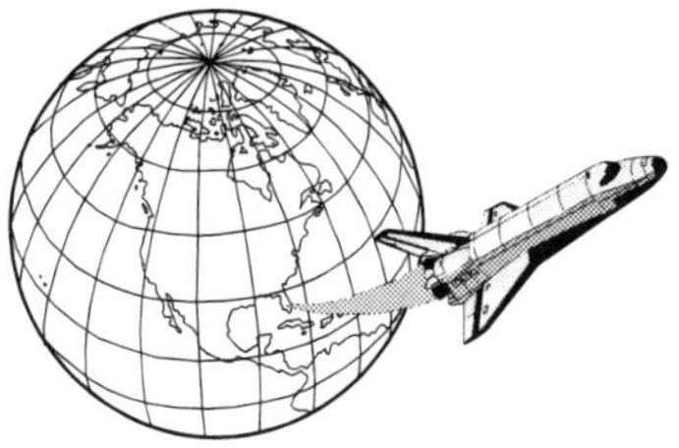

Orbiting in Cyberspace

C/Net search

http://www.search.com

This is one of the nicest search sites on the Web. It's a blend of a free service and a commercial service. Search.com actually blends its own commercial service in with other search engines. On the home page, for example, you'll see a link to search for shareware (see Figure 13) that looks like all the other links. That link, however, is owned by C/Net, the creators and sponsors of this site. Nice job, but a little bit of a sneaky trick on unsuspecting Newbies.

Jargon Cutter

Shareware - Software that is *distributed* free by its authors so that you can "try before you buy" during a trial period. But the software is not free, so to comply with copyright law you must register the software and pay the author if you choose to use it after the trial period.

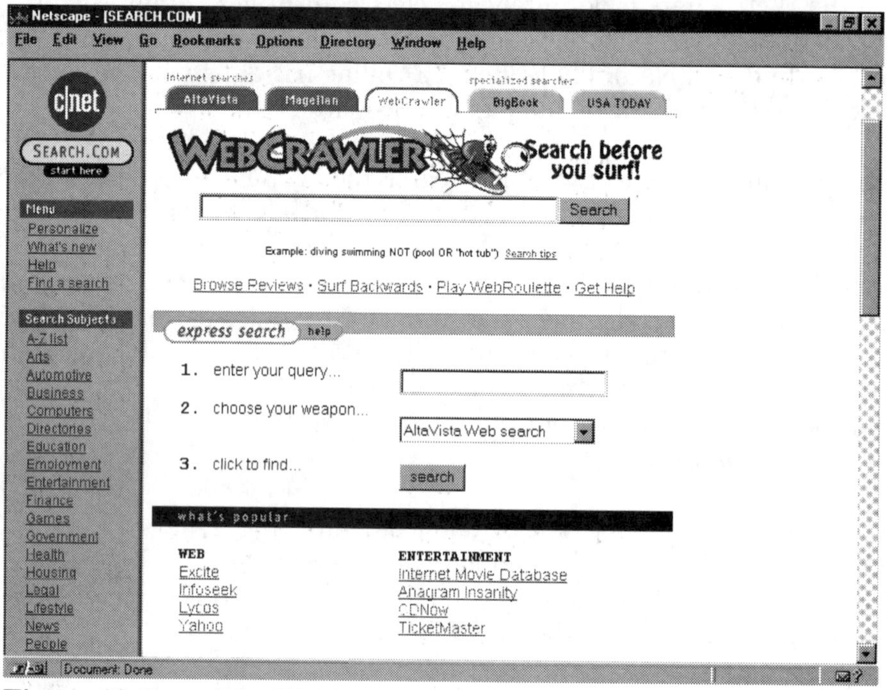

Figure 13 One of the Web's very best searching services

Deja News
http://www.dejanews.com

This service was profiled earlier in this chapter as an extension of Yahoo!, but it's a stand-alone service that has its own domain name (see Figure 14). You can add it to your Bookmarks so you can access it without going through Yahoo! Deja News is extremely efficient and fast. Even searches that span huge quantities of data are finished on the server in a few seconds, and it's got the largest collection of archived, indexed Usenet newsgroup documents that can be found anywhere!

Figure 14 Deja News an archive of Internet newsgroups

11

Cyber•Books: Libraries and Bookstores

Get comfortable with a snack and a drink nearby because you'll be in for a shock at how rapidly the publishing world has made the transition to cyberspace. But if you don't find enough resources through this chapter's featured library and bookstore sites, you always can go to a search engine and find even more sites—there's no shortage of material. The trick is to find useful sites and that's what this chapter does.

We'll first show you some on-line bookstores, then present some on-line libraries and finish with a collection of reference sources that will either help you find information or find links to other reference sources. The Orbiting in Cyberspace section will point you to some more resources, including general reference sources.

Bookstores

On-line bookstores come in two basic categories. Some are an electronic version of traditional bookstores—this means that when you enter them you can browse through conventional printed books by author, title or subject. Some of them improve upon the storefront bookstore by letting you search for books by keywords. But their main business is selling you printed books. The second category is a truly cyberspace bookstore that lets you directly download entire books. Of course some of these may also sell printed books, but their main business is electronically-published material.

Internet Book Shop

This site wins a gold star for the most on-line titles: 912,000! Every book they have listed has been classified into one of 2,000 categories. Once you locate a book, ordering is simple and they list the shipping and handling charges. Their Web address is: *www.bookshop.co.uk* (see Figure 1). Visit them today for a real literary treat.

This site's value extends well beyond being a convenient book source. They've got in-depth studies of various authors that includes cross-referencing more than 350 authors with more than 3500 titles in a "Good Reading Guide." Each month they profile one new book as their "Book of the Month."

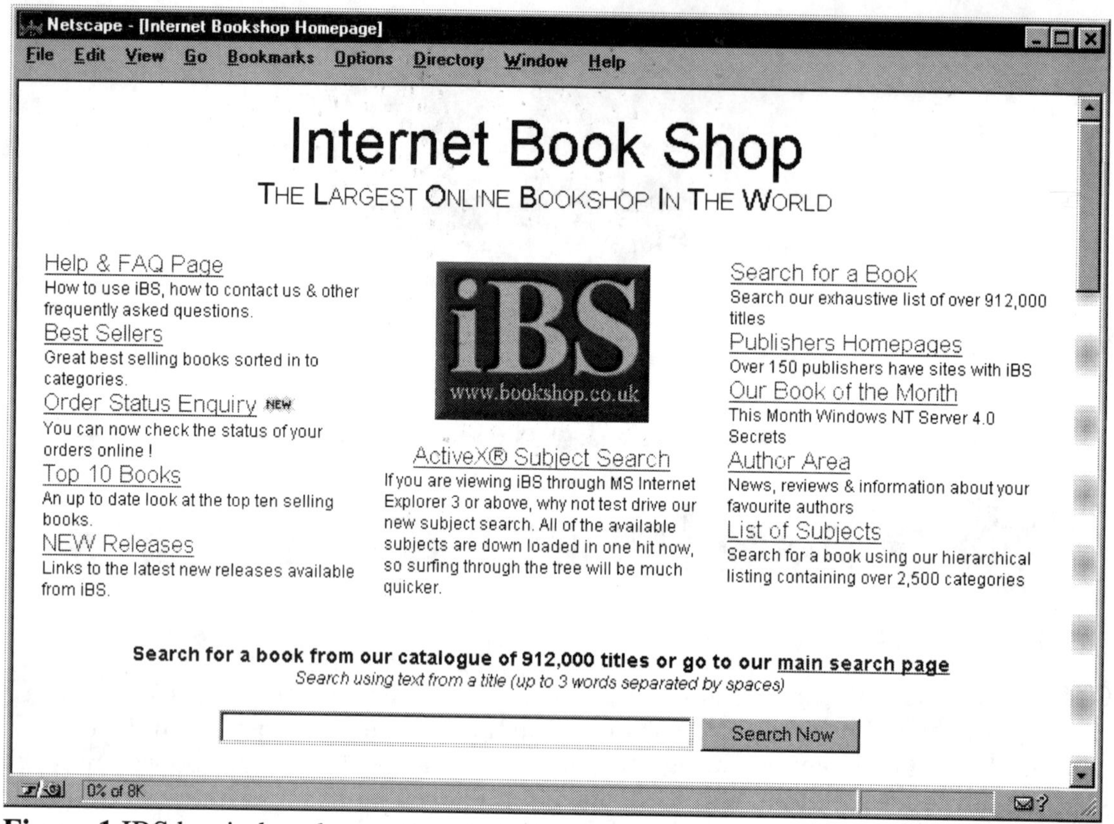

Figure 1 IBS has indexed more than 912,000 titles

You will also find special promotions, new developments and a special section for new titles. And in case you don't find what you need here, they've included a section that lists links to other interesting sites. But even if you just remain at this site, you'll find a rich variety of resources:

- On-Line publications (literature, general, zines and alternate publications, Internet and cyber-culture);
- Authors' pages, publishers and other on-line bookshops;
- Archives and libraries;
- Resources, art and music.

And they've created a powerful search engine that will locate books for you by title, author, ISBN number, publisher or topic (see Figure 2).

Jargon Cutter

Zines - On-line Internet magazines. They come in a vast array of topics from around the world. If you don't find one that covers your favorite topic, then start one yourself—you'll need nothing more than a Web site, some material and some Web publishing skills.

While this is a commercial service, it's still worthy of a Bookmark listing because it offers so many value-adding features. You will probably find it useful for locating information on a variety of topics—it's definitely *not* limited to selling books.

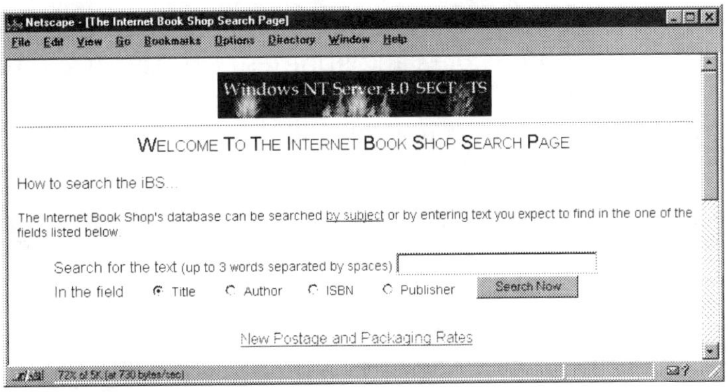

Figure 2 IBS book search

BookWire

Since the Internet Book Shop is in the U.K., using them might cause you shipping delays or currency exchange problems, so we've included some local bookstores. Of course, these days "local" means in the same country. The first featured site is BookWire, at *www.bookwire.com*, where you'll find an information-rich home page filled with links to book categories (see Figure 3).

From the home page, you can start with the link "BookWire Navigator" that brings up all of their links by category on one easy-to-browse page. Starting from this page, you should be able to satisfy all of your book needs.

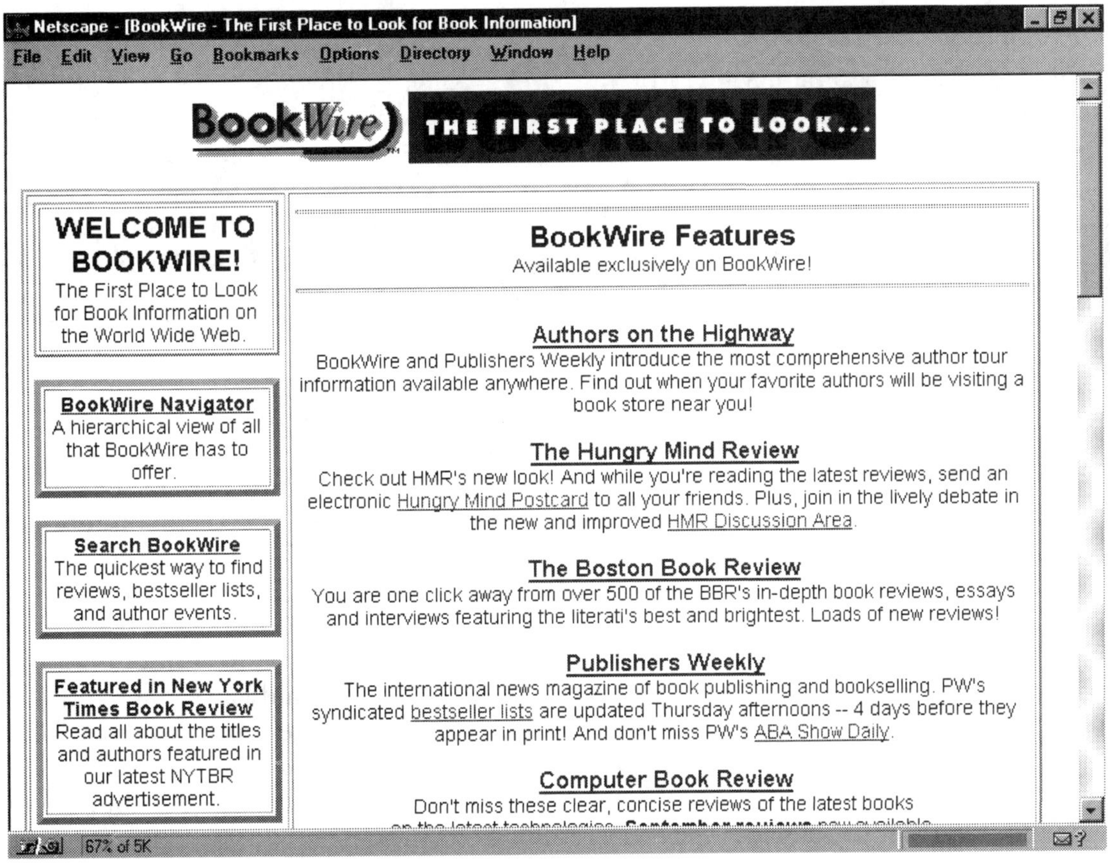

Figure 3 Complete on-line book information

And, just in case there isn't enough here, the folks at BookWire even include a link to other Web book resources. If you can't find the link, you can jump directly to this page at *www.bookwire.com/links/online_booksellers/online_booksellers.html* and find other virtual bookstores and libraries. This is a nice touch and a model for your own Web site, should you ever develop one: If you can't give your visitors what they need, graciously point them to sites that can.

Another nice touch is the modern, cool-looking home page they've created without resorting to bandwidth-grabbing graphics. Even though it almost appears graphical, it's just simple hypertext that uses a table layout.

How To Get Published

Does seeing all of these books stir up your own urge to get published? But you have no idea about how to begin? You won't be surprised that the Web can help you get your own book added to the lists you see here.

You can visit a cyber-literary agency in Washington, D.C., Adler & Robin Books, where you'll deal with Bill Adler, Jr. and Lisa Swayne. The agency's claim to fame is being "Number 1 in New York Times Bestsellers." They are also the second largest computer book agency in the world. If you want to know how they achieved such success, visit their Web site at *www.adlerbooks.com*. Bill and Lisa know the publishing industry inside out and share on-line some of their knowledge. Your best bet is to jump to the link on how to get published.

Their client list reads like a Who's Who directory: Dan Rather, Dick Clark, Ed McMahon, Fran Tarkenton, Geraldo Rivera, Helen Hayes, Howard Cosell, Jeff Smith (The Frugal Gourmet), Joan Lunden, Charles Osgood, Larry King, Margaret Truman, Mickey Mantle, Mike Wallace, Nolan Ryan, Pelé, Tom Shales, Ronald Reagan, Nancy Reagan, Sally Jessy Raphael, Senator Gary Hart, Senator George Mitchell, Senator William Cohen, Steve Allen, Tom Seaver, Willard Scott, Phil Donahue, Robert MacNeil and Ronald L. Wagner.

The Adler Books Web site includes postings of book ideas for which they are seeking writers, so check it out to see if you fit in? Already got a hot book idea? Then post a note and tell them about it.

The Bookstore

The Bookstore is a full-service on-line store at *intertain.com/store/welcome.html* that lets you browse by author or title and then order the book directly (see Figure 4). The Bookstore lets you create a profile that they keep on file for your future visits. Once your profile is registered you can browse the site, read synopses of books that interest you, and click on the "Buy" button to add to your shopping list. They offer a variety of shipping methods, so you have options on the shipping costs.

In addition to the author and title searches, you can search by keyword. For example, let's search for a book entitled *The Weather Sourcebook* (by Ronald L. Wagner and Bill Adler, Jr., Globe Pequot Press, 1994). With a search on the keyword "weather," it appeared on a list of 84 other weather books. If you get a similar list, you'll be able to click a check box in front of each entry that interests you, then click a "More" button to see the full description of each selection you checked.

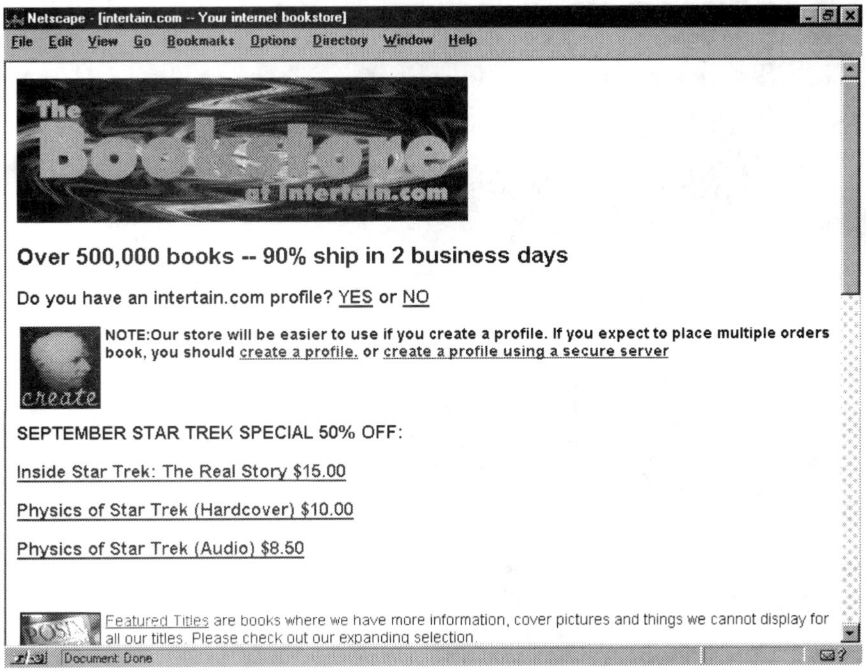

Figure 4 Keep a profile on record at the Intertain bookstore

While you're visiting, be sure to hit the button for "The Village." The Bookstore is just one shop in The Village at Intertain, a collection of stores available 24 hours a day, 7 days a week. The Village has many places to explore, to exchange ideas with other people and, of course, to shop.

Virtual libraries

First we'll present the newest form of library in the world: the virtual library. These are not usually affiliated with a traditional, physical library, but exist only in cyberspace. They can point you to a vast collections of information. Some actually store information on-site, but most are a collection of links to other Web resources. After showing you a few virtual libraries, we'll give you pointers to the Web sites of some real-world libraries that have gone on-line. You'll find something in these libraries for the whole family—and many of them should make the grade for your Bookmarks list.

World Library

The World Library presents a well-done, user-friendly front end that will speed your on-line information quests. Visit the home page, *www.scescape.com/WorldLibrary*, but make sure you've got a frames-capable Web browser such as your Netscape Navigator (see Figure 5). The right side of the screen gives you a separate scrolling window with links to different categories.

The left side of the screen displays a list of publishers. You can scroll through this window to find links to the publishers' home pages. In addition to the category links, you'll find a link to their on-line searching service. This is not, however, a Web search—it looks only at the resources cataloged at this site. Through the category links, however, you'll be pointed to global resources on a rich variety of information.

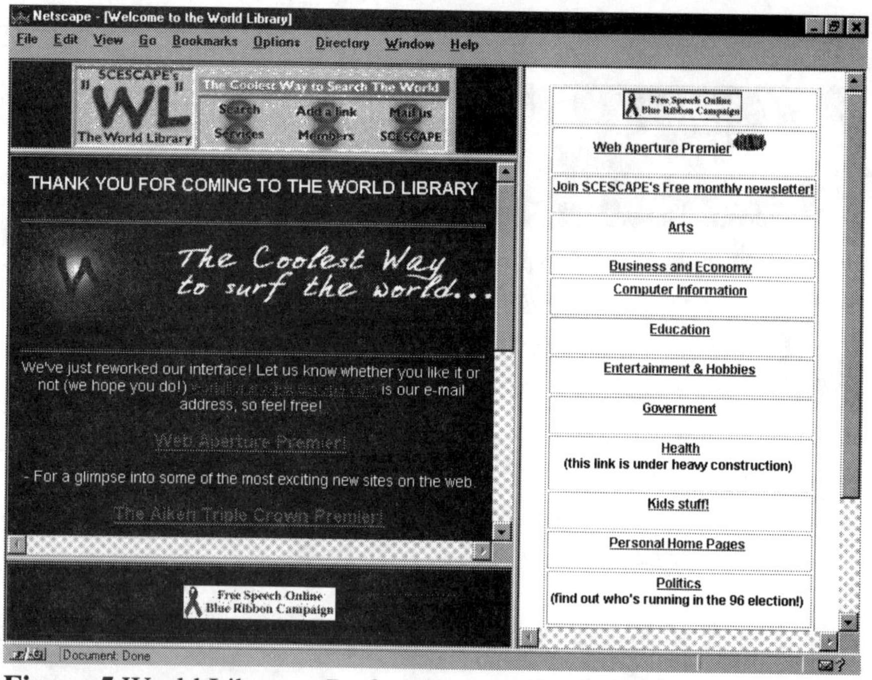

Figure 5 World Library - Perfect for your Bookmark list

WWW Virtual Library

The WWW Virtual Library uses a distributed subject catalog for topic organization. The home page, therefore, is a long listing of major topics for which they have references. The Web address is *www.w3.org/vl*, (see Figure 6). We've included it because it's a nice contrast to the World Library featured earlier. This service uses the simplest possible Web page interface and you might want to recommend it to friends who aren't fortunate enough to be enjoying the speed of Erol's Internet access. And it's also a good choice for anyone using a slow computer. The pages here won't tax your computer's resources, which is quite a switch from some of the other virtual book sources.

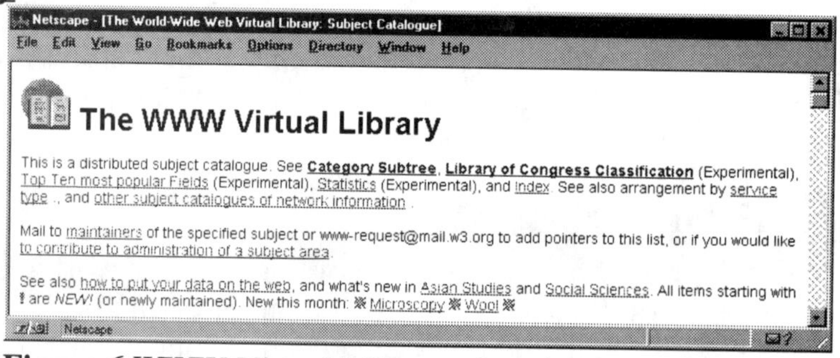

Figure 6 WWW Virtual Library - keeping it simple

The links at the top of the page give you a variety of display options for the topic listing. The Catalog Subtree link expands the listings shown here into subtrees that go as deep as three levels (two levels under the major topics). The Library of Congress Classification redisplays the screen with a much shorter list of standard topics. There's also a link that lists resources by Subject, which is so comprehensive we've included it in the Orbiting in Cyberspace section. Don't let its plain appearance distract you from the wealth of knowledge that you can tap through this site—the plain appearance is a resource-friendly gesture.

Real libraries

The sites featured here are on-line outlets of traditional, physical libraries. Some have provisions for borrowing material via mail, but many only let you use their service to search their archives and catalogs.

You'll find the whole spectrum, from the massive Library of Congress, to small Presidential libraries, university libraries and all the way down to small, community libraries. This is a rapidly-growing area on the Internet and it's hard to predict what's on-line and what's not.

There are countless libraries in cyberspace, so we'll begin with a representative overview and some resources that will point you to more. From those resources you'll find links you can follow to find everything that's available on-line in libraries.

Library of Congress

LOCIS (Library of Congress On Line) is the Library of Congress' mainframe-based collection of databases that includes a public access catalog of bibliographic information, federal legislation, copyright registered works, braille and audio materials, guides, organization descriptions and foreign law abstracts. From the home page, which is located at *www.loc.gov* (see Figure 7), you can find links to connect to LOCIS through a variety of Internet methods.

Figure 7 Library of Congress - a national treasure

You'll be able to get Web pages that offer Web and Gopher searches of the databases, as well as links that let you connect via Telnet (see Telnet sidebar on page 177) or Telnet 3270, a Z39.50 Gateway, or through the FTP.

Even the U.S. Government is joining us mainstream folks out here in cyberspace because they offer links here to other Internet search services such as The Awesome List, Whole Internet Guide and Catalog, Clearinghouse for Subject-Oriented Internet Resource Guides (University of Michigan) and the Categorical Catapult.

Presidential Libraries

Yahoo! has a one-page listing of all the Presidential Libraries that have established an on-line presence: *www.yahoo.com/Reference/Libraries/Presidential_Libraries*. Check out the Yahoo! page for an updated list. From there, for one example, you might jump to either of the two on-line Jimmy Carter Libraries.

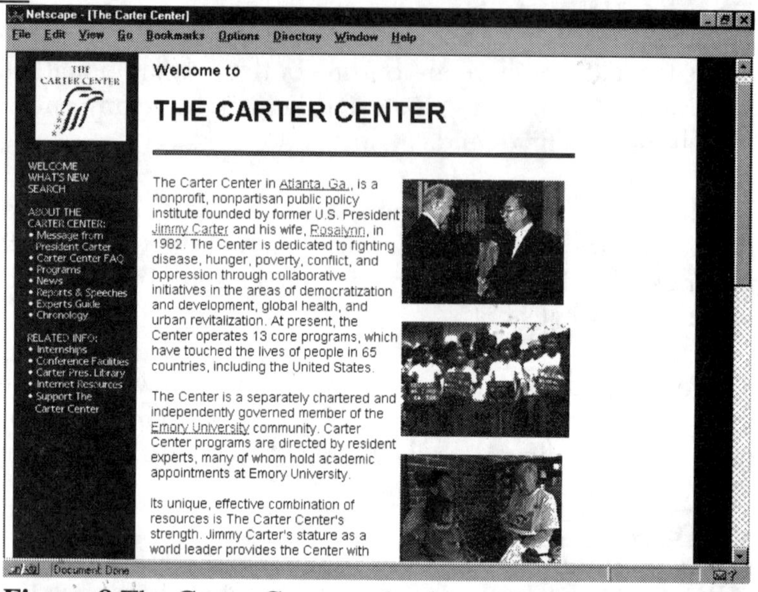

Figure 8 The Carter Center - check your local area

Presidential Libraries might be "small" libraries, but they have enough to keep you busy for the rest of your life if you did nothing else. Here's an example of what's available at the Jimmy Carter Library: "Over 26 million pages of material from the Carter White House are housed there, along with more than a million photographs, motion picture film, videotape, audiotape, and gifts to the President. The documents range from exchanges between President Carter, heads of state, diplomatic treaties, records of what was served for dinner, and how many paper clips were used by the White House staff. The audio and videotapes and photographs document a wide variety of activities, ranging from the visit of world dignitaries to a footrace between the President and his daughter."

If you live near any of the Presidential Libraries, you can check their home pages for information on scheduled events and special programs held at the libraries, such as events at the Carter Center (see Figure 8).

University libraries

Jump into Yahoo! and click on the home page link **Reference, Libraries**, then click on **University Libraries**. As this book was being written, Yahoo! displayed a list of 204 choices! Is that enough? The first nine at the top were marked "New," which means that this list is going to be much larger by the time you click on the same links.

The Yahoo! page has a **Special Collections** link at the top of the list that only had eight selections—at least something here is manageable. The Special Collections link is a good list to remember if you're having difficulty finding obscure information or rare books or images. These links truly have some unique research materials that could give students an edge when they prepare reports for school.

When you start clicking on the university library links you need to be ready for anything. Most of them use hypertext Web pages, but you'll find Gopher and Telnet links. These shouldn't be any problem with Netscape Navigator 2.0 or later because

Gopher is built-in and Telnet can be added as a helper application. Gopher pages will hardly look much different from Web pages, except for appearing very plain.

Telnet

Many libraries let you tap into their main computer via a Telnet connection. Telnet is an Internet protocol that lets your PC become a remote terminal to a larger computer. Telnet allows you to establish a connection and login so that all of your keystrokes are sent to the remote server. In this mode, you will see the screen output of the server as if you were operating a terminal directly connected to that machine. With a Telnet application you can establish a Telnet session using a dial-in modem and have access to the character-based Internet services available on the machine to which you have connected.

Windows Telnet applications are a snap to use and making the connection is easy, but you're on your own once you're connected. Try it now if you'd like, using *lib.dartmouth.edu* as the host. Once you're in, you can search for books by author, title or topic, using Dartmouth Library computer commands. To end the Telnet session, just close the window or press **ALT+F4**, then confirm **OK** to terminate the connection.

To get Telnet software, visit *www.state.ky.us/software/windows.html*, download the latest version, install it and configure it, then add it as a helper application to your Netscape Navigator (a Step-by-Step exercise on adding helper applications was included in the Netscape chapter). You might want to bookmark this page to get upgrades and for all the other links it contains to various Windows TCP/IP client applications, such as WS_FTP, Eudora e-mail Archie, Finger and Ping.

Local libraries

There's no pattern to the libraries that have established Web sites. You'll find many small communities with an active on-line library presence and yet some major communities that are not yet on-line. For example, Fairfax County, Virginia has the highest average education and income level in the U.S., so you'd expect it to have been among the leaders in cyberspace libraries. But this reveals a dilemma for large information systems: vast information resources come up against budget considerations. If Fairfax County were smaller, they'd be able to get on-line quickly, but putting such a huge collection on-line in today's tight budget environment isn't easy.

Clearwater Public Library

We browsed through a few local libraries and selected one that we found to be a excellent model of what can be done by community libraries. The Clearwater, Florida Public Library (see Figure 9) has done an outstanding job of presenting their on-line research and resource services as well as giving local patrons a comprehensive source of information on hours, locations, library policies and special events. See for yourself at *public.lib.ci.clearwater.fl.us/cpl*.

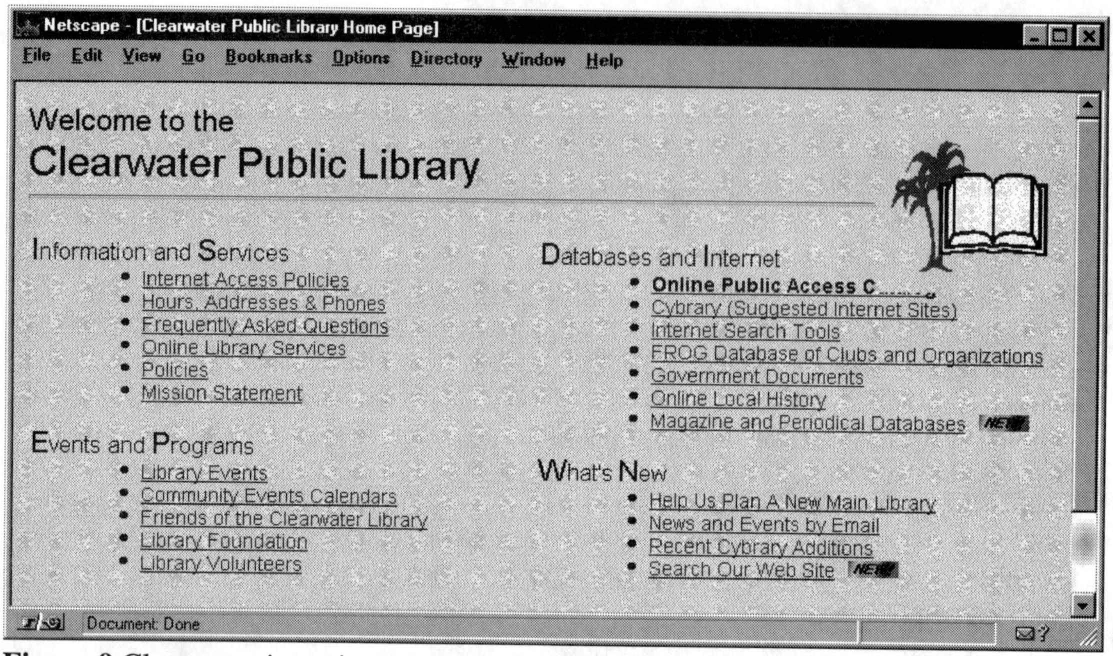

Figure 9 Clearwater is setting standards for local libraries

The "Cybrary" link to Internet Resources on the Clearwater home page (see Figure 10) is especially a real treat. The Cybrary link jumps to a whole menu of valuable features available in this cyber-library: the Card Catalog (Telnet to access their catalog file); the Reading Room (divided into Bibliographies, Literature, Nonfiction and Periodicals); the Reference Desk; the Youth Room; and FROG (Florida Resource and Opportunity Guide). FROG is a wonderful resource that area residents can use to track activities, organizations, events, and programs that meet the daily information needs of citizens, businesses, and community organizations in the Tampa Bay Area. While you probably won't use this directly, you can use it to lobby your local library system for better service—it's a well-done site for a local organization.

And, this site deserves a Bookmarks listing for its Reference Desk link alone—thank goodness there's so much more. The Reference Desk has everything from an e-mail link to "Ask a librarian," to international currency rates, to Bartlett's Quotations, to nationwide Lottery Numbers. And you can even find the Vital Records offices in every state, which means—believe it or not—that you actually can locate the right address to order a copy of your birth certificate! If you've ever tried to do that before the Internet, you know what a wonderful service this is.

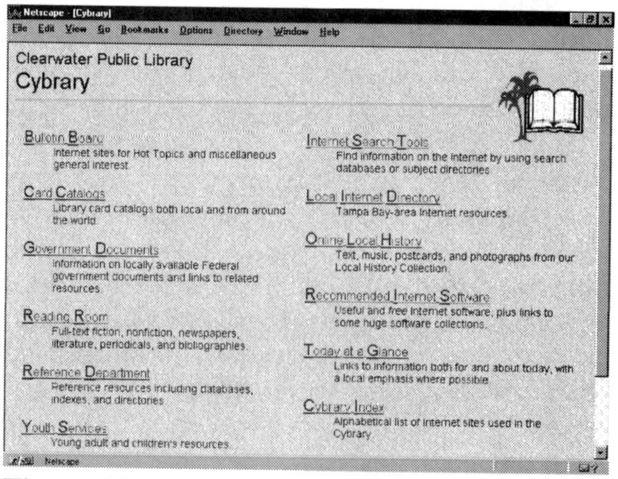

Figure 10 Cybrary - a true cyberspace library

Local library summary

There are several ways to find out if your local library system is on-line. First, of course, you can call a local phone number and ask, or you can stop at a local branch for information about the system's on-line status. Or, without leaving home, you can use standard Web search tools—after all, it's not mandatory that you use the Web only to find far-away places. A Yahoo! or Lycos search for the name of your city or county may be all you need. If that doesn't do the trick, jump directly to the page on community libraries at *www.yahoo.com/Reference/Libraries/Public_Libraries*. If your area library system isn't yet on-line you might be able to help them, using some of the existing sites, such as Clearwater, as examples. If you're thinking of developing your HTML authoring and Web publishing skills, volunteering to help a local library could give you excellent experience as well as a very public showcase for your talents.

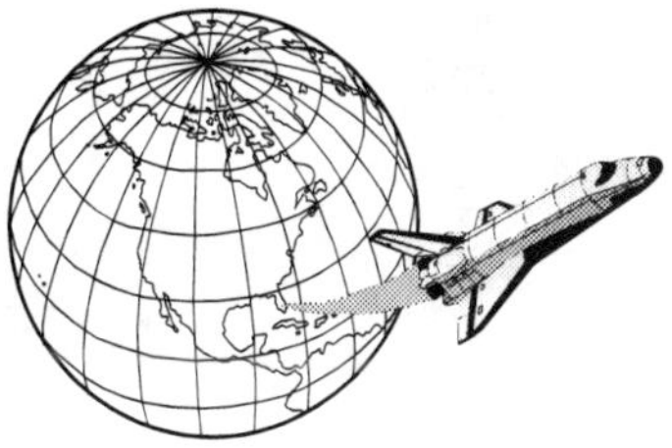

ORBITING IN CYBERSPACE

BookWire library index
http://www.bookwire.com/links/libraries/librarymenu.html

Here's a rich listing of Web-accessible libraries from around the globe. This is an excellent model of what the Internet does best. In fact, this site may make you run screaming from your computer. You could literally spend the rest of your life exploring just the links on this site and still tap into but a fraction of all that it offers. You can use this site to locate almost any information you want from libraries in these basic groups: Asian, Australian, Canadian, European, United States and Others. For example, the European option on this page can lead you to hundreds of world-wide resources through the Bodleian Library at the University of Oxford.

Internet Public Library
http://ipl.sils.umich.edu

This is a *must see* source on the Web for all kinds of information (see Figure 11). It's the home of "WebInk," an on-line newsletter for kids. Other features include "Introductory Tutorials" (helps use the Internet), "Interactive Classroom" (learn about computing) and the "Exhibit Hall" (permanent exhibits as well as an ever-changing array of temporary exhibits). Overall, lots of computing and Internet resources.

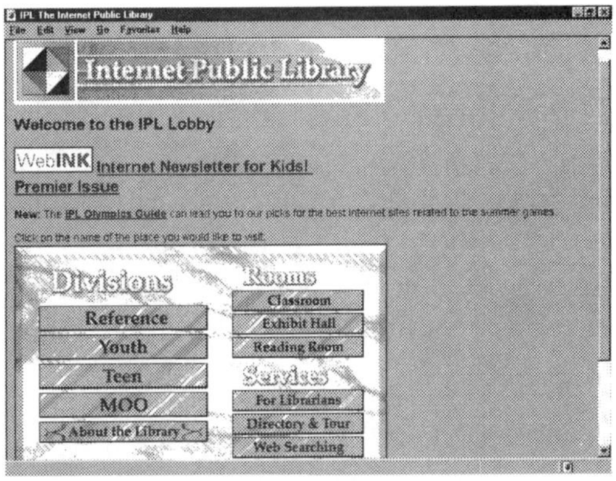

Figure 11 Internet Public Library

WWW Virtual Library
http://www.w3.org/hypertext/DataSources/bySubject/Overview.html

Here's a topic-oriented Internet reference site. Instead of keywords, you look for topics that interest you—or ones that intrigue you—there's something here for everyone. This is not like other topic-oriented sites like Yahoo!; it really is an on-line, hypertext library.

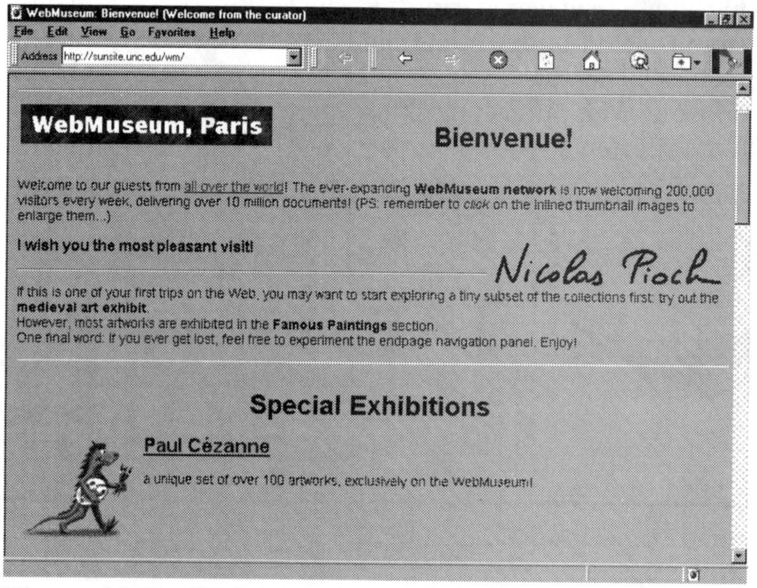

Figure 12 The Web Museum - all the way from Paris

Web Museum
http://sunsite.unc.edu/wm

This is a remarkable collection of Internet resources (see Figure 12). It's a free art museum created by Nicolas Pioch, a student studying economics at the École Nationale Supérieure des Télécommunications in Paris. It's a personal creation that has no support, no funding, and practically no personnel. In fact, they'd like your help because the WebMuseum is a collaborative work that encourages visitors to contribute to the site and improve the WebMuseum. This site is a past winner of a "Best of the Web Award."

Reference Shelf
http://www.nova.edu/Inter-Links/reference.html

The Reference Shelf is a potpourri of reference sources collected from around the Web. It's just one page, but it's a top candidate for your Bookmarks because you could stay busy for days exploring its links. A few valuable examples are City/Zip Code Lookup (with geography info), plus facts and maps for nearly every country in the world. The Perpetual Calendar link alone is worth bookmarking the list—where else can you instantly find a suitable-for printing calendar for any month of any year?

12

For the People: Government On-Line

This chapter could boost your faith in government. In it, we're going to show you some remarkable ways in which your tax dollars have been at work in cyberspace. It's truly heartening to see how the Internet can be used to make our governments more accessible and responsive. All kinds of previously obscure government information can now be tapped quickly and accurately right from your home. Just think, you might never need to stand in line again at a government office if governments continue to jump onto the Internet bandwagon.

It's amazing, actually, that the U.S. Government isn't the main focus of the Internet. We're lucky. Somebody back in the early 1960s was wise enough to realize that the Internet would be more robust if government stayed out of it. They were right, and fortunately, the government still doesn't control the Internet, although they have tried to impose some new restrictions.

But now that 30 years of freedom for the Internet has created a powerful, universal Web that connects us all, government is slipping back into the party—but mostly as an equal guest. Instead of controlling the Internet, the government sites you'll see here are very much like their civilian counterparts: they try to bring value to Web visitors.

The Web is an excellent resource for government information because we all need it and it's always hard to find. Before the Web, a search for government information was often a frustrating game of passing the buck. Perhaps when President Truman said, "The buck stops here," a lot of government agencies took that to heart and have tried to pass everything on up to the Oval Office. With the Internet, finally, the buck stops wherever you want it to stop.

You can find on the Web just about everything you'd want to know about the U.S. Government as well as your state and local governments:

- Congressional records, laws, regulations, Supreme Court rulings, Executive decisions;

- Indexes to agencies with phone numbers and addresses, current information on-line;
- Copies of birth certificates, marriage licenses, business licenses, applications for forms, sources for forms;
- Business hours, phone numbers, directions.

We'll give you some sample of sites from all levels of government: Federal, State and local. Of course you'll only see a few here, but they'll help you know what you can expect to find. Finally, the Orbiting in Cyberspace section will give you some good resources to track down Web sites from which you can obtain the government information you want.

Federal Government

The last chapter included a taste of government Web sites through its descriptions of a local library in Clearwater, Florida as well as the Library of Congress. Even though we've already covered the Library of Congress, we'll mention it here because it is an excellent resource for a large amount of Federal government information. The Library of Congress includes information on:

- Federal Government: General Resources, Executive Branch and Independent Agencies, Legislative Branch (includes Congress), Judicial Branch, and the Military, FOIA (Freedom of Information Act);
- State and Local Government: Indexes for state and local information, state maps, Council of State Governments, and the National Center for State Courts;
- Foreign and International Government: General information by country, CIA Factbook, State Department information, world constitutions, foreign relations, NAFTA, GATT, the United Nations and much, much more.

The Internet is rapidly removing many of the traditional geographical barriers to business that kept many businesses working close to home. But through these resources, you may be able to find opportunities to do business with faraway governments. Or, you might use these services to obtain information about doing business in other cities other states or even other countries—not other planets, though, not yet anyway. Before the Internet, setting up an out-of-town business and getting all the required business licenses was a chore. But now, even a small, home-based business can expand to just about anywhere in the world.

So, how will you find the information you need from governments? Well, certainly the Library of Congress site will give you lots of valuable information that can help you in your work and in your personal life. But we covered that in the last chapter, so now we'll profile a few other services that almost everyone can use. We'll profile some U.S. Government sites and then give you a sample of state and local governments that will get you on-track in your own community.

United States Postal Service

If you've got a mailing address but no zip code, you can use the USPS Web page at *www.usps.gov/ncsc* (see Figure 1). The Zip Code Lookup link on this site can deliver a complete, 9-digit, USPS-regulation address. Or, you can use it to check an address or find out the city that goes with a zip code.

Figure 1 Locate or verify any zip code in the U.S.

Here's a Step-By-Step exercise that will demonstrate how to use the USPS Zip Code Lookup.

STEP-BY-STEP

GOAL: Learn to correct an address with the USPS Web site.

- ✔ Start the Netscape Navigator.
- ✔ Press **CTRL+L**, type *www.usps.gov/ncsc* and press **ENTER**.
- ✔ Click **Zip Code Lookup**.
- ✔ Click in **Mailing Address**.
- ✔ Type *3000 timberwood* and press **TAB**.
- ✔ Type *herndon, va*.
- ✔ Click on **Process Address**.

  Note that the address has been corrected (it's actually three words now) and the full 9-digit Zip Code has been added.
- ✔ Press **ALT+LEFT ARROW** to return to the previous screen.
- ✔ Click **Clear the Form**.

  Enter your own address, but make a couple of errors. For example, if your address ends with "Drive" then reverse the abbreviation and use "rd." Leave off your zip code or reverse a digit when you type it. If you make too many errors, the database can't figure out what you meant, but it will handle quite a few problems.
- ✔ Press **ALT+LEFT ARROW** until you return to the first USPS page.

The USPS Web site can give you much more than this, including complete, current postal rate tables for every form of mail. You can even find out how to buy mail-order stamps. This Web site has made a lot of Bookmark lists.

Census Bureau

You pay for the Federal census, but how could you have used the collected census information before the Web? It hasn't been easy, but the Web changes that. Maybe a better question is, now that you can get it, what do you do with it? There is such a rich source of information available at the Census Bureau's site at *www.census.gov* (see Figure 2) that almost anyone in business can find something here to use. For example, before planning an expansion, a new product or moving your family across the country, you can check the Census Bureau's Internet demographic information to help you make the decision.

Figure 2 You've answered their questions—now see what they do with your answers

Try the Market Place link to learn how to order Census Bureau information in hard copy or on CD-ROM, or you can try Data Access Tools to get a lot of the information on-line. The Economy and Geography links are fabulous resources for developing business plans and proposals. And, if you're not sure how or where to find what you want, click on Ask The Experts to send an e-mail question. This is a wonderful site that makes public a lot of valuable, yet previously obscure, information.

Small Business Administration

The Internet has revolutionized almost every existing business, but it has also spawned countless new business ideas. A massive wave of corporate and government cutbacks, downsizing and layoffs have pushed a lot of displaced workers to form small or home-based businesses. If you need to form your own business or if you work for a small business, then the Small Business Administration (SBA) Web site at *www.sba.gov* (see Figure 3) should be on your bookmark list.

You'll find links to the SBA's Program Offices, Special Interests and Great Business Hot-Links. They also have an extensive shareware collection of more than 538 titles for applications that can help you run a small business. The shareware listing can be arranged either by an index, in one long listing or by searching.

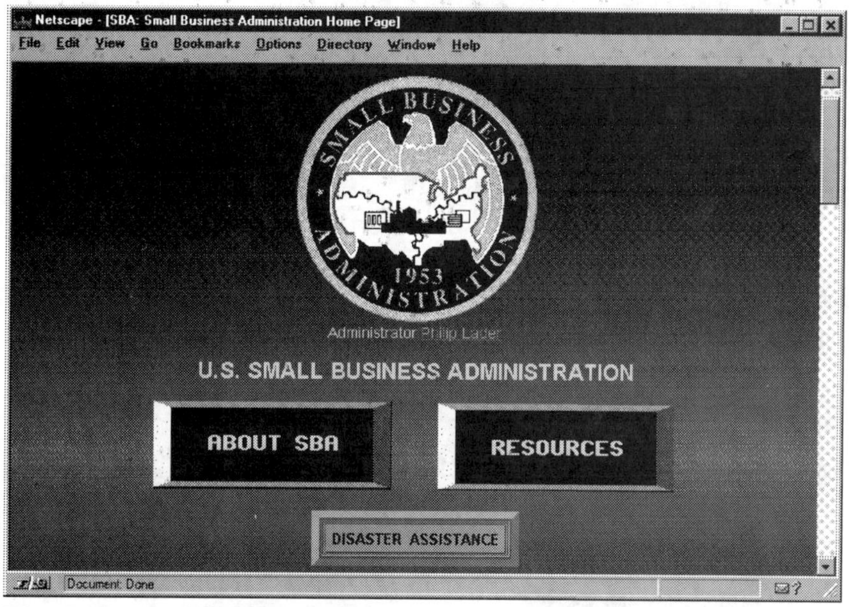

Figure 3 A good resource for small- or home-based businesses

The new business links are "Starting Your Business," "Financing Your Business" and "Expanding Your Business." They lead to pages with compiled information, gathered from the Web and other government agencies, that offer information or assistance.

Congressional E-Mail Directory

There was a time when you could take pride in just finding out the phone number or address of your Congressional Representative and Senators. Now, thanks to the Web site at *www.webslingerz.com/jhoffman/congress-email.html*, you can get complete contact information on them (phone, fax, snail mail, e-mail) and jump to their Web sites. The Congressional E-Mail Directory is a sure-fire hit for your Bookmarks (see Figure 4). When you get to your state page you can click on a link for the Web page and on another to e-mail directly from the Web site.

Figure 4 Tell 'em exactly what you think

This site is an excellent example of Web publishing because it has a high-quality look and a user-friendly interface, but hasn't resorted to bandwidth-hogging graphics. So, bookmark this site for two reasons: an outstanding information source and a model for good Web site design.

State Governments

Your first stop for state government information can be one of the major search engines. To save time you can jump directly to a Yahoo! page that lists links to every state, alphabetically by entering *www.yahoo.com/Government/U_S__States*. These links aren't the state Web sites—in fact not all states had Web sites as this was written—but it will give you a list of links related to any selected state.

Figure 5 A complete resource for state governments

State Technologies, Inc., which has run conferences and seminars on how government can use technology, now runs an Internet database of sound government practices (see Figure 5). The service is called Government On-Line and it's located at *www.gol.org*.

Government On-Line

Government On-Line's (GOL) niche is helping government entities embrace and use technology better, especially in an age in which corporate America has already jumped in so deeply and government has faced the need to cut costs. The Web can help budget-crunched agencies improve the way they deliver services, and GOL can help you work with these agencies. If you do any work with state governments, visit this site and hit the Doing Business with State Govern-

Figure 6 The Monthly Market Bulletin could give you some great business ideas

ments link. This presents a screen with such valuable services as links entitled "Opportunities," "News Flash" and "Monthly Market Bulletin" (see Figure 6).

The state-specific links are rich resources on doing business with a state. For example, you'll find links to "Market Profile," "How to do Business" and "New Opportunities" that can help you understand the state's needs and to instantly locate the contacts you need. For example, you can learn about authorization procedures by contract value threshold, so you'll know what work would qualify under discretionary budget rules and what levels would require a full, sealed bid process.

Inside Info

Remember to check the Library of Congress for state and local government information. The Web page at *lcweb.loc.gov/global/state/stategov.html* gives you a meta-index of state and local information, state maps, links to state home pages and some organizations that pertain to state and local government issues.

Local governments

There are too many local governments on-line to even begin to profile, but a good search engine will help you find the ones that represent your local area. County governments have reported that their Web sites have attracted new businesses to relocate or open branch offices. And, they've helped many companies learn how to do business with both the government as well as other companies within the area. You'll find them very useful for looking up hard-to-find records or, perhaps while researching the family tree.

The challenge, as always on the Internet, is finding the site you want. Of course, you can turn to Yahoo! or Lycos and search the state name. But if you're looking for a good Bookmarks list site that can be a ready reference to information pertaining to local governments, try visiting *www.civic.net/lgnet* (see Figure 7). This site is maintained by the Local Government Network (LGNet), a service of The Innovation Groups and The Center for Civic Networking.

Figure 7 LGNet includes detailed information on most major U.S. cities

Information available here includes training, workshops, conferences, on-line help, publications and an on-line resource directory. If you do business with local governments, be sure to list your products and services with the "Vendor Directory and Information." This is a central location for state vendors to publicize contacts, on-line catalogs, purchase schedules, and special offers. This link leads to a forms-based database that will accept your information directly from this page.

Cities

There are too many cities to count, right? Well, not too many for the Internet. There is one Web site that lists on-line information on 2,039 cities and 745 other destinations! City.Net, at *www.city.net*, is the Internet's most comprehensive guide to communities around the world (see Figure 8). City.Net is updated every day to provide easy and timely access to information on travel, entertainment and local business, plus government and community services.

Figure 8 You'll know more than the mayor's office

Once you locate the city you want, you'll learn things about the city that even the mayor doesn't know. Radio stations, television stations, newspapers, city directory, transportation, maps, sports teams, universities, magazines and zines, virtual tours, schedules of events, parks and tourism information. If you travel a lot, this is another "must have" bookmark site because if you check here before you go, you'll feel like a native when you arrive. Naturally not every city is represented, but the most popular travel destinations have extensive coverage.

If your ties to your hometown have fallen victim to our high-tech, high-mobility society, use this site to savor a taste of home. No, no, only kidding—Netscape doesn't have a taste and smell plug-in for the Navigator—yet.

Airports

Picture this. You're late catching a flight. You've jammed your clothes into your suitcase, rushed out the door without eating and driven like a NASCAR racer to make it on time. You burst through the doors, knock down three people getting to a scheduling monitor to check your gate. Then you see it: it's delayed an hour, or worse, CANCELED. What would you have given to have seen that monitor at home?

Commercial airline information is a valuable commodity and it's perfectly suited to the Internet. You can't yet get it in real-time, but major airports are regularly going on-line (see Figure 9) and before long, you'll be able to check departure and arrival screens at home. For now, you can Bookmark the Commercial Aviation Resource Center and check back frequently to track the industry's progress at going on-line (*w3.one.net/~flypba/AIRLINES/carc.html*).

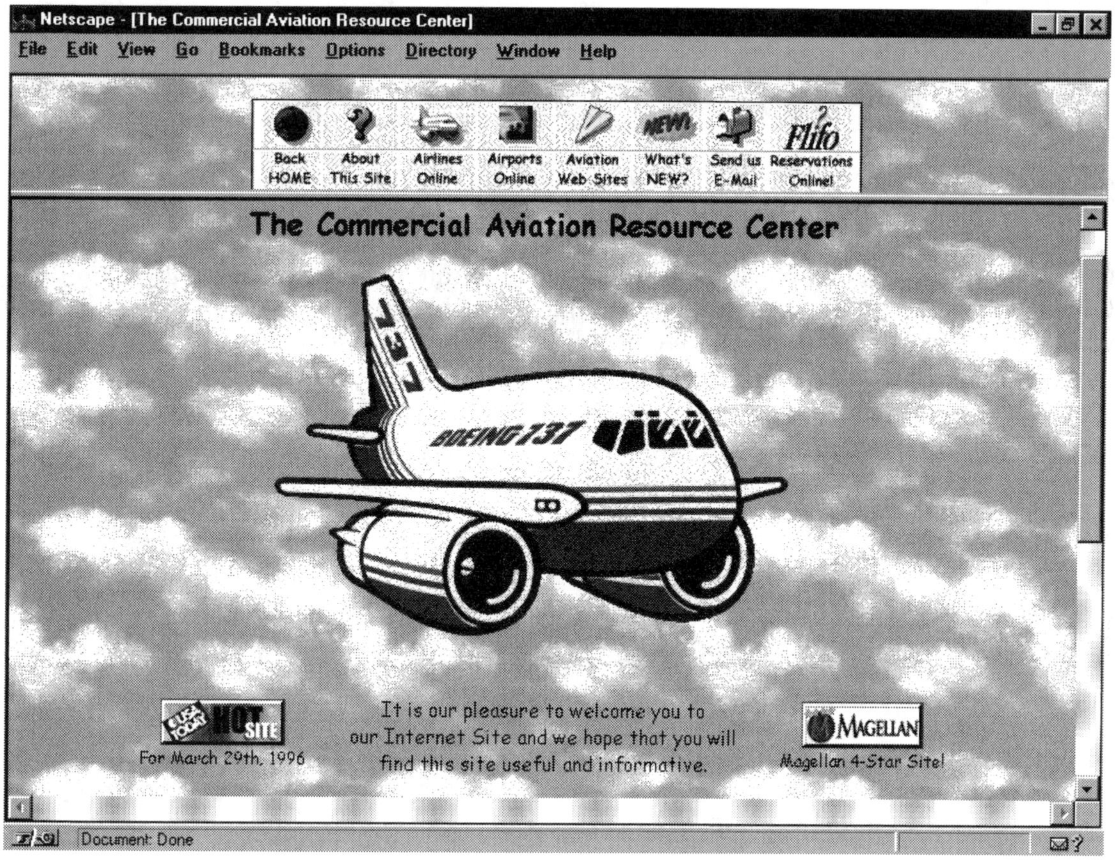

Figure 9 A complete commercial aviation resource center

Only a few airports are on-line as this is written, but many airports are working on their Web sites. Most of the ones that are on-line have major upgrade plans. That's good because there's much to be done. But the Oklahoma City Will Rogers World Airport is an example that shows what a good airport Web site eventually will do for us. It's located at *www.flyokc.com*, where the home page has links to several on-line services. The Airline Schedule link held promise, but turned out to only show what will be. At present, it's just a static, monthly schedule of flights with no real-time information (see Figure 10).

As we browsed airports, we saw a graphic illustration of the one-world, global community that we're building in cyberspace: the Sheremetyevo-2 Air Gateway in Moscow. When the Internet was first conceived in the early 1960s, can you imagine what the founders would have thought if they had known that one day anyone in the U.S. could pull up a map of the gates at the Moscow airport? To old Cold Warriors, that would have been a terryifying thought. Now, it's only slightly amazing—we accept it quickly and start wondering when they'll offer real-time flight schedules.

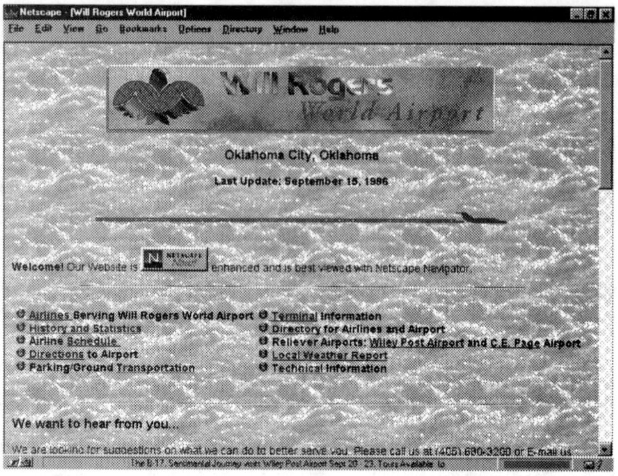

Figure 10 A vision of things to come—soon!

Shortcomings aside, current airport Web sites illustrate how the Internet is changing our lives by conveniently bringing us valuable, hard-to-find information—no matter where in the world it's located. If you think about it in absolute terms, it's almost barbaric that we've had to go to airports without seeing the schedule monitors until *after* we're there. It's too late then! But the Internet is growing rapidly to bring airport screens—and countless other such timely information services—into our homes in real time.

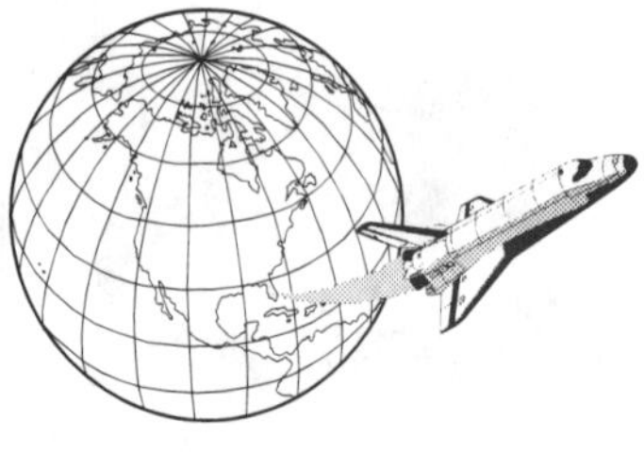

Orbiting in Cyberspace

Federal Government
http://www.fedworld.gov

FedWorld is a hypertext menu of various Federal Government computer resources. The National Technical Information Service (NTIS) introduced FedWorld in November, 1992 to help with the challenge of accessing U.S. Government information on-line (see Figure 11). Most of the links are to other Web sites, but it also includes Telnet links to several Federal computer systems. You'll find most links under the "Index of Subject Categories," but you will find direct links to some popular sites, including Web, FTP, Gopher and Telnet sites.

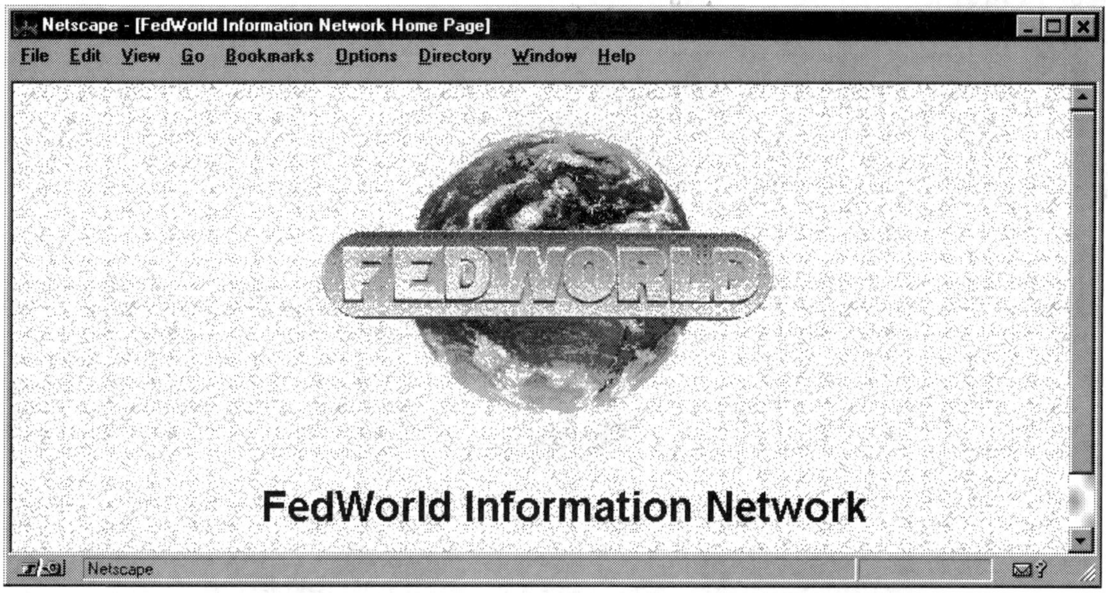

Figure 11 Start here if you don't know a specific government Web address

Yahoo!
http://www.yahoo.com/Government

The Yahoo! search engine has an excellent one-stop page for government information. This page lists links to government by category, so it offers a different slant from some of the other listings. You could use this if you had only a vague idea of the type of information you wanted, but had no idea what agency could help you. A key to using this site well is to click on the **Sub Category Listing** link to expand the categories into a myriad of sub categories. You also can click on **Indices** to get a listing of other Web sites that can help you find even more government information.

Federal Government Web Locator
http://www.law.vill.edu/Fed-Agency/fedwebloc.html

Sponsored by Villanova University Law School, this site lists more than 200 Federal Government Web sites. This site has a search engine that is an excellent tool if you've got a question about a topic but don't know which agency could handle your request. For example, what agency would you contact if you wanted to know about the progress on cleaning up the Exxon Alaska oil spill? A search on the words "oil spill" produced a link to the Oil Spill Public Information Center.

U.S. Government Web site
http://sunsite.unc.edu/govdocs.html

This site enables you to search for U.S. Government documents on the Web, such as press releases, speeches (including some audio and video clips) and the National Trade Data Bank. Take careful notes because many of the references you find here may be good value-added links for which you can provide links on your own Web site.

USA CityLink
http://banzai.neosoft.com/citylink

You can use this site to find information on cities around the U.S. and you can submit links to your own city. The USA CityLink Project (see Figure 12) lists cities, states and freenets. Here's what they say on their home page, "The USA CityLink Project is a city's interface to the world. It is the Internet's most comprehensive listing of World Wide Web pages featuring U.S. states and cities."

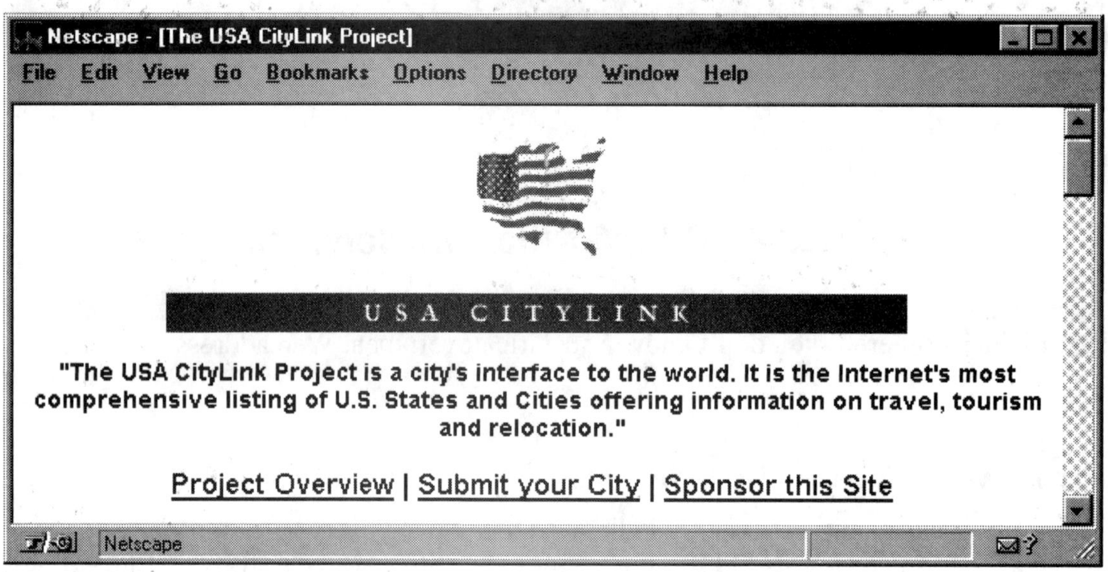

Figure 12 If your city isn't on this list, they'll let you submit it yourself

StateSearch
http://www.state.ky.us/nasire/NASIREhome.html

StateSearch is a service of the National Association of State Information Resource Executives (NASIRE) and is a topical clearinghouse of state government information on the Internet (see Figure 13). In addition to listing links to some featured special-interest Web sites, StateSearch provides links to information on commerce, state governments, state home pages, energy, tourism, state treasures, licensing and regulations, records, education and employment.

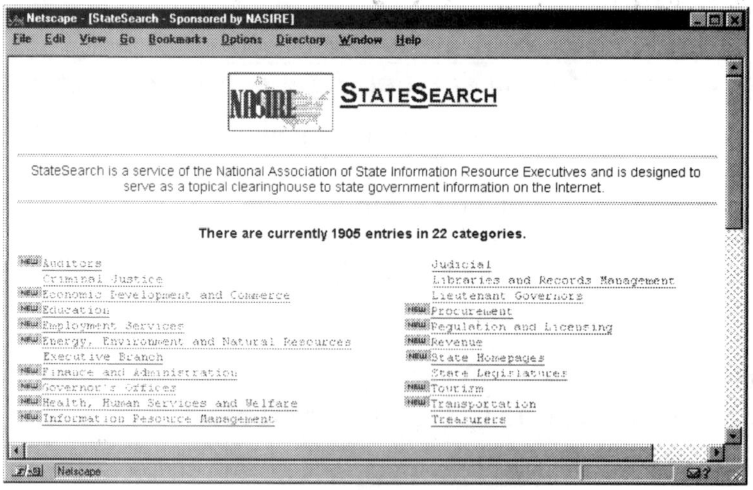

Figure 13 You'll find thousands of entries

13

Making It Pay: News, Business and Finance

This chapter focuses on several types of Internet news and business information services. First we'll cover on-line news services that can deliver more news than you ever wanted to know about any topic you can imagine. Blessedly, you also can use these services to filter out everything you *don't* need to know and get just the slice of news you truly need.

Major, traditional newspapers, such as *The Washington Post* and *USA Today*, are on-line. In addition, many innovative forms of news delivery bypass traditional news distribution systems. You'll see examples of both.

Next we'll give you some financial news links that can deliver stock quotes as well as track news that will affect corporate stock prices. These services can be used to track a personal portfolio, a major corporate investment plan or even the ups and downs of your competitors. You'll also get some good resources for marketing tips and general business information and consulting services.

General news

The nation's newspapers and magazines are scrambling to go on-line. As this is being written, there are 26 newspapers on-line just among full-service, primary newspapers that serve metropolitan areas with more than 1 million in population. Most assuredly that number will be higher by the time you read this. And that doesn't even count the smaller regions or smaller publications.

Pathfinder

Time Warner maintains this "mega site" of news, information and entertainment from the company's various magazines, book publishers, record labels and television and movie studios. Most of Pathfinder is "low bandwidth" to accommodate the millions of users who visit the site daily using telephone dial-up connections to access the site at *www.pathfinder.com*.

Pathfinder contains content offerings from more than 70 different information providers. Pathfinder management has announced that parts of the site will soon require registration and payment. But, for now, at least, all of Pathfinder's contents are free and available without restriction.

NewsLink

If you live in a large metropolitan area, you can find out if your area's newspaper is on-line by checking out the NewsLink page at *www.newslink.org* (see Figure 1). If you don't find it there, try searching Lycos or Yahoo! for the paper's name. Of course you could call them, too, but that's not very high-tech—it wouldn't be right to use a phone to get a cyberspace address!

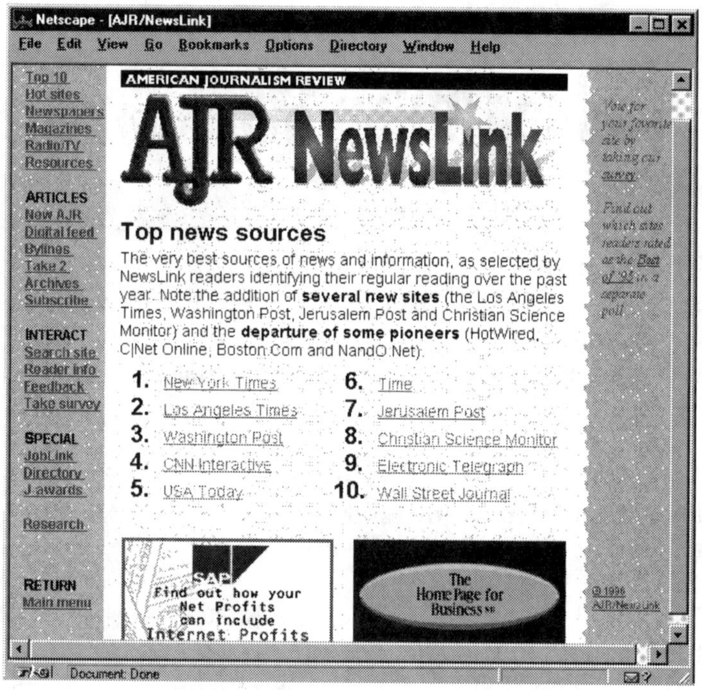

Figure 1 American Journalism Review

The NewsLink service is a must for your bookmark list. It's got listings and ratings for on-line versions of traditional newspapers, magazines and broadcast news as well as links to Internet-oriented news services. You will probably find all the news you need by visiting their Top 10 list or their best-of-the-year list. And each week NewsLink features one or more services that have made a particularly interesting addition to their list of on-line publications.

You may be interested in a commercial research report available via NewsLink. To learn more about the report, entitled "Tomorrow's News Today," click on the "Research" link on their home page. "Tomorrow's News Today" taps hundreds of academic and professional resources to provide in-depth, up-to-date thinking on content, design and marketing, with each source fully documented. This is not, however, merely facts, figures and random opinions. You'll find well-reasoned analyses that are geared toward helping you make wise investments today and in the growing cyberspace world of tomorrow.

Broadcast news on-line

Both radio and television stations are creating cyberspace versions of their traditional formats. Perhaps one or more of your local television stations features its Internet site during newscasts. For example, in the Washington area, NBC's Channel 4 offers an on-line weather service that supplements their broadcast weather. Increasingly, television stations are embracing cyberspace as additional programming outlets.

The Channel 4 News Web site (at *wxnet4.nbc4.com*) offers in-depth weather reports, historical statistics and updates on school closings that are affected by weather (see Figure 2). They also sponsor special events. For example, when the Comet Hyakutake passed near the Earth, they offered viewing information and downloadable images of the comet that they collected from viewers around the Washington region. And, if you'd like to see the actual weather in your nation's capital, just click on the WeatherNet 4 live camera links.

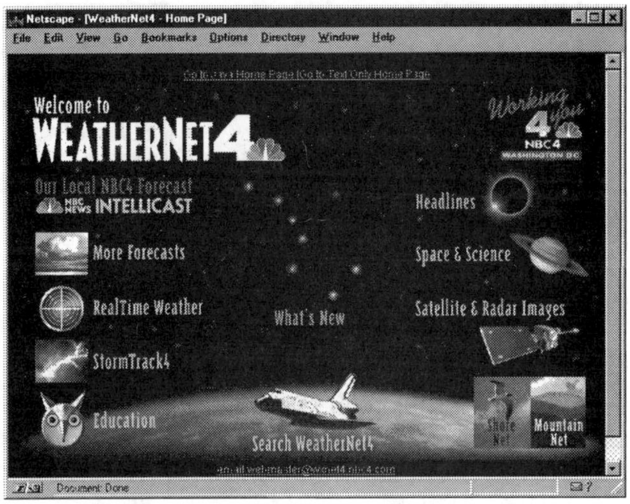

Figure 2 Washington, D.C. weather

The Washington Post

The Washington Post (at *www.washingtonpost.com*) has an on-line news service that's a one-stop site for national, international and Metro-Washington, D.C. news and information (see Figure 3). Here you'll find the information resources of *The Washington Post*, including background information, Post archives, photographs, news and classified ads. These resources, from news bureaus throughout the world, are available to anyone; not just *Post* subscribers.

Figure 3 *The Washington Post*

Local users will enjoy The Post's detailed metropolitan and neighborhood news and its comprehensive guide to entertainment in the Washington, D.C. metropolitan area and surrounding suburbs.

And even if you're not a local, you might find it interesting to see what's going on in the U.S. Capitol. Or you can try searching the past week's classified ads and maybe you'll find a chance to buy a used car from a Congressman.

The Post's Web site gives you the opportunity to participate in national—no, make that global—debates on the hottest political news topics in Washington. Check out the interactive section, in which you can post a response to a selected Post article and read other responses from around the world.

Another valuable service is the Post's free, easy-to-use, "Personal Portfolio" service (see Figure 4) that lets you build a targeted stock and financial news report from its Business section. Even if you don't build a personal portfolio, you can obtain current stock quotes and detailed financial news, and check out the latest economic calendar. The Financial section also has a global currency exchange report that would be an excellent Web browser bookmark for any world traveler or international investor.

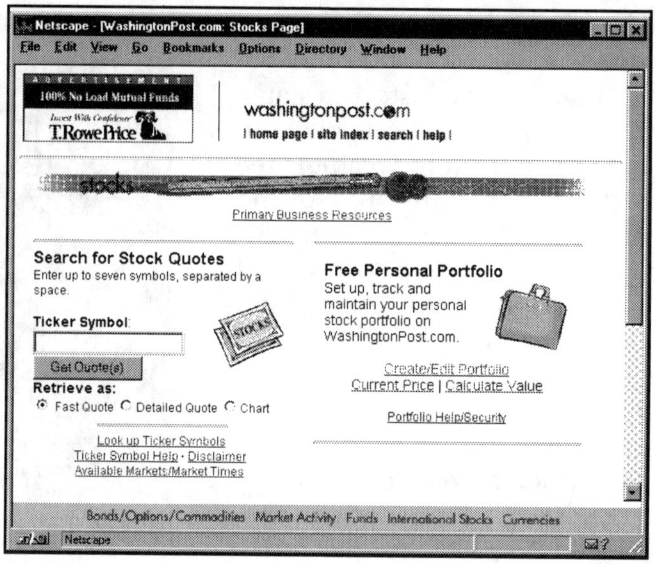

Figure 4 The Post - personal stock portfolio

If you're planning to visit Washington, D.C., bookmark the Post's home page and read it regularly for a few weeks before your trip. Not only will you get a feel for upcoming special events, you'll find virtual tours of interesting local spots. Save these reports and then take the tour in person when you're visiting. Even if you never come, this could be a fun way to learn more about the most historic area in the U.S.

Inside Info

Remember, *The Washington Post* is but one example of many on-line newspapers. We've included it because it carries so much news that is of national and international interest. Be sure to use an Internet search engine to check your local papers—or any city in the world.

Tailored news services

In cyberspace, you no longer have to seek the news. Lucky you, with Internet news services, the news will seek you through a tailored news service. Tailored news services have many different forms, but they all have one principle: they spare you the burden of being smothered by a crush of over-information that you don't need.

Figure 5 The China News Digest

As helpful as tailored news services are, there is a disheartening number of these services available and the list is growing all the time. Worse, there is no more a "right" service to choose than there is a "right" pillow to choose. The good news is that these services are inexpensive, they offer free samples, they are easy to find and subscribing and unsubscribing is simple. Hence, the best strategy for choosing the right Internet news service for your needs is to sample a lot of them and then decide.

One obvious way to start your search for on-line news services is to check out the major search engines such as Yahoo! and Lycos. Nearly all search engines have a news link. This will mostly likely point you to a mixture of news services, but you can browse through them to find the tailored services that filter the news for you.

You can get global news services from *potter.cc.keele.ac.uk/depts/li/eljourn.htm* (see Figure 5). The page is a lengthy collection of international, electronic newspapers, news services and journals. So, if you're interested in going directly to international news, this service lets you bypass everything else and get right to it. And, it features a link to the "IDEAL World Wide Web service" that gives you electronic access to academic press journals.

CRAYON

With so many services from which to choose, we needed some very scientific criteria to select one tailored news service to feature here. So, after much browsing and careful consideration, we used the highly scientific method of picking one because it's got a cute name: CRAYON (CReAte Your Own Newspaper). The CRAYON news service is at *crayon.net* (see Figure 6). Though it made the cut because of its name, CRAYON turned out to be a marvel of Internet technology.

Figure 6 Create a tailored on-line newspaper

Creating your own newspaper with CRAYON is simple. Imagine going to your local paper office and telling them exactly what you want and do not want to read, and then the next day they deliver to your door a tailored version of their newspaper. Getting the information you need then would be faster and more efficient than ever before. This is how CRAYON works. You can even specify your own title, giving you a little taste of how it must feel to be Rupert Murdoch (see Figure 7).

Figure 7 Create a personal edition of the news

In addition to selecting the type of news you want you can specify if the associated images are to be downloaded as part of your paper or included as on-line links. If you download them, be prepared for your daily paper to gobble more connect time.

You can also select the order in which you want your sections arranged. You can include multiple selections from any of the major headings: U.S. News, Regional and Local News, World News, Politics as

Usual, Weather Conditions and Forecasts, Information and Technology Report, Arts and Entertainment, SportsDay, The Funny Pages, The Tabloid Page and New and Cool Web Sites.

CRAYON generates a Web page with links to the news features you select. This generated page can be delivered one-section-at-a-time or in one big page. The one big page averages about 60k—which might cause problems with some computers and browsers—but it presents your selections in one continuous page.

Inside Info

After CRAYON generates your paper, you'll need to save the file. You then can open the page and add it to your Netscape Navigator Bookmarks. Then you'll be able to get to this page quickly anytime you want to see it.

If you notice that today's CRAYON paper has yesterday's images or text, you need to remember that the Netscape Navigator caches Web pages and images that it's previously downloaded. If the information on any page is stale, click on the refresh button, or press **CTRL+R** or click **View, Reload**. This will force your Netscape Navigator to bypass the cache and to download the page and images directly from the server.

Jargon Cutter

Cache - Web browsers store the pages you load into a memory buffer called a cache. This cuts down on Internet traffic because if you want to return to a page you've recently seen, the browser will pull the page from the cache instead of going back out to the Internet again. We covered this in depth in the Netscape chapter in Phase 2.

Also, remember that you can return to CRAYON anytime and generate a new Web page, changing the links you select, the title or the order of the sections you've chosen.

It could hardly be simpler and definitely can't be cheaper. Just watching this service work is an interesting experience. A word of caution, though: the page you generate with this service could be addictive. Starting from here, you could spend an entire day surfing through the ever-increasing cascade of links that your selected pages unveil. This is a "must get" service.

Investment management

You'll find that the Internet offers just about as many financial services as it does news services. You'll be able to track stock portfolios, get real-time stock ticker tape, receive special alarm notices via e-mail if certain maximum or minimum stock prices are triggered, track financial headlines and order tailored financial news reports.

You also will be able to access an incredible wealth of information on every company that trades stock publicly. This can be a boon when you're considering making an investment, or even if you're just curious about how your biggest competitor is faring.

We'll continue by showing you an excellent, full-powered stock reporting service that will give you automated, tailored financial reports, headlines, stock quotes and complete portfolio tracking. A top-notch stock service is Quote.Com (see Figure 8), which you can visit at *www.quote.com*.

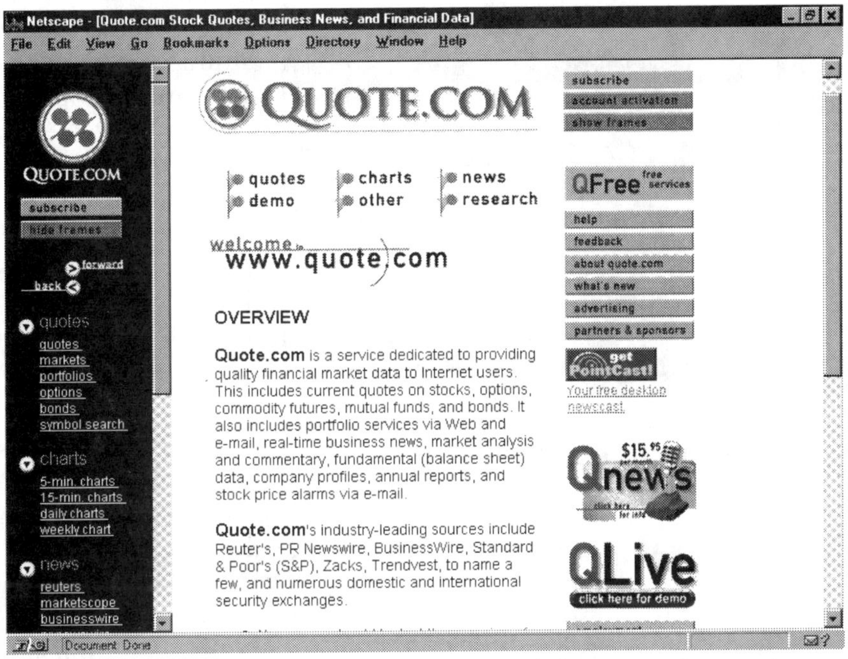

Figure 8 Quote.Com - a full line of financial news and reporting

Inside Info

Remember, you don't have to own a stock to track it. You can sign up with a stock service simply to track the players in your field of interest or to practice dealing with stocks or to test your market theories. You can set up a portfolio with 100 shares of the target stocks so you can easily decipher the impact of stock price swings.

NYU EDGAR

New York University maintains a terrific site for investors or anyone who needs to research company histories or statistics at *edgar.stern.nyu.edu*. The EDGAR (Electronic Data Gathering and Retrieval) site was developed by the NYU Stern School of Business Information Systems Department. Perhaps one of its most valuable features is the Profile Search that lets you search and view corporate profiles by entering keywords.

If you're investigating companies, you'll find plenty of uses for the links to the "RR Donnelley Library of SEC Materials" and "Corporate SEC Filings." One of its richest resources is the link called "Reciprocal Links" that will point you to a whole world of financial Web links. Be sure to check out their "Interesting Links" jump for such tidbits as the "Economics of Networks."

Tracking investment stocks

While we will profile only one of the many different services available, you can see more by visiting the Web page at *edgar.stern.nyu.edu/reciprocal.html* and checking out its array of related links. Quote.Com is a good choice because it offers one-stop shopping for all types of the stock services and has a range of subscription levels that will allow you to tailor your service to your needs.

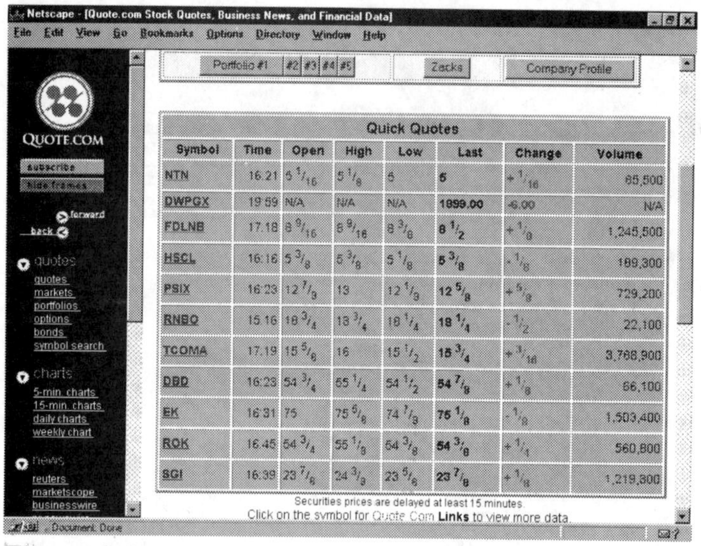

Figure 9 Sample on-line stock portfolio

To retrieve your portfolio, you'll have to enter a login and password. You'll then be able to select from a list of multiple portfolios such as the sample portfolio displayed here (see Figure 9). From this page, you can see that there are links to pick up Quick Quotes on other stocks, check financial news headlines, view a daily chart, consult an on-line stock guide, view a history file, or check your other portfolios. The buttons to Zacks Investment Research and to Trendvest are available at extra cost for basic subscribers or free for higher-level subscribers.

This portfolio is configured for on-screen viewing, but they offer several common formats that will permit you to easily enter this information into other applications. For example, they have ASCII comma-delimited, Quicken and spreadsheet formats.

And here's the best part: you don't have to visit the Quote.Com Web site to track your portfolio. Quote.Com e-mails you a summary of your portfolios at the end of the business day so they'll be ready for you in the morning.

Financial news & reports

Quote.Com includes with each report it sends to you links to related stories on the stocks you've selected to track. If you've chosen a high enough level of service, you'll be able to read the full text of these stories free. If you have the basic service, you'll be charged one dollar per story that you select to read.

In addition to stories that affect your stock portfolio, you can enter the Quote.Com home page directly and search for stories on other companies. Perhaps if you find something interesting that pertains to your industry or business, you might add that stock to your portfolio, even if you have no plans to invest in that company.

AT&T Business Network

The AT&T Business Network service can keep you current on critical industry and business news. You can access its extensive reference sources, connect with a dynamic community of other business networkers and take full advantage of a host of Internet business sources at *www.att.com/bnet*.

The AT&T Business Network features an incredible collection of on-line resources from leading publishers. We've assembled the current list in alphabetical order: Bunker Hill Consulting Group; BNA (Bureau of National Affairs); Business Travel News; CCH Incorporated; CNN Interactive; Cowles Business Media; Cowles New Media; Dow Jones Business Information Services; Dun & Bradstreet Information Services; Entrepreneurial Edge; Entrepreneur Magazine Group; Seth Godin Productions; Guerilla Marketing International; Individual, Inc.; Information Access Company; Inso Corporation; Investext Industry ReportsR; The Kiplinger Washington Editors; Nightly Business Report; Standard & Poor's; Thomas Register of American Manufacturers; Thomas Food Industry Register; TRW Business Information Services; TV HOST; Weather Services Corporation; Weissmann Travel Reports; and Meg Whittemore, Whittemore & Associates. As amazing as that list is, it's growing steadily (see Figure 10).

The AT&T Business Network will give you a free subscription, so it's a real information bargain. Imagine what it would have cost for at-home access to all of that information just a few years ago.

Figure 10 AT&T Business Network

Now that you've seen so many Internet resources for business and financial news, you ought to be able to make so much money that you can retire to a tropical island with nothing but a beach and your Internet connection. But there are more ways to earn money than just through investing. Let's move to the next step: using the Internet to sell your professional skills—or just to sell the wind chimes you build for a hobby.

Marketing sites

Internet marketing sites provide the full spectrum of marketing information. You can get help for selling products and services you produce in a home-based business and even for selling the business itself. You can find on-line advertising agencies, marketing consultants, marketing software, and advertising forums. The Internet has brought us all a whole new world of marketing possibilities and channels. Fortunately, it also has brought us the tools to explore these new possibilities.

Inside Info

The next time you need to buy or sell a car, or even your home, be sure to check for Web sites. This is a rapidly changing field and new sites come on-line constantly. A search with Yahoo! or Lycos will be a good start, of course. But keep an eye out for newspapers and magazines that put classified advertising on their Web sites.

Often the key to finding the services or contacts you need will be to use the search engines profiled in the last chapter. To get you started, however, we've included some helpful sites here. As with most sites, you'll find links here to other, related Web sites.

Marketing consultants

Marketing in cyberspace is a paradox: on the one hand it's completely different from any other marketing and on the other hand it's the same as it's been for thousands of years. It's different because it's interactive and buyers can tailor their own presentation. But then it's the same as always because even the coolest, high-tech Web site won't sell much if it doesn't focus on delivering value. But you might need some professional advice to help you learn to merge the new with the traditional.

Fortunately, expert help is available on-line. Let's begin with one of the best, Poppe Tyson (pronounced "poppy tyson"), a venerable, well-established agency that has been at the forefront of the move into cyberspace.

Figure 11 Internet marketing leaders

Poppe Tyson

Poppe Tyson (see Figure 11) is an international advertising agency owned by Bozell, Jacobs, Kenyon & Eckhardt, the world's fourth largest marketing communications company. But there's more to them than size: they were selected as the 1995 "Agency of the Year" by *Marketing Computers* magazine. Check them out at *www.poppe.com*.

Some of Poppe Tyson's clients prove its ability to handle cyberspace marketing. For example, they are handling the marketing for one of largest Internet service providers in the U.S., PSI Net of Herndon, Virginia. You may have seen one of their most visible projects: bringing major auto races into cyberspace.

During 1995 Memorial Day weekend, the Web site for the world's most famous race was introduced during commercial breaks by Valvoline Motor Oil, one of Poppe Tyson's clients. They coordinated both the marketing content and the technical expertise required to bring the Indy 500 Web site to life (see Figure 12). Now the Valvoline site includes many of the major Indy-car and NASCAR races.

Figure 12 Valvoline brought racing into cyberspace

Inside Info

Poppe Tyson's Web site is a marvel of cyberspace value and marketing expertise. They've got links that give you a behind-the-scenes view of the people and equipment that put the Indy 500 on-line. Of course, they hope to attract your business while you're surfing their site, but that's what well-done Web sites are all about.

GoSite

If you need a service that can develop hypertext versions of existing materials and transform logos, graphics and photos into Web formats that are ready to go on-line world-wide, check out the GoSite service at *www.gosite.com* for details. Costs for using a company such as GoSite will be lower than with a full-service agency such as Poppe Tyson, but then that doesn't include paying for the development of an advertising program. GoSite can create Web graphics that fit an existing, traditional marketing program and help format existing material into a valuable, user-friendly Web site. They can also create a complete Web server, register a domain name, upload the completed Web files and maintain the entire site.

GoSite is a nice compromise between a full-service agency and a total do-it-yourself Web service provider. One tool they use to bridge the gap between the two is the GoGadget Administrator, an Internet site manager that makes simple work of some otherwise complicated tasks. GoGadget makes maintaining a Web Site as simple as clicking a mouse. It will automatically consolidate the files between a company's computer and its GoSite Server by clicking a button. Even Internet novices will be able to set-up and control e-mail accounts, forward files and create auto-responding e-mail.

So if you want to market your handmade wind chimes but you've got a limited budget, then this is a good place to start. But beware—we discovered one fellow who had run a quiet little business selling parts for classic Ford Mustangs from his garage. He put it on the Internet and was so successful that he actually had to remove it for a while and then rent commercial space and hire help before he could go back on-line!

Your Marketing Coach

If you need to market, but you wish marketing would go away, you need Your Marketing Coach. Designed for businesses that market consulting and professional services, Your Marketing Coach is a do-it-yourself marketing program that's based on a principle called Client-Centered Interneting. Coach's home page is *www.marketing-coach.com*.

Coach works best for home-based businesses, sole proprietorships and small businesses such as accountants, engineers, architects, public relations consultants, writers, consultants and computer programmers. These professions are rarely filled with good marketers, but they can't survive without marketing. Coach makes marketing easy with a software application called Market Keys that analyzes an existing practice and recommends ways to capitalize on its client list to bring in clones of its best clients.

The Coach Web site features regularly updated tips on marketing your consulting and professional services and getting new clients. It also has links to many other sites that provide valuable help for small and home-based businesses. It's best touch is the free marketing manuals that you will be sent if you complete the on-line questionnaire. Just fill in your mailing information and request the manual you want.

Businesses For Sale

Here's a Web site that was under construction as this book was being written, so you'll want to check it out today to see how it's evolved. "AFC's Businesses For Sale" is a meeting place for people who want to buy and sell businesses. If you're a seller, you can list your business here. If you're a buyer, you can search for businesses under a variety of categories. For example, geographic location, revenue size, type of business. They also list links to several other business-for-sale Web sites. Visit their home page at *www.afc-inc.com* and check out the Orbiting in Cyberspace section for other similar services.

Department of Commerce economic data

This service offers up-to-date worldwide economic information, on everything from copyright issues to international currency exchange rates. It's not technically on the Web because it's a Gopher-search site maintained by the University of Michigan. Most likely this site soon will find its way onto the Web, but its information is too valuable to exclude just because it hasn't yet made the transition.

You can access the site by entering the URL *gopher://una.hh.lib.umich.edu/11/ebb*. You'll see a long list of folders that contain documents on various business topics. Many of the folders produce lists of sub-folders. Eventually you'll get down to a document you want, which can be retrieved by clicking on the document icon or the hypertext title. If browsing a long title list doesn't appeal to you, click on the link "Keyword Search of File Titles" at the top of the page. This link brings up a searchable Gopher index that lets you enter keywords.

Inside Info

The Gopher keyword searches performed on this Gopher site look for all terms separately. If you want to narrow a search by using more than one search term you must manually insert terms such as AND or NOT.

Better Business Bureau

The Better Business Bureau (BBB) is a classic, traditional source for lots of business information. Visit the Better Business Bureau site at *www.bbb.org* (see Figure 13).

Figure 13 The BBB is keeping up with the times

Like the rest of us, this venerable institution has moved into cyberspace to keep up with the times. For example, in 1996, the Council of Better Business Bureaus announced 15 finalists for their first annual "Better Business Bureau Torch Award for Marketplace Ethics." The award finalists were selected for demonstrating a commitment to exceptionally high standards of ethical business practices. Surely there's some inspiration for your own excellence lurking in the stories about such select companies.

The "Better Business Bureau Code Of Advertising" page is an excellent information source for use in reviewing a marketing plan. For example, with all of the "free" things floating around on the Internet, you might want to read the "Free" topic in these guidelines before you apply that often-misleading word to your products or services. Another company-saving topic is their "Scam Alert" link that can keep you up-to-date on the latest con schemes. A good example is an exposé entitled "Don't Get Scammed By Office Con Artists," that reveals the explosion of fake offices that are being established to hide con artist activities. Expect to see these same principles mushroom on the Internet.

Inside Info

Newsgroups aren't a part of the Web, but they're an integrated part of your system and they're easy to use. Start your newsgroup reader, then browse through the list of newsgroup headings until you see a folder named: **biz.*** Open this folder to reveal the topics inside, then click on any sub-heading that interests you.

Selling your house

Increasingly, the Web is becoming an alternate real estate marketing tool. New real estate sites are springing up weekly and existing ones are expanding. None of them is fully developed, none of them is fully national in scope—yet. As you browse through real estate Web sites you're quite likely to discover that your own state has no listings, or a city to which you want to move has no listings. Before long, however, expect this to become a booming business that will permanently alter the way residential real estate is bought and sold.

Figure 14 IRED - Internet Real Estate Directory

Since this aspect of the Web is changing so rapidly, we suggest that you use the major search engines to find real estate sites. Yahoo! has extensive resources dedicated to real estate listings, news, classified ads, interest rates and mortgage information. Another valuable resource for real estate information is the Internet Real Estate Directory (IRED) at *www.ired.com* (see Figure 14). IRED has countless links to every topic you'd want. And, of course, those links will lead to more links and more links and more links. Before long you won't even remember you started out just looking for real estate information—but that's why the Web is so popular, isn't it?

The Web's real estate content is not restricted to on-line companies—there are lots of individual listings, many of which are put up by private individuals who hope that someone on the Internet will find their listing and buy their home. If you'd like to find listings for your area, we suggest you go to Lycos or Yahoo! and perform a search on the keywords: "real estate listings XXXX." (Substitute the target state or city for the XXXX).

Listing your own house on the Web can be a snap. Many of the sites have simple forms for sellers to complete that will automatically place your listing on their site. Others let you mail them the information, including photos, and they'll publish your listing for you. Expect to pay a fee if the service does the work, perhaps in the $50 to $250 range.

Another option for listing your home on the Web is to start with Phase 4 of this book and learn about Web publishing. In those chapters, we not only get you started with the basics of Web publishing, but we help you learn how to get your site indexed into the Web search engines so that others can find your site.

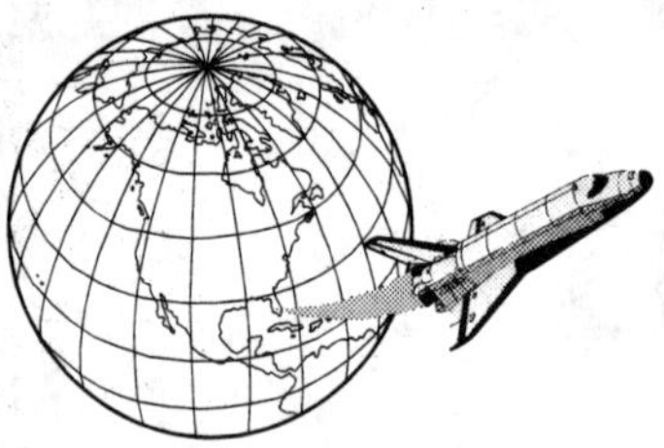

Orbiting in Cyberspace

Open Market commercial sites index
http://www.directory.net

Open Market, Incorporated develops and markets software, services and custom solutions that facilitate electronic commerce on the Web. Open Market applies both advanced technology and a business perspective to the expansion of business into an electronic marketplace. They offer solutions that address the needs of small companies and global businesses alike.

BizQuest
http://www.bizquest.com

BizQuest is a business service that maintains a database of international business transfer information. They list both "general" businesses (up to $2,000,000 in sales) and "mid-market" businesses ($2,000,000-$50,000,000) in sales. You may perform free searches for business buyers, sellers, brokers, appraisers, lenders and other services, but you'll have to complete a registration form before each search. For an annual fee, they'll give you a password that allows you to search without having to register each time you return to the site.

Figure 15 One of the Internet's most extensive directory services

World Wide Web yellow pages
http://www.yellow.com

Here's an easy-to-remember URL that should find its way onto thousands (perhaps millions?) of Bookmark lists (see Figure 15). You can use this page to search for a wide range of businesses with a Web presence. World Wide Yellow Pages is a trademark of Home Pages, Incorporated.

M&A Marketplace
http://www.mktplc.com/cfnet

The M&A Marketplace Web site is designed for buyers and sellers of companies and for financial intermediaries who are involved in mergers and acquisitions (M&A), divestitures and corporate finance. They've got links that let you explore companies for sale, buyers seeking sellers, joint ventures, financial sources and a host of other related topics. Full searching and browsing capabilities are reserved for visitors with paid memberships (currently $9.95 per month). They even provide an area on the site for members to network directly with other members.

GoGlobal Real Estate Search
http://www.goglobal.com

Here's a free, on-line real estate searching service. It has more than a million listings and is increasing daily. You can search directly for listed properties, for real estate firms, for real estate professionals, or for general, related information. Of course you also can list your own property so other surfers can find your house for sale. It's possible, however, that you'll just mark this as a Bookmark and check back later because a lot of states are not yet covered.

Certified business brokers
http://www.mgroup.com/cbb.html

Certified Business Brokers is a professional firm with a broad range of business skills and experience available to assist you in the sale or acquisition of a privately owned business. With over 60 years combined experience in business sales and acquisitions and a track record of over 1,000 businesses sold, Certified Business Brokers can be an essential element in buying a business or selling your current business.

Socially responsible business mailing list archive
http://www.envirolink.org/archives/srb

To quote from the site's home page, "At last, a place for the enlightened discussion of Socially Responsible Business and Investing. This is THE forum for discussion and information exchange focused around aspects and topics of socially responsible business (SRB) and investing (SRI)." The SRB and SRI topics are combined to create a more accessible and popular conference area by combining the two inter-related subjects. You can click on the "Subscribe" link to join the mailing list or you can browse through this archive and view documents sorted by author, subject or date.

Small and Home-Based Business Links
http://www.ro.com/small_business/homebased.html

A wealth of information for small and home-based businesses (see Figure 16). This site includes coverage of small and home-based franchises, business opportunities, small business reference material, information to help you run and market your small- or home-based business, small and home-based newsgroups, searching tools and services for small business; just about anything related to small and home-based businesses can be found in these links.

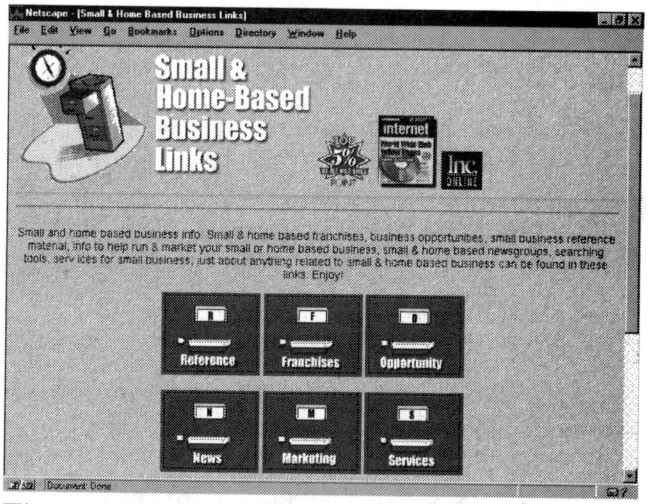

Figure 16 On-line help for your small business

IOMA
http://www.ioma.com

This site is home to the Institute of Management and Administration (IOMA) and Information Services for Professionals. It's an excellent guide to business resources on the Internet. IOMA, a leading publisher of management and business information, offers sample articles from a variety of newsletters, as well as 90-day trial subscriptions. Whether managing a law or accounting office, a defined contribution investment plan, or a computer network, professionals from virtually every industry can find invaluable, career-enhancing information in these IOMA newsletters.

Figure 17 Eliminate trips to the printshop and pick up hot tips

Printshop 2000
http://www.printshop2000.com

The computer revolution has hurt some print shops, but a few are using it to increase business. A top-flight example is the Printshop 2000 site where you may be able to handle all of your printshop needs on-line (see Figure 17). They'll take your order over the Internet, let you e-mail in your files and then they'll ship out the completed job. No more running out for special printing projects because you now have a printshop in your PC. This is a fabulous resource for small and home-based business owners who can't spare the time to run print shop errands and it includes workshops that will help you keep pace with the rapidly-changing printing industry.

Business Exchange Network
http://www.biz-exchange.com

The Business Exchange Network is a "clearinghouse" of information for the buying and selling of small-sized to mid-sized businesses. Sales are handled through their Web site, as well as through several traditional avenues. They publish a monthly newspaper, "Businesses for Sale," and two weekly publications, "Business Buyers Weekly Report," and the "Business Brokers, Agents, and Intermediaries Report." They offer another non-cyberspace option for the information on their Web site through a fax-on-demand system. If you're considering using such a service, you might want to read their articles dealing with all aspects of buying and selling businesses.

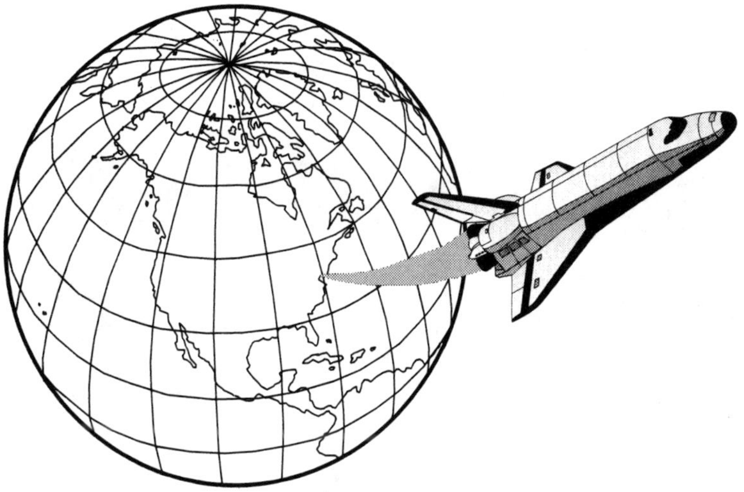

Phase 4

Phase 4: Web Publishing

Now that you've seen what other people have done on the Web, it's your turn. What do you have to say or to show to the world? Whatever it is, you can make it instantly available to anyone, anywhere in the world.

Perhaps you've just bought a new home and you'd like all of your on-line relatives to see some photos. Is there some exciting announcement you'd like to share with friends and relatives? Or, maybe there's a new baby in your life. You can have the photos on-line within hours.

Please understand that these chapters will just get you started and show you the basics of creating a Web site of your own. Keep in mind that most of the world-class Web sites you've been surfing through were created and are maintained by full-time professionals who do nothing else but create and publish Web content. But, don't worry about creating a stunning, world-class Web site—after all, your friends and family just want to see those photos and they want to see them today!

- **Chapter 14** is a primer for **Web publishing**. You'll learn about the options available to you for creating your own Web pages. You may be surprised how easy it is to present basic information on the Web.

- **Chapter 15** introduces **Web graphics**. It helps you understand the different computer formats for Web graphics and what software tools you can use to create and edit graphic images. We even give you a Web site that offers a wealth of tips on scanning existing documents, drawings and photos into your Web documents.

- **Chapter 16** closes the book with a light-hearted look at **copyright issues** in the electronic age of cyberspace. You'll encounter a lot of text and graphics on the Web that you'll be able to quickly download, save and reuse. Usually, that information will be protected by copyrights. But the good news is that securing permission for reuse usually is a snap. We'll help you understand what you can and cannot reuse without permission and give you tips on getting the permission you need.

14

Web Publishing: Your Cyber•Spacestation

When the Web first appeared, writing hypertext, HTML-language pages required high levels of computer expertise, diligence and patience. But today, creating HTML can actually be enjoyable and as simple as using a word processor.

> **Erol's Web Hosting**
>
> As a benefit of your Erol's Internet service, you will be able to have an area on our servers in which to store your own Personal Web Page free of charge. You can e-mail your friends its unique URL and they will be able to see your handiwork from anywhere on the World Wide Web.
>
> There are limits to the amount of information (in terms of bytes of data) and the kind of information (it must not be a commercial site selling goods or services and its contents must fall within generally accepted community standards regarding decency and good taste) that can be on your Personal Web Page. Also, there are certain technical guidelines regarding the use of third-party plug-ins and server scripting routines that are permissible. Since this technology is constantly changing, contact Erol's technical support for details.

Producing World Wide Web documents has become so common that you can create them with WordPerfect for Windows and Microsoft Word for Windows. Both offer free add-ons that greatly simplify the once arduous challenge of creating simple hypertext documents. So, now you can use an old friend as you become part of the Web. We'll highlight the strengths and weaknesses of both word processors, and then we'll discuss more advanced, dedicated Web editors.

But there's more to writing for the World Wide Web than the technical side of producing hypertext documents. Knowing how to use tools doesn't make you a skilled craftsman. Since your Web site will instantly broadcast your image world-wide, you'll want to get it right the first time.

We've included some home page tips that will help you know what you can expect to do yourself and when you might need a consultant. When you've finished this chapter, you'll be fully prepared to become a player in the electronic world of the Web.

Tools, tools, and more tools

There are more tools available for publishing Web hypertext documents than anyone can count. New ones are released almost daily. Before the recent dramatic expansion of Web tools, only programmers and computer specialists had the skills to create Web pages. But the Web's popularity explosion has prompted major software developers to create tools that enable mainstream users to create Web pages.

It's become so easy, in fact, that you may already have created Web pages without knowing it. That's because you can convert existing documents—including graphics and tables—into perfectly-formatted Web documents.

Creating the *very best* Web pages still requires a technical expert because the leading edge of technology always stays ahead of the mainstream user. Someone will always be pushing existing technical limits and if you want to play on the frontier, you'll need the skills of a full-time professional. But today, most users can create attractive, professional Web pages. We'll cover basic Web-development tools in several categories:

- Word processor add-ons;
- Conversion programs;
- Stand-alone HTML editors;
- Graphics software;
- CGI tools;
- Java.

Each category will be covered in subsequent sections of this chapter. Some of the topics, however, will be covered here only briefly because they have a dedicated chapter later in the book.

Word processor add-ons

Corel WordPerfect 7 for Windows includes a built-in HTML editor as well as automatic conversion of files to and from HTML, .GIF and .JPEG (see Figure 1). WordPerfect for Windows 6.1/7.0 and Microsoft Word for Windows each have add-on packages that enable them to handle HTML files. The WordPerfect 6.1/7.0 version is called the Internet Publisher and the Word version is called the Internet Assistant. These word-processor-based HTML editors are ideal for casual Web publishers and for documents that are mostly text.

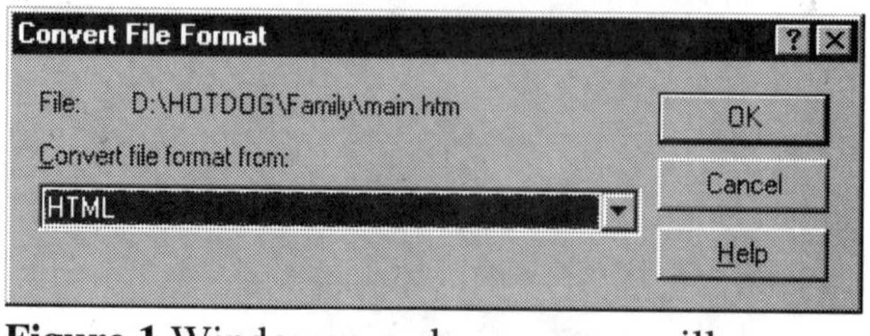

Figure 1 Windows word processors will convert HTML documents automatically

If you're converting documents for the Web and you don't need graphics or sound files, Word-

Perfect and Word are good choices because of their popularity.

In fact, users who won't give up their WordPerfect 5.1 for DOS can still create hypertext documents! The Styles feature in the trusty old 5.1 version (dating back to that ancient year 1989) enables documents to be turned into HTML by WordPerfect for Windows. This backward compatibility may be an important factor because some writers can't be dragged away from WordPerfect 5.1 even by the steamroller of Windows. The WordPerfect for Windows Internet Publisher enables almost anyone to write Web pages—even those who refuse to give up DOS or who still don't have a computer that can handle the demands of Windows.

You Say It's Easy, But How Do I Get Started?

Programmers long have learned their craft by analyzing the source code of existing programs. It's much easier to learn to program by example than it is to start from scratch. Often, programmers modify an existing program to fit their own needs. Using the same technique will help you learn to write HTML-encoded Web pages by studying and modifying existing Web pages.

When you encounter a Web page that has a feature you would like to learn, click **View, Source** to see its HTML source code. The default viewer is the Windows Notepad and you can use it for basic editing or to save the file on your system for later editing with a more sophisticated application. And it's certainly adequate if you just want to highlight a section of the page, copy it to your clipboard and paste it into another HTML document.

Even if you're content with Notepad's limited abilities, some Web pages are too large for it, so you may need to designate another editor as your viewer. But the Notepad is a good choice for most users. To change Netscape's default HTML viewer, follow the steps in the next Step-By-Step exercise.

Step-By-Step

GOAL: Set Netscape Navigator's HTML source code viewer

- ✔ Click **Options, General Preferences**.
- ✔ Click the **Apps** tab.
- ✔ Double-click in the **View Source** text entry box.
- ✔ Enter the name and path of your favorite application.

  You can enter any Windows editing application. If you don't know the application's full path and filename, click on **Browse**, then select an editor such as the Windows Notepad, the Windows Write program, the Windows 95 Wordpad or your favorite word processor.
- ✔ Click **OK** to save the change.

Of course, if you want to save the entire source code you can click **File, Save As File...** and use the dialog box with the **Save File as Type** set to **HTML (*.htm, *.html)**. Often, however, you only want to save a small piece of a document's HTML code, so just highlight the chunk you need, press **CTRL+C** to copy it to your clipboard and then paste it into your HTML editor.

As this was written, Microsoft Word didn't include HTML functions on their original distribution disks. Before you can create Web pages with Word, you'll need to download the application's Internet add-on and then install it. This also is true of the WordPerfect for Windows 6 versions. But Corel WordPerfect 7 now has built-in HTML support as well as built-in support for .GIF and .JPG graphics.

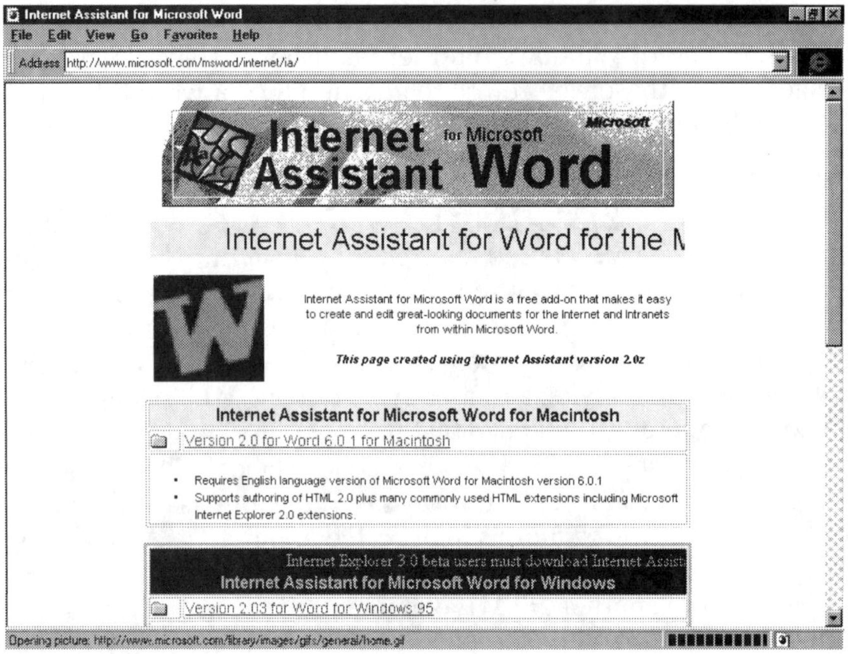

Figure 2 Internet Assistant - brings HTML authoring to Word

Downloading an HTML Add-on

WordPerfect Internet Publisher

If you use Corel WordPerfect 7, the Internet Publisher is included with the Corel Suite, enabling you to publish on the Web just about anything you can create in WordPerfect—including graphic presentations and spreadsheets.

If you still use WordPerfect 6.0/6.1, then go to WordPerfect's Web site at *www.wordperfect.com*. Click on the generic **Internet Publishing** link, click on the **Internet Publisher** link, then click on the download link. This will transfer the file *wpipzip.exe* to your hard disk. You'll need to put this file in its own directory, then execute it. It will install itself into your copy of WordPerfect for Windows 6.0/6.1. After that, you'll enjoy the freedom to create Web documents right inside your faithful, familiar friend.

Microsoft Word Internet Assistant

Start at the Microsoft Web site at *www.microsoft.com*. You might have to scroll down to see it, but look for a link to "Downloads" and a drop-list that says "Select a Product." Click on the drop-list and select "Internet Products." You'll find a link for the "Internet Assistant" on this page, under the heading "Authoring Tools." This page has links for Word 6, Word 95 and Word for the Macintosh. Download the file, *wordia.exe*, into a newly created directory on your hard disk. Do not place *wordia.exe* in your Word system directory because it needs to run in its own directory. Run the file from its directory and it will complete the installation and enable you to create HTML documents within Word. The download page itself was created with the Internet Assistant (see Figure 2).

HTML conversion applications

HTML conversion applications will convert existing documents, databases and other file types to HTML format. They often do a better job than the word processor add-ons. Conversion applications can be especially valuable for productivity if you need to Web publish a large number of existing documents. We'll introduce you to two popular applications from Skisoft:

- ❖ Web Publisher;
- ❖ Web Presentation Service.

Skisoft Web Publisher

This application can be a major efficiency tool for organizations converting reams of documents. One of its biggest selling points is its batch conversion mode that can convert hundreds of documents in a single pass. It's not perfect, but it's a big leap up from using the Internet Assistant add-on for Microsoft Word and manually working through each document.

The Skisoft Web Publisher automatically converts files from Word, WordPerfect, AmiPro and Excel, but it doesn't convert the native format of any of these applications. Instead, it accepts documents in the Rich Text Format (.RTF). All four of these applications can save files in the .RTF format. So, the Skisoft Web Publisher won't directly convert your archives of ancient WordPerfect 5.1 text without first converting all of them into .RTF. But even that process can be automated.

Tables in your word processing documents are converted directly into HTML tables. And the Web Publisher converts normal word processor images into .GIF files. Plus, it builds a cross-linked table of contents and an index of key terms with each item in the index linked to the appropriate text in your documents.

If you've spruced up your word processing documents with numbered lists, bullets and style headings, you'll be thrilled to know that the Web Publisher will convert all of these into HTML. It even converts bullets nested within numbered lists. Your styles can be converted into standard HTML heading codes.

Downloading the Skisoft Conversion Tools

Go to *www.skisoft.com* (see Figure 3) and you'll find links to both of the products reviewed here: Web Publisher and Web Presentation Service. Before you download, read their FAQ file that may answer any questions you have about the products. The free usage license for the downloaded applications is only for 30 days, then you'll need to register them to comply with copyright requirements. This site includes samples of documents and images that have been converted using Skisoft products.

Web Presentation Service

Skisoft also offers the *Web Presentation Service* that publishes your Microsoft PowerPoint presentations on the World Wide Web. Web Presentation Service converts a presentation of up to 20 slides into a linked collection of HTML text files and .GIF graphics files that are ready to post on your Web Server. Each presentation slide becomes a full-color Web page. It automatically creates buttons beneath each slide that lets site visitors jump forward or backward as they view your presentation. It also creates an Outline page that has a hyper-linked heading to its related slide.

Figure 3 SkiSoft - converts your existing documents into ready-to-use Web pages

So, Skisoft gives you several user-friendly methods to create great-looking Web pages without needing to become a techno-wizard. Actually, you will soon find that even the stand-alone HTML editors don't require a technical genius. Let's graduate now to the next step up the HTML development ladder.

Inside Info

Have you ever wondered how HTML originated? HTML is based on SGML (Standard Generalized Markup Language), which was developed in the 1980s and became a formal standard in 1988. HTML used part of the SGML, added URLs (Uniform Resource Locators) plus the HTTP (Hypertext Transfer Protocol) and created the Web. This is making a long story very, very short, but you can read all about it at *www.brainlink.com/~ben/sgml.*

Stand-alone HTML editors

Stand-alone HTML editors are dedicated Windows applications designed specifically for creating HTML files. They offer more hypertext features, better control and more flexibility than word processor add-ons or conversion applications. As a trade-off, however, they require a greater learning curve and they lack some of the advanced word processing features you've come to expect in Windows applications.

Here's a method you might use to ease your transition into Web publishing. Create your first Web pages in WordPerfect or Word, or convert some existing documents. After these HTML files are saved on your hard disk, open them in a stand-alone

HTML editor. Seeing your own pages in HTML format is a good learning experience. And, most likely you'll fine-tune some things that didn't convert as you expected. You may be surprised how quickly you pick up HTML using this method and learn to create Web pages directly in an HTML editor.

We've chosen two editors to profile here because they each have distinctively different features, strengths and weaknesses. The editors we've selected are:

❖ HotDog Pro

❖ HTML Assistant Pro

HotDog Pro

HotDog Pro (see Figure 4) is a loyal puppy for many Web authors, so you, too, may choose it as your own HTML editor. There are some disadvantages, however, in using HotDog instead of an HTML add-on. Editing in it is similar to working full-time inside the WordPerfect "Reveal Codes" screen. That means that while the codes clearly delineate commands, the effects of the codes don't appear on the editing screen while you're working. So, you must work for a while and then use the "Preview" mode to check the appearance. But HotDog gives you control that you simply don't have with an add-on. Blessedly, HotDog lets you install any Web browser as its previewer and then places that browser's icon on its main button bar.

Figure 4 HotDog - the Web editor from "Downunder"

> **Downloading HotDog**
>
> Actually HotDog comes in two versions: HotDog and HotDog Pro. The Pro version costs a few dollars more and has enough additional features that it's worth the small cost difference. Most of the features that we're discussing here, however, are built into both versions. But the Pro version simplifies the use of most of those features and has an HTML spell checker. And the Pro version gives you greater control over setup preferences to suit your needs.
>
> We'll just use HotDog here generically to mean whichever version you decide to use. You can download a free, trial version of HotDog so you can test it before you buy it. HotDog is a product of Sausage Software, located at *www.sausage.com*. Both versions give you a 30-day free trial period after which you should register and pay the registration fee.

HotDog gives you positive control

HotDog gives you complete control over all codes. This isn't true in the add-ons. For example, WordPerfect Internet Publisher prompts you to enter a title for your home page. It then uses the text you enter as the actual document title and as the main heading at the top of the document. In HTML, however, you are not required to display the title at all. This is important because if you create your title properly, you probably won't want it displayed.

HotDog lets you create a true HTML title that doesn't display on your Web page. This frees you to optimize the document title so that people can find your site easily with Web search engines. For example, with the word processor add-ons that we discussed earlier, you could be forced to have both the main heading and the title say, "Welcome to the Acme Company Home Page!" That's fine if someone searches for "Welcome" or "Acme Company." But what about people who are searching for the products or services you offer?

A more productive choice would be to keep "Welcome to the Acme Company Home Page!" as your first heading, but make your title—which won't be displayed on the screen—say, "Power Tools, Socket Wrenches, Oil Field Supplies." Then any search on those key words will place your Web page high on the list of search results.

Overall, there are many similar control improvements that you'll enjoy with a dedicated HTML editor. Many people begin with an add-on and then switch to an HTML editor after they get frustrated with the limitations of the add-on application.

HotDog Snaglets

The folks at Sausage are trying hard to make life easy for Web authors. They offer a set of tools that embellish HotDog and help you create special effects and implement advanced HTML features. They call these tools "snaglets," which is derived from the Australian name for a HotDog: snag.

They've got one tool, called FrameGang (see Figure 5), that will help you automatically create a Web page with frames. With some basic knowledge of HTML frames and your trusty mouse, you can point and click your way through frame generation for your Web pages. Using frames allows you to display multiple HTML documents on one Web page, and allow hyperlinks in one frame to interact with another frame.

Another great tool is CrossEye, an image-map editing utility that enables you to create clickable hotspots on graphic images, without having to use the CGI script that is normally required to perform this task. These hotspots may be linked to URL addresses, providing your Web visitors with a graphical jump to any Web link you choose. This a wonderful tool because few people who build Web pages are able to use CGI scripts, either through lack of programming skills or because their Web service provider doesn't permit them. CrossEye allows nearly any HTML author to create "client-side" clickable image maps that don't require CGI scripts or special skills.

These are only two of the snaglets Sausage offers. Be sure to check their Web site often for updates on these as well as for releases of new snaglets.

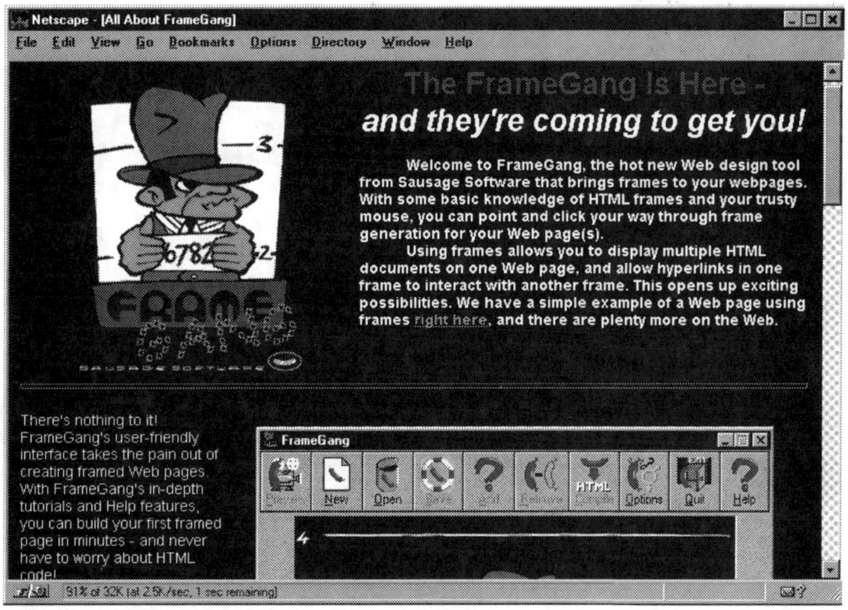

Figure 5 More from HotDog - frames not only look great, now they're easy to create

HTML Assistant Pro 2

HTML Assistant Pro 2, a product of Brooklyn North Software Works in Bedford, Nova Scotia, is much like HotDog Pro: a point-and-click editor for making Web pages. Running under Windows 3.1 and Windows 95, HTML Assistant Pro simplifies Web page authoring by using push button tools so you don't have to remember complicated codes. Adding hypertext links involves simply copying and pasting the URL for the page to which you want to point.

HTML Assistant Pro has a special feature called the Automatic Page Creator that lets you create a Web page by filling in blanks. This features simplifies the creation of forms and tables to simply clicking a button. Also similar to HotDog, it lets you designate any Web browser for previews so you'll be sure you're creating the look you want your visitors to see.

HTML Assistant Pro handles any size file, so your only size limitation will be in what you believe your visitors will be willing to wait for. As a bonus, Brooklyn North Software offers instant help via e-mail, a step-by-step tutorial that guides you through the creation of your Web page, a complete HTML Tag Reference and a beginner's guide to understanding the HTML.

HTML Assistant Pro has excellent aids for building tables and forms into Web pages. The syntax on both of those structures can be tricky, but this application lays out a sample for you after you select the basic format with a user-friendly dialog box. All you need to do is substitute your own text into the sample.

Choosing between HotDog Pro and HTML Assistant is going to come down to personal choice. They are both excellent products, although HotDog Pro has a lead right now. Still, you might bookmark the Web pages of both sites and follow the changes yourself. A good HTML editor can save you hours of work, so tracking updates will be time well spent.

Getting Your Copy of HTML Assistant Pro 2

You'll have to order HTML Assistant Pro 2 with a credit card via e-mail, fax or telephone. The current price is US $99.95 (Canadian $139.95) plus $10 shipping within the U.S., Canada or Mexico and $15 to other destinations. Canadian residents must include $10.50 GST and Nova Scotia residents must add $17.65 PST. Federal Express shipping to the U.S. is available for $25.

Mail orders: Brooklyn North Software Works, Inc.
25 Doyle Street
Bedford, Nova Scotia
Canada B4A 1K4

E-mail orders: sales@brooknorth.bedford.ns.ca
Phone orders: 800-349-1422
Fax orders: 902-835-2600

Graphics software

Once you begin writing HTML pages, you won't get far without wanting to add some graphics. The popularity of color printers and the color graphics that now adorn millions of Web pages has encouraged development of a slew of advanced graphics programs. "Corel Draw" and "Adobe Photoshop" are popular commercial products, while "PaintShop Pro" and "LViewPro" are popular shareware products for graphic image manipulation.

Graphics tools let you make Web pages attractive and interesting. And with these tools you can create image maps. Image maps are graphic images that are hypertext links on which users can click to jump to other Web information.

HTML extensions now include support for "client side" image maps that can be implemented without programming skills. Before the client side function was added, image maps could only be created through computer programming that was beyond the level of the average Web author. But clickable image maps are so simple now that HotDog even has a snaglet that automatically creates the HTML codes required to configure a clickable map on your Web site.

If you want to know more, read the next chapter, which is devoted entirely to Web graphics. But for now, let's get an overview of Common Gateway Interface (CGI).

Common Gateway Interface tools

Common Gateway Interface (CGI) is a programming specification for Web servers that makes it possible to have HTML pages tell the Web server to run programs that make your Web pages interactive.

CGI is called "server side" because it uses the server's processor to run the program. Input for the program is transmitted from the client to the server-based program. After the program runs, its results are transmitted back to the client.

User-friendly CGI tools include a wealth of valuable "pre-canned" programming scripts that can be referenced—called by the Web server—in existing hypertext documents. In other words, you won't have to start from scratch for every specialized function you want your Web site to perform. Advanced tools such as "Cold Fusion" enable Web authors to create sophisticated database applications without doing any actual programming.

Two of the most common uses on the Web for CGI programs have been clickable image maps and e-mail forms. The use of CGI for clickable image maps is certain to drop now that HTML includes "client side" image maps that do not rely on the server's processor. But, for now at least, CGI formmail routines can interface with HTML forms on your Web page to create a user-friendly feedback form.

Jargon Cutter

Formmail - a program used on Web servers that enables users to send e-mail to the host organization by completing a standard form. The advantage of formmail is that Web authors can design forms that ask for specific information, rather than letting each visitor ask questions in free form.

Java and JavaScript

Java and competitive variants enable a Web browser to download programming code from a Web server. The downloaded code extends the functionality of a browser so that it can perform elaborate tricks that are not built-in. Leading Web sites may use Java to nearly eliminate all Web browser limitations. The programming language required to implement Java applications is not yet for mainstream users, but you can hire a Java programmer to write some code if you've got an application in mind.

As opposed to CGI, Java is a "client-side" program. Because Java code runs on the client computer after being downloaded by your Web browser, it transfers the computing demands from the Web server to client computers. This permits a server to handle more traffic because Java is transferred to the client computer, and uses the client's processor.

Many users have computers that will not perform well while running Java applets. So, until your average Web visitor has a Pentium, consider the computing limitations your visitors might face before you implement an elaborate Java application.

While we're on the subject of considering the computing limitations of your Web visitors, we'd like to present some pointers for testing your Web site.

Java Restrictions

Many users have computers that will not run Java applications. The computer could lock up, causing the possible loss of data or requiring the intervention of a computer technician to restore the computer's operation. If you employ Java (or other advanced and potentially unstable technologies as Shock Wave and VRML, for example) in your Personal Web Page, Erol's may refuse to host your page on the server with these elements in it.

These technologies are changing, however, and may soon be supported fully when Erol's engineers determine that the software has demonstrated its stability and widespread acceptance in the consumer marketplace.

> If you still want to experiment with Java and other "beta" technologies on your Personal Home Page there are companies that will host your page for a fee. These hosting services, sometimes called Internet Presence Providers have restrictions too and their prices vary according to the amount of data you put up and the technical support it may require from them.

Testing your Web site

If you are involved in authoring Web pages and creating a Web site, you will most likely also be involved in the testing process. To create a truly user-friendly Web site, you'll need to consider four basic factors:

- Modem speed;
- Web browser;
- Windows screen resolution;
- PC processing power.

Even if you're not involved with the testing, be sure that you find out if the tests included consideration of these factors.

Test with a slow modem

Most likely your Web site's tests will be conducted on a hard drive in your own PC or on a network. No doubt you'll be quite satisfied with its performance. Then you'll look at the Web using your own Erol's Internet connection. But you'll have no idea how it will look to a visitor with a 14.4kbps modem and a slow Internet service provider. Not everyone is lucky enough to have the speed you enjoy right now, so your site needs to offer something incredible if it makes users wait. Of course you may not be concerned about appealing to visitors with slow modems—the use of those modems is fading rapidly.

As a minimum, you can offer a text-only option at the top of your home page so that visitors with slower computers can bypass any fancy graphics your site might include. On the other hand, ask yourself why you've chosen to include fancy graphics. These days, it's pretty tough to create a graphic that will earn a "Wow, that's cool" response. But it's real easy to create one that will earn, "Forget it, I'm not waiting that long."

Test with different browsers

The differences have narrowed between the appearance of the displays in the top Web browsers. At first, every browser seemed to have its own unique interpretation of HTML and you could hardly recognize the same page on two different browsers. But now the field has been narrowed to two dominant browsers that are reasonably similar in their displays. Whether you design your pages for Netscape or for the Microsoft Internet Explorer, be sure to test it with the other browser. Netscape remains the top Web browser, by far, though the Internet Explorer is changing Netscape's total dominance of the Web-browser market.

What about all the other browsers on the market? Don't worry about pleasing visitors with other browsers. Anyone these days who uses something other than Netscape Navigator or the Internet Explorer is someone who wants to be different from the majority. They have grown accustomed to weird displays, they relish the differences and they've learned to ignore the messages that say, "Designed for Netscape, click here to download your copy now."

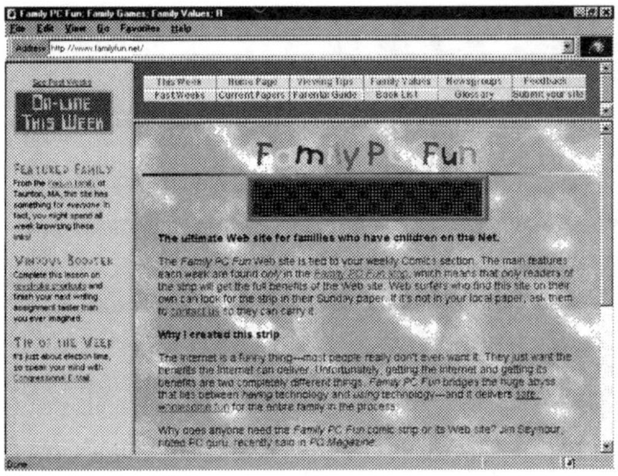

Figure 6 800 X 600 resolution

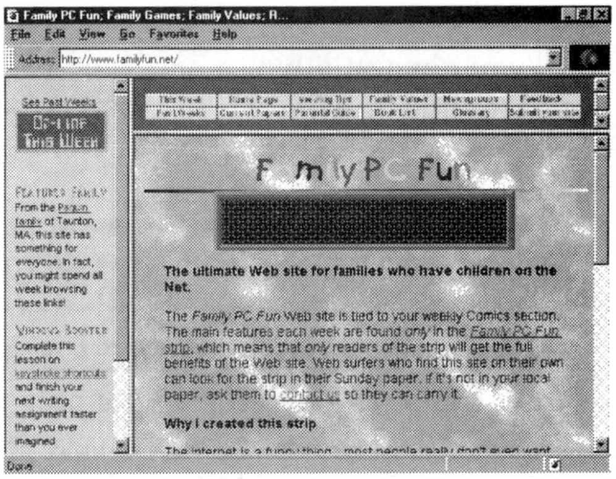

Figure 7 640 X 480 resolution

Test with different Windows screen resolutions

Here's a tricky factor to consider. What are the implications of different screen resolutions? You can create a Web site that looks great on your own monitor at 800 X 600 (see Figure 6), but that falls apart at 640 X 480 (see Figure 7). For example, a heading that fits neatly across a page in the higher resolution may wrap into two lines at the lower resolution. People who view your page at higher resolutions won't experience such problematic differences (see sidebar on page 234).

Changing screen resolutions in Windows is not a quick procedure because you must restart Windows after every resolution change. However, some premium video cards include a special driver that permits "on-the-fly" resolution changes without restarting Windows after each adjustment.

HTML Width Percentage Commands

Did you wonder how the buttons in the box at the top of the example site fit into that box even at different resolutions? According to the theory we're giving you here, they should have been jammed up at the 640 X 480 resolution. So, what gives?

HTML lets Web authors specify the width of graphic images, normally in pixels. (Pixels are the dots that make up a computer screen.) But a fixed number of pixels doesn't work because if the buttons fit at 800 X 600, they'd take up three rows at 640 X 480. And if they fit at 640 X 480, there would be a lot of blank, wasted space on 800 X 600 screens.

Fortunately, HTML includes a percent option on width specifications that can help your Web site accommodate visitors with varying screen resolutions. The buttons above all use the command **WIDTH=16%**. That means these six buttons occupy 96 percent of the width of the box no matter what the current screen resolution.

We can't give you a Step-By-Step lesson to change resolution with a special driver because each one works differently. Investing in such a card might be wise if you plan to regularly test a Web site in different resolutions. Of course if you're testing over a network, you may be able to borrow PCs from other users who are running other resolutions so that you can compare your site's appearance on a variety of systems. And, Microsoft has a special tool kit for Windows 95 that adds a utility that permits on-the-fly resolution changes with almost any video card.

Until you get a utility or a new video card, here's a Step-By-Step exercise that will show you how to adjust Windows screen resolution. If you've got at least a 15-inch monitor, you'll probably enjoy using a resolution of 800 X 600.

STEP-BY-STEP

GOAL: Learn to adjust Windows screen resolution

- ✔ Right-click an empty spot on your desktop.

  If your desktop isn't visible, click the right mouse button on the Taskbar, click on **Minimize All Windows**, then right-click the desktop.

- ✔ Click **Properties**.
- ✔ Click the **Settings** tab.
- ✔ Move the **Desktop Area** marker to 800 X 600.

  The Windows 95 default is 640 X 480. If your system has been changed to 800 X 600, then click **Cancel** now and skip the rest of this exercise.

- ✔ Click **OK**.

  Depending on your video driver, you may have to restart your system for the resolution change to take effect. If so, follow the prompts to shut down and restart your system now. When it reboots, you may have to readjust your monitor's display controls to resize or reposition the screen image.

Visitor PC processing power

Eventually we'll see Web standards that are as universally implemented as those on television. But until that time, consider the potential computer limitations that your visitors might face.

First, remember that a lot of visitors will be using 486 PCs that will be strained to run a complex Java application. This is changing rapidly because now it's difficult to buy a new 486. Thus, before long you can create your site to work best on a Pentium or better and just not worry about 486 traffic.

Decisions, decisions... too many choices

Are you feeling stressed over all of this information? It is *a lot* to absorb. And there are more products appearing every week to handle a constantly increasing array of Web features—trying to keep up is futile.

To simplify your decision-making, we'll present a couple of situations that might apply to your needs for Web publishing.

Family Web sites or home-based business Web sites

Families, small companies (1 to 20 people), partnerships and sole proprietorships will need to look for a Web service provider that can provide space for your Web site. A small business might hire a Web provider that also offers Web consulting services.

Keep in mind that no one who uses your Web site will know its geographic location, so it can be maintained anywhere in the country—so you're free to find a deal on Web server space a thousand miles away.

Tools

Families and small organizations often begin their Web site with a word processor add-on. Nearly anyone who is skilled in a Windows word processor can put basic information on a Web page. They'll use either the Internet Publisher for WordPerfect for Windows or the Internet Assistant for Microsoft Word for Windows that we discussed earlier. They are also likely to use one or more of the Skisoft programs to quickly convert some existing material to the required Web format.

Inside Info

Would you like to see some examples of well-done family Web sites to help you get started on your own? Check out Family PC Fun at *www.FamilyPCfun.com*, the Web site of a newspaper Sunday comic strip. The Web site includes lots of great family links but you'll really like the weekly "Featured Family" that showcases the best of family Web sites. Once you get yours up and running be sure to submit it and maybe you'll get your family in the paper!

If you own a small or home-based business you may want to contract with a local Web-page designer to fill in your weak points after you create the basics. College campuses are a good place to find HTML authors. You will probably find a suitable HTML author with a notice on a student union bulletin board or through an ad in the school paper. But then again, HotDog Pro has enough features that many average computer users learn it fast enough that their businesses don't suffer.

A small business also may need an ad copywriter to help with the writing and an advertising consultant and an artist to help with graphics and design. If you've used such marketing professionals before, you will probably find that they have expanded their services to include Web technology. In fact, students in most college marketing courses are developing Web pages in class exercises. So, perhaps a college student would be satisfactory in this aspect of your Web site development, too.

If information on your Web site needs frequent changes, you can update your Web site quickly if you use a Web service provider that permits you to FTP updates directly into your site's home directory. You don't want the accuracy of your information to depend on someone else's schedule for doing the updates. Web services are often staffed by people who may not understand the importance of responding to your schedule. But direct FTP capability will ensure that you have control over your Web site's content.

Summary

Well, that's a solid introduction to Web publishing. Internet technology changes too rapidly for us to put any more details in a book. You can probably see by now that Web site development can be fairly simple or it can be a never-ending story that becomes a full-time job. Don't get discouraged early. People who are able to create top-notch Web sites can earn more than $100 per hour for HTML development work. You can't expect to match the impressive technical level of the best sites on the Web without devoting a lot of time to it.

The important thing to remember in Web site development is to get started and become a participant instead of merely a spectator. You can improve your site as you learn more, and that will enrich the Web for us all. See you in cyberspace!

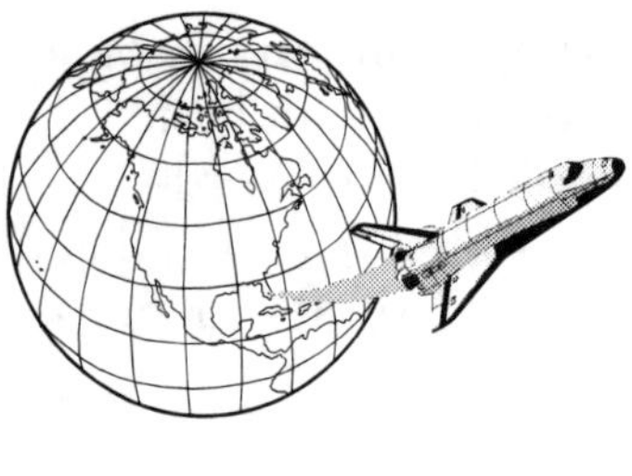

ORBITING IN CYBERSPACE

Digiweb
http://www.digiweb.com

We promised earlier in the chapter to include contact information for Internet Presence Providers that will permit you to load Web pages with Java, JavaScript and CGI applications. Check out Digiweb as a host for your interactive Web site. They offer the best rates we've found, as low as $20 for complete service. They don't provide technical support, so you'll need to know how to upload pages yourself via an FTP client and you'll be on your own if your HTML pages need trouble-shooting. For their low fees, Digiweb provides only the server, the domain registration and the Internet connection.

MindSpring
http://www.mindspring.com

Here's another candidate for hosting your Java-powered Web site. Their rates are a bit higher than Digiweb's rate, but they offer more services. For example, they have a technical support line that you can call with questions and help in troubleshooting your HTML pages. Your best bet is to visit these two sites and compare, then, perhaps use a service such as Yahoo! to search for other Internet Presence Providers.

O'Reilly Associates
http://website.ora.com

O'Reilly Associates has emerged as a powerhouse of technology on the Internet. They've published a library of more than 80 excellent technical reference guides that delve into details far more deeply that we have in this book. Actually, mainstream users may find the topics covered in this site to be too technical, but if you are performing or managing the hands-on work involved in publishing your organization's Web site, then you absolutely *must* place O'Reilly's URL on your Bookmark List.

Random tips and hints on constructing Web pages
http://www.nd.edu/PageCreation/TipsAndHints.html

Here's a Notre Dame University site that gives tips and hints on constructing HTML documents (see Figure 8). Be sure to check out the "Clickable Graphics" tutorial that gives you a clickable graphic map demonstration-tutorial. This site is not an encyclopedic presentation on creating HTML documents—and it admits to being "Maccentric" on some points—but it does address a number of issues that are encountered frequently. Bookmark this URL because this Web site is also a good place to track HTML changes as well as other changes in Web technology.

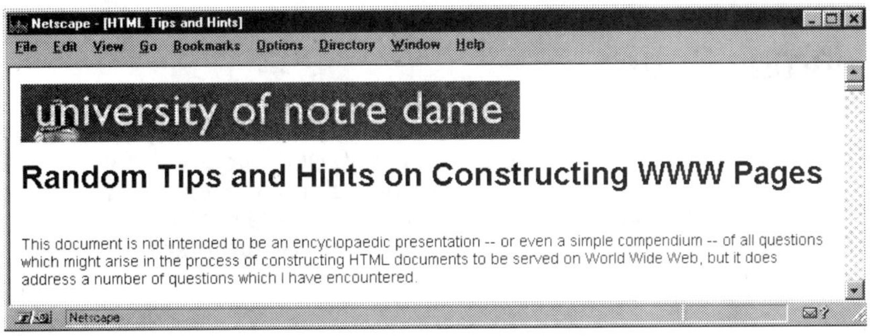

Figure 8 HTML tips - everything from the basics to video

Jeff Mallett's Web Authoring Page
http://www.cruzio.com/~tao/html.html

Here's an on-line guide to publishing on the Web by Internet guru Jeff Mallet. Click on any one of these headings to jump to fact-filled text that can help you get started with your Web publishing: Authoring HTML, Web Authoring, Authoring CGI Scripts, Java and Authorization.

Self-taught Web publishing
http://www.lne.com/Web/Books/HTML

This is the home page for the books *Teach Yourself Web Publishing with HTML in a Week* and *Teach Yourself More Web Publishing with HTML in a Week*, both by Laura Lemay. These books describe how to write, design and publish information on the World Wide Web. In addition to describing the HTML language itself, they provide extensive information on using images, sounds, video, interactivity, gateway programs (CGI), forms and imagemaps. Through the use of dozens of real-life examples and actual HTML source code, the books help you not only learn the technical details of writing Web pages, but also teach you how to communicate information effectively through the Web.

The World Wide Web Handbook
http://www.ucc.ie/~pflynn/books/wwwbook.html

This is a Web site for the book, *The World Wide Web Handbook An HTML Guide for Users, Authors and Publishers* by Peter Flynn, published by International Thomson Computer Press. It profiles the book, including its Table of Contents and includes a downloadable version of the "HTML Reference Card" that is included with the printed edition of the book.

HTML specification 3.0
http://www.w3.org/hypertext/WWW/MarkUp/MarkUp.html

Here's a link to the table of contents for the complete HTML 3.0 specifications on-line manual. This is not a user-friendly guide to HTML, but it is a highly detailed reference source about all aspects of HTML, its development and its specifications.

HTML 3.0 has been designed to be created in a variety of different ways. It is simple enough to type manually and can be authored using WYSIWYG editors for HTML or generated via export filters from common word processing formats or other SGML applications.

Jargon Cutter

WYSIWYG (pronounced "whizzy-wig") - Stands for What You See Is What You Get. Windows word processors are WYSIWYG because what you see on-screen is pretty much what you get when you print. DOS programs weren't WYSIWYG because they displayed text as plain characters, and you had to print to see how your document looked. Windows HTML editors are not WYSIWYG—yet. So far, they display only text, so you must use your Web browser to see how they'll look on the Web.

Fill-out forms overview

http://www.ncsa.uiuc.edu/SDG/Software/Mosaic/Docs/fill-out-forms/overview.html

This site focuses on creating fill-out forms for your Web pages. One of its most valuable features is a listing of 13 forms done in HTML (at last count) that you can use as examples. They range in complexity from "ludicrously simple" to extremely advanced. It's a good place to download sample pages that will help you develop your Web publishing skills.

15

Pictures in Space: Web Graphics

A picture is worth—how much is it? A thousand words? Ten thousand? Whatever the number, the Web is a perfect illustration of that ancient adage. Remember that for nearly thirty years the Internet existed in text-only format, distributing technical and academic information between large institutions. And in its text-only format, the Internet remained the realm of scientists and academics. But the creation of the Web permitted the Internet to go graphic and the graphics are what made it go public.

Well-done graphics can lend an appealing look to static, boring technical information. Graphics can also create simple explanations for difficult concepts and convey messages quickly and efficiently. And, graphics can bypass language barriers by creating universal, pictorial labels and instructions—perfect for the World Wide Web.

Unfortunately, Web graphics have been a double-edged sword. While cutting easily through difficult concepts and making the Internet interesting to us everyday folks, graphics have also cut severely into Internet bandwidth. The result is that the Internet—designed to carry efficient, text-only documents—is now clogged with millions of graphic images. But that's a price we're willing to pay because without the graphics few people would ever venture into cyberspace.

There will be a happy ending to this, however, because technological advancements will soon alleviate Internet bandwidth problems. Your Erol's Internet service offers high-speed ISDN service already, which will greatly alleviate your personal bandwidth limitations. Nonetheless, most of the rest of the Internet is shackled with more limited technology, which will hold you back—until they catch up with the high-speed access that we deliver.

Until most of the Internet has a bandwidth capacity that matches Erol's Internet system, please go easy on the graphics for Web sites you design and create. Still, you should begin now to master Web graphics because they are here to stay and your visitors will expect you to use graphics to improve your site's value.

Web graphics primer

You'll see two file formats in common use on the Web: .GIF (Graphics Interchange Format) and .JPEG (Joint Photographics Expert Group). .GIF is the more common of the two, but .JPEG is catching on fast. There are pros and cons to both, so you'll have to decide for yourself which to use on your own Web site.

We'll present an overview of both major formats, tips on choosing the right one for a given application, overviews of graphics drawing, editing and conversion software, plus tips on graphics saving and editing. You'll find many excellent graphics resources from around the Web, including links to other Internet books that deal specifically with graphics and scanning.

.GIF graphic files

The .GIF format (Graphic Interchange Format) is good for all types of images and is compatible with a wide variety of graphics applications. .GIF was developed in 1987 by CompuServe to be a device-independent method of storing pictures. .GIF allows high-quality, high-resolution graphics to be displayed on a variety of graphics hardware and is intended as a common exchange and display mechanism for graphic images. A .GIF picture file has an extension .GIF.

The 1987 .GIF format was upgraded and released again in 1989, but used the same .GIF extension. Some graphic applications distinguish the two .GIF formats as GIF87 and GIF89. Even though the .GIF 8 bits/pixel format only supports 256 colors and has relatively large file sizes, .GIF remains one of the most popular choices for storing images. .GIF format is best when used with images containing flat areas of color that have little or no shading. .GIF is well-matched to inexpensive computer displays because it can store only 8 bits/pixel (256 or fewer colors) and most PCs can't display more than 256 distinct colors at once.

Sizing Web Graphics

The graphic images used on the Internet are sized by pixels. Pixels are dots on your screen. A typical Windows screen is made up of 640 pixels horizontally and 480 pixels vertically. For short, this is called a 640 X 480 screen resolution. But Windows has other resolutions. Another common Windows resolution is 800 X 600. Thus an image that is 240 pixels high would run 50 percent of the height of a 640 X 480 screen, but would occupy only 40 percent of the height of a 800 X 600 screen.

If your graphic image displays in different sizes on different screens, you'll have difficulty planning the text so that it will fit around the graphic. Fortunately, HTML gives you two important—but little-used—tools to help control the relationship between text and graphics on your Web pages.

The clear break command

HTML has a code, <BR>, that causes a line break. You could use a series of consecutive <BR> commands to push your text down below the bottom of a graphic image. But if you put in just enough of them to push the text down past the graphic on a 640 X 480 screen, then the page will look different on a 800 X 600 screen. The solution is not to use multiple <BR> commands, but to use an option with the code that forces the next line break to occur *after* it clears the current graphic image. Use the code <BR CLEAR=LEFT> or <BR CLEAR=RIGHT> depending on which side of the screen the image lies.

The percentage width command

HTML lets you control the width of graphic images with the WIDTH command that normally is expressed in pixels. But instead of using pixels, you can use a percent so that the size will be uniform across all screen resolutions. For example, if you used <IMG SRC="image.gif" WIDTH=25%>, the image would be 160 pixels wide at 640 X 480 and 200 pixels wide at 800 X 600 resolution.

Inside Info

.GIF Internet images are downloaded in 16 X 16-pixel blocks. Knowing this can help you increase your site's download efficiency. For example, if you size a graphic to be exactly 160 X 80 pixels it will download in 10 blocks by 5 blocks, or 50 blocks. But if you sized the same image at 162 X 82 it would require 11 blocks by 6 blocks, or 66 blocks. This would increase the download time, yet the on-screen size difference would barely be noticeable—a real waste of bandwidth.

.JPEG and .JPG graphic files

JPEG (pronounced "jay-peg") is a standardized image compression mechanism. The name .JPEG is derived from the original name of the committee that wrote the standard, the Joint Photographic Experts Group.

.JPEG is designed for compressing either full-color or gray-scale images of natural, real-world scenes. It works well on photographs, naturalistic artwork and similar material, but not well on lettering, simple cartoons, black-and-white or line drawings. A .JPEG picture file has an extension .JPEG or .JPG.

.JPEG stores full color information: 24 bits/pixel (up to 16.7 million colors). Therefore, with full-color hardware, .JPEG images can look far better than .GIF files. And, .JPEG files can be much smaller than GIFs so they are *usually* superior to .GIF in terms of disk space and transmission time.

We say "usually" because applications that save images in .JPEG files or convert images to .JPEG files permit adjustments to the image that alter the image quality and file size. Both the compression method and the percentage of compression are user-controllable and directly correspond to the quality of the compressed image.

It is possible to save a .JPEG image in a file that is larger than its .GIF counterpart. Of course it also can be smaller. The trick is to learn to adjust the quality optimally because there is a point of diminishing returns with every image. In other words, eventually you'll reach the point that increasing the quality adjustment doesn't improve quality, but does continue to increase the file size. That's why .GIF can be a nice trade-off because it creates a reasonable middle-of-the-road file in terms of balancing quality versus file size—and requires no tweaking skills.

.JPEG files often use a file extension of .JPG because of file naming limitations in MS-DOS and Windows 3.x. For example, if you use a Windows 3.x application to save a .JPEG graphic file, your system will convert the extension to .JPG. There will be no difference between the two files and you can rename it with a .JPEG extension if you transfer it back to a Unix, a Windows 95 or a Windows NT system.

Capturing images from Web sites you visit

You'll see a vast array of graphics as you surf the Internet, and your Netscape Navigator makes it easy to save them to your hard drive. Of course you'll have to keep in mind that almost all Internet graphics are protected by normal copyrights, but you can easily e-mail the source site for reuse permission. If you want to include a graphic on your site because you're cross-linking to the source site, they will probably be happy to grant permission to increase their site's exposure.

Inside Info

If you're seeking permission to reprint or reuse a graphic image from a Web site, where do you start? First, go to the bottom of the home page of the Web site and look for a link to e-mail to the "Webmaster." Since Webmasters are responsible for the design and maintenance of Web sites, they'll know the source of the graphics. Often, you'll be told that the graphic is "public domain" and you're free to use it. But even if it's not public domain, most places will be glad to grant you permission to use their graphics if you'll link to their site and give them credit.

Once the copyright considerations are handled, you can have a field day collecting graphics all over cyberspace. Here's a quick Step-By-Step exercise that shows you how to capture a graphic to your hard drive.

STEP-BY-STEP

GOAL: Learn to save an Internet graphic image

- ✔ Start Netscape Navigator.
- ✔ Press **CTRL+L**.
- ✔ Type *www.fedworld.com*, then press **ENTER**.
- ✔ Place the mouse over the logo image at the top of the screen.
- ✔ Click the right button.
- ✔ Click **Save Image As...**

  Select an appropriate directory in which to save this image before you complete the next step.
- ✔ Click **Save.**

  You can open a saved graphic image in Netscape at any time, or you can reference it in one of your own HTML pages.

That was easy, but what about capturing the background image? That, too, is easy with the Netscape Navigator.

Jargon Cutter

Background image - A .GIF or .JPG image file that is used as a background behind the text on a Web page. Usually the image is small so it downloads quickly. Then the Web browser repeats the image on the screen, like a wallpaper pattern. Many Web pages have no background image—they're plain white or they just use a color—so there's no background image to capture.

Step-By-Step

GOAL: Learn to save an Internet background graphic

- ✔ Start with the same page used in the previous exercise.
- ✔ Click the right mouse button on any blank area of the page.
- ✔ Click **Save Background As...**
- ✔ Click **Save** to save the image on your hard drive.
  Select a directory and change the name as desired.

Windows 95 also lets you save a Web page background image to your clipboard so you can paste it into your favorite graphics application. And, the Netscape Navigator lets you designate a Web page background image as your desktop wallpaper.

Tips On Selecting an Image Format

The best graphic format to use depends on the application and the desired effect. So, to make some sense out of your choices, we'll share these tips from Kody Kline of *Extreme D.T.P.* in Tulsa, Oklahoma (see Figure 1). Kody is a master computer graphics artist. See for yourself at: *www.ionet.net/~kkline*.

Transparent background

All graphic images are rectangular in shape, even if they store pictures of irregularly-shaped objects. If you want an irregularly-shaped object not to have a rectangular outside shape, you'll need to use the GIF89a format because only GIF89a lets you make a transparent background for your image. A transparent background creates the illusion of an irregularly-shaped picture because the transparent background allows the colors behind the picture to show through the transparent color, even though the actual image outline remains rectangular.

File efficiency

If you want to reduce the download time of your large graphic images, you'll find that a moderately-compressed .JPEG image can cut the file size and download time by approximately 70 percent with only minor loss of quality. Much greater detail can be obtained in full-color photographic quality in a low compression .JPEG versus .GIF because of the .GIF color limitations.

Interlacing

Although the flashy 16.7-million color .JPEG images may look excellent on your computer, remember that many people who access your Web site will not have adequate video hardware or the higher speed modems to handle these images efficiently. .GIF format supports an "interlaced" option that quickly displays a blurred full-size image of the .GIF, then, during repeated passes, fills in and sharpens the image. This doesn't reduce overall download time, but at least it gives visitors a quick taste of the image that may entice them to wait.

Whichever format you select, a compromise between a high-quality photographic image and concerns for long transmission times can result in a usable graphic that can deliver pizzaz without visitors needing a nap during download.

Figure 1 DTP Extreme - a top-notch Web graphics designer

Original graphics art

Creating a world-class site requires world-class graphics. Very few part-time graphics users can create the level of the very best graphics that you'll see today on the Web. And even if they could, they probably lack the expertise to optimize the balance between image quality and file size. Creating world-class Web graphics is truly a professional job.

For a home-based or small business, or for your family's Web site, you don't need world-class, eye-popping graphics. A simple, colorful graphic image will spruce up your site and you won't have to quit your job to create it. So, perhaps your creative juices are stirring and you want to try your own hand at Internet graphics. If so, then we'll give you do-it-yourselfers a quick introduction to creating Internet graphics.

Graphic drawing packages

A review of all the good graphics programs would be a book in itself, so we'll trim the list and show you some of the most popular—in other words, some of the most inexpensive—applications. In fact, some of them are *extremely* inexpensive—for example, free! These won't create the top-of-the-line world-class graphics, but you'll save money. Everything involves trade-offs. Besides, if you're a novice, you most likely wouldn't be able to justify the time it would take to learn to use those highly-specialized tools.

Client-side Clickable Maps

Until recently, Web authors needed to use CGI programs—runing on the Web server—to enable users to navigate via clickable image maps. The need for CGI programming skills put clickable maps out of reach of most Web authors. But a new HTML standard—called "client-side" clickable maps—is simple enough that most Web authors will be able to create clickable image maps.

Client-side clickable maps means that the action occurs on the client computer. Once the Web page is downloaded, the server won't need to be involved with handling the site's clickable maps. This helps alleviate some of the Internet bandwidth problems, lessens the strain on Web servers and simplifies the work of Web authors.

In the last chapter, remember we outlined the HotDog HTML editor? HotDog has an add-on application, CrossEye, that automates the tedious job of mapping coordinates on an image map. You can get CrossEye from the Sausage Software Web site at: *www.sausage.com*. With CrossEye, you won't have to write, test, compile and upload a CGI script to handle the jumps. Instead, it generates simple HTML code and puts it in the Windows clipboard. All you have to do is paste the code into an HTML page that you're editing in HotDog. Then, once your Web page is loaded into a visitor's browser, the image map code on your page handles all hyperjumps.

CorelDraw

Since its acquisition of the complete line of WordPerfect products, Corel now has the most complete line of business software in the industry. Check out their latest product line at *www.corel.com* (see Figure 2). For years their CorelDraw graphics application has been an industry leader. The merging of the two product lines will help the WordPerfect word processor remain a leader in Web page development.

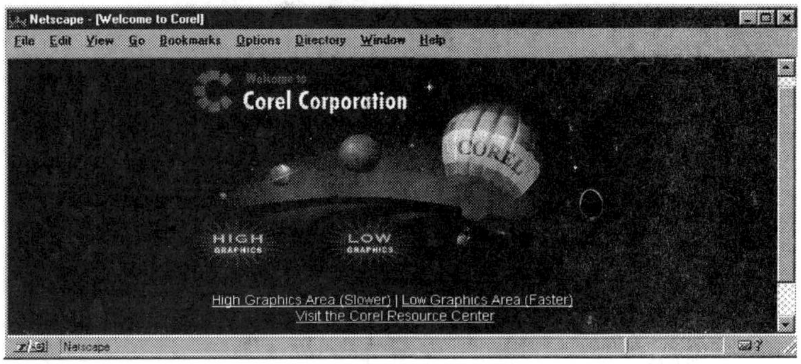

Figure 2 Corel - keep up with latest developments in Web graphics

Another benefit to using CorelDraw is that it is available in many versions. Unlike most software vendors, when CorelDraw creates an upgrade, it keeps its older versions on the shelf. This gives users a range of prices and a range of features. You can pay top dollar for the latest version, or you can buy a deeply-discounted, slightly older version that may still serve all of your graphics needs.

Corel also bundles these older versions with high-quality hardware products such as video display cards and scanners. If you're just getting into the Web and graphics and you've realized that your old video card is sapping your computer's performance, shop around for a card that includes a recent version of CorelDraw. These cards are no more costly than comparable video cards and give you an excellent $150 to $350 drawing package free.

For example, CorelDraw 3.0 is currently free with a Diamond Stealth video card and Corel Photo Paint 5.0 is free with a Hewlett-Packard HP-4c scanner. These bundled products may be all you need, so check for bundling deals when you're shopping for a new computer or computer hardware. Then test the bundled software thoroughly before investing in upgrades that you may not need.

Features for the Web

When you're selecting which version of CorelDraw you'll use, check if yours is recent enough to handle .JPEG files. The older versions, Version 3.0 for example, do not. But even Version 3.0 handles .GIF files, so you can use it for basic Web graphics jobs.

Even older versions of CorelDraw can create a wide array of special effects, including objects that appear as 3-D. You'll be able to control blending in shaded objects so you can adjust the appearance of their resolution. And, Corel imports and exports most of the major graphics formats. Considering the Internet's bandwidth limitations, which means that you should apply graphics sparingly, even older versions of CorelDraw may be all you'll need for a couple of years.

3-D Graphics

Even though CorelDraw and others have some 3-D capability, there are some stand-alone, top-end 3-D graphics packages available. 3-D graphics is a very hot topic as this book is being written. You'll need to check the latest versions on store shelves, read magazine reviews or check out the Web sites of the various graphics application vendors. The bottom line: with moderate graphics experience you can expect to create some stunning 3-D graphics with the tools now available.

Paint Shop Pro

Paint Shop Pro is a shareware graphics application. This means that you can download a limited-license version and test it before you pay (see Figure 3). Paint Shop Pro is a user-friendly, powerful image viewing, editing and converting program. With support for more than 30 image formats, and several drawing and painting tools, this may be the only graphics program you will ever need. It comes in both 16-bit and 32-bit versions. The 32-bit version runs under the Windows 95 and Windows NT operating systems and takes full advantage of these 32-bit operating system. The 16-bit version is an excellent choice for anyone using Windows 3.x.

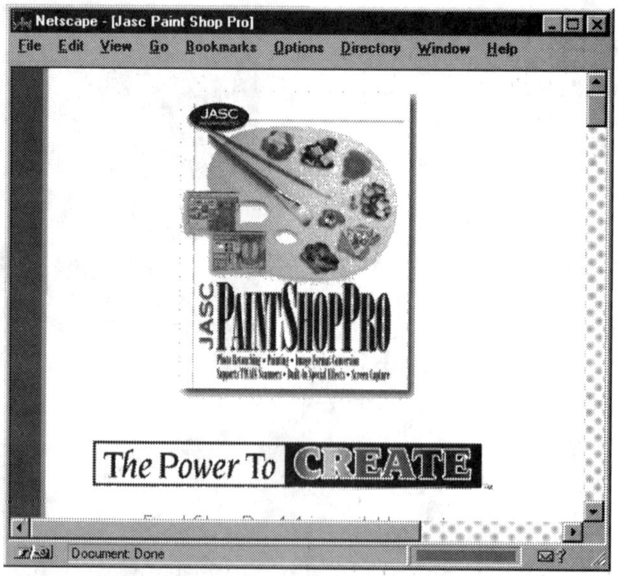

Figure 3 Paint Shop Pro - one of the Web's best graphics bargains—a great way to start

Paint Shop Pro is an excellent graphics tool for Web-authoring beginners. It handles all required formats to get you started. The home page is at *www.jasc.com/psp.html* where you can read about it, check its lengthy feature list and download a free, trial copy. You won't beat this deal on a graphics program. If you like it, you can register and pay the fee to get technical support and upgrades.

Even though Paint Shop Pro is not the most powerful graphics application, it's got plenty of professional-level features and can create some terrific graphics. For the money, this is the best value for Web graphics. But if you're not on a tight budget and you're ready to tackle the intricacies of some truly world-class graphics features, check out the next topic.

World-Class Graphics

Adobe Photoshop graphics software enables designers and photographers to create original artwork, correct color, retouch and composite scanned images and prepare professional-quality separations and output with complete flexibility. With such a wealth of powerful painting and selection tools, plus multiple layers, special effects filters, and lighting effects, Adobe Photoshop is a professional's dream application. You can learn more at *www.adobe.com* (see Figure 4).

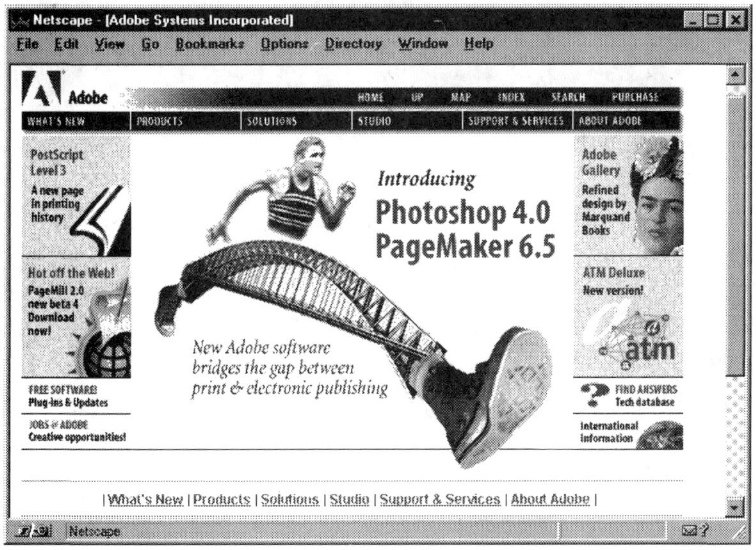

Figure 4 Adobe - world-class Web graphics for the most demanding artist

Photoshop includes more than 40 standard filters, including multiple choices for image sharpening, softening, stylizing, distortion, video, and removal of noise, scratches and dust. Its powerful lighting effects let users apply multiple light sources to an image and choose from a range of colors, intensities, and angles.

With Photoshop, you can create an original image or start with a scanned image. It lets you create effects in separate layers—like transparent sheets of acetate—upon which you can combine graphic elements, paint and edit without changing the original background image. Photoshop's user-friendly interface lets you drag-and-drop selections from different files or from different layers. And you can save the finished image in a wide variety of different file formats, including .GIF and .JPEG. Its .GIF support extends to the GIF89 format that lets you create transparency and interlacing.

LView Pro

Somewhere in between the full-featured graphic applications and the beginner's applications, you might find that you lose some graphics conversion abilities. Via the Web you can download an excellent, shareware graphics conversion application, called LView Pro, that was authored by Leonardo Haddad Loureiro of MMedia Research. You'll be free to distribute LView Pro to others for trial and leisure utilization. If you decide to use it in business, however, you'll need to register your copy with MMedia to comply with copyright regulations.

You'll find an amazing array of features considering that you can download this application free from the Internet. It lets you flip, rotate, resize and crop images, and it gives you a full-range of powerful image enhancement tools. LView Pro can handle importing of .BMP, GIF87, GIF89, .JPEG, .PCX, .TIF, .TGA, .PPM, .PGM, .PBM and .DIB formats. Its .GIF features include a transparency that uses a simple "dropper" that lets you touch a background color that you want made transparent. A simple menu selection lets you tell LView Pro to automatically save all of your .GIF files in interlaced format—an excellent choice if you expect your visitors to be using dial-up modems to browse your site.

Figure 5 LViewPro - a must for conversion

To get your copy of LView Pro (see Figure 5), check out the LView home page at *www.lview.com*. You'll have a choice of either a Windows 3.x or a Windows 95 version. The registration fee for commercial use is only $30, a true software bargain. While you're there to download the application, you might as well check out the link entitled, "Transparent color" and save it or print it so you can create transparent backgrounds for your .GIF images.

Oh, No, There's More!

Just when you nailed down the facts on Internet graphics, things changed. A new graphics format is emerging. It's all about law suits and patents, but the result to you is a new format. After .GIF had become a standard on the Web, some lawsuits were filed over alleged patent infringements. Someone thought they'd suddenly be able to collect royalties from everyone who uses .GIF.

The real result? .GIF had been showing its age in a number of ways even before the lawsuit, so the announcement only hurried the development of a new and much-improved replacement. Now we all have a new graphics format with an extension of PNG (pronounced "ping"). The PNG format (Portable Network Graphics) was developed as free software and CompuServe intends it to be free of patent infringements.

For more information on PNG, check out its home page, which is maintained by Greg Roelofs at *quest.jpl.nasa.gov/PNG*.

HiJaak graphics software

HiJaak 95 changes the way you work with graphics by integrating its graphics technology directly into Windows 95. Without ever having to run a separate application, you'll be able to view, organize, convert and print graphics naturally and easily. HiJaak 95 also includes superb capture, convert and image management tools—with a choice of how to work: from the HiJaak application window or directly in Windows 95.

HiJaak 95 has extended Windows 95 with thumbnails of more than 75 graphics formats and has added to the Windows 95 shortcut menu searching, viewing, printing, thumbnail updating and converting. This unprecedented level of integration means that HiJaak 95 can help you perform your graphics tasks more efficiently than ever before. Its conversion feature handles every graphic format you'll encounter.

HiJaak 95 performs all the usual graphics enhancing tasks that you'll need and includes a flexible and powerful screen capture application that enables you to capture and to save any image you can see on your screen.

Also, the HiJaak Graphics Suite is an integrated set of graphics utilities that lets you easily add great graphics to your Web pages. And you don't have to be a professional to get excellent results with HiJaak Graphics Suite. HiJaak Graphics Suite includes HiJaak Browser, HiJaak Smuggler, HiJaak Paint, HiJaak Draw and HiJaak Pro. With the Suite, you can browse, search, find, manage, create, draw, edit, paint, view, convert, trace, capture, scan and print. As a bonus, it includes a clip art library on CD-ROM that has thousands of images indexed by the HiJaak Browser so you get visual access to specific images without entering keywords.

Image Scanning

Scanning is a computer function that transforms existing photos, graphic images, drawings, sketches, maps, illustrations or even your child's museum piece. Once stored digitally, the captured image can be manipulated with computer graphics software. Scanned images can be retouched in the computer to optimize their on-screen appearance or they can be printed or included in a word processing document. Your primary use of a scanner will probably be to capture images and save them in either .GIF or .JPEG formats that you can use in your Web documents.

Since some quality is always lost during the scanning process, make sure that your original image is the best quality you can get. For best results the images should have high contrast and be perfectly sharp. Very much as with photocopiers, you may need to adjust the brightness and contrast to capture an acceptable image. You will quickly discover that there's a bit of an art to optimally scanning images, but we've included some excellent scanning resources in this chapter and in the Orbiting in Cyberspace section at the end of this chapter.

Scanner basics

For professional results you should consider only flatbed scanners that are used on a desktop. A flatbed scanner is a scanning device that accepts flat art (photographs, drawings, clippings, illustrations). Most flatbed scanners are designed to handle 8.5 x 11 inch originals in *reflective media*—images that reflect light. Some flatbed scanners will handle transparent media (such as Ektachrome transparencies and 35mm slides), but you may have to add a special transparency adapter to activate this function.

Figure 6 TWAIN - permits you to scan images directly into your word processor

For increased flexibility in paper handling, you can find scanners that accept legal-size documents. If you need to scan a large number of existing documents, be sure you select a scanner that includes a document feeder option because flatbed scanners normally accept only one document at a time.

Scanners will include scanning software, but the quality and features vary greatly. You're not likely to find a full-featured application bundled with any scanner, though all are adequate. If possible, stick to applications that give you the ability to scan and save in all the common file formats that you will want to use (especially .GIF and .JPEG). Good scanning software should also allow you to crop and rotate before or during saving. It's an absolute must that your scanner have a TWAIN (Technology Without An Interesting Name) module. TWAIN is a crucial feature because it's supported by all major applications and allows you to scan directly into non-image processing applications such as WordPerfect, PageMaker, CorelDraw, etc. It's fun to watch WordPerfect ingest a color photo directly into a document (see Figure 6). What a way to spruce up a report, newsletter or family announcement!

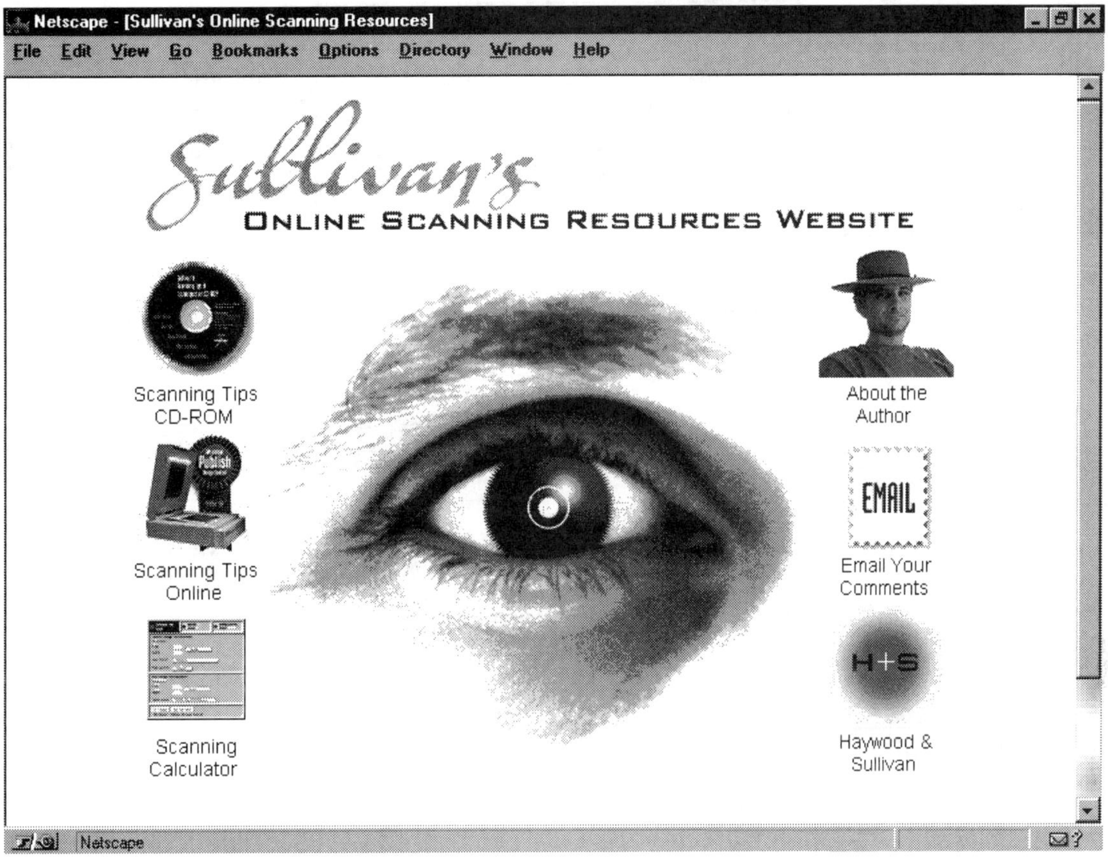

Figure 7 Michael Sullivan - for advanced scanning tips and resources

If you're interested in going beyond the basics of scanning, the next sidebar will take you about as far as you could want to go. A note of caution, though: this could become a full-time job.

Advanced Scanning and Graphics

Below, we'll show you where to access on-line graphics lessons that will teach you advanced scanning and other graphics techniques. You can learn everything from how to produce transparent backgrounds (a must for irregularly-shaped images) to optimizing your graphics for size and download speed.

Advanced scanning

For some productivity-enhancing scanning tips, check out Michael J. Sullivan's Web site at *www.hsdesign.com/scanning* (see Figure 7). This a fabulous scanning resource, but it's only the tip of the iceberg. For in-depth lessons and tips you can buy Michael's book, *Make Your Scanner a Great Design and Production Tool*, North Light Books, 1995.

Michael is partner and artistic director of Haywood & Sullivan in Quincy, Massachusetts, an award-winning full-range design firm that excels at communication design using various media. He also is founding partner of Pilgrim New Media in Cambridge, Massachusetts, a multimedia titles publisher.

Advanced graphics

Jump to *www.warwick.ac.uk/~cudbh/I3course/graphics.html* where you'll find a full set of graphics lessons from Bronwen Reid at the University of Hull, in the U.K. Lessons here include backgrounds, transparencies and interlacing. Also, you can use this site as a jumping-off point for other sites with graphics tips.

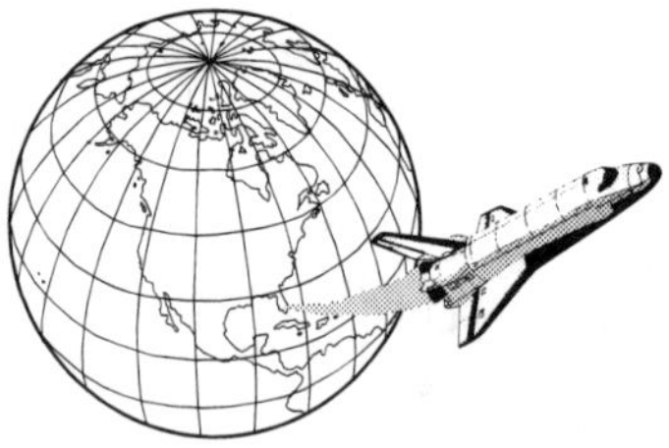

ORBITING IN CYBERSPACE

Computer graphics virtual library
http://www.dataspace.com/WWW/vlib/comp-graphics.html

This is a dazzling array of sources for graphics that you can use in publishing your Web page. You could spend all day at this site alone. Unfortunately, this trip—with countless graphic images to download—can be annoying during off-peak hours and impossibly slow during peak hours. Of course, with an ISDN Internet connection, time of day won't affect your speed as much as it will for other users. Keep this URL, though, for the day that will soon come when you've got more bandwidth than you know what to do with.

Graphics viewers, editors, utilities and info
http://www.w3.organization/pub/WWW/Graphics

This is the World Wide Web Consortium's collection of links to graphics shareware, demos, and information files available over the Internet. You'll find in-depth FAQ files for several major graphics formats as well as recently-posted messages on graphics formats and an on-line archive of past messages. They also include links that can guide you to Usenet newsgroups for different graphics formats and topics. Links to applications are accompanied by a designation for each particular platform: Windows, MS-DOS, UNIX and Macintosh.

Yahoo! .GIF files
http://www.yahoo.com/

Computers_and_Internet/Software/Data_Formats/GIF

Yahoo! has an entire category for .GIF graphics. This is the direct URL for the page. From within Yahoo!, you can step manually through the categories: Computers and Internet, Software, Data Formats, .GIF. This page probably includes more on .GIF than you'll ever need to know. .GIF licensing has been a mess for years, but if you're a .GIF graphics developer you can check here to make sure you're up to speed on the latest word on licensing of the .GIF technology.

Adobe
http://www.adobe.com

We mentioned Adobe earlier when we presented graphics drawing applications. But Adobe offers one of the widest, most powerful selections of Internet graphic tools of any software vendor. In addition to their Photoshop graphics application, they have publishing applications, including a Web publishing application, called SiteMill, that gives you drag-and-drop Web authoring. Browse around and discover a rich resource of other graphics links on the Web. To help you learn more, they include not only other Web sites, but newsgroups and mailing lists to which you will want to subscribe.

Usenet graphic FAQs files
http://www.cis.ohio-state.edu/

hypertext/faq/bngusenet/comp/graphics/top.html

Now that's a long URL, but it's equally long on content. This could be a primary contact point for graphics information, answers and updates. If you've been elected to be your organization's computer graphics expert, you should put this URL on your bookmark list because eventually you will need something listed on this page.

Web graphics sources
http://redtape.uchicago.edu/users/mdmendoz/art.html

This page says it best itself, "Have you ever needed a picture of an armadillo but didn't know just where to start looking for it? Well, hopefully this page will contain some help for you. From clipart to fonts to graphics, the links below will connect you to a wealth of art and graphics resources. Have fun!" This page is a perfect bookmark candidate for anyone who needs to locate graphic images for Web sites. At least start here, because many of the pages listed here will have other links and you can always return for that armadillo.

Scanning FAQs
http://www.infomedia.net/scan

This page contains a wealth of scanning FAQs, presented by Jeff Bone, formerly Electronic Media Coordinator, University of Alabama at Birmingham, School of Medicine; and more recently founder and president of Infomedia, Inc., a top-flight, information systems integration and development company, serving the southeast. To give you easy access, the topics on scanning artwork and photographs have been broken down into four primary categories: line art, halftones, greyscale and color. In addition to these tips, you also can read about tricky, yet very important, resolution issues and copyright issues. If you don't yet own a scanner, be sure to check out the "Scanner Roundup" here before you buy.

16

Cyberspace Copyrights: Top 10 Myths

While you're working in cyberspace, you're going to encounter more written material than you've ever before been able to access. After all, that's the exciting part about the Internet—it brings into our homes and offices just about any information we want, instantly. And, this book has not only taught you how to access information instantly, but you've learned how to use it instantly by copying and pasting information from the Internet into reports, e-mail, newsgroup postings and your own Web site. But instant access doesn't give anyone instant rights to copyrighted material.

There are a lot of myths in cyberspace about the status of copyrighted material. There is a tendency to think that anything you can bring up on your monitor belongs to you. Usually, this is not true. Electronic material is protected by copyright law just as well as traditional, printed material. We want to leave you with some food for thought about electronic copyrights so you don't put yourself in a bind over some material you've copied and pasted from the Internet.

This is one of those proverbial "good news—bad news" situations. The bad news is that violating copyright laws is very easy to do and it can get you trouble even if you did it accidentally. The good news is that it also is very easy to stay out of trouble.

So, we've compiled answers to what are ten common myths about copyrights as applied to the Internet. This information was created by Brad Templeton, the publisher for ClariNet Communications Corporation's news service. ClariNet, founded in 1989, is the Internet's first and largest electronic newspaper. This chapter covers issues related to most aspects of the Internet.

Please note that while most of the principles covered here are international in scope, some are derived from Canadian and U.S. law. Brad created this document to clear up some common misconceptions about intellectual property law that are often seen on the Internet. It is not intended to be a complete treatise on all the nuances of the subject, but it lays the groundwork of understanding.

Inside Info

Note: Do not e-mail Brad Templeton for legal advice—use other resources or consult a lawyer. You can, however, check out Brad's personal Web page at ClariNet: *www.clari.net/brad* (see Figure 1).

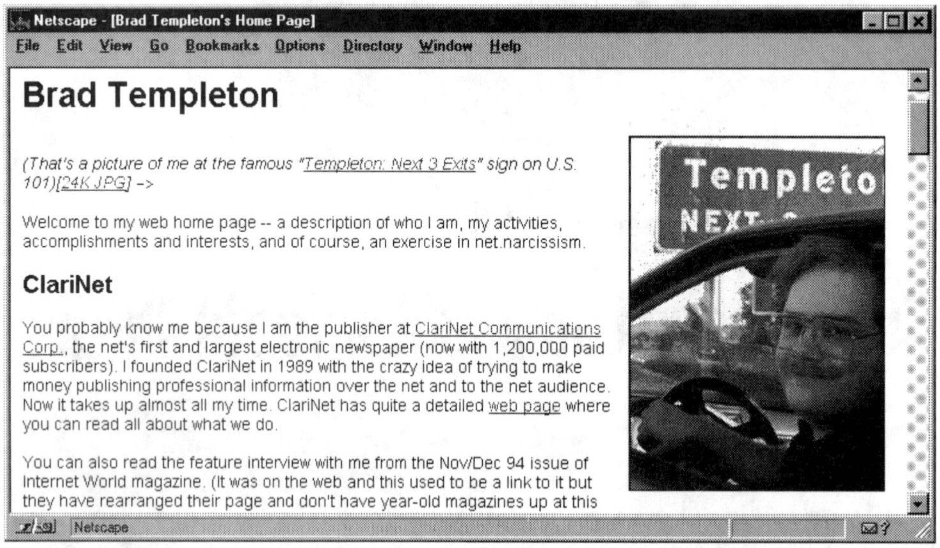

Figure 1 The founder of the ClariNet news service

Copyright myths

Here's the text of Brad's 10 Big Copyright Myths, followed by a summary of the main points. Be sure and check out the Orbiting in Cyberspace section at the end of the chapter in which we point you to some other Internet sources on copyright issues.

1) If it doesn't have a copyright notice, it's not copyrighted

Not true. This was true in the past, but today almost all major nations follow the Berne copyright convention. For example, in the U.S., almost everything created privately and originally after April 1, 1989 is copyrighted and protected whether it has a notice or not. The default you should assume for other people's works is that they are copyrighted and may not be copied unless you *know* otherwise. There are some old works that lost protection without notice, but frankly you should not risk it unless you know for sure.

It is true that a notice strengthens the protection, by warning people, and by allowing one to get more and different damages, but it is not necessary. If it looks copyrighted, you should assume it is.

This applies to pictures, too. You may not scan pictures from magazines and post them to the Internet, and if you come upon something unknown, you shouldn't post that either.

The correct form for a copyright notice is:

"Copyright (dates) by (copyright holder)."

You can use the copyright symbol © instead of the word "Copyright" but "(C)" has never been given legal force. The phrase "All Rights Reserved" used to be required in some nations but is not now needed.

2) If I don't charge for it, it's not a violation

Absolutely false. Whether you charge can affect the damages awarded in court, but that's essentially the only difference. It's still a violation if you give it away—and there can still be heavy damages if you hurt the commercial value of a protected property.

3) If it's posted to Usenet it's in the public domain

False. Nothing is in the public domain anymore unless the owner explicitly puts it in the public domain. Explicitly, as in you have a note from the copyright holder stating, "I grant this to the public domain." If not those exact words, then words very much like them.

Some argue that posting to the Usenet newsgroups implicitly grants permission to everybody to copy the posting within fairly wide bounds, and others feel that Usenet is an automatic store and forward network where all the thousands of copies made are done at the command (rather than the consent) of the poster. This is a matter of some debate, but even if the former is true (and in this writer's opinion we should all pray it isn't true) it simply would suggest posters are implicitly granting permissions "for the sort of copying one might expect when one posts to Usenet" and in no case is this a placement of material into the public domain. Furthermore it is very difficult for an implicit license to supersede an explicitly stated license of which the copier was aware.

Note that all this assumes that the poster had the right to post the item in the first place. If the poster didn't, then all the copies are pirate, and no implied license or theoretical reduction of the copyright can take place.

Copyrights can expire after a long time, putting something into the public domain, and there are some fine points on this issue regarding older copyright law versions. However, none of this applies to an original article posted to Usenet.

Note that granting something to the public domain (PD) is a complete abandonment of all rights. You can't make something "PD for non-commercial use." If your work is PD, other people can even modify one byte and put their name on it.

4) My posting was just fair use!

The "fair use" exemption to copyright law was created to allow things such as commentary, parody, news reporting, research and education about copyrighted works without the permission of the author. Intent and damage to the commercial value of the work are important considerations. Are you reproducing an article from the New York Times because you needed to in order to criticize the quality of the New York Times, or because you couldn't find time to write your own story, or didn't want your readers to have to pay to log onto the on-line services with the story or buy a copy of the paper? The first is probably fair use, the others are not.

Fair use is almost always a short excerpt and almost always attributed. (One should not use more of the work than is necessary to make the commentary.) It should not harm the commercial value of the work—in the sense of people no longer needing to buy it (which is another reason why reproduction of the entire work generally is forbidden.)

Note that most inclusion of text in Usenet follow-ups is for commentary and reply, and it doesn't damage the commercial value of the original posting (if it has any) and as such it is fair use. Fair use isn't an exact doctrine, either. The court decides if the right to comment overrides the copyright on an individual basis in each case.

There have been cases that go beyond the bounds of what's been covered here, but in general they don't apply to the typical Internet misclaim of fair use. It's a risky defense to attempt.

5) If you don't defend your copyright you lose it

False. Copyright is effectively never lost these days, unless explicitly given away. You may be thinking of trade marks, which can be weakened or lost if not defended.

6) Somebody has that name copyrighted

You can't copyright a name or anything short like a name. Titles usually don't qualify, but you could not write a song entitled: "Everybody's got something to hide except for me and my monkey." (J.Lennon/P.McCartney)

You can't copyright words, but you can trademark them, generally by using them to refer to your brand of a generic type of product or service. Like an "Apple" computer. Apple Computer "owns" that word applied to computers, even though it is also an ordinary word. Apple Records owns it when applied to music. Neither owns the word on its own, only in context, and owning a mark doesn't mean complete control—see a more detailed treatise on this law for details.

You can't use somebody else's trademark in a way that would unfairly hurt the value of the mark, or in a way that might make people confuse you with the real owner of the mark, or which might allow you to profit from the mark's good name. For example, if I were giving advice on music videos, I would be very wary of trying to label my works with a name like "MTV."

7) They can't get me, defendants in court have powerful rights!

Copyright law is mostly civil law. If you violate a copyright you usually would get sued, not charged with a crime. "Innocent until proven guilty," is a principle of criminal law, as is "proof beyond a reasonable doubt." In copyright suits, these don't apply the same way or at all. It's mostly which side and set of evidence the judge or jury accepts or believes more, though the rules vary based on the type of infringement. In civil cases you can even be made to testify against your own interests.

8) Copyright violation isn't a crime

Actually, recently in the U.S., commercial copyright violation involving more than 10 copies and value of more $2500 was made a felony. So use caution. (At least you get the protections of criminal law.) On the other hand, don't think you're going to get people thrown in jail for posting your e-mail. The courts have much better things to do than that. This is a fairly new, untested statute.

9) It doesn't hurt anybody—in fact it's free advertising

It's up to the owner to decide if he or she wants the free ads or not. If he or she wants them, you'll get a reply. Don't rationalize whether it hurts the owner or not, ask them. Usually that's not too hard to do. Time past, ClariNet published the very funny Dave Barry column to a large and appreciative Usenet audience for a fee, but some person didn't ask, and forwarded it to a mailing list, got caught, and the newspaper chain that employs Dave Barry pulled the column from the Internet. Even if you can't think of how the author or owner gets hurt, think about the fact that piracy on the Internet hurts everybody who wants a chance to use this wonderful new technology to do more than read other people's flamewars.

10) They e-mailed me a copy, so I can use it

To have a copy is not to have the copyright. All the e-mail you write is copyrighted. However, e-mail is not, unless previously agreed, secret. So you can certainly report on what e-mail you are sent, and reveal what it says. You can even quote parts of it to demonstrate. Frankly, somebody who sues over an ordinary message might well get no damages, because the message has no commercial value, but if you want to stay strictly in the law, you should seek permission.

On the other hand, don't go nuts if somebody posts your e-mail. If it was an ordinary non-secret personal letter of minimal commercial value with no copyright notice (like 99.9 percent of all e-mail), you probably won't get any damages if you sue.

In summary

Almost everything written today is copyrighted the moment it's written and no copyright notice is required.

Copyright is still violated whether you charged money or not, though damages usually increase if you charge money.

Postings to the Internet are not granted to the public domain. And, they don't grant you any permission to do further copying except perhaps the sort of copying the poster might have expected in the ordinary flow of the Internet.

Fair use is a complex doctrine meant to allow certain valuable social purposes. Ask yourself why you are republishing what you are posting and why you didn't rewrite it in your own words.

Copyright is not lost because you don't defend it—that's a concept from trademark law. The ownership of names is also from trademark law, so don't say somebody has a name copyrighted.

Copyright law is mostly civil law where the special rights of criminal defendants you hear so much about don't apply. Watch out, however, as new laws are moving copyright violation into the criminal realm.

Don't rationalize that you are helping the copyright holder by increasing the exposure of his or her information. The Internet has made it easier that ever to secure permission, so be sure to ask first.

Posting e-mail to a newsgroup is technically a violation, but revealing facts from e-mail isn't. And, for almost all typical e-mail, nobody could wring any damages from you for posting it anyway. Again, why not just e-mail the original author first for permission?

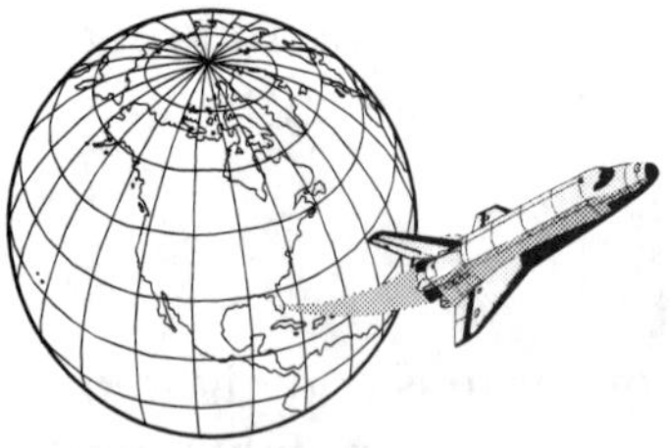

Orbiting in Cyberspace

Copyright Clearance Center Online
http://www.copyright.com

This is the on-line version of the Copyright Clearance Center, a non-profit organization that provides collective copyright licensing services. It's an excellent resource for electronic copyright information. They help ease the permission burdens and consolidate payment rights for organizations of all sizes and types.

Electronic Freedom Frontier's intellectual property law primer
http://www.eff.org/pub/CAF/law/ip-primer

This is a primer written by J. Diane Brinson and Mark F. Radcliffe to help you understand intellectual property law issues as they apply to the development and distribution of multimedia works. The information was derived from the Multimedia Law Handbook (Ladera Press, 340 pages, 1-800-523-3721).

U.S. Copyright Office Automated Information Service
gopher://marvel.loc.gov/11/copyright

For an actual connection to a directory listing within the U.S. copyright office in Washington, D.C., begin by clicking on the first document on the list, entitled, "Introduction to the Copyright Office." After reading it, return to the first page and click on any of the directory folders that you need to access.

Brad Cox on Electronic Property
http://www.virtualschool.edu/mon/TTEF.html

Brad Cox is a professor at George Mason University in Fairfax, Virginia. He's the author of *Superdistribution: Objects as Property on the Electronic Frontier*, an in-depth study of the problems of product distribution in the electronic age. On the Web home page listed here, Brad covers four different aspects of our cyberspace world: Electronic Commerce, Electronic Money, Electronic Goods and Electronic Property (see Figure 2).

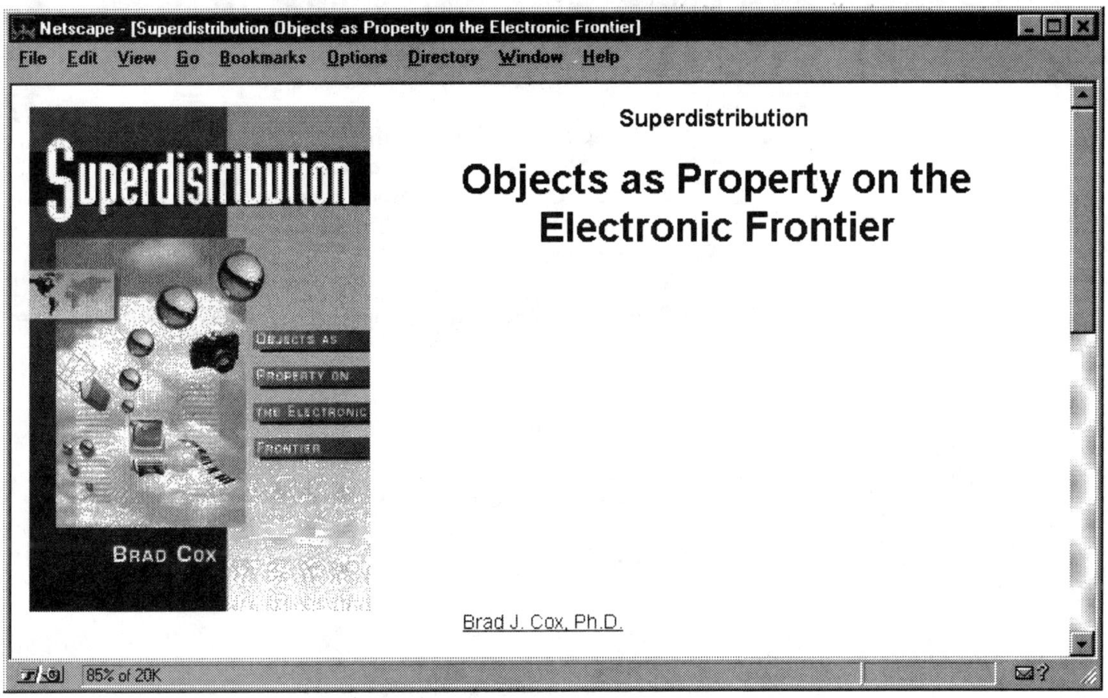

Figure 2 Brad Cox's book on rights for electronic intellectual property

Cornell University
http://www.law.cornell.edu/topics/copyright.html

This is a comprehensive Web page with hypertext links to just about every aspect of intellectual property law in which you could be interested. It includes a hypertext version of U.S. copyright law from the Legal Information Institute (LII) and a hypertext version of the Berne international copyright convention.

The United States Patent and Trademark Office (USPTO)
http://www.uspto.gov

The USPTO provides a Web page (see Figure 3) entitled, "Basic Facts About Registering A Trademark." Topics include securing trademark rights, submitting applications, who may apply, how to search for conflicting, previously-registered trademarks and rules for using (tm), (SM) and "circled R" symbols. Some of the information here can help you sort out the relationship (or lack thereof) between Internet domain names and registered trademarks.

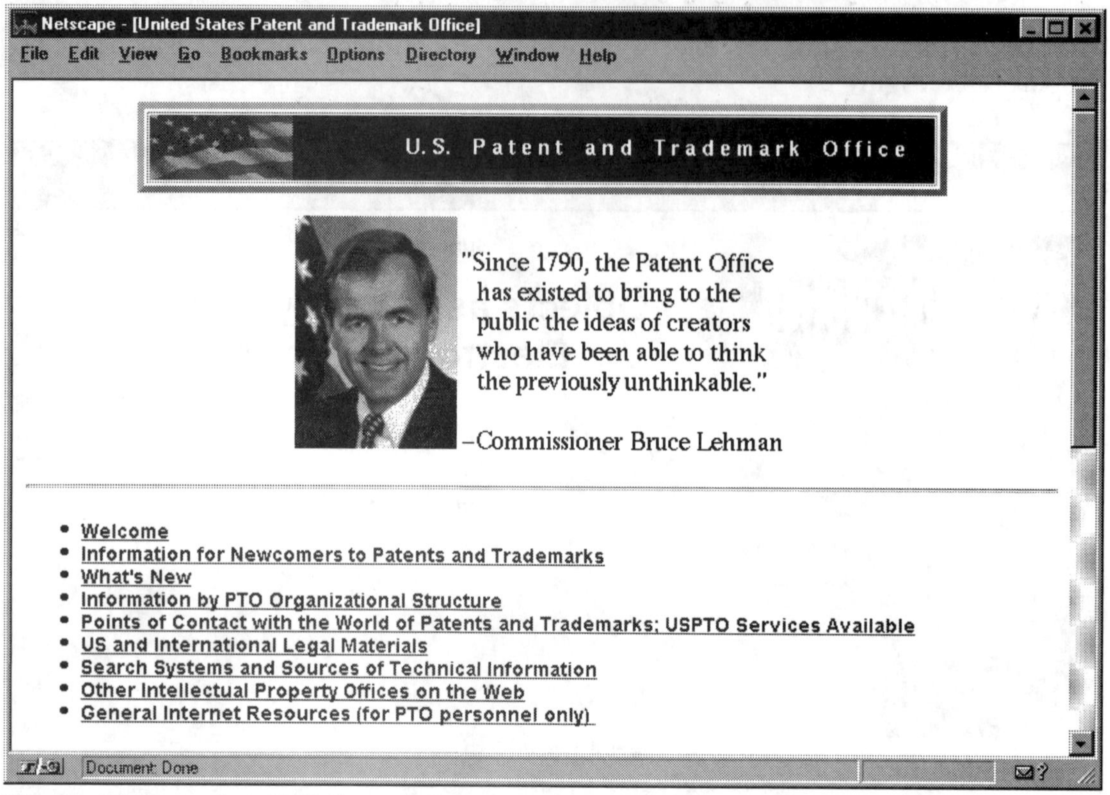

Figure 3 Mecca for all U.S. copyright and trademark issues

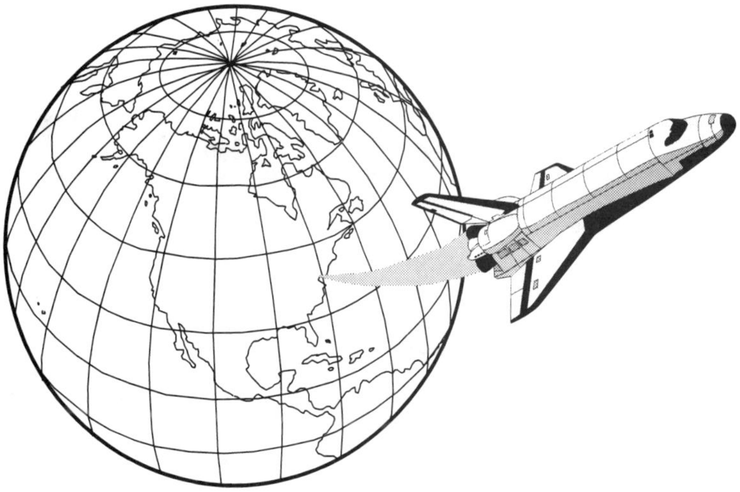

Appendix

Glossary

Inside Info

Erol's has an on-line glossary of computer and Internet terms on our Web site. You can access it by starting at our home page (*www.erols.com*) and clicking on links until you get to it.

anonymous FTP - Using the FTP function of the Internet anonymously by not logging in with an actual, secret login ID and password. Often permitted by large, host computers who are willing to share openly some of the files on their system with outside users who otherwise would not be able to log in.

Archie - An ancient Internet search tool, not used much since way back in the good old days of 1994. It's an archive of filenames maintained at Internet FTP sites. Don't pine its passing, you didn't miss anything—the Web is much more fun.

bandwidth - The transmission capacity of the lines that carry the Internet's electronic traffic. Historically, it's imposed severe limitations on the ability of the Internet to deliver all that we are demanding it deliver, but the high-speed cables of Erol's Computers and Internet have removed many of your bandwidth problems. And we offer ISDN service at the same rates as our regular service so you can enjoy more of the bandwidth that we're capable of supplying.

browser - Software that enables users to browse through the cyberspace of the World Wide Web. Netscape Navigator and Microsoft Internet Explorer are the primary Internet browsers today.

CGI - Common Gateway Interface. A programming function used on Web servers that gives Web pages the ability to interact with Web visitors.

ClariNet - A commercial news service that provides tailored news reports via the Internet. You can access ClariNet news within Usenet newsgroups. There is a whole series of them, dedicated to a wide range of broad topics. In general, you can find them on news servers at clari.*.

client/server - Computer technology that separates computers and their users into two categories: clients or servers. When you want information from a computer on the Internet, you are a client. The computer that delivers the information is the server. A server both stores information and makes it available to any authorized client who requests the information. You may hear this term frequently, especially if someone says, "You can't contact us today because our Web server is down."

dial-in - An Internet account that can connect any stand-alone computer directly to the Internet. The account is used by having a software application dial-in to an Internet service provider (ISP). The software connects with the ISP and establishes a TCP/IP link to the Internet that enables your software to access Internet information. The computer that accesses a dial-in connection needs either a modem to connect via a regular phone line or a terminal adapter (TA) to connect via an ISDN phone line.

e-mail - (Electronic mail) Messages transmitted over the Internet from user to user. E-mail can contain text, but also can carry with it files of any type as attachments.

FAQ - (Frequently Asked Questions) Files that are maintained at Internet sites to answer frequently asked questions so that experienced users don't have to bear the annoying burden of hearing newbies repeatedly ask the same questions. It's good netiquette to check for FAQs and read them. It's extremely poor netiquette—and a good way to get flamed—to post questions that already are answered in the FAQ.

Finger - An Internet function that enables one user to query (finger) the location of another Internet user. Finger can be applied to any computer on the Internet, if set up properly. For example, the most famous finger site of all was a Coke machine at Carnegie-Mellon that students wired to the Internet so they could finger it and track such important information as how many bottles of which beverage remained and how long the bottom bottle in each stack had been in the machine—so they wouldn't walk all the way to the machine and find it empty or purchase a warm soda. You won't use this, but it was fun while it lasted. Most sites have disabled Finger because it helps hackers crack a system.

firewall - A combination of hardware and software that protects a local area network (LAN) from Internet hackers. It separates the network into two or more parts and restricts outsiders to the area "outside" the firewall. Private or sensitive information is kept "inside" the firewall.

flames - Insulting, enraged Internet messages. The equivalent of schoolyard brawls in cyberspace. Unfortunately, a good schoolyard brawl would be preferable because at least then the only people who suffer are the dummies who fight. On the Internet, everyone suffers as resources are squandered on ridiculous, infantile behavior. But you won't be using flames, of course.

FQDN - (Fully Qualified Domain Name) The "official" name assigned to a computer. Organizations register names, such as "ibm.com" or "utulsa.edu." They then assign unique names to their computers, such as "watson5.ibm.com" or "hurricane.cs.utulsa.edu."

FTP - (File Transfer Protocol) The basic Internet function that enables files to be transferred between computers. You can use it to download files from a remote, host computer, as well as to upload files from your computer to a remote, host computer. (See Anonymous FTP).

gateway - A host computer that connects a network to other networks. For example, a gateway connects a company's local area network to the Internet.

GIF - (Graphics Interchange Format) A graphics file format that is commonly used on the Internet to provide graphics images in Web pages.

Gopher - A tool that organizes information by means of a hierarchy of menus. Gopher is now buried under mountains of WWW pages—don't bother learning how to use this directly. You sometimes will find a Web link that takes you to a Gopher site, but at that point, if you're using Netscape, its usage will be obvious and will look a great deal like the Web.

host - A system that includes TCP/IP and runs applications that provide files or services or that shares the system's resources.

HTML - (Hypertext Markup Language) The basic language that is used to build hypertext documents on the World Wide Web. It is used in basic, plain ASCII-text documents, but when those documents are interpreted (called rendering) by a Web browser, the document can display formatted text, color, a variety of fonts, graphic images, sound, video clips, run programs, perform special effects and handle hypertext jumps to other Internet locations anywhere in the world.

HTTP - (Hypertext Transfer Protocol) The protocol (rules) computers use to transfer hypertext documents.

hypertext - Text in a document that contains a hidden link to other text. You can click a mouse on a hypertext word and it will take you to the text designated in the link. Hypertext is used in Windows help programs and CD encyclopedias to jump to related references elsewhere within the same document. The wonderful thing about hypertext, however, is its ability to link—using http over the World Wide Web—to any Web document in the world, yet still require only a single mouse click to jump clear around the world.

IP - (Internet Protocol) The rules that support basic Internet data delivery functions. (See TCP/IP.)

IP Address - An Internet address that is a unique number consisting of 4 parts separated by dots, sometimes called a "dotted quad." For example, 198.204.112.1. Every Internet computer has an IP address and most computers also are assigned one or more Domain Names that are easier to remember than the dotted quad.

IRC - (Internet Relay Chat) Currently an Internet tool with a limited use that lets users join a "chat" channel and exchange typed, text messages. Few people have used IRC, but it is going to create a revolution in communication when the Internet can provide the bandwidth to carry full-color, live-action video and audio. Once that occurs, the IRC will provide full video-conferencing. Even today, while limited for all practical purposes only to text, the IRC can be a valuable business conferencing tool, already providing adequate voice communication.

ISDN - (Integrated Services Digital Network) A set of communications standards that enable a single phone line or optical cable to carry voice, digital network services and video. ISDN is intended to eventually replace our standard telephone system and today is used by many people for Internet service. Erol's lets you connect with ISDN service at no extra cost for your Internet service—although the telephone company will charge you extra for the ISDN phone line to your home or office.

JPEG - (Joint Photographic Experts Group) The name of the committee that designed the photographic image-compression standard. .JPEG is optimized for compressing full-color or gray-scale photographic-type, digital images. It doesn't work well on drawn images such as line drawings, and it does not handle black-and-white images or video images.

kbps - (kilobits per second) A speed rating for computer modems that measures (in units of 1,024 bits) the maximum number of bits the device can transfer in one second under ideal conditions.

kBps - (kilobytes per second). Remember, one byte is eight bits.

leased line - A leased phone line that provides businesses with a full-time, dedicated, direct connection to the Internet. The advantage to a leased line is that there is no connection delay while a modem dials in, connects and verifies your logon information. If you use Erol's ISDN service, then you'll hardly need a leased line because you'll be able to connect to us in about 10 seconds.

listserv - An Internet application that automatically "serves" mailing lists by sending electronic newsletters to a stored database of Internet user addresses. Most lists let users subscribe and unsubscribe automatically, not requiring anyone at the server location to personally handle the transaction. But for a "reflector" mailing list, the request to join goes to a human being's mailbox who must manually perform the subscribe or unsubscribe transaction.

mailing list - An e-mail-based discussion group. Sending one e-mail message to the mailing list's list server sends mail to all other members of the group. Users join a mailing list by subscribing. Subscribers to a mailing list receive messages from all other members. Users have to unsubscribe from a mailing list to stop receiving messages forwarded from the group's members.

MIME - (Multipurpose Internet Mail Extensions) A set of Internet functions that extends normal e-mail capabilities and enables computer files to be attached to e-mail. Files sent by MIME arrive at their destination as exact copies of the original so that you can send fully-formatted word processing files, spreadsheets, graphics images and software applications to other users via simple e-mail, provided the recipient has a MIME-capable e-mail application (most of them today are).

modem - An electronic device that lets computers communicate electronically using regular phone lines. The name is derived from "modulator-demodulator" because of its function in processing data over analog phone lines.

netiquette - Internet etiquette, good netiquette will keep you out of trouble in newsgroups.

newsgroup - An electronic, community bulletin board that enables Internet users all over the world to post and read messages that are public to other users of the group. Some estimates say that there were 26,318 public newsgroups in mid-1996, collecting far more than 100 megabytes of data daily. But no one really knows.

NNTP - (Network News Transfer Protocol) An Internet protocol that handles Usenet newsgroups at most modern Internet service providers.

POP - (Post Office Protocol) An Internet protocol that enables a single user to read e-mail from a mail server.

PoP - (Point of Presence) A site that has an array of telecommunications equipment: modems, digital, leased lines and Internet routers. An Internet access provider may operate several regional PoPs to provide Internet connections within local phone service areas. An alternative is for access providers to employ virtual PoPs (virtual Points of Presence) in conjunction with third party provider.

protocols - Computer rules that provide uniform specifications so that computer hardware and operating systems can communicate. It's similar to the way that mail, in countries around the world, is addressed in the same basic format so that postal workers know where to find the recipient's address, the sender's return address and the postage stamp. Regardless of the underlying language, the basic "protocols" remain the same.

router - A network device that enables the network to reroute messages it receives that are intended for other networks. The network with the router receives the message and sends it on its way exactly as received.

shell account - A software application that lets you use someone else's Internet connection. Instead of using your own, you connect to a host computer and use the Internet through the host computer's connection. It's a long way from having your own, direct Internet connection and Erol's Internet subscribers have no need for this type of service.

signature file - An ASCII text file, maintained within e-mail programs, that contains a few lines of text for your signature. The programs automatically attach the file to your messages so you don't have to repeatedly type a closing.

SLIP/PPP - (Serial Line Internet Protocol/Point-to-Point Protocol) Two different, basic sets of rules that let Internet traffic travel point to point. Both SLIP and PPP are used by all kinds of Internet hosts and routers.

SMTP - (Simple Mail Transfer Protocol) The simple, classic protocol used to handle the Internet's e-mail functions.

spam - Anything that nobody wants. Applies primarily to commercial messages posted across a large number of Internet Newsgroups, especially when the ad contains nothing of specific interest to the posted Newsgroup.

T-1 - An Internet backbone line that carries up to 1.536 million bits per second (1.536Mbps), which is very fast, but still far, far slower than the connections to the Internet that Erol's uses.

T-3 - An Internet line that carries up to 45 million bits per second (45Mbps). Erol's connects to the Internet with multiple T-3 lines so that you'll enjoy the fastest possible dial-in service available today.

TA - See Terminal Adapter.

TCP/IP - (Transmission Control Protocol/Internet Protocol) The basic programming foundation that carries computer messages around the globe via the Internet. Co-created by Vinton G. Cerf, former president of the Internet Society, and Robert E. Kahn.

Telnet - An Internet protocol that lets you connect your PC as a remote workstation to a host computer anywhere in the world and to use that computer as if you were logged on locally. You often have the ability to use all of the software and capability on the host computer, even if it's a huge mainframe.

Terminal Adapter (TA) - An electronic device that interfaces a PC with an Internet host computer via an ISDN phone line. Often called "ISDN modems." However, because they are digital, TAs are not modems at all. (See modem definition.)

Unix - The computer operating system that was used to write most of the programs and protocols that built the Internet. The need for Unix is rapidly waning and mainstream users will never need to use a Unix command-line prompt. The name was created by the programmers who wrote the operating system because they realized that while they were developing the operating system they essentially had become eunuchs.

URL - (Uniform Resource Locator) A crucial term. It's your main access ticket to Internet resources. It's the equivalent of having the phone number of a place you want to call. You will constantly use URLs with your Internet software to identify the protocol, host name and file name of resources you want.

Usenet - Another name for Internet Newsgroups. A distributed bulletin board system running on news servers.

Veronica - Archie's companion—not really, because Veronica actually helps you find information on Gopher menus. It's an acronym for "Very Easy Rodent-Oriented Net-wide Index to Computerized Archives." You will probably never use it, however, because Web searches are faster and more extensive and Veronica is now considered "ancient" technology on the Internet.

World Wide Web - (WWW) (W3) (the Web) An Internet client-server distributed information and retrieval system based upon the hypertext transfer protocol (http) that transfers hypertext documents across a varied array of computer systems. The Web was created by the CERN High-Energy Physics Laboratories in Geneva, Switzerland in 1991. CERN boosted the Web into international prominence on the Internet.

Windows Primer

If you're new to Windows, some of the Step-By-Step exercises in this book might be confusing. So, we'd like to give you a brief Windows overview so you'll understand the basic terms. If you're already comfortable with Windows, however, you can skim this section. But note the tips we've included in this appendix so you can point it out to friends, family members and coworkers who need help getting started.

Common User Access

Everything that you do with Windows takes place within an object on the screen called a window—pretty clever name, isn't it? Every window you'll use has common characteristics, a fairly common set of menu commands, a common set of keystrokes, and a common set of controls for interacting with users. Put those factors together and you've got something called Common User Access (CUA).

When programmers write a Windows application, they don't start from scratch and make up their own rules, keystrokes and menus. Instead they abide by the CUA standard. This is terrific for you because all applications take on a similar look and feel so that learning new ones becomes simpler. And, when you switch back and forth between applications, you don't have to mentally shift gears each time and use a completely different set of standards.

Inside Info

Nothing involving humans is truly standard, is it? Well, Windows is no exception. While we've just told you that Windows has common components throughout all applications, the creative human element shines through as well. That means that you'll see more than the basics because programmers have created some of their own tools and user-interaction devices. Still, even these original Windows creations will have similarities with the basics. Use Windows with an eye toward seeing as much commonality as you can, and don't be thrown off-balance by the differences.

You can buy whole books on Windows and take full-day Windows classes, so these few pages are by no means a complete Windows lesson. But we can give you the basics so you can at least perform the Step-By-Step exercises in this book. As you do that, your Windows knowledge will increase naturally because you'll learn as you go. The plan here is to give you four basic components: windows, keystrokes, menus and user interaction tools.

Windows components

We'll begin with a picture of a window and a description of its components (see Figure 1). The components are labeled on the image. Look them over, then we'll run through each labeled item.

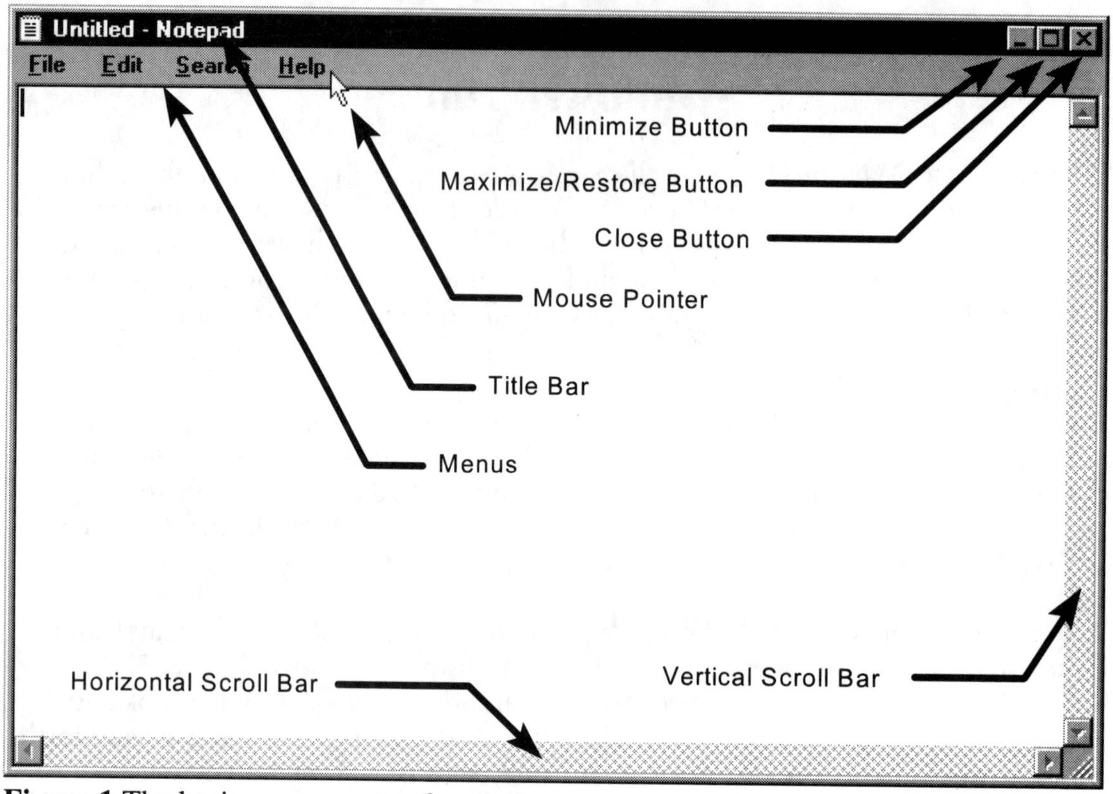

Figure 1 The basic components of a window

Mouse Pointer

When we tell you to **click** something, we mean to use the computer's mouse to move this pointer over the object, then quickly press (click) the left mouse button.

When we say to **double-click** something, place the mouse over the object and click the left mouse button twice in quick succession, *without moving the mouse* as you make the two clicks.

When we say to **right-click** something, place the mouse over the object and click the right mouse button, then release it *without moving the mouse*. A right-click will bring up a short menu of commands.

Inside Info

Many experienced mouse users don't truly understand how to use a mouse pointer. When we say to put the mouse on something, we mean the **tip of the pointer** only. The rest of the mouse is there just to make the pointer visible. So, it's possible to put 99 percent of the mouse on an object, but to actually have the **tip** positioned on another object. If you think you've clicked on one thing and something else happens, try again and be sure you get the very tip of the pointer on the targeted object.

Scroll Bars

The horizontal and vertical scroll bars let you use the mouse to scroll through documents that are too large to fit on the screen. To scroll through a document, you use the mouse on the arrows at the ends of the scroll bars.

Minimize Button

When you click on the minimize button, the current window drops to the bottom of the screen. You'll then see either the desktop or any other windows that were open underneath the window you minimized. A minimized window is still open, and is quickly accessible through commands you'll learn later. In Windows 95, a minimized application remains visible as a button on the Taskbar.

Maximize/Restore Button

When you click on the maximize button, the current window expands in size to fill the entire area it's allowed to fill. Some people believe that maximize means to make a window fill the screen, but you'll see that that's not true. Once a window is maximized, this button changes appearance and becomes a "Restore" button. Clicking on a restore button, restores the window to the same size, shape and location it was before being maximized.

Windows that contain applications will generally fill the entire screen when maximized. Thus, maximizing an application window will generally cover all other open applications. (The other applications remain open, they're just covered by the maximized window.)

Applications have windows within them that are used to contain documents. These windows are called "document windows" even though they may hold a spreadsheet file or an e-mail message. Document windows cannot exist on their own; they only exist as children of an application. The application window is the parent, and the document window is the child. So, when a document window is maximized it cannot fill the screen—it can expand no farther than the size of its parent window.

Close Button

The button with the "X" in it closes the associated window. If the close button is on a document window, that document is closed. So, if you click on the close button of an e-mail "In" box, only the In box closes and the application remains open. When you click on the close button of an application window, the entire application closes. If any of the open documents within that application needed to be saved, you'll be asked to save them before the application closes.

Title Bar

This is the solid-colored line at the very top of a window. The title bar includes the name of the application and the name of the active document in use by that application. You can use the title bar to drag the window around to different places on the screen.

If a window is not maximized, you can double-click on the title bar to maximize it. If a window is maximized, you can double-click on the title bar to restore it.

Menus

Menus are list of commands that can be selected with the mouse or with keystrokes. To activate a Windows menu with the mouse, place the pointer over the word (read the tip above), then click. A list of commands will drop down. You then can click on one of those commands—and then, perhaps, another.

When we tell you to activate a menu command, we'll depict it like this:

✔ Click **File**.

When we tell you to activate a series of menu commands we'll depict it like this:

✔ Click **File, Document, Properties**.

Keystroke commands

Most mouse operations have equivalent keystroke commands. We'll show the keystroke commands in bold and all caps. So, when we tell you to use a keystroke command (for example, to hit the Enter key), we'll depict it like this:

✔ Press **ENTER**.

Keystrokes that require you to use one or more keys together will be tied together with a plus sign. So, when we tell you to use a combination keystroke command (for example, to hold down the Control key and press the F4 key while you're holding down Control), we'll depict it like this:

✔ Press **CTRL+F4**.

A series of keystrokes will be strung together and separated with commas, like this:

✔ Press **ALT+F, O, ALT+V, ENTER**.
✔ Press **CTRL+SHIFT+F1, ALT+O, C, ENTER, ENTER**.

The ALT key

You can use the **ALT** key in lieu of clicking on almost any menu command. Notice that every menu command has one underlined letter (see Figure 2). You can activate a menu by holding down **ALT** and pressing the underlined letter.

Once a menu has been activated you perform the sub-menu commands by pressing just the underlined letter. Hitting **ALT** once a menu has been activated will cause the menu to close.

For example, you could save a file with this command:

✔ Press **ALT+F, A**

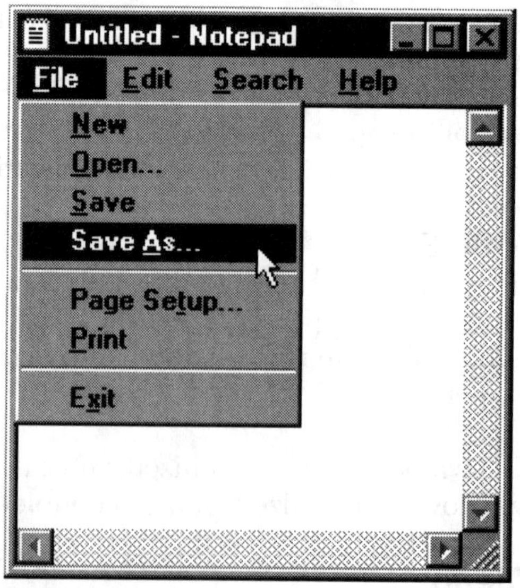

Figure 2 Using the **ALT** key

Common controls

When an application needs to show you information or get information from you, it uses a control called a "dialog box" (see Figure 3). The name describes very well what's happening because the application uses a dialog box to have a dialog with you.

Dialog boxes can be as simple as just presenting a text message. But they usually present controls you can use to perform some action within the current application. Dialog boxes use a lot of different types of controls—we can't list them all here. Because there are so many controls and because they can be arranged in so many different ways, dialog boxes have nearly an infinite variety of appearances. Even though there is such a wide range of possibilities, we'll show you some of the basic dialog box controls.

Figure 3 A commonly-used dialog box

Radio buttons

When a dialog box needs to give you a set of choices and you are only allowed to select one of the choices, they often use a radio button control (see Figure 4). In this example (taken from the Solitaire game), there are two sets of radio buttons. Each set is independent of the other.

If we tell you to make a radio button selection, we'll depict it like this:

✔ Under **Scoring**, select **Vegas**.

Check boxes

Check boxes are similar to radio buttons in that they present a set of selections. The difference is that marking one check box does not exclude other selections.

On a dialog box with multiple check boxes, you can check or uncheck as many as you wish. And you can change your mind as many times as you like because the selection doesn't take effect until you click the **OK** button. If you click **Cancel**, then all of the selections you've made will be ignored.

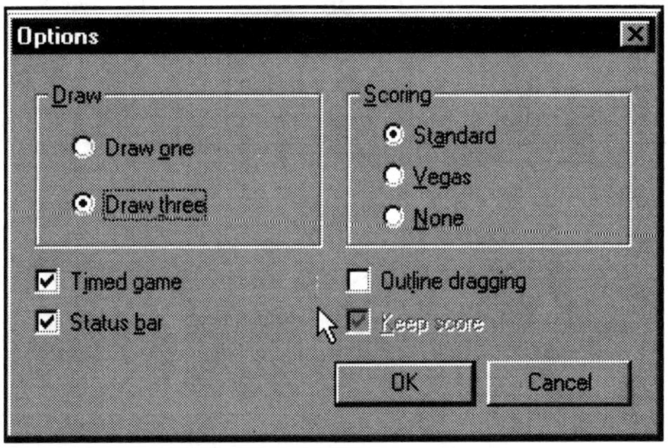

Figure 4 Radio buttons and check boxes

If we tell you to make a check box selection, we'll depict it like this:

✔ Check **Outline dragging**.

✔ Uncheck **Timed game**.

Inside Info

You can use radio buttons and check boxes with keystrokes, too. Each control has one letter underlined. In the example above you could select Vegas scoring by pressing **ALT+V**. And, hitting **ENTER** is the same as clicking on **OK**. So, you could switch to Vegas scoring with: **ALT+V, ENTER**.

Spin buttons

Sometimes programmers use a tool called a "spin button" (see Figure 5) that lets you select a choice from a list. The spin button does the same thing as a radio button, but can only see the selected choice.

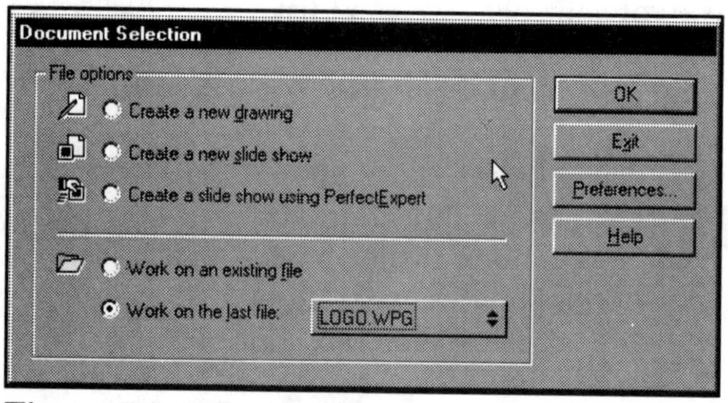

Figure 5 Spin button near the bottom of the box

To use a spin button you must hold down the left mouse button on the spin button and then—while still holding down the left button—you highlight your selection. Releasing the mouse selects the highlighted menu item, and then you can click **OK**.

If we tell you to make a spin button selection, we'll depict it like this:

✔ Select **Iconic Symbols**

Text entry box

Text entry boxes let you enter information into an application (see Figure 6). After typing the information you can press **ENTER** to tell the application you're through. Of course clicking on **OK** will do the same thing, but when you're entering text, hitting **ENTER** will be much quicker than stopping to pick up the mouse and then moving the mouse pointer and then clicking **OK**.

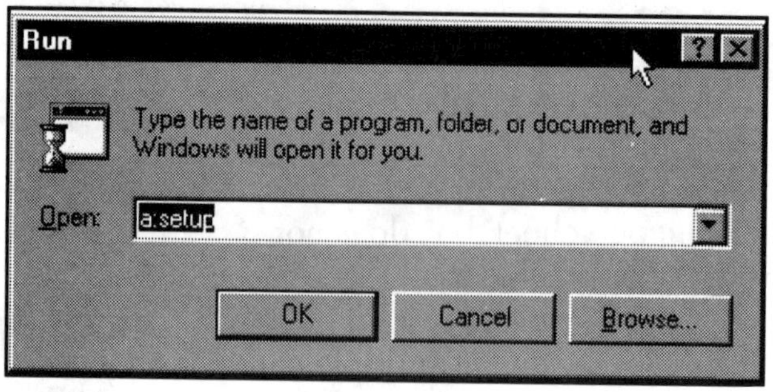

When we tell you to enter text, we'll depict it like this:

✔ Type *a:setup* and press **ENTER**.

Congratulations for sticking with these lessons. You've learned enough now to get you through our Step-By-Step exercises. Go back now and do something fun.

Index